12-19

Black History

AFRICA, THE CARIBBEAN, AND THE AMERICAS

Rosemary Sadlier
Gregory Birkett
Derek Grant
Kathleen James
Alyson Van Beinum
Joy Martyr-André
Colleen Birkett
Maureen Birkett
Mark Campbell
Ian Hundey

2009
Emond Montgomery Publications Limited
Toronto, Canada

PUBLISHER
Anthony Rezek

NATIONAL SALES & MARKETING MANAGER
Lindsay Mascherin

MARKETING MANAGER
Christine Davidson

DEVELOPMENTAL EDITORS
Loralee Case
Rena Sutton

CONTRIBUTING WRITERS
Jennifer McPhee

SUPERVISING EDITOR
Jim Lyons, WordsWorth Communications

PRODUCTION & COPY EDITOR
Gillian Scobie

PROOFREADER
Debbie Gervais,
WordsWorth Communications

IMAGE RESEARCHER & PERMISSIONS EDITOR
Karen Becker

MAPS
Visu*TronX*

COVER DESIGNER, INTERIOR DESIGNER, & COMPOSITOR
Shani Sohn,
WordsWorth Communications

INDEXER
Paula Pike, WordsWorth Communications

Emond Montgomery Publications Limited
60 Shaftesbury Avenue
Toronto ON M4T 1A3
http://www.emp.ca/school

Printed in Canada.

We acknowledge the financial support of the Government of Canada through the Book Publishing Industry Development Program (BPIDP) for our publishing activities.

ISBN 978-1-55239-265-2

Reviewers

Malik Adams
Halifax Regional School Board

Nicole Aloise
Toronto District School Board

Dr. Henry Bishop
Executive Director, Black Cultural Centre for Nova Scotia

Jocelyn Dorrington
Chignecto-Central Regional School Board

Dr. Maureen Finlayson
African Canadian Services Division, Nova Scotia Department of Education

Dr. Patrick Kakembo
African Canadian Services Division, Nova Scotia Department of Education

George MacLean
Cape Breton–Victoria Regional School Board

Donald MacMillan
Cape Breton–Victoria Regional School Board

Kirk Moss
Toronto District School Board

Randy Niedzwicki
Toronto District School Board

Lisa Reid
Halifax Regional School Board

Cheryl Rock
Durham District School Board

Tim Stapleton
Department of History, Trent University

Sheldon States
Annapolis Valley Regional School Board

Moira Wong
Toronto District School Board (formerly), Equity Reviewer

Table of Contents

Introduction

The time has come to reaffirm our enduring spirit; to choose our better history; to carry forward that precious gift, that noble idea, passed on from generation to generation: the God-given promise that all are equal, all are free, and all deserve a chance to pursue their full measure of happiness.

President Barack Obama, in his inauguration speech, January 20, 2009

January 20, 2009, is a day that will live on in the memories of millions of people around the world. It is the day that Barack Obama—the American-born son of a Black immigrant from Kenya and a White mother from Kansas—was sworn in as president of the United States of America.

Taking the oath of office on inauguration day, January 20, 2009

Barack Obama, with his wife Michelle and daughters Malia and Sasha, stood before a crowd estimated at between 1.5 and 2 million people gathered to witness history in Washington, D.C.

Obama's remarkable accomplishment is an inspiration to people of African heritage everywhere. His success fulfills the dream of Dr. Martin Luther King Jr., that "one day this nation will rise up and live out the true meaning of its creed: 'We hold these truths to be self-evident, that all men are created equal.' "

Celebrating Obama's inauguration in Kenya

At the University of Nairobi in Kenya, where Obama's grandmother lives and his late father was born, thousands of people gathered to watch the inauguration. In countries around the globe, people of African heritage shared a new sense that the world was theirs, too.

A symbol of change: Living in the White House

Following his inauguration, Barack Obama and his family moved into the White House—a house that was built in large part by enslaved Blacks more than 200 years ago. Obama's election marked a seismic shift in the American psyche and sent a signal to the world that it was time to break from the prejudice and injustices of the past.

Obama's election would have been unthinkable just a generation ago. Why did it take so long to elect a Black president? In this book, you will have the opportunity to explore the long and troubled history that led to this historic occasion. Starting at the beginning, you will investigate Africa as the birthplace of humanity. You will learn about some of the great civilizations that once flourished all across the African continent. You will discover the devastating impact that the Europeans' quest for global power and wealth had on Africa as they captured and enslaved African peoples, then took over their lands when they colonized the continent. You will see how different African cultures resisted their oppressors and gave birth to new nationalist movements which empowered them to reclaim their lands. You will look at the experiences of Black people in the Caribbean and North and South America, both in the past and the present. Finally, you will explore Africa as it is today and learn about the issues, challenges, and choices facing the people of Africa.

Features of This Text

The features of *Black History* open windows onto the significant events, movements, and people in the history of the African diaspora.

Image Analysis	**Image Analysis** presents different visual materials that encourage you to develop your media literacy skills.
IDEAS	**Ideas** allows you to explore some of the important ideas and movements that have shaped Black culture, in either Africa, the Caribbean, or the Americas.
ORIGINALS	**Originals** focuses on a diverse selection of people of African heritage in a variety of areas, including politics, social reform, music, and the arts. It provides an overview of their achievements and analyzes their significance in the African diaspora.
EXPRESSIONS	**Expressions** provides descriptions and analyses of various forms of cultural expressions in Black art, dance, and music. It explores the significance of these works and their connections to key ideas, events, and struggles of the time.
REVIEW AND REFLECT	**Review and Reflect** questions and activities at the end of each main section in a chapter allow you to assess your understanding and reflect on your learning.
The Historian's Craft	**The Historian's Craft** is a full-page feature at the end of each chapter that guides you through the theory and practice of such skills as historical inquiry, research techniques, detecting bias, documenting evidence, and using primary and secondary sources. It gives you the opportunity to practise the skills of the historian on your own. You can learn more about this feature in the Introduction to The Historian's Craft on the next page.
STUDY HALL	**Study Hall** provides an extensive set of end-of-chapter activities that cover Knowledge and Understanding, Thinking, and Communication and Application skills.

Introduction to The Historian's Craft

The Historian's Craft features focus on the nature of historical thinking and the work of the historian. Their premise is that the most valuable studies are those that are authentic—that is, they require you to work as practitioners of a craft. In these features you will read how historians approach their work, undertake research, interpret evidence, use historical imagination, refine their thinking, and present their conclusions. You will also consider how historians help us understand today's world and your place in it. Each feature includes questions that relate the Historian's Craft to the chapter content and that encourage you to think and act as a historian.

A common theme running through all of these features is the recognition that historians act out of intellectual curiosity. Even when they are experts in a topic, they are ready to look more deeply into matters. They undertake formal inquiry through the research of historical sources. From your previous studies in history you may know that these sources fall into two categories. *Primary sources* are those that were produced at the time historical events took place. *Secondary sources* are works that are produced after the events, and are based on primary sources and earlier secondary sources. In writing this book, the authors have relied on both kinds of sources, but have taken care to include a wide range of primary sources.

History textbooks written 50 or 100 years ago would not be as rich in primary sources as this textbook. If these earlier texts included primary sources at all, they were limited to government laws, proclamations, and other official documents. In this book, however, you will find not only official documents but other kinds of evidence, including stories and myths, poems and songs, paintings and cartoons, and maps and photographs. This variety of historical evidence helps you and your classmates engage in history in a more meaningful way using different learning styles and multiple intelligences.

It is important to include such a range of primary evidence for two reasons. First, the past voices of those who expressed themselves in visuals, in craftwork, and in writing are allowed to speak. Second, such a wide range of evidence helps you and your classmates to engage with African history in more meaningful ways. In doing so, you will deepen your appreciation of the historian's craft.

UNIT 1

Early African History: The Land and Its Peoples

TABLE OF CONTENTS

A sunrise over the African savannah

All peoples on earth have evolved from Africans who first inhabited this diverse continent.

CHAPTER

1

Africa: The Birthplace of Humanity

A People's Story

Within the huge continent of Africa, different peoples developed their own distinct civilizations. They were advanced societies with well-developed social structures. They built large cities. They created complex governments. They had distinct religious beliefs. They had systems for recording their histories. While the ancient civilizations of Africa were isolated from the civilizations of Europe and Asia, within the continent they had contact with one another. Through contact, they shared their knowledge of science and technology and developed distinct languages and cultures.

In this chapter, you will have the opportunity to learn about Africa as the birthplace of humanity. You will see how Africa's diverse geography shaped African peoples. You will learn about some elements of African culture. As you read, think about the fact that human beings originated in Africa and what that means for all people today. Think about the ways in which our knowledge of Africa and its people may have been shaped by misconceptions that are created when people look at the world from a Eurocentric perspective. As you learn, reflect on the importance of seeing the world through other people's eyes.

KEY CONCEPTS

IN THIS CHAPTER, YOU WILL:

- discover why Africa is called "the cradle of humankind"
- recognize the roots of Africentricity
- learn about the first African diaspora
- examine the diversity of African geography and culture
- discover the birth of civilization along the Nile River

Earliest evidence of pre-human hominid species	Hominid species in Ethiopia	*Homo habilis* (handy man) appears	*Homo erectus* (upright man) appears	The first modern humans, *Homo sapiens* (wise man), emerge in Afric
BCE 4 million	4–2 million	2.5 million	1 million	100 000

Image Analysis

FIGURE 1.1 Mercator projection versus Peters projection

Some of our perceptions about Africa may have been formed from maps. But maps can be misleading. Map projections distort size, distance, and area. Look at these maps.

The top map uses the Mercator projection, designed in Europe in 1569. The shapes of the continents and countries are accurate, but their sizes are distorted. The further away land is from the Equator, the larger it looks on the map. For example, Greenland looks bigger than Africa. But in reality Greenland is about 2 000 000 km^2 and Africa is more than 30 000 000 km^2!

The bottom map uses the Peters projection. It was created in 1974. It is an equal-area map. It shows countries, continents, and oceans according to their actual shapes and sizes. There is no distortion.

Who would have created these maps? Who was the intended audience for each map? How does each map influence your understanding of how Europeans viewed Africa?

North Africans begin iron mining in Nile Valley	Art begins to flourish in Africa	North Africans begin farming in Nile Valley	East Africans domesticate cattle in what is now Kenya	Ancient African civilizations flourish in Nile Valley
43 000	20 000	17 800	15 000	4000–1000

The Cradle of Humankind

No one is quite certain exactly when or how humankind evolved. But scientific evidence proves that human life began in Africa.

Archaeological Discoveries

archaeologist
a person who studies human history and prehistory through the excavation of sites and the analysis of physical remains

anthropologist
a person who studies human beings, especially their societies and customs

hominids
a species that includes the human family

Much of what we know about the first human species, *Homo habilis* (handy man), is due to the work of two famous **archaeologists** and **anthropologists**, Louis and Mary Leakey. Without the groundbreaking work of Mary and Louis Leakey, the story of human evolution might still be unknown. For decades they scoured the Olduvai Gorge in East Africa searching for evidence that humans originated there. They uncovered the fossils of extinct animals and many stone tools. But they had yet to uncover significant evidence that hominids had once lived there.

FIGURE 1.2 The Olduvai Gorge

The Olduvai Gorge is a part of the Great Rift Valley in East Africa. Many of the places where archaeologists have uncovered significant evidence of the fossilized remains of early humans were on or near a river or lake.

What conclusions can you reach based on this information?

Then, in 1959, a fragment of bone on the ground caught Mary Leakey's eye. After brushing away the dirt, she saw teeth embedded in the bone. Over the next three weeks, the Leakeys uncovered more than 400 pieces of skull fragments that made up almost an entire skull. Scientists used a process called **radiocarbon dating** to determine the age of the fossils. They concluded that the fossils were 1.75 million years old. This was the first evidence that the human species had its roots in Africa.

radiocarbon dating
the determination of the approximate age of an ancient object, such as a fossil, by measuring the amount of carbon 14 it contains

The Leakeys' discoveries led to more archaeological digs in Africa. In 1960, Mary Leakey and her son Jonathan found another, smaller form of hominid at Olduvai Gorge. They believed this one was different and more advanced than the species they had found before. There was evidence that it was the first species to use tools. They called it *Homo habilis.*

The Leakeys' spectacular discoveries shone the spotlight on the field of **paleoanthropology**. The publicity prompted governments and organizations like the National Geographic Society to fund more archaeological digs.

paleoanthropology
the study of the origins of humankind

In 1974, Donald Johanson, an American paleoanthropologist, made another major discovery when he uncovered the fossil remains of Lucy in Ethiopia. The discovery of Lucy was significant for two reasons: her remains dated back 3.2 million years, and almost half of her skeleton was found, unlike most fossil finds, which are just fragments. Later, not far from where he found Lucy, Johanson found the remains of at least 13 people. He called them the First Family. The evidence suggests that the group died together 3.2 million years ago, perhaps in a flash flood. It was the first evidence that people had lived together in groups.

FIGURE 1.3 The skeleton of Lucy

With 40 percent of her skeleton intact, Lucy is the oldest and most complete adult human ancestor found in Africa.

Why did her discovery change what we know about evolution?

In 1978, Mary Leakey and her team uncovered one of the greatest prehistoric finds ever: a trail of hominid footprints about 3.6 million years old. They were formed as three early hominids walked across volcanic ashes at what is now known as Laetoli in Tanzania. A light rain was falling. As the hominids walked, their footprints were cast into the mixture of muddy ash. When their impressions dried, they left behind two rows of footprints. Experts believe they are the footprints of two adults and one child—the child followed behind, stepping in the larger adult footprints. These tracks provide some of the oldest evidence of **bipedalism**. They provided additional proof that modern humankind evolved in Africa.

bipedalism
the process of walking upright on two legs, a major milestone in human evolution

FIGURE 1.4
The footprints at Laetoli

Only 50 years before hominid footprints were found at Laetoli, few scientists believed that Africa was the birthplace of humanity. Finding the footprints provided further proof that Africans were the first people.

Why do you think bipedalism helped scientists understand human evolution?

DIFFERING CONCLUSIONS

From these and other discoveries, some researchers concluded that a group of *Homo habilis* lived near the water at Olduvai Gorge. They made tools to hunt elephants and buffalos. They ate and slept alongside the water's edge. Not everyone agreed with these conclusions, though. Other archaeologists thought that early hominids were not hunters, but scavengers—that is, that they ate the dead carcasses left behind by animal predators. These archaeologists doubted that early humans would have slept on the ground because they would have been exposed to night predators.

From Homo Erectus to Homo Sapiens Sapiens

Eventually, *Homo habilis* disappeared and *Homo erectus* emerged, 1.8 million to 300 000 years ago. *Homo erectus* was taller and more robust than *Homo habilis. Homo erectus* had a larger brain, which enabled them to design more sophisticated tools such as scrapers and axes. They were meat eaters, so they had a more nutritious diet. They built shelters out of tree branches. There is evidence that they learned how to make fire. This provided them with warmth and protection.

Between 200 000 and 140 000 years ago, *Homo sapiens* evolved in sub-Saharan Africa. This species used fire for cooking as well as for smoking and drying meat to preserve it. They were capable of complex speech. Another evolutionary step followed around 120 000 years ago when the species evolved into *Homo sapiens sapiens*—modern humankind.

OUT OF AFRICA

In the past, there have been conflicting theories about how *Homo sapiens sapiens* gradually spread throughout the world. Today, however, the most widely accepted theory is the Out of Africa theory. It states that modern humankind evolved from a single population of *Homo sapiens* living in Africa 140 000 to 200 000 years ago. As Figure 1.5 shows, beginning 100 000 years ago, *Homo sapiens sapiens* gradually spread around the globe in the first African **diaspora**.

diaspora
a group of people who are dispersed around the world

DNA Evidence

The Out of Africa theory is supported by DNA evidence. In 1986, scientists using DNA analysis concluded that all humans were descended from a single woman who lived in Africa about 200 000 years ago. They analyzed DNA taken from the *mitochondria*, a specific part of the human cell. This DNA is different from other DNA. It is passed down only through the female line. Scientists compared this DNA from women of different cultures to build a family tree of the human race. At the base of the tree is "Mitochondrial Eve." She is the 10 000th great-grandmother of every person living on earth! This does not mean that she was the only woman alive at that time. It means that it is her **lineage** that has survived through the ages. Today, African archaeologists and anthropologists are continuing the process of unearthing evidence of Africa's place as the birthplace of humanity.

lineage
line of descent; family or descendants

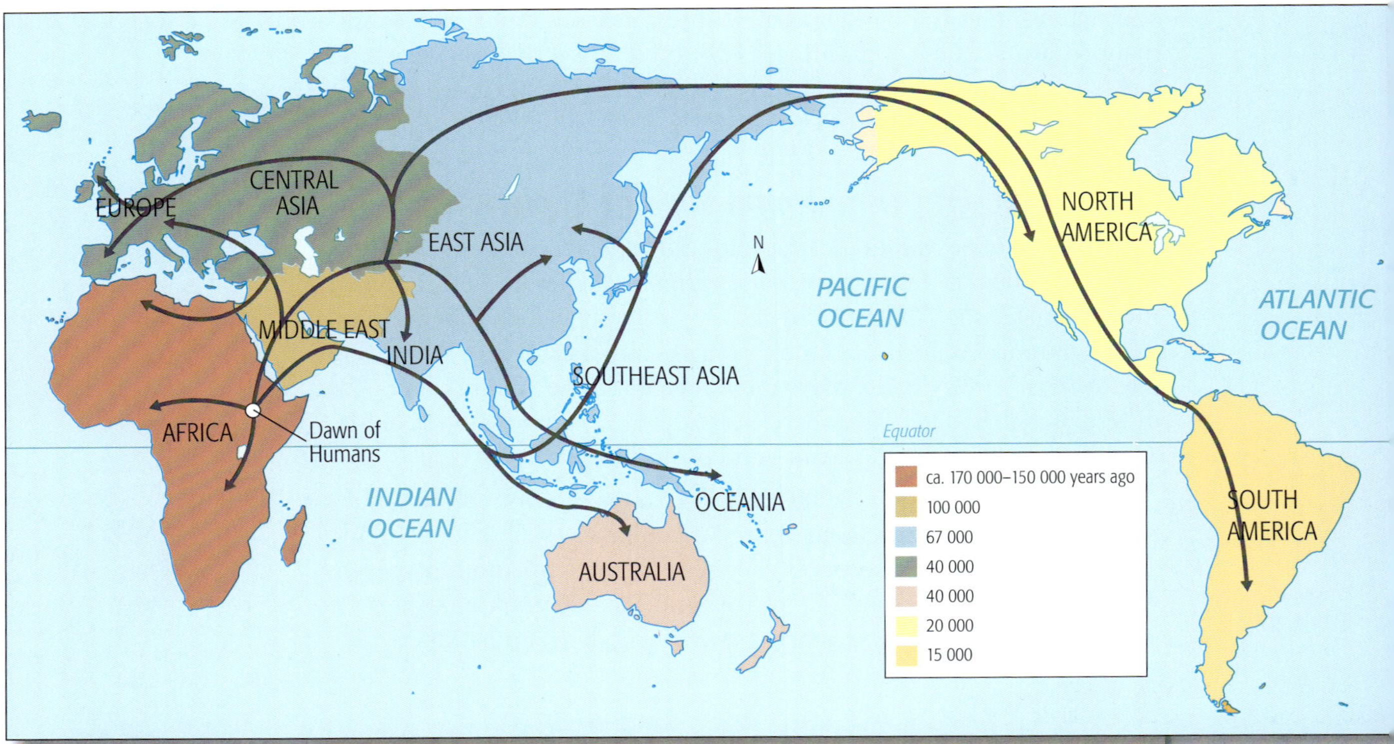

FIGURE 1.5 Great migrations out of Africa

From their origins in Africa, modern humans spread throughout the world.

Where was the last region to be settled? Why do you think this was?

REVIEW AND REFLECT

1. What have scientists learned from uncovering ancient fossils? Why is this important?
2. Think about what you have learned in this section. Record your ideas in brief notes, a web, or a sketch. Then share what you have learned with a partner.

IDEAS

ORIGINS OF RACE

There are many physical differences among the cultures that make up the species known as *Homo sapiens sapiens*—that is, the human race. Yet despite these physical differences, genetically all modern humans are remarkably similar. The concept of different races is fairly recent. It did not exist in ancient times. Back then, language, religion, status, and social standing were more important than physical appearance.

Over time, ideas and definitions of race have changed. Western anthropologists used to believe that Africans, Asians, and Australian Aboriginal peoples evolved from *Homo erectus* and that Europeans evolved from the Neanderthals who once populated Europe. This made Europeans different from Africans, Asians, and Aboriginal peoples. But as you have discovered, DNA analysis has proven this theory wrong.

The concept of race did not originate in science. Rather, in the late 18th century, science was used to validate existing ideas about race and to "prove" that there was a natural social order among groups. In Europe and North America, this placed people of European descent at the top of this social order.

Today, evidence suggests that the concept of race has little meaning. The physical differences traditionally assigned to race, such as the colour of people's skin or the shapes of their eyes and noses, really only reflect the different ways that humans have adapted to their environments.

Today, social scientists confirm race based on social values and attitudes—in other words, race is whatever a society says it is. In the United States, the government historically applied a "one drop of blood" system to establish race. When the government conducted a census, a person who had one Black great-grandparent and seven White great-grandparents was classified as Black. The system had nothing to do with genetics. It reflected the social values that historically existed in the United States. The "one-drop" system was controversial because it applied only to people of African heritage and did not recognize the blending of different cultures.

FIGURE 1.6 Physical adaptations

The physical features of different groups of people are caused by our environment. Skin colour reflects the latitude where people live. In tropical climates like Africa, people developed darker skin as protection from the harmful effects of the sun. In cold climates like Canada, people developed long, narrow noses because they are better able to warm cold air as they breathe it in.

In what other ways do you think humans have adapted to their environments?

My mother is English; my father is Ghanaian. My sisters are married to a Nigerian and a Norwegian. I have nephews who range from blond-haired kids to very Black kids. They are all first cousins. Now, according to the American scheme of things, they're all Black—even the guy with blond hair who skis in Oslo.

Kwame Anthony Appiah, Professor, Philosophy and African American Studies departments, Harvard University, *The New Yorker*, July 24, 1994

In 1997, under pressure from interracial couples and their children, the US government relaxed its "one-drop" system of racial classification. Now when a census is conducted, individuals are allowed to identify themselves as members of more than one race.

Think It Through

In your opinion, what should be the criteria for classifying a person's heritage and cultural background? Explain your response.

A Continent of Geographic Diversity

Africa is a huge continent. It makes up 20 percent of the world's total land mass. There are many distinct regions in Africa. The climate of each one is influenced by its distance from the sea, wind direction, ocean temperature, and elevation. As a result, the African environment includes snow-capped mountains, tropical rainforests, grassy savannahs, and windswept deserts.

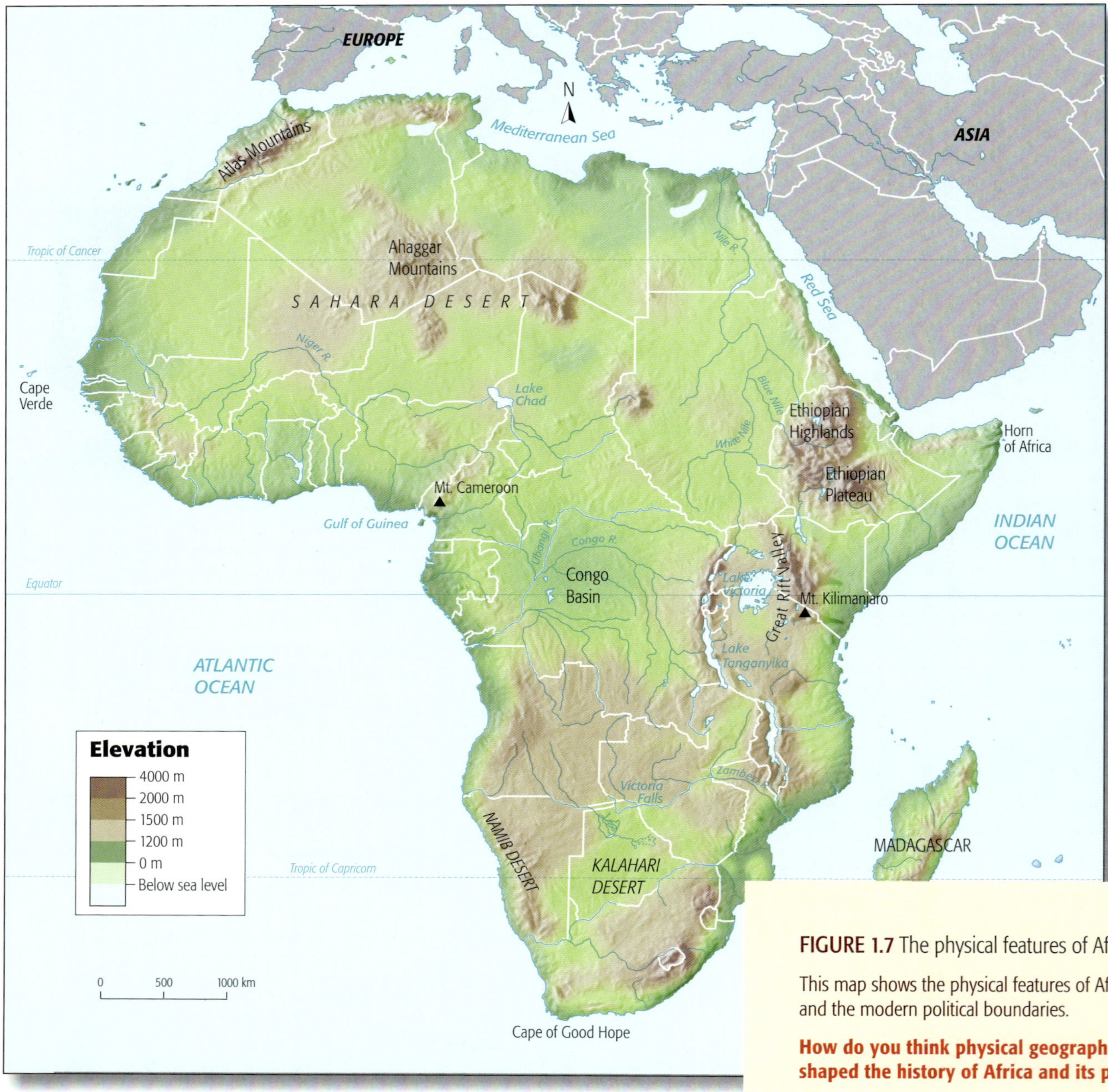

FIGURE 1.7 The physical features of Africa

This map shows the physical features of Africa and the modern political boundaries.

How do you think physical geography has shaped the history of Africa and its people?

SOME FACTS ABOUT AFRICA

- It is the second-largest continent on earth, spanning over 30 000 000 km^2.
- It stretches approximately 8000 km north to south, from its most northern point at Ras ben Sakka in Tunisia to its most southern point at Cape Agulhas in South Africa.
- It stretches approximately 7400 km east to west, from its most eastern point at Ras Hafun in Somalia to its most western point on the island of Cape Verde in the Atlantic Ocean.
- It is bounded by the Atlantic Ocean on the west, the Mediterranean Sea on the north, the Red Sea on the northeast, and the Indian Ocean on the east.
- Several islands are a part of Africa, including Madagascar, the fourth largest island in the world at 587 000 km^2.
- The highest point is Mount Kilimanjaro in Tanzania at 5895 m. The lowest point is Lake Assal in Djibouti at 156 m below sea level.
- Africa contains the Sahara Desert, the largest hot desert in the world at 9 065 000 km^2. The largest body of fresh water in Africa is Lake Victoria, which covers 69 500 km^2.
- There are 54 countries in Africa. The largest is Sudan at 2 505 816 km^2. The smallest is the Seychelles at 453 km^2.

The Mountain Highlands

Mountainous regions in Africa are found in the Atlas Mountains of Algeria and Morocco and along the highlands that extend from Eritrea south through the Great Rift Valley into South Africa. Elevation is above 1500 m. This creates a cooler climate than is found in other parts of Africa. The highest peaks, such as Mount Kilimanjaro in Tanzania, are snow-capped. At lower elevations, commercial crops such as coffee, coconut, cotton, cashew nuts, and rice are grown. There are valuable mineral deposits, too, including diamonds, gold, and copper.

FIGURE 1.8 Mount Kilimanjaro in Tanzania

Mount Kilimanjaro's spectacular beauty attracts trekkers eager to reach the top. Global warming, however, is melting Kilimanjaro's famous glaciers. Since 1989, they have shrunk by 33 percent.

Experts predict the glaciers will disappear altogether within a decade or two. What impact do you think that will have on the region?

The Equatorial Rainforest

The rainforests are located along the West African coast close to the Equator and in the Congo basin. This is where the heaviest rainfall in Africa occurs. Most of the rain falls between June and September. The ample rainfall and warm temperatures create ideal growing conditions for rich vegetation, including dense forests. Mahogany and ebony trees are valued for their high-quality wood. Palm oil from the heart of the palm tree is another valuable forest resource. Farming is possible in some parts of the rainforest. Crops include rice, corn, yams, and bananas. In other places, though, heavy rains wash out the soil, leaving the land infertile.

FIGURE 1.9
The equatorial rainforest

In popular culture, the rainforest is known as "the jungle." But in fact it is a complex ecosystem. The towering trees admit only slivers of sunlight to the decaying undergrowth below. By day, the rainforest is a silent world. By night, it comes alive with the sounds of the rich diversity of wildlife that lives there.

The Savannah Grasslands

As rainfall decreases, the tropical rainforests give way to woodlands before turning into savannah grasslands. The savannah is dotted with trees. It covers about 25 percent of the continent. Rainfall is unreliable, but there is usually enough to support farming and herding. Sometimes, though, excessive rains lead to flooding. At other times, a lack of rain can cause drought. Both of these acts of nature can destroy crops and herds. Livestock and crop farming are the most important industries on the savannah. Cattle and sheep are the most important livestock. Wheat, peanuts, bananas, and cotton are among the important crops.

FIGURE 1.10 Cattle grazing on the savannah

Once, the grasses of the savannah were eaten mainly by natural herds of grazing animals, such as zebras and gazelles. Now livestock herds eat the grasses, too. This competition for food has led to overgrazing. The balance of nature is also upset when herders kill natural predators, such as lions and hyenas, when they hunt near their herds.

The Desert

The savannah gives way to bush and scrub before merging with the desert. There are two major deserts in Africa: the Sahara in the north and the Kalahari in the south. The Sahara is the world's largest desert. It extends over much of the northern part of the continent. This vast stretch of wasteland appears to be an impenetrable barrier for travellers. But African traders have been crossing it since ancient times. The Kalahari Desert is much drier than the Sahara. Only the most skilled hunters and gatherers have adapted to life there.

FIGURE 1.11 An oasis on the Sahara

The Saharan landscape once contained lakes, rivers, and lush grassland. People lived throughout the region. About 5000 years ago, though, the amount of rainfall began to decline. Over time, the lakes and rivers dried up. The only signs of the old Saharan landscape today are the occasional oases where water from underground springs allows a few palm trees to grow.

How would these oases benefit animals and travellers?

The Rivers

Africa is home to some of the world's longest and largest rivers. Rivers such as the Nile, the Niger, the Zambezi, and the Congo have linked the regions of Africa for thousands of years. Rivers that originate in the interior descend steeply through a series of waterfalls and rapids. These obstacles protected the interior from outsiders. But they provided excellent transportation for the people living in the interior. Silt from seasonal flooding nourishes the soil and turns the river valleys into fertile farmland. The shores along the rivers have been the sites of many great African civilizations.

FIGURE 1.12 The Nile River

The Nile is believed to be the world's longest river. It is almost 7000 km long. The White Nile begins at Lake Victoria in Uganda. The Blue Nile emerges from the highlands of Ethiopia. The two rivers merge in the Nubian Desert in Sudan. From there they flow northward to the Nile Delta before emptying into the Mediterranean Sea. The river floods the Nile Valley. As it does, it leaves rich silt deposits along the banks. This creates fertile soil that is ideal for farming.

The Wildlife

The Sahara Desert created a barrier that allowed unique forms of animal life to emerge in sub-Saharan Africa. There are at least 100 different species roaming the savannah, the rainforests, and the highlands. The **herbivores** include zebras, elephants, hippos, and warthogs. The **bovids** include gazelles, antelope, wildebeests, and giraffes. The **primates** include monkeys, baboons, gorillas, and chimpanzees. All of these animals are prey for **carnivores** and **reptiles**. The carnivores include lions, cheetahs, leopards, and hyenas. The reptiles include cobras, pythons, lizards, and crocodiles. Africa also hosts a vast array of migratory birds. Millions of birds migrate from Europe and Asia each year to nest in Africa. Africa's lakes and rivers are also teeming with a wide variety of fish and marine life.

herbivore
an animal that feeds on plants

bovid
a family of hoofed, hollow-horned animals

primate
the highest order of mammals

carnivore
an animal that feeds on flesh

reptile
a cold-blooded, scaly animal

FIGURE 1.13
Wildlife in Africa

Africa's wildlife is legendary. Today, however, many species are **endangered**. Population growth, resource use, and urban development threaten natural habitats. Many environmental groups are working with local people to develop and manage protected areas. Their goal is to ensure the survival of some of the most fascinating wildlife on earth.

endangered
in danger of becoming extinct

REVIEW AND REFLECT

1. How would the way of life of people in the equatorial rainforest differ from that of people in the savannah? Explain your response.
2. Which of the environments you have read about in this section do you think would be the most challenging to live in? Give reasons for your ideas.

A Continent of Cultural Diversity

Africa's geographic diversity has contributed to its cultural diversity. Hundreds of different peoples live on the continent and its islands. In many places, these people have mixed with one another through intermarriage. As a result, the peoples of Africa have various skin colours and genetic features.

Language Families

The variety of African cultures is reflected in its many languages. There are six major language families on the African continent:

- Afro-Asiatic
- Niger-Congo A
- Niger-Congo B
- Khoi-San
- Nilo-Saharan
- Austronesian

The Niger-Congo and Nilo-Saharan languages are spoken exclusively in Africa and in all parts of the continent. The Afro-Asiatic language family is also spoken in the Middle East. Within these main families, more than 1000 languages are spoken, with as many as 8000 **dialects**.

dialect
a form of speech peculiar to a particular region

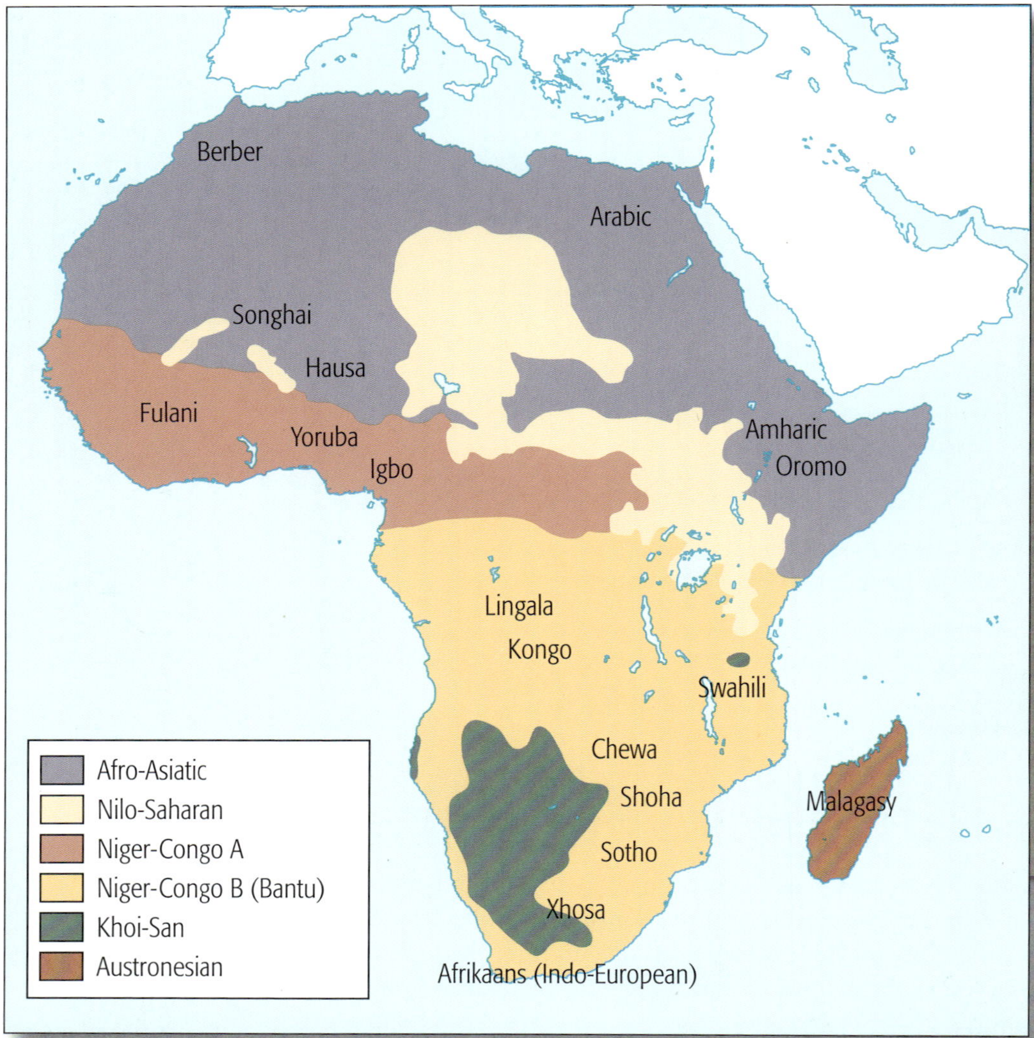

FIGURE 1.14 Language families of Africa

This map shows the six major language families in Africa and some major African languages. The largest family is the Niger-Congo B, or the Bantu languages.

Compare this map with a political map of Africa in an atlas. In what countries are the Bantu languages spoken? In what countries are the Afro-Asiatic languages spoken? Why do you think the Austronesian language is confined to the island of Madagascar?

Many Africans speak more than one local language. Many of these languages have no written form. Traditionally, African societies passed down their histories orally through the stories they told. There are some exceptions. The Nubian language in the Nilo-Saharan family has written records dating back to the 8th century **CE**. Today, the use and development of written languages has become increasingly important as African peoples work to protect their language heritage.

CE
the Common Era

The Oral Tradition

For thousands of years, African peoples passed down their histories through the **oral tradition**. These traditional stories are rich and varied. They include creation stories, **myths**, songs, poems, folk tales, riddles, and **proverbs**. Oral traditions among African cultures are very symbolic and can be highly intellectual.

oral tradition
the telling of stories and histories by word of mouth

myth
a symbolic account of the origin of things

proverb
a short saying that embodies a general truth

Most African societies had well-developed systems of passing down their histories. Some cultures, particularly in West Africa, have professional historians called *griots*. These are men and women who are specially trained to preserve their oral histories. They memorize the important events and the names and actions of rulers going back for hundreds of years. It is an effective way of preserving the records of their culture's achievements.

A Creation Story

This creation story is told by a group of cattle herders known as the Fulani in Mali. Their mythology centres on milk.

At the beginning there was a huge drop of milk.
Then Doondari came and created the stone.
Then the stone created iron;
And iron created fire;
And fire created water;
And water created air.
Then Doondari descended the second time. And he took the five elements
And he shaped them into man.
But man was proud.
Then Doondari created blindness and blindness defeated man.
But when blindness became too proud,
Doondari created worry, and worry defeated sleep;
But when worry became too proud,
Doondari created death, and death defeated worry.
But when death became too proud,
Doondari descended for the third time.
And he came as Gueno, the eternal one,
And Gueno defeated death.

African Literature, Britannica Online Encyclopedia

A MYTH

In Namibia, people have a myth that explains how the crocodile got its textured skin.

The crocodile originally had a smooth golden skin, and it stayed that way because the crocodile would spend all day in the muddy waters and only come out at night. All the other animals would come and admire its beautiful golden skin.

The crocodile became very proud of its skin and started coming out of the water to bask in the other animals' admiration, even while the sun was shining. He began thinking he was better than the other animals and started bossing them around. The other animals became bored with his change in attitude and fewer and fewer started showing up to look at his skin. But each day that the crocodile exposed his skin to the sun it would get uglier and bumpier and thicker, and soon it was transformed into what looked like bulging armor. Crocodile never recovered from the humiliating shame and even today will disappear from view when others approach, with only his eyes and nostrils above the surface of the water.

The Namibian Oral Tradition Project, *The Secret of the Crocodile*

Recognizing African Culture and Heritage

In the past, Western historians did not accept the oral traditions of African peoples as a legitimate form of historical evidence. They extended this **bias** to all **indigenous** peoples around the world, including First Nations and Inuit peoples in Canada. Western historians judged African culture from their own **Eurocentric perspective**. Because most African cultures had no written histories, they concluded that African peoples had no histories at all. As a result, for centuries the rich cultural heritage and the significant achievements of African cultures were dismissed by Western scholars. This lack of knowledge and understanding led to the **prejudice** that created many **stereotypes** about Africa and its people.

Today, historians understand that the history of Africa did not begin with the arrival of Europeans on the continent in the 1500s. They recognize that African history has been ongoing for thousands of years. They know that diverse and prosperous cultures have thrived on the continent, just as they did in Europe and other parts of the world. They recognize that varied and distinct African cultures left behind rich heritages filled with great achievements. You will learn about some of these great civilizations in the next chapter.

Today, Africans want people to learn the real history of Africa. They do not want them to learn about Africa from a European point of view. They want people to learn about Africa from an African perspective. Only then can the true story of Africa be told.

bias
a prejudice that makes it hard to judge fairly

indigenous
born in a region

Eurocentric
focused on Europe and European peoples, especially in relation to historical and cultural influences

perspective
a view of the world that has developed from a people's collective experience

prejudice
a preconceived opinion for or against a person or group

stereotype
a preconceived and oversimplified impression of the characteristics of a person or situation

REVIEW AND REFLECT

1. Why did so many historians ignore the value of the oral tradition?
2. What stories are passed down in your culture or religion? Share one of these stories with a partner.

ORIGINALS

HEIKH ANTA DIOP (1923–1986)

eikh Anta Diop was one of the most influential Black intellectuals of the ı century. He was born in 1923 in the West African country of Senegal, tion with a long tradition of producing scholars and oral historians. Their k inspired Diop's interest in history, the humanities, and the social sci- es from an African perspective. He was one of the first historians to ent an *Afrocentric* view of world history—that is, a history that acknowl- es the importance of African people and culture and that positively cts African values.

n 1946, Diop enrolled at the Sorbonne at the University of Paris. ough he majored in physics, he was drawn to African studies and the ins of humanity and civilization. His first book, *Nations négres et culture gro Nations and Culture*) in 1955, challenged Western scholarship on a. In it, Diop charged that Africa's place in world history had been berately distorted by Western scholars and writers. He argued that the ent civilization of Kemet—known in the West as ancient Egypt—was a nct Black African nation that had no historic or cultural ties to either ope or Asia. His work made him one of the most controversial historians is time.

After Senegal reclaimed its independence in 1960, Diop returned to his neland. He established a radiocarbon laboratory at the University of ar, where he developed a technique to determine the skin pigment of Egyptian mummies to gain further evidence that ancient Egyptians were k. Many scholars hailed his test as an important breakthrough. Critics ied that the test was ineffective because skin pigment would be affected mbalming and deterioration over time.

n 1974, Diop published his groundbreaking work *The African Origin of ization: Myth or Reality*. He argued that ancient Egypt had influenced ancient Greek civilization in science, math, medicine, architecture, phil- ohy, literature, and the arts. Since modern Western civilization emerged n ancient Greece, Western civilization was in fact the offspring of ancient can culture.

The ancient Egyptians were Negroes. The moral fruit of their civilization is to be counted among the assets of the Black world. Instead of presenting itself to history as an insolvent debtor, that Black world is the very initiator of the "western" civilization flaunted before our eyes today. . . . We know that certain Biblical passages are practically copies of Egyptian moral texts. . . . It is simply a matter of providing a few landmarks to persuade the incredulous Black African reader to bring himself to verify this.

Cheikh Anta Diop, *The African Origin of Civilization: Myth or Reality*, translated by Mercer Cook, Chicago: Lawrence Hill & Company, 1974, pp. xiv–xv

FIGURE 1.15 University Cheikh Anta Diop

Diop worked to unite African peoples by restoring their cultural identity and reclaiming their history. After his death, the University of Dakar changed its name in 1987 to the University Cheikh Anta Diop to honour the Senegalese scholar and politician.

One of Diop's most controversial issues was the definition of *Black*. He argued that the definition should not be confined strictly to the peoples of sub-Saharan Africa. Instead, it should be a broad definition that encompasses the people of northern Africa as well, just as the definition of *White* covers a broad spectrum of people in Western civilization.

When he died in 1986, many of Diop's ideas were still controversial. Today, however, more than 20 years after this death, his contribution to the history of Africa inspires and influences new generations of African scholars and students around the world.

Think It Through

Why were Diop's ideas so controversial? Why do you think European scholars rejected Diop's claim that ancient Egypt was a Black African nation? Explain your response.

EXPRESSIONS

AFRICAN MASKS

One way in which African cultures have traditionally expressed themselves is through their art. Masks are a particularly important element of African art. The use of masks can be traced back to the development of the first stone tools thousands of years ago. Masks are dramatic portraits of spirits, departed ancestors, and invisible powers. Each mask is made according to a traditional style and is worn only by a trained performer. Masks are part of elaborate costumes worn to the accompaniment of vibrant music and stylized dances.

Find Out More

What are some of the spiritual symbols in your culture? How are they used in ceremonies and celebrations? Present your work in a visual presentation.

FIGURE 1.16 Spiritual faces: the female mask Nimba, of the Baga peoples, Guinea

This Nimba mask is used extensively throughout sub-Saharan Africa. It symbolizes the power of women's fertility and portrays women as powerful and beautiful. The Nimba mask is worn during the planting and harvesting of rice. Men compete for the honour of wearing the heavy wooden headdress. The women sing and throw rice as the man dances vigorously to the beat of the drums.

FIGURE 1.17 Powerful forces: the Kifwebe mask of the Songye peoples, Democratic Republic of the Congo

Members of the Kifwebe society use sorcery to help their political leaders maintain power. The abstract shape and design of the mask symbolize supernatural powers. Female masks are created in light colours that signify peace, beauty, wisdom, goodness, and fertility. Kifwebe dancing invites the spirits to produce many children. The face of the mask combines powerful features that are associated with certain animals. For example, the eye slits represent termite holes, while the chin represents the snout of a crocodile.

FIGURE 1.18 Portraits of rulers: the elephant mask of the Bamileke people, Cameroon

The elephant mask signifies kingship and wealth. Traditionally, it was worn by powerful members of an elite society that included royalty, wealthy landowners, and powerful warriors. The elephant mask is lavishly decorated with coloured beads. The red beads symbolize life, women, and kingship. White symbolizes the people's ancestors and powerful medicines. Black denotes the relationship between the living and the dead. The masks were worn during funerals for members of the society and for the king's public celebrations.

The Historian's Craft

BUILDING YOUR INTELLECTUAL CURIOSITY

To be a good historian, you have to exercise your intellectual curiosity. But what motivates you to ask new questions or investigate new ideas? Sometimes this may be an extension of your own work. As you research a topic, you discover new things that you want to find the answers to. Sometimes you may be inspired by the discoveries of others. In this chapter, you have read about a few of the important archaeological discoveries in Africa. This may have stimulated your curiosity about new discoveries scientists may have made.

CURIOSITY AND INQUIRY

Whenever you study history, you must always think like a historian. You have to find out enough about the topic you are investigating to ask relevant questions. For example, if you were doing further research into African masks, you might ask, "Who would have worn this mask? Why did they wear it? Has the mask's symbolism changed over time?" Sometimes your questions may result in immediate answers. Other times they may lead you to reach inferences or tentative conclusions. When this happens, you need to follow up and do more research to find concrete answers.

Before you do your research, as a historian you need to formulate a thesis statement that states your position. For example, your thesis statement might be: "Masks played a central role in many early African societies." Alternatively, you may form a question for inquiry: "What did masks most often symbolize to early peoples in Africa?" A question for inquiry suggests a number of possible answers. Then you gather evidence to find the possible answers.

SCIENTIFIC METHODS, HISTORICAL IMAGINATION, AND PERSPECTIVE

Conducting historical research is rigorous work. You must look for evidence that not only supports your hypothesis, but that could weaken or disprove it, too. In the process, you may have to revise your hypothesis. When researching a question for inquiry, historians gather evidence for all possible alternatives. Sometimes they must develop new alternatives or ask new questions if the evidence warrants it.

Once you have gathered your evidence, as a historian you need to ask critical questions about its reliability. (See the Historian's Craft on page 108 in Chapter 3.) Then you have to consider whether you have omitted some possibilities and recheck your interpretation of the evidence. Remember to always ask critical questions about your evidence and methods of research. Only then can you draw conclusions and communicate your findings.

This all sounds very scientific. But as a historian, you can use your historical imagination to create empathy by trying to imagine what life was like at a particular time and place. Imagine yourself in someone else's shoes! This can help you gain new perspectives on the past. Remember: rely on both critical inquiry *and* your imagination to help you develop the historian's craft.

TRY IT!

Develop a question for inquiry for one topic in this chapter. Then do research to find possible explanations that answer this question. When you have finished, write a thesis statement to answer the inquiry question.

STUDY HALL

KNOWLEDGE & UNDERSTANDING

1. Create a graphic organizer to record information about the three hominid groups *Homo habilis*, *Homo erectus*, and *Homo sapiens* under these four key points:
   - geographic location
   - earliest and latest known time period in which this species existed
   - physical characteristics
   - social and intellectual characteristics.
2. List the main pieces of evidence that led scientists to believe that Africa is the birthplace of humanity.

THINKING

3. "The physical differences traditionally assigned to race, such as the colour of people's skin or the shapes of their eyes and noses, really only reflect the different ways that humans have adapted to their environments." Do you agree with this statement? Prepare arguments for a debate either supporting or rebutting this statement based on further research.
4. Scientists have concluded that Africa is the birthplace of humanity. How does this affect your understanding of race and racism? Express your ideas in an opinion paragraph.
5. The animals of Africa are as much a part of the environment as the landscape itself. How would a decrease in savannah grasslands affect some animals' ability to hide? What would happen to these animals if they could no longer hide? Discuss your ideas with references to specific animals in Africa.

APPLICATION & COMMUNICATION

6. Imagine you are going to interview Mary and Louis Leakey. Write down three important questions you would ask that would help the public understand the significance of their research.
7. Conduct further research into the Out of Africa theory. Then write a magazine article that provides evidence to support this theory.
8. Masks reflect African cultures and traditional beliefs. Create a modern mask that reflects your culture and beliefs. Then write a one-paragraph summary of the symbolism behind your mask.
9. Research the creation story traditionally told in your culture. Write the story as you would tell it to an audience of your peers.

CHAPTER

2 Early African Civilizations

A People's Story

For thousands of years, at different times and in different places, great civilizations flourished across Africa. As in civilizations in other parts of the world, the different peoples of Africa—the Egyptians, the Kush, the Soninke, and the Malawi, to name just a few—pursued trade and built empires that led to great wealth and prosperity. They developed cultured societies with their own distinct values, beliefs, and traditions. They invented new technologies and created unique art forms. They developed their own worldviews that continue to this day.

In this chapter, you will have the opportunity to learn about some of the great civilizations of Africa. You will discover that there were many different cultures and ways of life all across the continent. You will learn what factors helped these cultures build great societies. You will see how, as in other civilizations throughout time, these African civilizations flourished before they eventually declined. As you read, think about the accomplishments of these great civilizations and the impact they had on their societies. As you learn about the rich heritages these civilizations left behind, reflect on the great diversity of African history and culture.

KEY CONCEPTS

IN THIS CHAPTER YOU WILL:

- learn about African culture and history
- discover the historical and geographic location of different early African civilizations
- explore the evolution of kingdoms and empires from early African civilizations
- understand the political, economic, and social systems of early African kingdoms
- examine the influence of African art on Western art

Agriculture reaches the Nile Valley	Ancient Egyptian civilization begins	Kush conquers Egypt	Use of iron spreads across Africa	End of the Kush Empire	King of Axum converts to Christianity	Ghana rises to pow as a kingdom of city-states
BCE 7000	3100	750	500	CE 300	324	500

Image Analysis

FIGURE 2.1 Ships of the desert

Camels can survive five to seven days without water. Long double eyelashes help keep the sand out of their eyes. They have two hoofed toes on each foot. They spread their toes wide apart when they walk to prevent their feet from sinking into the sand.

Why do you think camels helped open new trade routes in Africa? What challenges do you think African traders faced as they made these journeys across the desert?

Ghana controls the salt-gold trade in West Africa	Swahili city-states emerge in East Africa	Great Zimbabwe emerges in southern Africa	Empire of Ghana falls	Mali gains control of salt-gold trade	Mansa Musa makes pilgrimage to Mecca	Mali absorbed by the Songhai Empire	Songhai Empire falls
700	900	1000	1076	1240	1324	1464	1591

Knowledge About the Past

How do we know about the early civilizations of Africa? Most of the histories of these ancient civilizations are unwritten. Knowledge of the past is passed down through the oral tradition. The keepers of historical knowledge, such as the *griots* of West Africa, chronicle the history of their peoples through stories, music, poetry, dance, and drama. They pass down these histories from generation to generation.

> **I teach kings the history of their ancestors so that the lives of the ancients might serve them as an example, for the world is old, but the future springs from the past.**
>
> Griot Mamadou Kouyaté, Intellectual Heritage Program, Temple University, Philadelphia

FIGURE 2.2
Early African kingdoms

Many great African civilizations emerged at different times and places across the continent. In this chapter, we will look at a few of these ancient societies: Egypt, Kush, and Axum in northern Africa; Ghana, Mali, and Songhai in western Africa; and Great Zimbabwe and the Swahili city-states in southern Africa.

The Arab world developed written languages earlier than many other cultures. Muslim scholars who travelled during these early times, such as Ibn Battuta in the 14th century and al-Maghili in the 15th and 16th centuries, recorded their observations about African societies. These **primary sources** have added to our knowledge about African civilizations.

primary source
a first-hand account or an artifact created by people who witnessed or participated in a historical event (see The Historian's Craft on page 66)

Archaeology reveals the part of history that lies hidden beneath the surface. Archaeology has told us a lot about the ancient civilization of Egypt in northern Africa. Yet much less has been uncovered at the sites of many other great African civilizations. Today, archaeologists are working to uncover more evidence that will help us learn about these early African societies.

What we do know from all of these sources is that between 3000 **BCE** and 1600 CE, powerful African empires and kingdoms prospered and flourished from trade. Widely separated geographically and culturally, they reflected the diversity of life on the African continent.

BCE
Before the Common Era

REVIEW AND REFLECT

As a class, brainstorm ideas about what makes a civilization great. Think about such things as education, technology, government, and art. Then create a graphic organizer to record all of your ideas.

Egypt: Land of the Pharaohs

Egypt is an African nation. The people of ancient Egypt called their land *Kemet*. They called themselves *Kemmui*, which means "black" in their ancient language.

The Nile: Giver of Life

Early hunters likely moved into the Nile Valley from the Great Rift Valley in East Africa. Around 8000 BCE, the lush Saharan landscape began to dry up. Hunters began migrating into the valley of the Nile River where water and wild game were plentiful.

Archaeologists believe that by 7000 BCE agriculture had reached the Nile Valley. In time, early farmers were able to grow enough food to support permanent settlements. Artifacts reveal that between 5000 and 4000 BCE the people became full-time farmers. By 3500 BCE, there were many small farming villages clinging to the shores of the Nile.

Over time, these settlements grew into political states. In 3100 BCE, the 3000-year civilization of ancient Egypt emerged in northern Africa. This great civilization lasted longer than any other in the history of the world.

FIGURE 2.3
The Nile River

The Nile is the longest river in the world. It flows north from Lake Victoria in central Africa to the Mediterranean Sea, some 6672 km away. In ancient times, the Nile was the source of life. It still is today. Without the Nile, Egypt would be a desert.

FIGURE 2.4 The Great Sphinx

Much of what is known about ancient Egypt comes from the archaeological excavations of the pyramids. These were elaborate tombs built for the pharaohs. The Great Sphinx is a portrait of the pharaoh Khafre. It was sculpted from an outcrop of rock. It stands in front of Khafre's funeral pyramid at Giza.

Religion

Religion was deeply woven into Egyptian society. It was a complex religion based on many gods and **mythologies**. The Egyptians believed the gods controlled the forces of nature. Gods had the power to produce abundant harvests or devastating crop failures. They held the power of life and death over everyone.

mythology
a collection of stories and traditions about people and institutions

The Egyptians believed in life after death. In the afterlife, people continued to live the way they had in their first lives. Egyptians planned for the afterlife carefully. The pharaohs built huge stone pyramids for their burials. They filled them with the food, furniture, and treasures they would need in the afterlife. Wealthy Egyptians built elaborate tombs called "Houses for Eternity." They painted scenes of their journey to the afterlife on the walls of the tombs. Even poor Egyptians made simple preparations for life after death.

PRESERVING THE DEAD

mummified
embalmed and preserved

The bodies of the dead were preserved before being buried. This was an important part of Egyptian religious ritual. The Egyptians believed the soul returned to the body after death. Therefore, they **mummified** the bodies to preserve them. The process of mummification took about 70 days. It was a remarkably effective technique. This system of preservation has made it possible for modern scientists to examine the bodies and learn about health problems and causes of death among the ancient Egyptians.

FIGURE 2.5
Egyptian mummies

After the body was mummified (top photo), it was placed in a specially decorated coffin like the one shown below. The body was buried with spells written on papyrus and funeral statues to

A System of Writing

Scientists believe that the need to keep records of their religious rituals led the Egyptians to develop a system of writing called *hieroglyphics*. The earliest evidence of hieroglyphics dates from about 3100 BCE. These were simple *pictograms*, or pictures of objects, such as animals or tools. Gradually, the hieroglyphics became more complex. The Egyptians began creating *ideograms*. These were pictures that symbolized ideas and actions. A picture of a person reclining, for example, meant sleep. Later, the Egyptians added pictures in a sequence that symbolized the sounds of words.

At first, the hieroglyphics were carved onto stone or wood. As they developed more sophisticated technologies, the Egyptians flattened papyrus reeds into strips and wrote their hieroglyphics using brushes and ink.

Today, scholars are able to decipher the meaning of the hieroglyphics through the Rosetta Stone. This is an ancient slab of black rock with carved text that was created in 196 BCE. It was found in Egypt in 1799. The Rosetta Stone contains an inscription in three scripts: hieroglyphics and the known languages of Coptic and Greek. A French scholar, Jean-François Champollion, spent years comparing the words with the hieroglyphics to crack the code of Egyptian writing. By 1822, he had translated the entire inscription. His work paved the way for the translation of thousands of Egyptian hieroglyphic records.

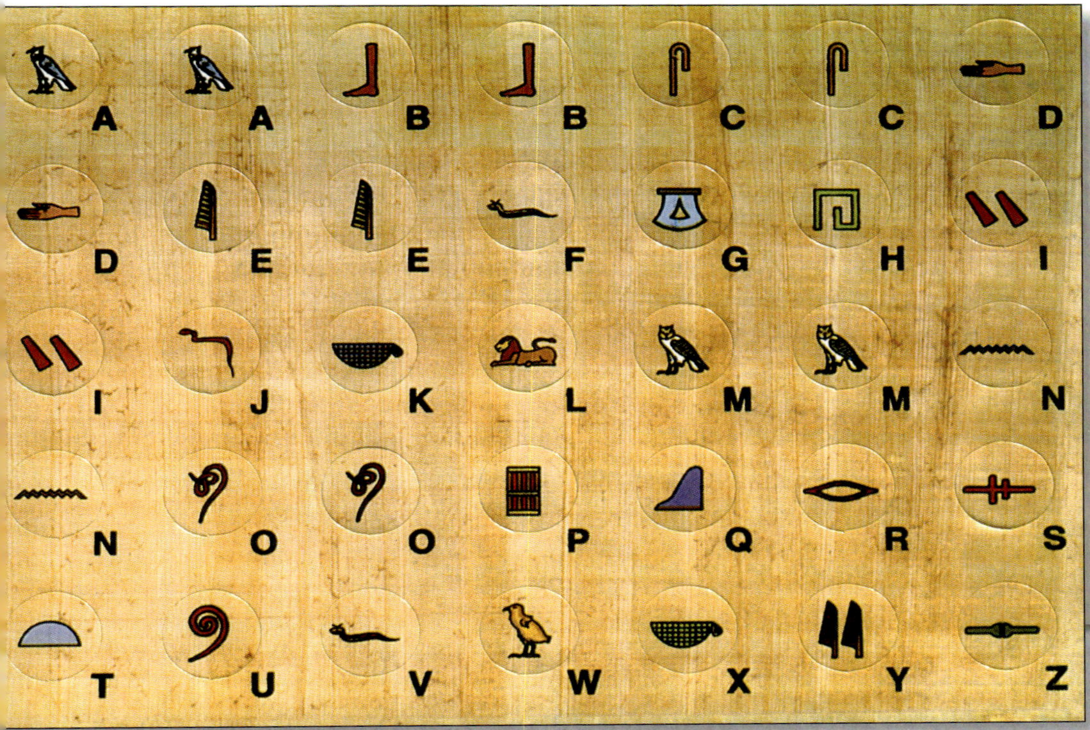

FIGURE 2.6 Egyptian hieroglyphs and the alphabet

This chart shows Egyptian hieroglyphs and their corresponding letters in the alphabet.

Find the letters in your name. Then write your name in hieroglyphics.

Government

With the ability to translate hieroglyphics, researchers were able to learn a great deal about government in ancient Egypt. The villages that had emerged along the Nile were divided into two kingdoms: Upper Egypt and Lower Egypt. Around 3100 BCE, the ruler of Upper Egypt conquered Lower Egypt to unite the two kingdoms. Between 2700 BCE and 1090 BCE, there were at least 30 dynasties in Egypt. They are divided into three major periods: the Old Kingdom (2700 BCE–2200 BCE), the Middle Kingdom (2050 BCE–1800 BCE), and the New Kingdom (1570 BCE–1090 BCE).

THE OLD KINGDOM

During the Old Kingdom, the Egyptian pharaohs were all-powerful. They had absolute control over people's lives. They owned all of the land and its resources. They shared these with the people in return for tax payments and total obedience.

The Old Kingdom has been called the Age of the Pyramids. It was a period of great technological achievement. The Egyptians developed the engineering skills they needed to build elaborate burial tombs for the pharaohs. Though the pyramids are a simple design, they are an incredible feat of engineering. No one knows for sure how they were built. Archaeologists and engineers have been able to piece together clues from unfinished pyramids and tomb paintings. They know it took thousands of workers many years to build a single pyramid. But just how many workers and how many years no one knows for sure.

There are different theories about how the pyramids were built. One suggests that the Egyptians used ramps to haul the stone blocks on wooden sleds. The ramps were lubricated with water to make it easier to pull the sleds. Another theory suggests they might have used a wooden crane with a stone counterweight on one end to lift the stone blocks. Many scientists dispute this theory, though, because there were no trees in ancient Egypt strong enough to do the job. Another possibility is that the Egyptians used pulleys to hoist the blocks up the ramps. Scholars know that pulleys were used on ships at the time, so they could have been used on land, too.

For now, how the pyramids were built remains an unsolved mystery. But scholars know that many workers lost their lives in the process. In time, the people grew to resent their rulers. The cost of the pyramids began to drain the royal treasury. The power of the pharaohs began to weaken. By 2200 BCE, the Old Kingdom was fading. Egypt experienced 150 years of discontent and disorder before a new **dynasty** emerged.

dynasty
a line of hereditary rulers

THE MIDDLE KINGDOM

Around 2050 BCE, a new dynasty restored order in Egypt. The pharaohs of the Middle Kingdom treated their people with greater respect than their predecessors. In the Old Kingdom, only the king and the wealthy could be mummified. In the Middle Kingdom, the people were granted the right to have their bodies mummified so that they, too, could experience the afterlife.

The pharaohs of the Middle Kingdom embarked on some remarkable projects. New technology allowed them to drain the swampland in the Nile Valley. This created thousands of hectares of new farmland. A canal was dug to connect the Nile River to the Red Sea. This opened up transportation and trade. It enabled the Egyptians to have greater contact with other civilizations and to exchange knowledge and technologies. Contact with other civilizations contributed to the flourishing of Egyptian literature and art.

FIGURE 2.7 The temple at Luxor

During the Middle Kingdom, the pharaohs built two huge temples along the east bank of the Nile, one at Luxor and the other at Karnak. The temple at Luxor was the centre of important festivals in the Egyptian capital of Thebes.

What impressions do you get about ancient Egypt from this site?

By 1800 BCE, Egypt was again in turmoil. A series of weak rulers led to civil war as strong nobles battled for power. This was followed by an invasion by the Hyksos of western Asia. They used horses and war chariots, both unknown in Egypt, to crush the disorganized Egyptians, who had only donkey carts from which to fight. The Hyksos ruled the state for about 200 years until a group of Egyptian nobles banded together to expel the foreign invaders.

THE NEW KINGDOM

During the New Kingdom, the power of Egypt reached its peak. Ambitious pharaohs conquered their neighbours as they built a vast empire. They looted the treasures of the lands they conquered to expand their own wealth. As trade flourished in the new empire, the Egyptian treasury overflowed with taxes from trade.

During the New Kingdom, women achieved new prominence in Egyptian life. In paintings and statues, women were often presented as prominently as their husbands. In the royal household, the queen was held in high honour because she was married to a god and was the mother of a future pharaoh. At times, the queen ruled jointly with her husband.

The world's first known female ruler reigned during the New Kingdom. Queen Hatshepsut ruled for 22 years. She launched a great trading expedition to territories beyond Egypt's southern borders. The Egyptian traders returned with a rich cargo of gold, ebony, ivory, and incense. The success of Hatshepsut's expedition is engraved on the walls of her funeral temple.

Hatshepsut's successor, her stepson Thutmose III, was a brilliant military leader. Under his rule, Egypt expanded to its greatest size as he conquered Palestine and Syria. Like other pharaohs, Thutmose raised monuments to his own greatness. He built tall pointed stone pillars called *obelisks* on which to inscribe his accomplishments.

The New Kingdom began to decline with the reign of Amenhotep IV. He tried to reform Egyptian religious beliefs by ordering the priests to worship only Aton, the sun god. But the priests opposed him. The military refused to support him. The people were afraid to abandon their traditional gods. As a result, Egyptian society began to weaken. When Amenhotep died in 1358 BCE, an eight-year-old boy inherited the throne. The young pharaoh's name was Tutankhamun. The boy king earned the support of his people by restoring traditional Egyptian religious beliefs.

FIGURE 2.8 Tutankhamun's tomb

The discovery of Tutankhamun's tomb in 1922 is considered the most important archaeological find of the 20th century. A treasure house of wealth was buried with the boy king. No one knows for sure why Tutankhamun died at the age of 18 or 19. But the treasures the tomb contained reveal a fascinating look at the life of the ancient pharaohs.

The Fall of Egypt

Following the reign of Ramses II, Egyptian power steadily declined. By 1090 BCE, civil wars had left Egypt too weak to defeat raiders and invaders from islands in the Aegean Sea. Eventually the Assyrians and then the Persians conquered Egypt. In 331 BCE, the Greeks occupied the lands around the Nile. Egypt's power and influence had faded. But the advances the Egyptians made in engineering, trade, literature, and art shaped not only their own civilization, but many other civilizations to come.

REVIEW AND REFLECT

1. What led to the creation of kingdoms in the Nile Valley?
2. Ancient settlers in the Nile Valley kept records of when the Nile flooded its banks. Why do you think it was important to know this?
3. How did Egyptian writing become more complex over time? How did writing contribute to the development of Egyptian civilization?
4. Create a timeline of the events in ancient Egypt described in this section.

IDEAS

CULTURAL NATIONALISM VERSUS CULTURAL INTERNATIONALISM

For centuries, foreigners have been removing historical cultural objects from their original locations. Sometimes they looted them to sell for profit. Sometimes they took them to enrich their museums. Today there is a powerful movement in many countries, including countries in Africa, aimed at returning the world's most prominent ancient treasures from foreign museums to the nations that created them.

The debate is over *cultural nationalism* versus *cultural internationalism*. Cultural nationalists argue that a nation's cultural property belongs within that nation's borders because it was created by the people of that nation. Cultural internationalists, on the other hand, argue that everyone has an interest in and benefits from cultural property regardless of where it is located.

Arguments for cultural nationalism	**Arguments for cultural internationalism**
◆ Cultural property is part of a nation's history. ◆ Many objects were stolen from their countries of origin. Not returning them endorses plunder and encourages it in the future. ◆ People should learn about a country's past while visiting that country, not while visiting a foreign land. ◆ It shows respect for the cultural rights of countries. ◆ It is the moral and ethical thing to do.	◆ The countries that created these objects do not always have the facilities to house and preserve them properly. ◆ Countries that now have these artifacts have spent millions of dollars restoring them. ◆ Many museums are international institutions designed to preserve world culture. ◆ Returning all cultural property would destroy the inventories of many museums. ◆ It would limit the number of people who could see these cultural treasures.

FIGURE 2.9 The Rosetta Stone

One argument foreign museums have presented in their refusal to return treasures like the Rosetta Stone is that they are too fragile to be transported.

What other reasons might these museums have for not returning these treasures?

Egypt would like its most cherished treasures, such as the Rosetta Stone in London's British Museum and the limestone bust of the Egyptian Queen Nefertiti in Berlin's Altes Museum, to be returned permanently. But these museums, and others, are unwilling to return these works. In the interim, Egypt has asked that they be returned on loan for the opening of the new Grand Egyptian Museum in 2012. But, so far, museum officials have denied Egypt's request.

Think It Through

Do you think that priceless cultural property that reflects a country's history and heritage should be returned to the states that created them? Debate this issue as a class.

Kush: Lost Kingdom on the Nile

While the ancient Egyptian civilization flourished, the Kingdom of Kush (also known as Nubia) emerged in what is now Sudan. For historians and archaeologists, Kush has been overshadowed by the great discoveries of ancient Egypt to the north. For many years, much of the archaeological evidence about Kush remained shrouded in mystery and myth.

Today, though, scholars are learning more about the culture and civilization of Kush. Modern archaeological research and Egyptian documents reveal that the Kingdom of Kush began around 3800 BCE. It flourished during its peak between 1500 and 300 BCE. It was a powerful empire. It had both the political skill and the military strength to control and influence a 1200 km stretch of land along the Nile Valley.

> **This makes Kush a more major player in political and military dynamics of the time than we knew before. Studying Kush helps scholars have a better idea of what statehood meant in an ancient context outside such established power centres of Egypt and Mesopotamia.**
>
> Geoff Emberling, archaeologist, University of Chicago, *The New York Times*, June 19, 2007

Trade

Kush was a land of natural wealth. One of its most important resources was iron ore. During the period known as the **Iron Age**, iron was critically important. It was used to make tools and weapons. Iron ploughs enabled farmers to grow more food. People who had iron weapons had an advantage over those who did not. With its abundant supply, Kush was the iron centre of ancient Africa. It was also one of the major producers of gold. Excavations in the ancient kingdom have uncovered artifacts that were once used in gold-processing centres.

Iron Age
the archaeological period that began around 1200 BCE when iron replaced bronze in the making of weapons and tools

As a result of its rich resources and strategic location, the Kingdom of Kush and its capital of Meroë became a centre for trade between the Nile River, the Red Sea, and sub-Saharan Africa. The merchants of Kush traded iron goods, gold, ivory, ebony, leopard skins, and wood for cotton, glassware, jewellery, and bronze lamps produced in Egypt and the Mediterranean. Elephants trained for use in warfare were exported to Egypt. The kings and queens of Kush used the wealth they accumulated from trade to build grand palaces, huge temples, and great burial pyramids.

Religion

Religion in Kush was strongly influenced by Egypt. Like the Egyptians, the people of Kush believed in an afterlife. They mummified their dead and placed them in pyramid tombs. These pyramids were similar to those of the Egyptians, except they were flat on the top. They worshipped some of the same gods as the Egyptians. Kushite nobles travelled to Egypt. They brought back Egypt's religious rituals and traditions.

In time, the Kushites interacted with Christians who came to the kingdom to trade. This led to a growing interest in the teachings of Christianity.

FIGURE 2.10 The Meroitic pyramids

These are the royal pyramids on the outskirts of the Kush capital of Meroë.

What cultural influences from Egypt can you identify?

The Fall of Kush

Assyrians
people from the ancient country of Assyria, now northern Iraq

In 751 BCE, the Kushite king Piankhi led his army north to conquer Egypt. For the next 80 years the rulers of Kush controlled an empire that stretched from the Mediterranean to what is now Ethiopia. They retreated when the **Assyrians** took control of Egypt and parts of Kush in 671 BCE.

From that point, Kush entered a long period of decline. The demand for iron ore had a devastating impact on the environment. The Kushites cut down an increasing number of trees to burn as fuel to make iron. The trees could not replenish themselves. Soon the land was stripped of its trees. Without fuel, Kush could not produce iron. Traders began to look elsewhere. As trade dwindled, the Kingdom of Kush began to weaken. With the land deforested, the soils eroded. People could not make a living from farming. By 300 CE, Meroë and the Kingdom of Kush had disappeared.

REVIEW AND REFLECT

1. What can scientists and archaeologists learn from studying the remains of ancient Kush?
2. What was the economic importance of Kush?
3. How did the exploitation of the environment contribute to the fall of the Kingdom of Kush?

Axum: Kingdom at the Crossroads

The decline of Kush paved the way for its neighbour, the Kingdom of Axum, to expand. Axum's location in the Ethiopian highlands near the Red Sea was ideal for trade. It was directly in the path of the growing commercial trade routes between Africa, Arabia, and India. The cities of Adulis, Axum, and Matara became three of the most cosmopolitan centres in the ancient world. They became a crossroads for a variety of cultures, from Egypt to the Middle East to India.

Trade

African traders from the interior of the continent brought gold, ivory, and animal hides to the port of Adulis on the Red Sea. Arab traders transported the goods to Egypt, the Middle East, and India. Adulis was alive with activity as it became a centre for world trade. It provided a vital link in the long series of ports along the central coast of East Africa and the Red Sea.

The Arab traders settled alongside the African farmers and merchants of Axum. As a result, the civilization of Axum blended African and Arab cultures. They accommodated religious minorities, too, including Jews, Nubians, Christians, and Buddhists.

FIGURE 2.11 Axum

The craftspeople of Axum created their own coins and produced luxury goods from glass and metal for export to Egypt and the Roman Empire. Today, the city of Axum is a **UNESCO World Heritage Site**.

UNESCO World Heritage Site an area or structure designated by the United Nations for preservation because of its global historical and cultural significance

mercantile
of or relating to merchants or trade

Axum took advantage of its location. It prospered from Greek and Roman **mercantile** technology and trade. Its advanced agricultural technology included irrigation and ploughing. Combined with a high level of literacy, this created a great deal of commercial activity in Axum. The people prospered as merchants. They sold ivory, rhinoceros horns, hippopotamus hides, gold dust, frankincense, spices, elephants, and enslaved peoples. These were traded for salt, cotton, and other goods from Egypt and the Mediterranean.

FIGURE 2.12
The obelisks of Axum

There were once seven large obelisks at this site. They were carefully cut from granite using stone and iron tools. All were decorated in the same style, with doors and windows and heavenly images on the top. The largest obelisk still standing today is 21 m high. There were taller ones, but they have crumbled away through the ravages of time. Obelisks were often used as tombstones to honour kings. The history of the ruler was inscribed on the stones.

Religion

In the 4th century, Christian scholars and merchants introduced Christianity to Axum. In 324 CE, the ruler of Axum, King Ezana, converted to Christianity. He then proclaimed Axum a Christian state. The king attempted to convert his subjects to Christianity. But the highlanders of

FIGURE 2.13
The Ark of the Covenant

The Axumites believed that they were the descendants of Menelik I, the son of the **Queen of Sheba** and **King Solomon**. They believed that Menelik went to Jerusalem and took the **Ark of the Covenant**. He brought it back to Axum. Today, replicas of the Ark are found in more than 20 000 churches in Ethiopia.

Axum were fiercely independent. They were slow to embrace the Christian faith. When they did convert, it was to a unique form of Christianity that blended their traditional beliefs with Christian values.

The conversion to Christianity paved the way for Axum to establish trade links with Greece in the eastern Mediterranean. But the spread of Islam across North Africa in the 7th century broke the connection between the Christian world and Axum. Christianity survived in Axum, though. Today, the people of Ethiopia trace their Christian culture back to the civilization of Axum.

Queen of Sheba
(ca. 1000 BCE–901 BCE) a mysterious and powerful woman who is immortalized in the world's great religious works, including the Bible and the Qur'an

King Solomon
(ca. 1000 BCE–922 BCE) in the Bible, one of the greatest kings of Israel, who ruled over a kingdom comprising most of the modern Middle East

Ark of the Covenant
a wooden box lined with gold containing the two tablets on which, according to the Christian faith, God wrote the Ten Commandments

The Fall of Axum

Axum reached its peak in power and prosperity in the 4th and 5th centuries. Then the kingdom slipped into decline. Like the Kingdom of Kush before it, Axum had taken its toll on the environment. The land had been stripped of its forests, leaving the hillside soils to be washed away by the rains. As Islam began to spread throughout northern Africa, Arabs took over the city of Adulis. This ended the kingdom's sea trade.

Axum was now isolated from the rest of the world. The people of Axum retreated further into the highlands in search of new farmland. They survived there for more than 1000 years. They created their own unique religious and architectural traditions in the new civilization of Ethiopia.

REVIEW AND REFLECT

1. What resources contributed to the wealth of Axum?
2. Do you think it is important to designate places like Axum as World Heritage Sites? What World Heritage Sites are you aware of in Canada? Discuss your ideas with a partner.

Ghana: Empire of Gold

The Kingdom of Ghana in West Africa originated with the Soninke clan and rose to power around 500 CE. It was located approximately 805 km north of present-day Ghana in what is now Mali, Senegal, and southeast Mauritania. Ghana benefited from its location between the Niger and Senegal rivers.

FIGURE 2.14
The location of the ancient Kingdom of Mali

People from the region travelled the rivers to trade. Camel caravans carried goods from northern Africa and the Mediterranean across the Sahara Desert to Ghana. The camels brought goods such as salt, textiles, and tools. They left carrying goods such as gold, ivory, and copper.

Trade

The gold and salt trade made Ghana wealthy. People in northern Africa wanted gold from West Africa. People in West Africa wanted salt from northern Africa. According to Arab writers, Ghana had the richest gold mines on earth. The traders who came to Ghana to trade in gold had to pay taxes when they entered and left the kingdom. The taxes were paid with salt, iron, silks, and spices. The accumulation of these resources made Ghana wealthy.

As trade prospered, towns began to spring up throughout Ghana. Kumbi Saleh was the capital of the kingdom. It was located on the fringes of the desert along the southern Saharan trade route. It consisted of two centres. The northern centre was home to Muslim traders, lawyers, religious leaders, and teachers. The southern centre was home to the royal palace. The homes of the city residents lay in between the two centres. Kumbi Saleh became the most dynamic and important city in the southern sphere of the trade route. More than 30 000 people lived in the city during the height of the Ghanaian Empire. In 1914, archaeologists found the ruins of Kumbi Saleh. They unearthed finely made weapons, farm tools, glass weights, and pieces of pottery.

Government

The king of Ghana was more powerful than anyone else. He was considered the father of all the Soninke people. He was the religious leader, chief of the army, and the highest judge in the land. People worshipped the king as if he were a god. He was known as the *Ghana*, which means "warrior king."

The kings of Ghana amassed great wealth from the taxes levied on trade. They maintained large armies to guard the trade routes and to keep the kingdom under control. As the kings grew richer, they conquered their neighbours. Local rulers were left in charge of newly conquered lands. But the people were expected to obey the king and to pay **tribute** to his kingdom.

tribute
a donation given as a sign of respect or to ensure peace and protection

Religion

The Soninke people practised their own traditional beliefs. They believed in a god that created the universe and regulated all things in it. They believed that all things on earth possessed a spirit. They respected and revered their ancestors. Disaster awaited anyone who displeased them. They believed that the best way to respect their ancestors was to live a decent life.

FIGURE 2.15 Ancient mosque at Larabanga

Unlike many of its neighbours, Ghana never converted to Islam. But the Ghanaian court allowed Muslims to settle in the cities. Many Muslims became advisers to the royal court. Since they were literate, they wrote about life in ancient Ghana. Much of what is known today about ancient Ghana comes from these Muslim records.

The People of Ghana

Most of the people in ancient Ghana were farmers. They worked together in family units and lived in farming villages made up of people who belonged to the same clan. According to Ghanaian custom, land could not be bought or sold. It was allocated by the village leader to each family based on need. The farmers produced crops such as cotton, groundnuts, rice, okra, pumpkins, watermelons, and sesame seeds. Not every crop was grown in every village, so trade among the villages became a part of daily life.

Within the villages, men and women divided the labour. Men hunted and farmed. Women harvested and prepared the food. They processed millet and other grains using special stones for grinding. While the women readied the food, the men built houses out of sun-dried mud or acacia wood. Both men and women made baskets, pots, utensils, and tools. Success was not measured by material wealth, though. It was measured by the productivity of the farm.

FIGURE 2.16
Life in Ghana

Farmers produced enough food to feed people in the cities. City dwellers enjoyed many luxuries. They wore expensive clothing. They had copper utensils. They created artwork. They obtained many foreign goods through trade.

The Fall of Ghana

By 1050 CE, Ghana had reached its peak. A prolonged drought had weakened the kingdom. The inability of the land to sustain crops and livestock led to widespread famine. The king lost his control of the gold and salt trade as new gold mines opened up further east. The kingdom began to disintegrate as states began to break away.

Weakened from within, Ghana was then vulnerable to attack from outside forces. According to Arab historians, around 1054 CE **Almoravid** Muslims from Morocco invaded and conquered Ghana. Others believe the Almoravids occupied Ghana peacefully and gradually converted the people to Islam. The Kingdom of Ghana finally collapsed after it was attacked by the Sosso ruler, Samaguru. Now Ghana was about to be eclipsed by the Empire of Mali.

Almoravid
the Spanish name of a Muslim dynasty in North Africa and Spain

REVIEW AND REFLECT

1. How did the farming villages of Ghana unite the people?
2. In what ways are the records written by the Arabs valuable sources of primary evidence?
3. What do you think was the most interesting feature of the Kingdom of Ghana? Present your ideas in an opinion paragraph.

Mali: The Golden Age

According to the *griots*, the decline of Ghana created the opportunity for a powerful **sorcerer** called Samaguru to build his own empire among the Sosso people. But he was challenged by another powerful sorcerer named Sundiata. In an epic battle, Sundiata triumphed over Samaguru. It was the beginning of great new empire in West Africa that would last for 200 years.

sorcerer
a living person who possesses special knowledge that allows him or her to use the spiritual powers of the ancestors

FIGURE 2.17
A West African *griot*

The Mandinke *griots* of West Africa still tell the 750-year-old story about the legendary hero Sundiata. Known as the Lion King, as a child he was an unlikely hero. He was unable to speak or walk until the age of seven. Then, according to legend, he was magically cured. He became a great warrior and leader who ruled Mali for 25 years before his death in 1255 CE.

Sundiata ruled the Kingdom of Mali from 1230 to 1255 CE. He maintained a strong army, which he used to take over nearby kingdoms. He expanded his empire north to the edge of the Sahara Desert, south into the rainforest, east to the great bend in the Niger River, and west to the Atlantic Ocean. Mali became big and powerful enough to take control of the trade routes across the Sahara.

Controlling the trade routes made Mali even richer and more powerful. The written Arabic language allowed the traders to write contracts and keep records of their trade. Sundiata taxed all trade transactions. This contributed greatly to Mali's wealth. By 1300, the Mali Empire was more than twice the size and had twice the population of the old kingdom of Ghana.

Religion

The rulers of Mali converted to Islam in the 11th century. Their new faith presented Mali with the opportunity to become part of the trade network the Muslim nations had created in northern Africa. Muslims played an important role in the government. But many people continued to practise their traditional religions. Muslim scholars credit the influence of Islam for Mali's advanced civilization. But in the oral histories passed down by the *griots*, there is little talk about Islam.

FIGURE 2.18 The Grand Mosque of Djenné in Mali

The Grand Mosque was the ancient centre of Islamic learning in Mali. It is the largest adobe, or mud brick, building in the world. The first mosque was built in the 13th century. The current structure was built in 1907. The entire community of Djenné takes part in the maintenance of the mosque during an annual festival to repair any damages to the structure.

The People of Mali

The people of Mali were farmers and herders. They kept sheep, goats, and chickens on the grasslands of the savannah. They lived in a cluster of villages on the savannah or in clearings in the rainforest.

Family life revolved around the children. Mothers raised the children until the age of 12. Then the boys became men and decided their future: to become **apprentices** in the **castes** of their uncles or to join the army.

apprentice
a person who learns a trade by being employed in that business for a period of time

caste
a hereditary social class

Girls were raised to become wives and mothers. The women were strong and attractive, which made them much sought after as wives. But they had no choice in their marriage partners. That was decided by the girl's father. Women did not have the same rights as men. Men could divorce their wives for being infertile, lazy, or a nag! They could have as many wives as they wanted. But if a woman committed adultery, she was put to death.

Mansa Musa

Mansa Musa is one of the greatest of all the kings of Mali. Musa's reign from 1307 to 1332 CE is known as the Golden Age of Mali. During this time, Mali expanded its territory and extended its trading routes. At its height, the Mali Empire under Mansa Musa was as large as Europe.

Musa was a devout Muslim. His pilgrimage to Mecca in 1324 established Mali as a powerful kingdom. Musa took 8000 attendants and two tonnes of gold with him.

TRANSATLANTIC EXPLORERS

Did the people of Mali explore beyond their own borders? According to Muslim scholars, Mansa Musa told the story of one attempt to cross the Atlantic Ocean.

> **The Sultan got ready 2000 ships, 1000 for himself and the men whom he took with him, and 1000 for water and provisions. He left me to deputise for him and embarked on the Atlantic Ocean with his men. That was the last we saw of him and all those who were with him.**
>
> **And so, I became king in my own right.**
>
> Mansa Musa, as told to the Syrian scholar al-Umari

Historians believe that Mali had the resources to launch an expedition such as Mansa Musa described. They disagree, though, on whether or not the Malians really did.

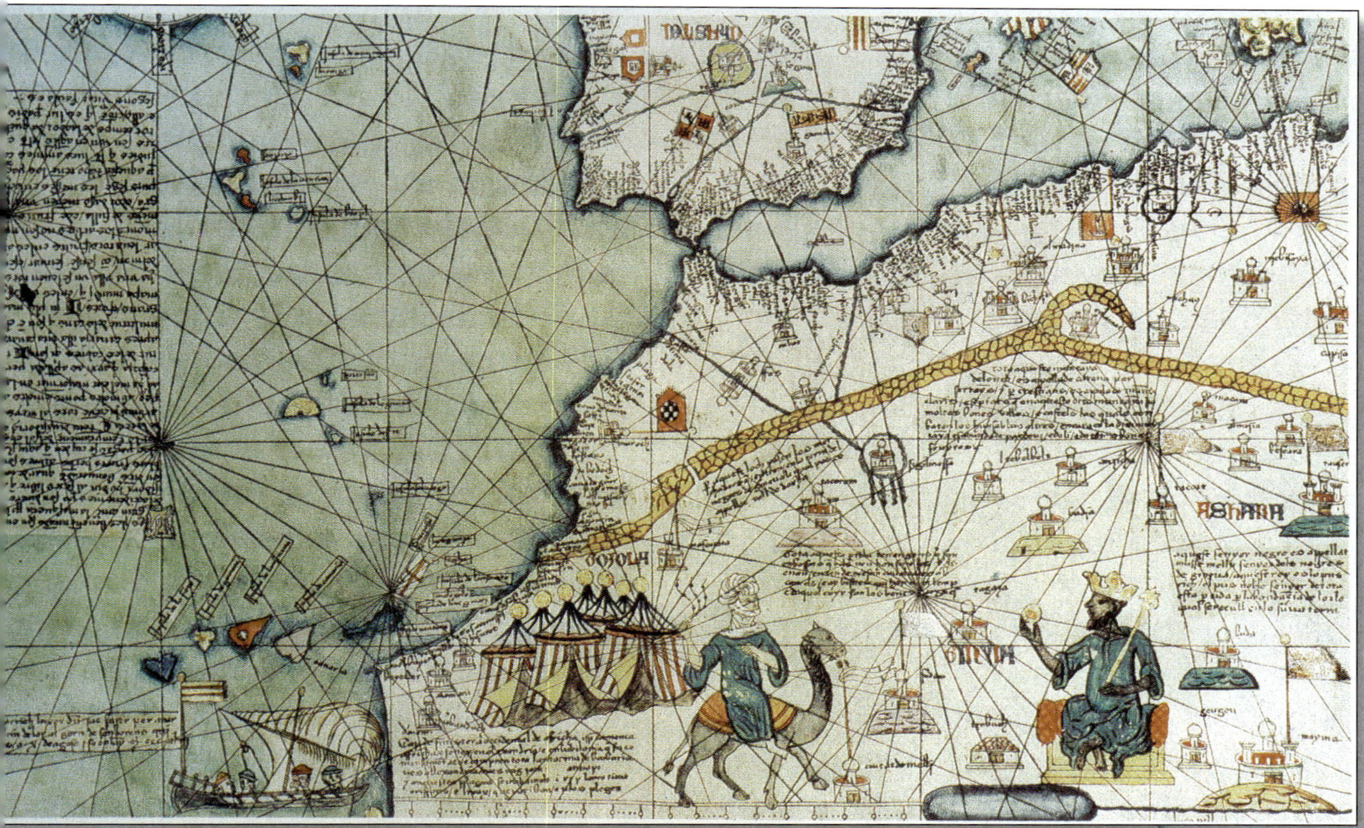

FIGURE 2.19 Mansa Musa

In 1324, Mansa Musa left the capital city of Timbuktu on a pilgrimage to the Muslim holy city of Mecca. He travelled through Cairo with hundreds of servants and camels loaded with gold. As he made his way through the city, he gave away gold nuggets. His generosity attracted attention in Europe.

How does this map, created by a Spanish cartographer in 1375, reflect the Europeans' view of the empire of Mali?

Timbuktu: City of Gold!

Timbuktu became famous around the world during the rule of Mansa Musa. Musa commissioned the design and construction of extensive libraries and Islamic universities. He supported the creation of elaborate works of art in gold and copper. Under his guidance, Timbuktu blossomed into a centre for commerce, learning, and culture. People from as far away as India came to Timbuktu to study. The university had great manuscripts highlighting the teachings of Islam in subjects such as astronomy, medicine, mathematics, chemistry, law, government, and conflict resolution.

FIGURE 2.20 Traders bound for Timbuktu

Many people travelled to Timbuktu for trade. Caravans arrived almost daily with salt to be traded for such treasures as gold, silver, and leather.

In Timbuktu, most people practised Islam. Although Arabic never became an official language, it was widely read, spoken, and written throughout the city. However, many Muslims were unhappy that Mansa Musa did not order everyone in Mali to convert to Islam. Under pressure from Islamic leaders, he tried to convince gold miners to convert. But the miners refused. When the attempts to convert them continued, they refused to work. Mansa Musa realized it was in the best interests of his empire to maintain religious freedom. He never tried to convert any of his subjects again.

The Fall of Mali

The death of Mansa Musa in 1337 marked the beginning of Mali's decline. His son, Mansa Maghan, inherited the throne. But he was not a skilled leader like his father. He could not prevent the kingdom from crumbling as smaller states Mali had once conquered began to break away.

Other groups quickly took advantage of the political instability. Aggressive raids by the **Mossi** and the **Tuareg** gradually reduced Mali's power. In 1468, the powerful Songhai army seized Timbuktu and the once-great Mali Empire collapsed.

Mossi
an African people living in what is now Burkina Faso and Côte d'Ivoire

Tuareg
African traders living in North and West Africa

> Mali is eternal. But never try . . . to pierce the mystery which Mali hides from you. Do not go and disturb the spirits in their eternal rest. Do not ever go into the dead cities to question the past, for the spirits never forgive. Do not seek to know what is not to be known.
>
> Griot Mamadou Kouyaté, "Sundiata: Lion King of Mali," ARTSEDGE, The Kennedy Center, 1997

REVIEW AND REFLECT

1. What made Timbuktu famous? What impact do you think the idea of a city of great wealth in Africa might have had on Europeans?
2. Reread the quotation from Griot Mamadou Kouyaté. What do you think his message is?
3. What is your impression of the ancient Kingdom of Mali? Present your ideas to your classmates using photographs and illustrations.

Songhai: Land of Royalty

The Kingdom of Songhai had been part of the Empire of Mali. Beginning in 1464 CE, the king of Songhai, Sonni Ali, took over lands that had once been part of the Kingdom of Mali. The Songhai army conquered Timbuktu and Djenné as part of Ali's plan to gain control of the Saharan trade routes. Timbuktu's importance as an intellectual centre and Djenné's gold and ivory resources would give the Songhai the tools they needed to thrive in trade and commerce and become a great empire. By 1492, Songhai controlled a huge kingdom and the important trade routes across the Sahara. It expanded to become the largest of the three great West African civilizations.

Sonni Ali accepted Islam and took a Muslim name. But he refused to give absolute loyalty to Islam or to forget the traditions of the Songhai people. During the conquest of Timbuktu, he killed Muslim scholars who did not respect Songhai religion. Muslims accused him of being an enemy of Islam. Ali had the respect and admiration of the *griots*, though.

Sonni Ali wanted to bring the different clans under his rule together in a peaceful and stable kingdom. He appointed people he trusted to govern the provinces. He allowed local leaders in the countries he conquered to hold on to power if they paid tribute and obeyed his orders. To make sure that law and order prevailed, Ali maintained a large and powerful army.

FIGURE 2.21 Songhai ruins

The ruins of towns and villages in the Songhai Empire remain today.

What does the evidence at this site tell you about the way of life of the Songhai people?

Mohammad Askia

In 1493, Mohammad Askia became king of Songhai. Mohammad embraced Islam. He understood that the wealth of his kingdom depended on the activities of the Muslim traders. Even though he was a devout Muslim himself, Mohammad allowed Songhai traditions to be practised throughout the empire. He did not force Islam upon his non-Muslim subjects. But in the cities, the daily work of the kingdom was based on Islamic traditions, laws, and beliefs. These helped to restore Timbuktu as an important centre of Islamic scholarship.

Mohammad appointed Islamic judges to make decisions based on Muslim law. He attempted to make Songhai a more equitable society. Positions in government were no longer passed down from father to son. Any man had the opportunity to advance in his government. Mohammad encouraged Islamic education. He opened many schools to teach students to read and recite the Qur'an and learn Islamic theology, law, language, and history.

The Glory Days of Timbuktu

Under Mohammad Askia, Timbuktu reached the peak of its power and influence. Many students and scholars were drawn to Timbuktu. At its height, the population reached 100 000 as Timbuktu blossomed as a centre of religion, education, science, and culture.

> Here are many shops of craftsmen and merchants, especially those who weave linen and cotton cloth. To this place Barbarie [Berber] merchants bring cloth from Europe. All the women of this region except maidservants go with their faces covered, and sell all necessary kinds of food. The inhabitants are exceedingly rich. Here there are many doctors, judges, priests, and other learned men that are well maintained at the king's cost. The inhabitants are people of a gentle and cheerful disposition, and spend a great part of the night in singing and dancing through all the streets of the city.
>
> Leo Africanus, a Moroccan scholar, upon visiting Timbuktu in 1510

Djenné was highly regarded for its medical knowledge and practices. Many people travelled to Djenné for medical attention. Doctors discovered that mosquitoes caused malaria. They performed eye surgery to remove **cataracts**. Their advanced medical knowledge and technology made a significant contribution to modern medicine.

cataract
a cloudiness on the lens of an eye

FIGURE 2.22
A traditional granary

These distinctive clay granaries are part of the traditional architecture of Songhai villages. Each family has its own set of granaries. They use them to store grain and other food stuffs.

The Trade in Human Lives

Slavery was an important element of trade in the Kingdom of Songhai. Horses, spices, and cloth were exchanged for captives of war, prisoners, enemies, and criminals. To keep up with the demand, Muslim leaders raided nearby provinces. They captured and sold people who practised traditional African religions. As a result, many people converted to Islam to protect themselves from capture. Under Islamic law, free Muslims could not be enslaved. But enslaved people who converted to Islam after being captured were not given their freedom.

Arabian and Moroccan merchants used the captives as porters to carry their goods. While travelling across the desert, they were often beaten and forced to walk long hours without water. Many people died during the ordeal. Those who survived were sold at markets as bodyguards, soldiers, and household servants. You will learn more about the trade in African peoples in Chapter 3.

The Fall of Songhai

Mohammad's son Musa led a revolt against his father. Mohammad renounced his throne and was placed under house arrest. When Musa was assassinated, Mohammad's other sons tried to rule the kingdom. But they all failed. The kingdom remained in disarray until Askia Daoud gained power and restored peace and order. It did not last, though. The wealth of the Songhai Empire made it the envy of its neighbours. Although the Songhai army was large and powerful, it was no match for the Moors from Morocco. The Moors wanted to find Songhai's secret gold mines. In 1591 CE, they invaded the kingdom armed with guns and cannons. When they could not find the mines, the Moors robbed the Songhai people and destroyed their towns. Timbuktu and Gao were quickly captured. Djenné followed soon after.

The Moroccan invasion divided the Songhai. It disrupted the lucrative trans-Saharan trade. Without trade, the Kingdom of Songhai quickly collapsed into poverty. All that remains today is a small ancestral homeland nestled along the Niger River where the descendants of the original inhabitants live.

REVIEW AND REFLECT

1. In what ways did the rulers of Songhai demonstrate their religious tolerance?
2. In your opinion, what factors contributed to the success of the Songhai Empire?
3. What impact do you think the destruction of Timbuktu had on West Africa? Discuss your ideas with a partner.

ORIGINALS

LEO AFRICANUS (1485–1554)

El Hasan ben Muhammed el-Wazzan-ez-Zayyati was a Muslim scholar and traveller. He was given the name Leo Africanus by Pope Leo X, who commissioned him to survey Africa in the early 16th century. His records provided Europeans with much of their knowledge about the African continent. He visited Timbuktu during the Songhai Empire. Although it was past its peak, Timbuktu was still a busy trading town and centre of learning.

> The royal court is magnificent and very well organized. When the king goes from one city to another with the people of his court, he rides a camel and the horses are led by hand by servants. If fighting becomes necessary, the servants mount the camels and all the soldiers mount on horseback. . . . The king has about 3000 horsemen and infinity of foot-soldiers armed with bows made of wild fennel, which they use to shoot poisoned arrows. This king makes war only upon neighboring enemies and upon those who do not want to pay him tribute. When he has gained a victory, he has all of them—even the children—sold in the market in Timbuktu.

Leo Africanus, *The Description of Africa*, 1526

FIGURE 2.23
Awaiting an Audience by Ernst Rudolphe

Like the subject of this 19th-century painting, Leo Africanus likely spent hours waiting for an audience with royal rulers and diplomats.

What impression of these royal households do you get from this painting?

Think It Through

What impressions do you get about the early civilizations of West Africa from reading this account? Is this a valuable source of primary evidence? Explain your response.

Great Zimbabwe: House of Stone

The kingdom of Great Zimbabwe was located between the Zambezi and Limpopo rivers in southern Africa. It was a strategic location along the trade route that linked the goldfields of the African interior with the east coast trading port of Sofala. From Sofala, the gold was shipped to Persia, India, and China in exchange for silks, spices, cotton, and porcelain. Among the ruins of Great Zimbabwe, archaeologists have found items from China and India that the people of Great Zimbabwe bought with profits from the gold trade.

> **Among the gold mines of the inland plains between the Limpopo and Zambezi rivers [there is a] . . . fortress built of stones of marvellous size, and there appears to be no mortar joining them. . . . This edifice is almost surrounded by hills, upon which are others resembling it in the fashioning of stone and the absence of mortar, and one of them is a tower more than 12 fathoms [22 m] high. The natives of the country call these edifices Symbaeo, which according to their language signifies court.**
>
> Viçente Pegado, captain of the Portuguese garrison at Sofala, 1531

The People of Great Zimbabwe

Knowledge about life in Great Zimbabwe is limited. Much of the archaeological evidence was removed from the site during early European excavations. Historians do know that the first settlers here were the ancestors of the present-day Shona people. Around 1000 CE, migrating farmers and herders settled here. Artifacts show that they were skilled craftspeople and metal workers. They made intricate objects out of gold and copper. They used iron to fashion tools. They carved flat wide dishes and other objects out of soapstone. They decorated them with intricate carvings of cattle, zebras, and other animals.

Archaeologists believe that Great Zimbabwe was likely a religious centre where Mwari, the supreme Shona god, was revered. Soapstone carvings found at the top of some columns suggest that birds had significance, too. Scholars believe they served as royal emblems. Birds remain a powerful symbol of rule in the modern era.

The Fall of Great Zimbabwe

For centuries, Great Zimbabwe was a stable, prosperous kingdom. At one point, its population may have been as high as 18 000 people. But in the 15th century, Great Zimbabwe began to decline. The gold trade moved further west as the gold supplies around Great Zimbabwe ran out. The grazing lands of the savannah were exhausted. The trees were gone. The soil was eroded. By 1450, the land could no longer support the people of Great Zimbabwe and the site was abandoned.

African Origins Denied

When Europeans first located the ruins of Great Zimbabwe, they refused to believe such skilfully constructed buildings had been built by Africans. Since they were unlike any other structures they had seen in Africa, they concluded they were built by foreign travellers.

Excavations by amateur archaeologists and treasure hunters removed much of the archaeological evidence that could prove Great Zimbabwe was built by Africans. The first archaeologist to investigate the site was David Randall-MacIver in 1906. He concluded that the ruins were in fact of African origin. Yet the British were still unwilling to accept the fact that the structures of Great Zimbabwe were of African invention. For the next several years, they banned archaeologists from conducting any further research.

The truth about the Zimbabwe ruins was finally confirmed in 1929. A British archaeologist named Gertrude Caton-Thompson led the first all-female excavation of the site. She determined from the remaining archaeological evidence that Great Zimbabwe was, without doubt, built by Africans. After the colonial state of Rhodesia gained its independence from Britain in 1980, the country was renamed Zimbabwe after this great ancient civilization.

The Ruins of Great Zimbabwe

Roughly translated, the name *Great Zimbabwe* means "Houses of Stone." The remains at the site of Great Zimbabwe provide evidence of a thriving culture in the heart of Africa.

The ruins of Great Zimbabwe reflect the advanced civilization that once lived there. The people began building in stone around 1100 CE. The site consists of three main structures: the Hill Complex, the Great Enclosure, and the Valley Ruins. These structures were made of rectangular blocks cut from granite and placed in layers without the use of **mortar**. This created stable, free-standing curved walls that were both high and wide. Archaeologists believe that the rulers and the wealthy lived in these stone buildings. They are among the most fascinating structures in Africa.

mortar
a mixture of lime with cement, sand, and water used to bond bricks or stones

FIGURE 2.24
The Hill Complex

The Hill Complex is the oldest of the three structures. The wall is in the shape of an oval. It is 100 m long and 44 m wide. The outer wall is nearly 11 m high. From its vantage point on top of a hill, the people of Great Zimbabwe had a bird's-eye view of invaders.

FIGURE 2.25 The Great Enclosure

Just below the Hill Complex lies the Great Enclosure. It was built when Great Zimbabwe was at the peak of its power. The enclosing wall is 240 m long and in some places over 9 m high. An inner wall runs along the outer wall, creating a narrow passageway 54 m long. Archaeologists believe the Great Enclosure served as the royal palace.

FIGURE 2.26 The Valley Ruins

The Valley Ruins lie in the valley between the two larger structures. These buildings were the last to be built, likely as the population of Great Zimbabwe grew and more housing was needed. The Valley Ruins contain hut-like structures made of dried earth, mud, and gravel. The commoners of Great Zimbabwe likely lived in these structures.

REVIEW AND REFLECT

1. Why do you think Europeans refused to believe that the buildings of Great Zimbabwe were built by Africans?
2. What do you find most interesting about the ruins of Great Zimbabwe? Give reasons for your response.

The Swahili City-States: Ancient Crossroads

Around 900 CE, the Swahili city-states began to emerge along the southeastern coast of Africa. Between the 12th and 16th centuries, these city-states flourished as ships from Arabia, India, and China called at their ports. They came for gold, ivory, and enslaved peoples from the African interior as well as for crops from the coastal plantations.

The Swahili culture integrated the Bantu-speaking peoples and the Arabs. The Bantu were farmers and cattle herders from the African interior. The Arabs were merchants and traders from Ethiopia. Together, they created a unique culture that laid the foundation for the **Kiswahili** language that emerged along the coast.

Kiswahili
a Bantu language mixed with Arab elements, from the Arab word *sawahil*, meaning "coast"

The people were united not just by their language, but by their Islamic faith. They created a literate population that read and spoke Kiswahili. They recorded their histories and traditions in the Kiswahili language. They translated the Qur'an into Kiswahili. They wrote profound poetry in elegant Arabic script.

Trade

Their Islamic faith connected the people to the world of international trade. They traded extensively with Persians, Arabs, Somalis, and Muslims in India and Indonesia. They exchanged goods from the African interior, such as ivory, gold, and ebony, for Asian products, such as silk, spices, and porcelain.

Trade brought wealth and prosperity to the Swahili merchants. They took great pride in showing off their good fortune. They built magnificent houses made of coral stone. Their homes had many rooms, including bathrooms with pit toilets. They ate delicious Swahili cuisine from fine porcelain dishes imported from China and Persia. They dressed in elegant and elaborate clothing made from silks and fine fabrics from India and China. Archaeological excavations have uncovered glass beads and vessels, semi-precious stones, and copper kohl sticks used to apply makeup—evidence that the Swahilis enjoyed the finer things in life and took pride in their appearance.

To maintain strong ties with their trading partners, the Swahili merchants often arranged marriages between their children and those of Arab and Asian merchants and African traders. These blood relations strengthened their commercial alliances and added to the Swahilis' prosperity.

The Swahilis developed advanced technologies that helped them prosper from trade. They built sturdy boats that were able to withstand the ocean's rough seas. They learned how to spin and weave cotton into cloth. They carved ivory and bone tools and utensils. They decorated clothing with intricate patterns using shells and semi-precious beads. They produced salt by evaporating large amounts of sea water.

FIGURE 2.27
The ruins of the city of Kilwa

Visitors to the city-states were likely impressed by what they saw. Their beauty and splendour reflected a culture that was urban, literate, and sophisticated. Kilwa was a large city of about 12 000 people. It had elaborate stone-terraced buildings and houses with exquisite woodwork. Walls and terraces surrounded the city. Beyond their walls the lush countryside was abundant with fruit trees and vegetable gardens. Swahili culture established Africa as a place of urban sophistication long before the arrival of Europeans.

The People of the Swahili City-States

The eight major Swahili city-states—Mogadishu, Barawaa, Mombasa, Gedi, Pate, Malindi, Zanzibar, Kilwa, and Sofala—were united by language and culture. But they remained fiercely independent. They competed against one another for the largest share of African trade. In the north, the city-states remained to themselves. They made little effort to influence African culture inland. In the south, though, the people of Sofala spread Islam and Islamic culture deep into the African interior.

The Arabs and Persians controlled trade. But the city-states themselves were controlled by an upper-class nobility of African origin, possibly mixed with Arab blood. Beneath the nobility were the commoners. These were the majority of citizens. They worked as artists and craftspeople, as government clerks and court officials, and as ship captains and crew members. The nobility lived in large stone houses and grand palaces. The commoners lived in clusters of small rectangular mud-and-thatch houses.

The Fall of the Swahili City-States

The Swahili city-states began to decline in the 16th century. Portuguese traders arrived along the coast. They conquered the Swahili city-states and pushed the African traders out of African trade. The city-states remained under Portuguese control until the late 17th century, when the **sultan** of Oman conquered the Portuguese in East Africa.

sultan
the ruler of a Muslim country

The cities that exist today on the sites of the former Swahili city-states bear little resemblance to the places they once were. Once-powerful cities like Mombasa and Malindi have retained little of their Swahili character. Only on the small island of Zanzibar, now part of Tanzania, is there a modern city that still maintains its Swahili roots.

FIGURE 2.28 Lamu Old Town

The city of Lamu is geographically isolated along the coast of modern-day Kenya. Its location helped the city preserve many of its Swahili customs and traditions. The Old Town is the oldest and best preserved Swahili city in East Africa. These carved wooden doors are traditional Swahili doors. They are still found today on many old buildings in Lamu. Lamu Old Town is a World Heritage Site and an important centre for education in Islamic and Swahili culture.

REVIEW AND REFLECT

1. Locate the Swahili city-states in your atlas. How did their coastal location benefit them?
2. In what ways did Islam work as a unifying force in the Swahili city-states?

EXPRESSIONS

AFRICAN INFLUENCES ON MODERN ART

You have seen how various African civilizations created rich and vibrant cultures for thousands of years all across the continent. Within these diverse societies, peoples created their own unique visual cultures, too. Through sculptures, masks, and other art forms, the people of Africa created one of the most diverse artistic legacies in the world.

Traditionally, the power of African art came from imagination and emotion. It expressed the spiritual, emotional, and psychological elements of life as it explored the people's mystical and religious experiences. They often presented their art as abstract interpretations of the natural world.

Traditional European art, on the other hand, was based on realistic representations of the world. To Europeans, art was a symbol of wealth, power, and possessions, unlike in Africa, where art was an integral part of a society's rituals, dances, and ceremonies.

In the early 20th century, artists like Pablo Picasso and Georges Braque wanted to break free of traditional European ideas about art. They found their inspiration in African art—art that was not meant to hang lifelessly in galleries and museums, but that played an integral part of people's daily lives.

> [I examined] these masks, all these objects that people had created with a sacred, magical purpose, to serve as intermediaries between them and the unknown, hostile forces surrounding them, attempting in that way to overcome their fears by giving them colour and form. And then I understood what painting really meant. It's not an aesthetic process; it's a form of magic that interposes itself between us and the hostile universe, a means of seizing power by imposing a form on our terrors as well as on our desires. The day I understood that, I had found my path.
>
> Pablo Picasso, "Stealing Beauty"

FIGURE 2.29 Sculpture by the Nok peoples

The earliest known sculptures were created by the Nok peoples of Nigeria around 500 BCE.

What are the interesting features of this sculpture?

FIGURE 2.30 *Head of a Woman* (1907) and an African mask

Picasso found new artistic inspiration at an exhibit of African art in Paris in 1907. Afterward, his work shifted in appearance and theme. He adopted the colour palettes found in many African pieces of art. On the left is his portrait *Head of a Woman*. On the right is an African mask from the Dan peoples of Côte d'Ivoire, Liberia, and Guinea.

In what ways did African artistic forms and technique influence this painting?

What Picasso found in African art was the key to a new way of seeing and representing the world. The influence of African art was evident in Cubism, the most influential movement in the history of modern Western art, founded by Picasso and Braque. After Cubism, the art world never looked the same again—a credit to the influence of African art.

Find Out More

Do some research to find other examples of modern art that were influenced or inspired by African art. Create your own art gallery catalogue showing these pieces of art. Include the name of the artist, the title of the work, and the year it was created. Add captions that explain how African art influenced each piece.

The Historian's Craft

PRIMARY AND SECONDARY SOURCES

This textbook includes evidence from both primary and secondary sources. *Primary sources* are first-hand accounts created by people who were there during the event. They are eyewitness accounts of history. They give you, the historian, the opportunity to find out first-hand what people did, said, and saw in the past. They create a sense that you are there that makes history come alive. Examples of primary sources include:

PRIMARY SOURCES		
Written	**Visual**	**Oral**
◆ diaries ◆ government documents ◆ journals ◆ letters ◆ on-the-scene newspaper reports	◆ contemporary maps ◆ paintings and carvings ◆ photographs ◆ cartoons ◆ video and DVD recordings	◆ speeches ◆ poems and songs ◆ music ◆ oral interviews

Secondary sources are accounts of events created by people who did not witness the events first-hand. After the fact, historians create secondary sources from primary sources and other secondary accounts. Secondary sources allow you to see the big picture. They give you the opportunity to find out what other historians think about a topic or event. Examples of secondary sources include:

SECONDARY SOURCES
◆ books and textbooks ◆ documentaries ◆ encyclopaedias ◆ journal articles ◆ newspaper and magazine articles and editorials ◆ modern maps

CAUTIONS ABOUT PRIMARY SOURCES

Primary sources are appealing. They let you read what history makers wrote, to see what they painted, and to hear what they sang. Primary sources allow you to slip into the shoes of historical people. Yet, as a historian, you have to approach primary sources cautiously. As you read through this book, enjoy the primary sources as an interested reader. At the same time, use the critical thinking skills of a historian to analyze and evaluate their value and validity as sources of evidence.

TRY IT!

Choose one piece of primary evidence from this chapter that gives you a strong sense of "being there." Explain why it speaks to you so strongly.

STUDY HALL

KNOWLEDGE & UNDERSTANDING

1. In a graphic organizer, compare the ancient kingdoms of Kush and Axum.
2. In a graphic organizer, compare and contrast the Swahili city-states with the West African empires.
3. Explain the significance of the degradation of the environment in the decline of many African civilizations.
4. Discuss your ideas on why African civilizations achieved greatness.

THINKING

5. How did trade affect the early civilizations of Africa? Outline the advantages and disadvantages in a graphic organizer.
6. Use a spider map to highlight the impact Islam had on the early civilizations of Africa.
7. Conduct further research on Mansa Musa and his pilgrimage to Mecca. Why did he make this pilgrimage? How did the pilgrimage benefit Mali? In what ways did the pilgrimage inform other nations about Mali?
8. Based on what you have learned about African civilization, write a rebuttal to the European description of Africa as the "Dark Continent."

APPLICATION & COMMUNICATION

9. Create a graphic organizer to highlight what you consider to be the two greatest achievements of each of the civilizations in this chapter.
10. If you could live in one of the African civilizations described in this chapter, which one would you choose? Give reasons for your response.
11. Imagine you are a trader in one of the African civilizations discussed in this chapter. Create a brochure to present to potential trading partners, highlighting the goods you have to offer.
12. Choose one of the civilizations identified on the map in Figure 2.2 that is not covered in this chapter. Conduct research into this civilization. Present your findings in a visual presentation or display.
13. Assume the role of a modern-day *griot*. Write a story you wish to tell about the history of your society. Then tell your story to the class.

UNIT 2

Africa Discovers Europe and the Americas

TABLE OF CONTENTS

The Door of No Return in the House of Slaves on Goree Island in Dakar, Senegal

From here, captured West Africans boarded ships bound for the Caribbean and the Americas and a life of slavery.

CHAPTER

3 Africa and Europe: The Devastating Connection

KEY CONCEPTS

IN THIS CHAPTER, YOU WILL:

- look at the East African trade in African peoples
- identify the European imperial systems that led to trade in African peoples
- examine the methods of acquiring African peoples for trade
- discover the economic benefits of Triangular Trade that fuelled the trade in African peoples
- examine how enslavement shaped the world socially, politically, and economically
- discover the ways in which African peoples resisted slavery
- learn what factors contributed to the abolition of slavery

A People's Story

The devastating trade in African peoples across the Atlantic Ocean lasted for more than 400 years. During this time, an estimated 12 million Africans—men, women, and children—were torn from their families and communities, enslaved, and shipped to the Caribbean and the Americas. Millions more died in the raids for African captives to be sold into slavery. The enslaved Africans were forced to work on plantations and in mines, enduring conditions that were brutal, cruel, and deadly.

In this chapter, you will have the opportunity to learn more about this devastating trade in human life. You will see what prompted Europeans to begin the transatlantic trade in African peoples and why this practice was accepted by so many people for hundreds of years. As you read, think about the role that race, class, and gender played as millions of people were denied basic human rights. Think about the effect slavery had on African peoples and on the African continent itself. Ask yourself about the impact slavery has had on people of African heritage whose ancestors were enslaved. Then reflect on the moral lessons of slavery, both in the past and today.

Zanzibar becomes main trading post in East African trade	Public sale of West African peoples begins in Portugal	Portugal builds first trading post in West Africa	The first direct shipment of enslaved Africans arrives in the Americas	Spain issues contracts for trade in African peoples	Britain joins trade in African peoples	The Netherlands transports first enslave Africans to North Amer
CE 700	1444	1482	1518	1528	1562	1619

Image Analysis

FIGURE 3.1 Slaves below deck of *Albanez*

This image is a rare, authentic view of a cargo hold for African captives making the journey across the Atlantic Ocean into a life of slavery. It was painted by an English sailor onboard a British anti-slavery ship that had just captured the vessel.

How would you describe the living conditions revealed in this image? How important is this image as a primary source of evidence? Explain your ideas.

1640	1700	1787	1807	1808	1833	1865
Britain transports first enslaved Africans to ibbean sugar plantations	Britain dominates global trade in African peoples	The Society for the Abolition of the Slave Trade founded in Britain	Britain abolishes trade in African peoples	United States abolishes trade in African peoples	Slavery abolished throughout the British Empire	Slavery abolished in the United States

The Origins of Slavery

Slavery has existed throughout history, in different forms, in different places, and at different times. It existed in the ancient civilizations of China, Greece, and Rome. It was practised in some indigenous cultures of North and South America. It is sanctioned in religious codes such as the Bible and the Qur'an.

Slavery existed in African cultures, too. In most African societies, enslaved people were domestic workers or **indentured servants**. They were not **chattel** to be bought and sold for profits. They were symbols of wealth and power. Some who distinguished themselves in military service gained social status.

indentured servant
a person who is contracted into the paid service of another for a specified period of time

chattel
a personal possession that is the legal property of the owner and can be bought, sold, or bequeathed at the owner's discretion

The Global Trade in African Peoples

The nature of slavery in Africa changed dramatically around 700 CE. African peoples were captured and exported against their will to foreign lands in exchange for other trade goods. It was the beginning of a global trade in human lives that would last for more than 1000 years.

The first global trade in African peoples was the East African trade. This was followed 800 years later by the transatlantic trade. Millions of Africans were captured and traded on global markets. No one knows for sure how many. The East African trade may have involved between 8 million and 17 million African people. The transatlantic trade may have involved between 11 and 20 million. In this chapter, you will have the opportunity to learn about the devastating trade in African peoples and its tragic consequences.

> **The course of human history is marked by appalling crimes. But even the hardened historian is filled with horror, loathing, and indignation on examining the record of African slavery.**
>
> Elikia M'bokolo, "The Impact of the Slave Trade on Africa," *Le Monde Diplomatique*, April 1998

REVIEW AND REFLECT

1. Complete a KWL (Know-Wonder-Learn) chart and fill in everything you know, or think you know, about slavery.
2. In what way was the traditional form of slavery in African societies different from the global trade in African peoples?
3. Why do you think it is difficult for historians to determine with certainty how many people were involved in the global trade in African peoples?

The East African Trade in African Peoples

The rise of the East African trade in African peoples in the 8th and 9th centuries marked the beginning of the longest trade in human lives in history. It coincided with the rapid expansion of Islam in the decades following the life of **Muhammad**. Muslims from the Arabian Peninsula began travelling into northern and eastern Africa spreading the Islamic faith. As they did, they created a vast trading empire that stretched from Arabia across North Africa into present-day Spain, through Mesopotamia and into Persia. A system of roads, caravan tracks, and sea routes connected these lands. They linked major African trading centres such as Tripoli, Algiers, and Cairo with trading centres in India and China.

Muhammad
(ca. 570–632 CE) the Arab prophet and founder of Islam born in Mecca

Middle Eastern traders captured people of all races. However, White captives were viewed as more valuable than Black ones. As Middle Eastern prosperity grew, so did hostility toward Black Africans. Racist attitudes were expressed by many Arabic writers and scholars. These new attitudes marked the beginning of the enslavement of African peoples.

> **Babatu [a famous Muslim slave trader] and others didn't see anything wrong with slavery. They didn't have any knowledge of what the people were used for. They were only aware that some of the slaves would serve others of the royal families within the sub-region.**
>
> Mohammed Ibrahim Babatu, great-great grandson of Babatu

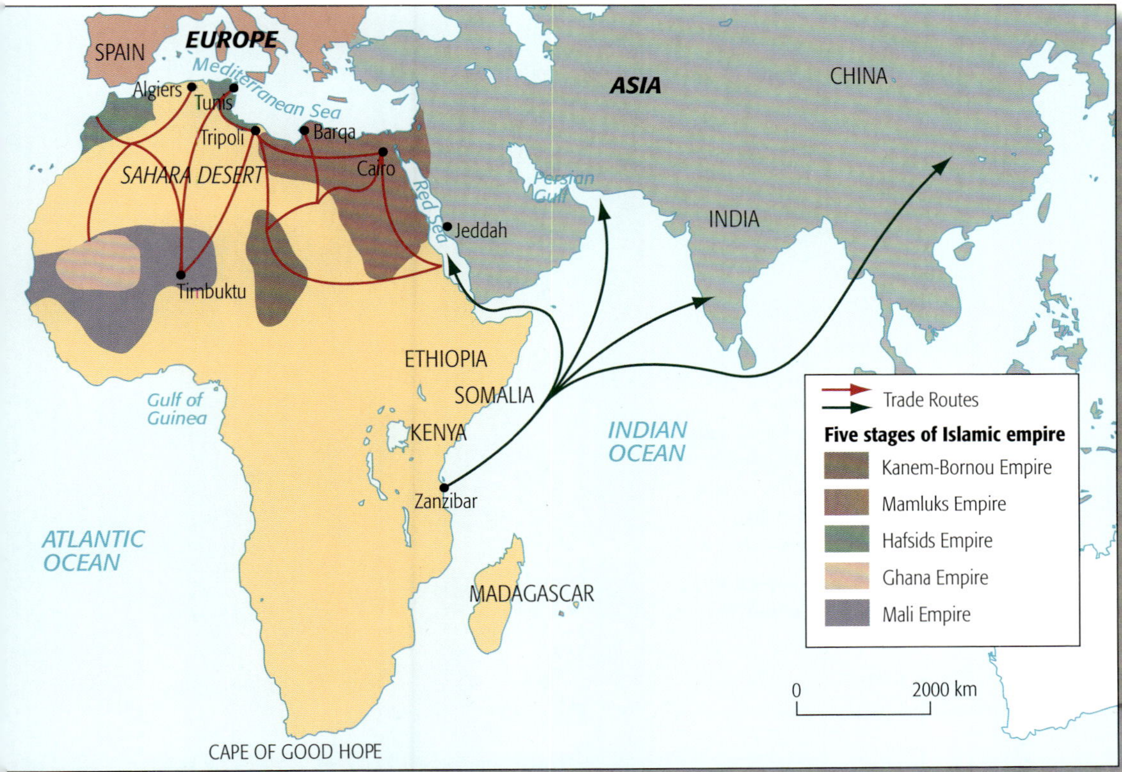

FIGURE 3.2 The routes of the East African trade in African peoples

There were two main trading routes. An overland route crossed the Sahara Desert. A sea route linked the east coast of Africa to the lands along the Red Sea and the Persian Gulf. Middle Eastern traders also operated in Ethiopia and Somalia, along the coast of present-day Kenya, and on the island of Zanzibar.

Raids

Although some enslaved Africans were acquired through conquest or tribute, most were captured during raids. Arab hunters raided unsuspecting African villages just before dawn. They killed off as many of the older villagers as they could. Then they abducted the young women and men. They forced the captives to endure long marches through the countryside, stopping to raid more villages along the way. The captives were bound together at the hand and neck. Many were beaten and raped during the long and torturous journeys.

Young women made up the bulk of the East African trade. Two women were captured for every young man. Most women were destined to become **concubines** in the **harems** in the households of wealthy and powerful men. They bore these men many children. It was a form of sexual abuse that lasted more than 1000 years.

concubine
a woman who lives with a man without being married, with few rights and low social status

harem
the part of a Muslim household reserved for the wives and concubines of the male head of the household

Enslaved young men toiled as domestic servants, labourers, and soldiers. Hundreds of thousands of young boys born into slavery between the ages of 8 and 12 were mutilated through castration. Their wounds were seared by hot coals to stop the bleeding, but many still bled to death. Those who survived were known as *eunuchs*. They fetched higher prices in the Middle Eastern markets. They served as guards or tutors and watched over the women in the harems.

FIGURE 3.3
A Middle Eastern slavery market

Middle Eastern traders travelled throughout the Arabian Peninsula. They captured both White and Black people for trade. The captives were transported to towns and settlements in North Africa and the Arabian Peninsula and to Arab lands bordering the Persian Gulf.

Who do you think created this painting? Whose perspective does it reflect?

The Expansion of Trade

The East African trade in African peoples remained relatively small until the late 18th century. Then demand escalated as the powers of Europe expanded their colonial empires. The focus of trade shifted from **domestic slavery** to **estate slavery**. A growing population in Europe increased the need for workers to produce food on the colonial plantations around the Indian Ocean. On the island of Zanzibar, the clove plantations of Middle Eastern sultans needed workers. British attempts to suppress the transatlantic trade in African peoples forced Atlantic traders to travel around the Cape of Good Hope to capture Africans from the Zambezi Valley and Mozambique.

From the 1860s to the 1880s, an increased demand for ivory in Europe gave another boost to the trade in African peoples in East Africa. Traders raided local villages to capture Africans to carry ivory tusks to coastal ports. The demand for ivory drew traders into the interior of the continent. By now, the traders were a diverse group of competitors: Arabs, **Swahilis**, **Prazeros**, and local peoples such as the Makua of Mozambique, the Nyamwezi of Tanzania, the Baganda of Uganda, and the Yao of Lake Malawi. The fierce rivalries among them fuelled the trade in African peoples. Each group scrambled to trade African captives for European firearms they could use against one another or to defend themselves against their neighbours.

domestic slavery
a form of slavery that forces people to work in other people's households for little or no pay

estate slavery
a form of agricultural slavery in which large numbers of enslaved workers perform labour in an impersonal relationship with the landowner, who has absolute power over them

Swahilis
people of Afro-Arab ancestry

Prazeros
people of Afro-Portuguese ancestry

FIGURE 3.4 Tippu Tip (1840–1905)

One of the most famous traders in the East African trade was Tippu Tip, also known as Hamed bin Mohammed. Tip, the grandson of an enslaved African, was a Swahili trader. In the1860s, he built a huge trading empire in central East Africa. He specialized in long and dangerous trips into the interior to capture or buy Africans. He was a ruthless yet clever man who grew wealthy through East African trade.

Throughout this period, only the traders benefited from the trade in people, ivory, and weapons. But the people who were enslaved, such as the Bantu, the Igbo, and the Yoruba, suffered from the violence and destruction inflicted upon their families and communities. Millions of people died during raids and on the dangerous journeys to the slavery markets of Zanzibar.

The East African trade in African peoples was the longest such trade in history. It lasted from approximately 700 CE into the early decades of the 20th century. It is impossible to know for sure how many Africans were sold during this time. Estimates place the number at around 14 million: 9.6 million African women and 4.4 million African men. When the East African trade ended, it was not out of an awakened moral consciousness. Changing economic factors meant the trade was simply no longer profitable.

REVIEW AND REFLECT

1. Using Figure 3.2 and your atlas, describe the trading routes of the East African trade in African peoples.
2. What factors led to the expansion of the East African trade in African peoples?
3. The figures about slavery are estimates. Who might be overlooked in these estimates? Who might not be included? Discuss your ideas with a partner.

The Transatlantic Trade in African Peoples

The transatlantic trade in African peoples was motivated by one overriding goal: the quest for wealth and power. In the 15th century, Prince Henry the Navigator of Portugal wanted to pursue trade in Africa, especially trade in gold. He organized and financed several Portuguese sailing expeditions down the west coast of Africa. (He never actually sailed on any of these voyages himself, though.)

Before the Portuguese voyages, European ships had never sailed beyond the Sahara Desert. Henry encouraged his captains to sail further south into uncharted waters. Initially, they landed along the coast of what is now Guinea. Eventually, they sailed all the way around the southern tip of Africa. They established a sea route to India. During their travels, they traded with the rulers of many African kingdoms.

Meanwhile, Queen Isabella I of Spain financed an expedition across the Atlantic Ocean in search of a water route to India. In 1492, Christopher Columbus arrived in the Caribbean. At first, he thought he had reached India. When he realized his mistake, he returned to Spain. He took some local people from the island of Hispaniola and samples of gold along with him.

Columbus's voyage launched a competition for wealth and power among the ruling monarchs of Spain, Portugal, England, and France. Other European explorers soon followed in his path. As they did, they claimed the lands they encountered for their European monarchs. In time, the European powers carved out vast empires in the Caribbean and North and South America. They were eager to tap the vast resource wealth of these colonial possessions. To do so, they needed mass labour. As you will discover later in this chapter, they turned to Africa to secure it.

Unprecedented Trade

The transatlantic trade in African peoples was unlike any trade that had gone before it. It involved the buying and selling of millions of Africans as property in the Europeans' quest for wealth and power. No one knows for sure how many African people were involved in the trade. Most historians today believe that it was likely around 12 million.

As monumental as this figure is, however, it does not tell the whole story. It does not include the people who were killed during raids on African villages. It does not take into account the people who died fighting local wars over trading rights. It does not include the millions of Africans who died from disease or abuse after being displaced from their villages. It does not account for the unknown number of African lives lost in the violence and devastation of slavery itself.

FIGURE 3.5 Christopher Columbus on the island of Hispaniola, 1492

Columbus planted the Spanish flag on the island to declare the land for Spain.

Who do you think created this painting? Who was the intended audience? Why do you think so?

The Key Players in Trade

The massive transatlantic trade in African peoples was a global partnership involving players from four continents:

- African traders (mostly chiefs) who captured other Africans for trade
- traders from Europe who bought and sold Africans into slavery
- colonists from the Caribbean and North and South America who kept enslaved Africans

THE AFRICANS

Many African peoples resisted the transatlantic trading of their people. Rulers such as King Tanja Musa of the Gwolu peoples tried to protect their people from being captured. In the early 1500s, the king of Benin banned the sale of male captives. In Senegal, a Muslim religious leader, Nasr al Din, denounced the trade and criticized kings who enslaved people.

Not all African rulers resisted, however. The rulers of powerful African kingdoms such as the Asante, Dahomey, Oyo, and Benin played an active role in the transatlantic trade in African peoples. They controlled the terms of trade along the West African coast. The Europeans needed their permission to build their trading posts. In return, European traders paid high prices to African leaders for strong young Africans.

The introduction of European firearms into the trade raised the stakes. Local rulers wanted these firearms to fight their enemies. Europeans took advantage of these local rivalries. They told African kings and chiefs that their enemies were trading Africans for firearms with other European traders. They persuaded them to trade people for firearms to ensure that they could defend themselves against their enemies.

In time, the motives for taking part in the trade in African peoples were influenced by other factors. Some rival kings and chiefs wanted to take control of the trading routes to expand their territories. Others were motivated by greed and a willingness to exploit their weaker neighbours. Some wanted to defend their people from the traders. Yet to do so, they needed guns and ammunition. To get them, they had to raid their neighbours and take captives because the Europeans only accepted captured Africans in exchange for weapons. Yet many African leaders, such as Queen Nzinga of Angola, resisted the trade in captive Africans, at great risk to their people.

But while many Africans participated in the trade in African peoples, the overwhelming majority of Africans were victims of one of the greatest tragedies in human history. Families were torn apart. Communities were wiped out. Entire nations were destroyed by raids, wars, and famines as people were forced to abandon agriculture.

THE PORTUGUESE

In 1441, a Portuguese sea captain named Antam Gonclaves kidnapped ten Africans off the coast of Cape Bojador on the west coast of Africa. This marked the beginning of European trade in African peoples. The next year, Portuguese ships captured 30 more Africans. Over the next ten years, thousands of West Africans were captured and transported to Portugal and its island colonies.

The Portuguese set up **factories** along the West African coast. Eventually, the coastline from Senegal to the Congo was dotted with these trading posts. But the Portuguese needed something of value to trade for African gold. They built sugar plantations on two uninhabited islands (São Tomé and Principe) off the west coast of Africa. They needed people to work the plantations, so they captured West Africans from the mainland.

factories
trading posts

In the early 1600s, the Portuguese set up sugar plantations in their South American colony of Brazil. However, the Europeans brought diseases to the colony for which the local people had no immunity. Thousands of indigenous people died. As a result, the local population could not provide a reliable and growing supply of cheap labour.

FIGURE 3.6 Portuguese traders being greeted by the king of Congo, late 1500s

In time, Portuguese traders exported Africans to markets in Portugal, Spain, and Italy. By the mid-1500s, there were more than 50 slavery markets in the Portuguese capital of Lisbon. Portugal was responsible for 40 percent of all transatlantic trade in African peoples.

Who do you think created this image? Who was the intended audience?

THE SPANIARDS

In 1492, Christopher Columbus claimed the Caribbean island of Hispaniola (now Haiti and the Dominican Republic) for Spain. His arrival in the Caribbean was disastrous for the indigenous people who lived there. Columbus exploited the local Tainos people. He tried to force them to work as labourers in his quest for gold. The Tainos resisted, but they were unable to overcome the firepower of European weapons. Most of the population was slaughtered. By the early 1500s, violence and European diseases had all but wiped out the Tainos.

Such human destruction repeated itself throughout the Spanish Empire as the Spaniards expanded their quest for gold and silver. Ancient civilizations such as the Incas of Peru and the Aztecs of Mexico all but vanished. Their material wealth was looted by the European traders. Their lands were given to European settlers. With local populations decimated, the Spaniards faced a shortage of workers for their mines and plantations. Like the Portuguese, they turned to Africa.

asientos
contracts issued by non-Spanish merchants and financiers by King Charles I of Spain

Spain had no trading posts of its own on the continent, so they sold ***asientos*** to foreign merchants and financiers. The winning bidders had the exclusive rights to sell Africans into slavery throughout the Spanish Empire. For the first 100 years, the Spaniards awarded their *asientos* to Portuguese traders. In the 1630s, they began issuing them to Dutch and British traders, too. Eventually, Spain, the Netherlands, and Britain became the most powerful forces in the transatlantic trade in African peoples.

FIGURE 3.7 Enslaved Africans carrying a barrel, 1839

Africans from many different cultures worked together, frequently performing back-breaking work, carrying heavy barrels like this one over long distances.

Who do you think created this image? Who was the intended audience? What message does this image convey?

THE DUTCH

The Dutch were latecomers to the transatlantic trade in African peoples. When they began setting up trading posts in Africa in the late 1600s, they came into conflict with the Portuguese. The Dutch prevailed. The balance of power in the transatlantic trade shifted. The Netherlands replaced Portugal as the dominant trading power. For the next 100 years, the Dutch shipped Africans to their colonies in Portuguese Brazil, the Caribbean, and Suriname. They were the first to import Africans to North America in their colony of New Amsterdam (renamed New York after the British took it over in 1664). In New Amsterdam, enslaved Africans built houses, roads, and defence walls. New York's famous financial centre, Wall Street, got its name from a long wooden wall built by these enslaved workers.

THE FRENCH

France joined the trade in Africans to exploit the resources of its Caribbean colonies. The French needed workers, so they seized Dutch trading posts on the West African coast. Between 1540 and the mid-1800s, French ships delivered 1.6 million enslaved Africans to the Caribbean colonies of Martinique, St. Christopher, Guadeloupe, and Saint-Domingue (now Haiti).

FIGURE 3.8 Whipping a fugitive, French West Indies, 1840s

Plantation owners had many instruments of torture. This man's arms and legs were pegged to the ground as he was whipped by a Black overseer. Other enslaved Africans were forced to watch.

How would watching scenes like this affect the thinking of enslaved Africans?

NEW FRANCE

In New France (now Quebec), the first enslaved African was a young boy named Olivier LeJeune. He arrived in the colony in 1628 and became a servant of a Jesuit priest, Father Paul LeJeune. In time, more enslaved Africans came to New France from the French colonies in the Caribbean. They worked as domestic servants in the homes of government officials and wealthy merchants and **seigneurs**. By 1759, there were 1132 enslaved Africans living in New France. When Britain gained control of the colony in 1760, they agreed that the enslaved Africans would remain enslaved under British rule.

seigneur
a holder of land in New France

THE BRITISH

A British sea caption named John Hawkins was one of the early pioneers in the transatlantic trade in African peoples. During the 1560s, he captured Africans in West Africa to sell in the emerging European colonies of the Caribbean.

For the most part, though, Britain did not participate in the trade in African peoples until the mid-1600s. By then, its colonies in the Caribbean and along the Atlantic coast of North America were flourishing. The sugar, coffee, and tobacco the plantations produced had become daily essentials in Britain. Like the other colonial powers, the British needed more workers. They, too, turned to Africa.

In 1672, the British king granted a monopoly over trade in African peoples to the Royal African Company. During the 1670s and 1680s, the company transported an average of 5000 Africans a year to British colonies. But when rival merchants demanded an end to the Royal African Company's monopoly, Britain opened up trade. The number of Africans captured for slavery skyrocketed to over 20 000 a year.

By the dawn of the 18th century, the British were in fierce competition with the Dutch and the French for supremacy in the West African trade. With its large and powerful navy, Britain seized control of almost all of the coastal trading factories. Britain now led the world in the trafficking of human lives.

BRITISH NORTH AMERICA

Trade in African peoples and slavery existed under British colonial rule in British North America, too. In 1780, about 4000 Black people lived in British North America. About 1800 were enslaved Africans. Most worked as domestic servants in the households of the political and social elite. Many came with the **Loyalists** who fled the United States following its war of independence against Britain. In 1793, the governor of Upper Canada (now Ontario) passed a law making it illegal to bring enslaved Africans into the colony. Those who were already enslaved, however, remained so until slavery was banned throughout the British Empire in the 19th century.

Loyalists
people who remained loyal to Britain following the American Declaration of Independence in 1776 and who migrated from the United States to British North America

British North America played an economic role in the colonial system that fuelled the trade in African peoples. Trade was brisk between Britain's northern and Caribbean colonies. Sailors from Newfoundland carried boatloads of salted cod fish to tropical isles like Jamaica. They traded the cod for smooth, delicious rum! The impact of this trade is still evident today. Salted cod, or salt-fish, is the national dish of Jamaica. Strong rum called Screech is the traditional drink of Newfoundland and Labrador. Britain also relied on its shipbuilding industry in British North America to build many of the ships it used to transport African peoples across the Atlantic. You will learn more about slavery in Britain's northern colonies in Chapter 5.

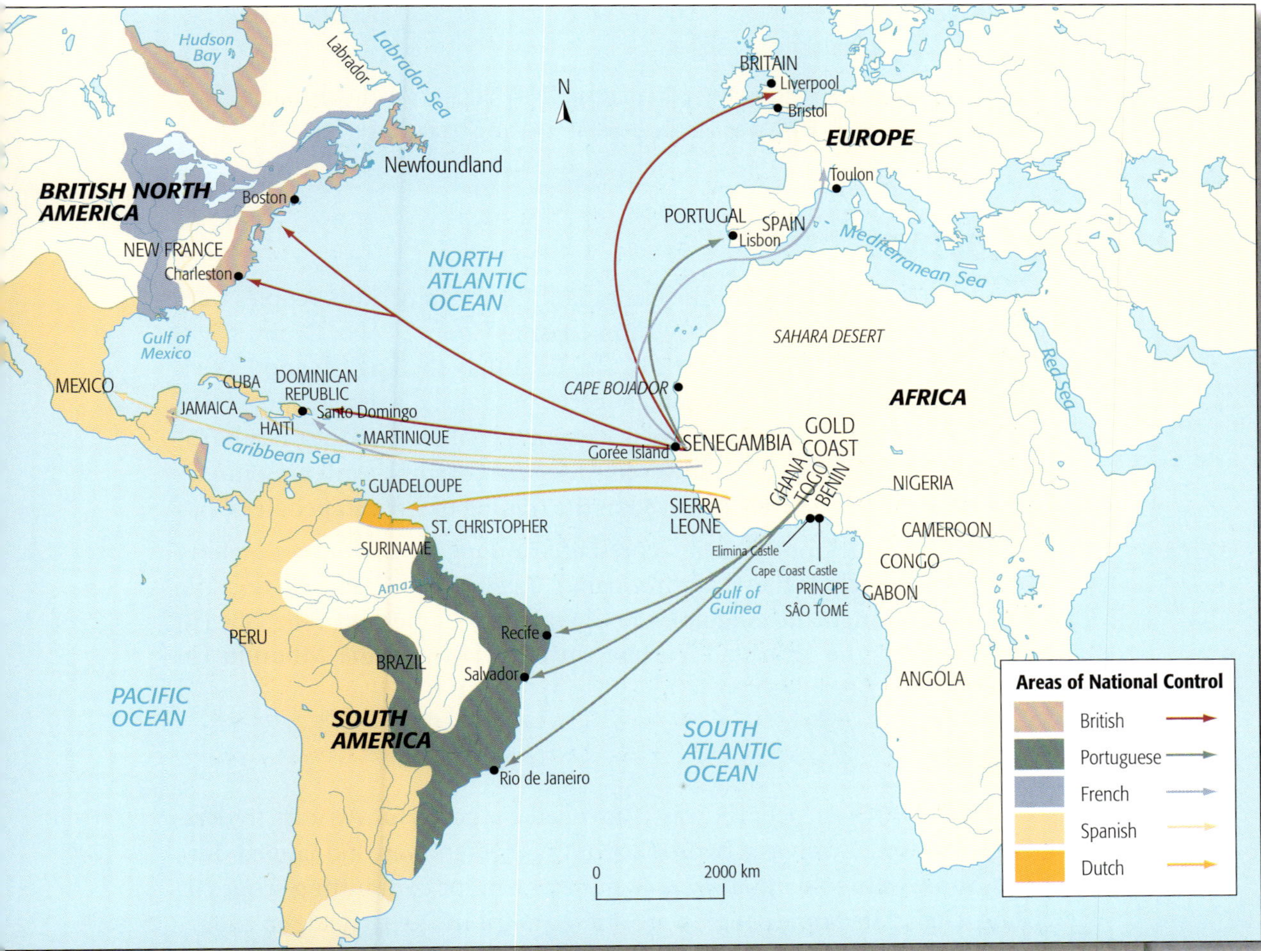

FIGURE 3.9 The distribution of enslaved peoples, 1500 to 1870

This map shows the distribution of enslaved Africans. The Portuguese transported over 4 million Africans to Brazil. Spain distributed 2.5 million Africans throughout its empire. The Netherlands shipped 500 000 captured Africans to its colonies. France sent 1.6 million African people to its colonial possessions. Britain transported 2 million Africans to its Caribbean colonies and another 500 000 to its colonies in North America.

What do these figures suggest about the impact the trade in African peoples had on Europe and on North and South America?

REVIEW AND REFLECT

1. What motivated African rulers to take part in the trade in African peoples?
2. What were the connections between the trade in African peoples and British North America?
3. Look back to Figure 3.8. What do you think would have been the purpose of having enslaved Africans punish one another?
4. Which European power transported the most enslaved Africans? Which transported the fewest? Create a bar or pie graph to illustrate the data for all countries in Figure 3.9.

The Captives

The main sources of captives for the transatlantic trade in African peoples were the current countries on the West African coast of Ghana, Togo, Benin, Nigeria, Cameroon, Gabon, Congo, and Angola. To supply the English and French sugar plantations in the Caribbean, Nigeria became a massive source for enslaved Africans beginning in the mid-17th century. Ghana had the most European trading forts. By the 1700s, however, the entire coastline from present-day Senegal to Angola was actively involved in the trading of African peoples.

The African peoples most heavily represented among the millions of captives taken from Africa include the Akan (in Ghana), the Bakongo (in the Democratic Republic of the Congo and Angola), the Chamba (in Cameroon), the Gbe (in Togo and Benin), the Igbo and Yoruba (in Nigeria), and the Mbundu (in Angola).

Captured

The capture of African peoples was controlled by powerful African traders. Some captives were taken as a byproduct of war. Others were kidnapped during raids. Some were sold into slavery as punishment for committing crimes or practising witchcraft. Some people were offered as tribute to persuade an enemy not to wage war.

Initial encounters between the captors and their captives were brutal. The captives fought desperately for their freedom. Many died during the struggle. Those who survived were forced to march to the coast in chains. Their journeys covered hundreds of kilometres. They lasted for weeks and even months. Along the way, the captives were traded many times over. Millions of African peoples were seized. Less than half survived the gruelling journey to the grim dungeons of the European trading posts.

FIGURE 3.10 Slave coffles on their way to the African coast (above); wooden restraints (below)

The captives were chained together in lines called *coffles*. Women and children were roped together with strips of rawhide. Men were forced to wear wooden restraints called *gorees* around their necks. The back of the neck was thrust into the fork-shaped stick. The two prongs of the fork were fastened together by a bar beneath the chin. This restricted the men's movements, making escape impossible.

ORIGINALS

OLAUDAH EQUIANO (1745–1797)

FIGURE 3.11
Olaudah Equiano

Michael Pascal gave Equiano a new name—Gustavas Vassa. Taking away people's identity and giving them new names was one way in which owners showed enslaved peoples they controlled them.

Olaudah Equiano was the son of a village elder. According to his memoirs, he was born in a village in the kingdom of Benin in what is now Nigeria. When he was 11, African traders abducted the young boy and whisked him off to be sold into slavery. He told his story in his memoirs, *The Interesting Life of Olaudah Equiano or, Gustavas Vassa, the African*, in 1789.

I was born in the year 1745, in a charming fruitful vale, named Essaka. The distance of this province from the capital of Benin and the sea coast must be very considerable; for I had never heard of white men or Europeans, nor of the sea. . . . One day, when all our people were gone out to their works as usual, and only I and my dear sister were left to mind the house, two men and a woman got over our walls, and in a moment seized us both; and, without giving us time to cry out, or make resistance, they stopped our mouths, and ran off with us into the nearest wood.

Equiano was forced onboard a ship bound for Barbados in the Caribbean. Conditions were appalling. The captives were held in the ship's hold, which was carpeted with vomit and human waste.

> When I looked around the ship . . . and saw a large furnace of copper boiling, and a multitude of black people of every description chained together, every one of their countenances expressing dejection and sorrow, I no longer doubted of my fate and quite overpowered with horror and anguish, I fell motionless on the deck and fainted. . . . I asked if we were not to be eaten by those white men with horrible looks, red faces, and long hair?

From Barbados, Equiano was sent to the British colony of Virginia. He was purchased by Michael Pascal, a British naval officer.

> We were conducted immediately to the merchant's yard, where we were all pent up together, like so many sheep in a fold, without regard to sex or age. . . . We were not many days in the merchant's custody, before we were sold after their usual manner, which is this: On a given signal, (as the beat of a drum) the buyers rush at once into the yard where the slaves are confined, and make choice of that parcel they like best.

Pascal and Equiano returned to England, where Pascal sent the young boy to school to learn to read and write. Equiano's education was interrupted periodically as he joined Pascal at sea during Britain's Seven Years' War with France.

After the war, Equiano was sold to a merchant named Robert King. He was shipped to the Caribbean island of Montserrat. By now, Equiano was well educated and too valuable to work in the plantation fields. Instead, he worked as a trader. King promised Equiano that he could buy his freedom if he raised enough money. In 1766, after three years, Equiano paid £40 for his freedom. At the age of 21, he was a free man.

Equiano returned to England. He became an outspoken advocate for the abolition of slavery. In 1789, he published his memoirs, *The Interesting Narrative of the Life of Olaudah Equiano or, Gustavas Vassa, the African*. His work gave a voice to the millions of Africans who had been captured into slavery but had left no records.

> Without scruple, relations and friends are separated, most of them never to see each other again. . . . Is it not enough that we are torn from our country and friends, to toil for your luxury and lust of gain? . . . Are the dearest friends and relations, now rendered more dear by their separation from their kindred, still to be parted from each other, and thus prevented from cheering the gloom of slavery, with the small comfort of being together; and mingling their sufferings and sorrows? Why are parents to lose their children, brothers their sisters, husbands their wives? Surely, this is a new refinement in cruelty, which . . . aggravates distress; and adds fresh horrors even to the wretchedness of slavery.

Equiano's memoirs focused attention on the horrors of slavery. The book sparked the first serious debates over the morality of slavery in the British Parliament. Today, however, some historians have raised questions about the authenticity of parts of Equiano's work. They claim that birth records show that Equiano was not born in Africa. He was born on a plantation in the British colony of South Carolina. They say there are inaccuracies in the stories about the first ten years of his life. They claim this is further proof that the stories about his early years were fabricated. They believe these stories reflect the oral histories of other enslaved peoples rather than first-hand accounts of Equiano's own life. He may have made up this part of his life story, they argue, to bolster his campaign to abolish slavery.

Other historians dispute these claims. They argue that any inaccuracies in Equiano's stories about his early life reflect the fact that he was a young child who had been abducted into slavery. The trauma of the horrific events he experienced at such a young age simply clouded his memory. They claim that stories of Equiano's life are accurate and can be verified by other sources.

The truth about Equiano's birthplace may never be fully revealed. Whether stories of his early experiences reflect his own life or those of other enslaved children, his work provides a lasting legacy about the horrors of slavery.

Think It Through

What can you learn from Olaudah Equiano's memoirs? Why is it important to understand Equiano's experiences? Do you think the controversy over his birthplace makes his memoir any less valid? Why or why not?

Imprisoned

After reaching the coast, most of the captives were held in the grim dungeons of the European trading factories. They waited for weeks, months—sometimes as long as a year—before being hoarded onto ships bound for strange and distant lands. About 5 percent of the captives died during their imprisonment.

At the factories, European traders inspected their captives before accepting or rejecting them. They preferred young males between the ages of 15 and 25 who were in good health and had strong, muscular bodies. Females and males between the ages of 8 and 15 or 25 and 35 fetched lower prices.

FIGURE 3.12
Elmina Castle, Ghana

Several trading factories, such as Elmina Castle (shown on the right as it looked during the trade in African peoples and below as it is today) are still standing. They serve as memorials to the millions of people who died there or who were forced to make the **Middle Passage**.

Middle Passage
the long journey of kidnapped African peoples across the Atlantic Ocean from Africa to the Caribbean and the Americas

FIGURE 3.13
The auctioning of captives and their transfer to the ships

After the captives were auctioned, they were loaded directly onto the ships. A typical ship held 300 captives. Sometimes, ships often waited weeks before their cargoes were full.

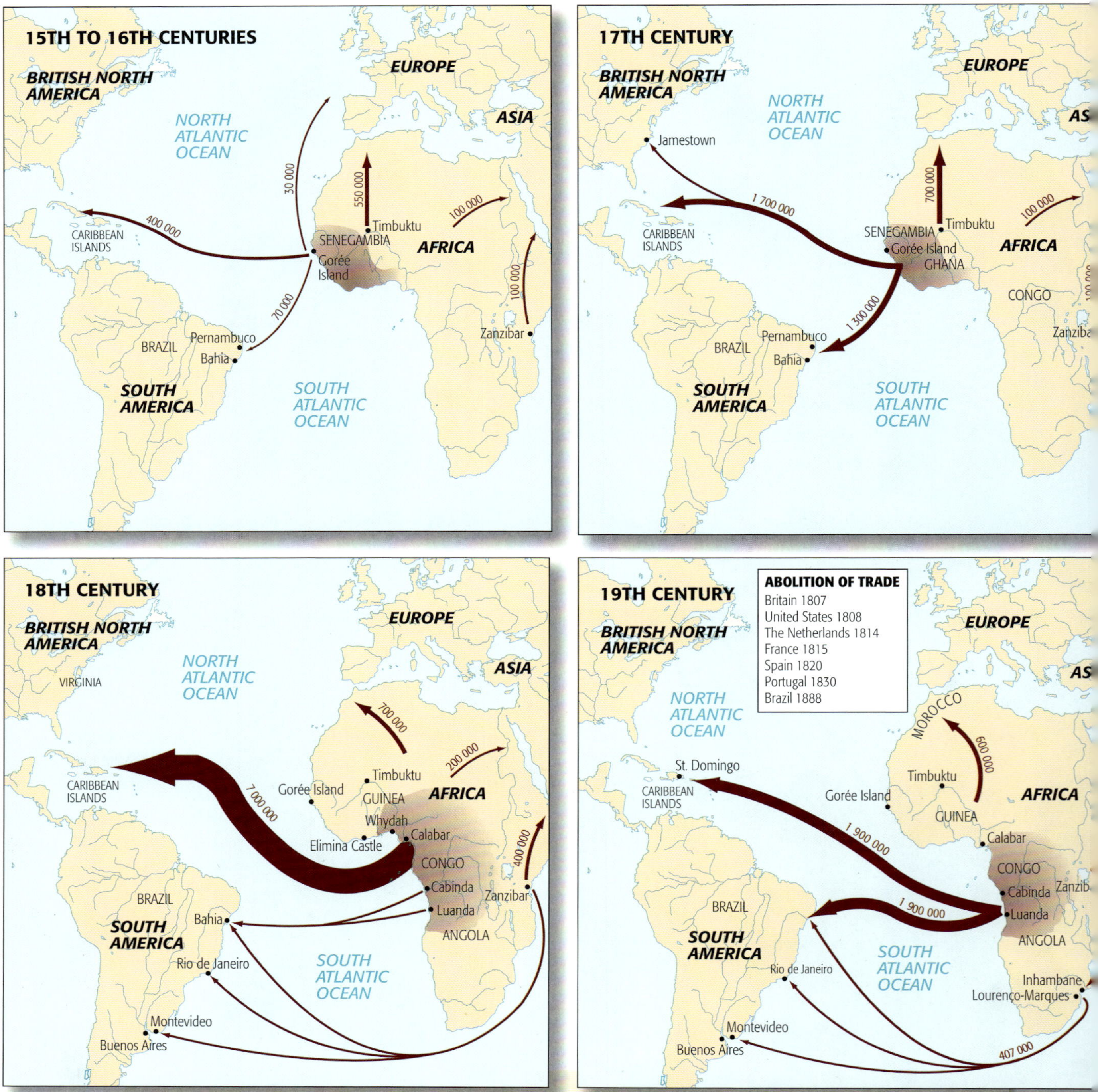

FIGURE 3.14 Enslaved peoples exported from Africa to the Americas on the Middle Passage, 1500 to 1870

These maps show the flow of captured Africans out of Africa between the 15th and 19th centuries. The figures are based on recorded data from ship manifests. Many historians believe they underestimate the real totals because they do not take into account the large number of Africans who were shipped by smugglers.

Triangular Trade

The trade in African peoples led to a complex trade route that linked three continents. This Triangular Trade route extended from Europe to Africa to the Caribbean and the Americas.

On the first stage of the route, ships carrying manufactured goods sailed from Europe to the west coast of Africa. Once there, they exchanged these goods for captured Africans. On the second stage of the route, the ships crossed the Atlantic Ocean to the Caribbean and the Americas. Once they reached the colonies, the captives were sold for cash or traded for other goods. The ships returned to Europe loaded with natural resources reaped through the exploitation of enslaved Africans. It was a hugely profitable business. Triangular Trade provided the money needed to fuel the **Industrial Revolution** in Europe.

Industrial Revolution
the transformation of society from an agricultural economy to an industrial economy characterized by manufacturing, which began in Britain in the mid-19th century

Most ships plying the Triangular Trade route were specially built to maximize profits. The African captives were chained in the holds for the Atlantic crossing. After they reached the colonies, the ships' holds were converted to carry as much sugar, rum, tobacco, molasses, rice, cotton, fur, and whale oil as they could. In Europe, these were manufactured into consumer goods and sold for big profits.

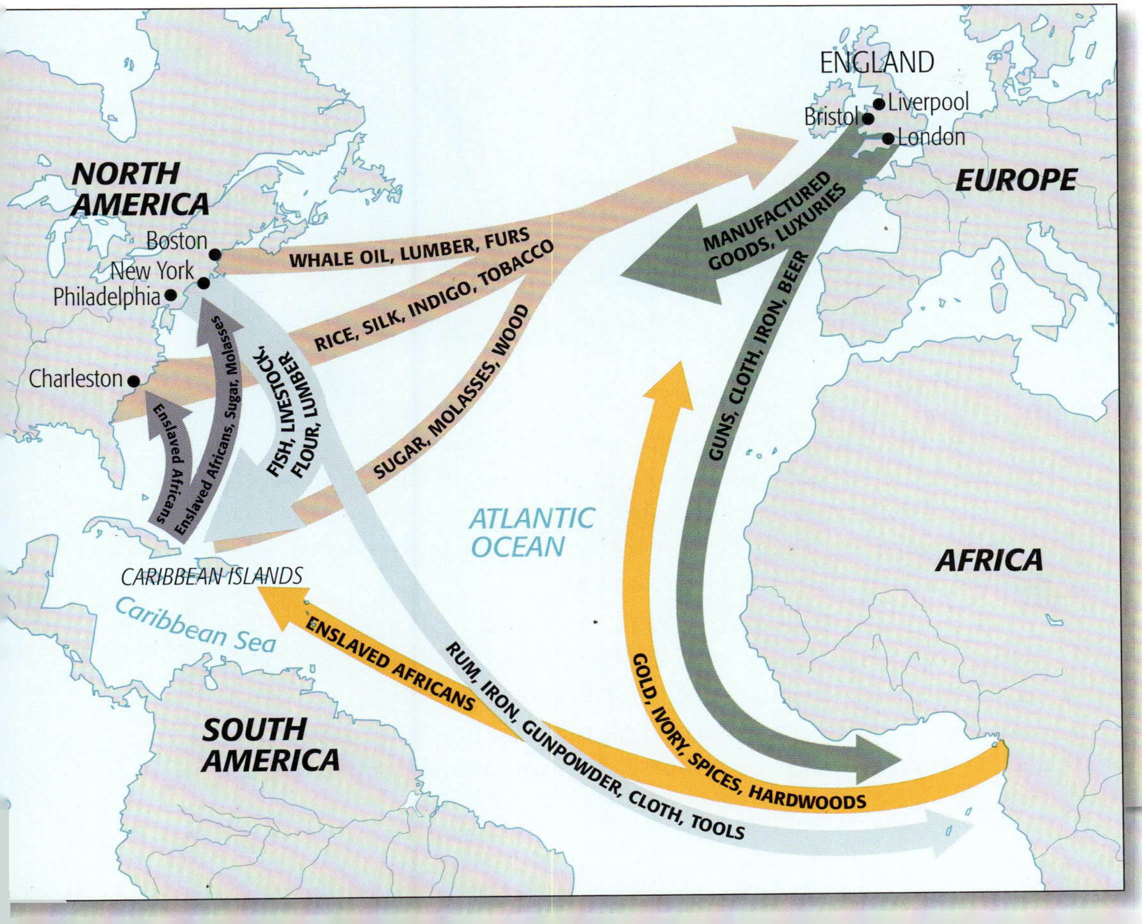

FIGURE 3.15 The Triangular Trade route

There was a lot of planning involved before setting sail on the Triangular Trade route. First, a good captain had to be found—one who could not only direct the voyage but deal with traders in Africa and the colonies. Timing was important, too. Captains tried to avoid the wet season, which increased the chances of the crew contracting deadly diseases such as malaria.

The Middle Passage

For the captives onboard the ships, the Middle Passage was a psychological, physical, and emotional nightmare. Many were grief-stricken. They were leaving Africa forever, never to see their families again. Terrified of what lay ahead, many people attempted to take their own lives. Some threw themselves overboard. Others refused to eat in the hope of starving to death. Many people simply lost the will to live and sank into a melancholy despair before dying.

FIGURE 3.16 Woman being punished for refusing to dance with the captain

The captives endured threats, beatings, forced feedings, and other forms of torture and humiliation. Many sailors witnessed these events, but few spoke publicly about them. They were afraid the powerful merchants, ship owners, and captains would refuse to hire them again.

Who do you think created this image? Who awas the intended audience?

Living conditions on the ships were unbearable. The men were chained and shackled together in pairs, although the women were usually spared this fate. Everyone was jammed into spaces so small they had to lie sideways. It was impossible to sit upright. During the summer, the heat was stifling, the air barely breathable.

The containers that served as toilets quickly filled to overflowing. The captives had to lie in their own vomit and waste. They were brought on deck to exercise and wash. But this did nothing to stop the spread of diseases such as dysentery, influenza, measles, and smallpox. Between 12 and 20 percent of captives onboard the ships died during the Middle Passage.

FIGURE 3.17
Captives onboard a slavery ship

The enslaved Africans were crammed onto the ships, usually naked or with little clothing. The public knew little about the conditions on the ships. The merchants and traders who controlled the trade in African peoples resorted to lies and deception to hide the truth. They were afraid bad publicity might lead authorities to regulate trade.

Do you think they would want the public to see images like this? Why or why not?

THE CASE OF THE ZONG

One of the most notorious incidents during the Middle Passage took place on the British slavery ship *Zong* in 1781. The *Zong* was bound for Jamaica when disease swept through the ship. The captain ordered 54 of the sickest captives to be chained together and thrown overboard. Two days later, 78 more ailing Africans were tossed into the sea. In the captain's mind, he had good reason to throw them overboard: insurance covered Africans who drowned but not those who died from disease.

FIGURE 3.18
Captives being thrown overboard

The *Zong* had been at sea for 12 weeks, carrying 417 Africans. By the end of the voyage, 132 of them had been murdered.

How do you think people might have reacted to this image?

Upon returning to England, the owners of the *Zong* filed insurance claims for all those who drowned. But news of the tragic conspiracy at sea had leaked to the public. The insurance company refused to pay. The owners took the case to court. The jury sided with the owners and ordered the insurance company to pay the claims. The insurance company appealed. The decision was overturned. The court ruled that the insurance company did not have to pay because the captives who died were people, not cargo. It was a landmark decision that contributed to public opinion against slavery in Britain and raised awareness about the emerging **abolitionist** movement.

abolitionist
a person who favours banning a practice or institution

Resistance at Sea

Many captives, desperate to be free from the horrors of the ships, plotted mutinies against their captors. Evidence suggests that there were more than 300 shipboard rebellions during the Middle Passage. Experienced captains tried to minimize the opportunities for mutiny. They gathered their captives from different places along the African coast. If the captives did not speak the same language, it was more difficult for them to conspire against their captors.

Those who did rebel faced brutal punishment. Rebel leaders were flogged to death. Some were even dismembered in full view for all to see. It was a warning to others: horrific death awaited all those who stood up to their captors.

MUTINY

Yet, despite the brutal intimidation, some captives succeeded in taking over their ships. One of the most famous acts of resistance took place onboard the Spanish ship *La Amistad* in July 1839. The ship was carrying 53 kidnapped Africans from West Africa. One man, a rice farmer named Sengbe Pieh—his Spanish captors named him Joseph Cinqué—broke free of his chains. He helped others break free, too. They seized control of the ship, killing the captain and his cook.

FIGURE 3.19 Mutiny on *La Amistad*; portrait of Cinqué (right)

La Amistad was on its way from Havana to Puerto Principe, Cuba when Cinqué took over the ship.

Cinqué ordered the ship's owners to sail *La Amistad* back to Africa. But they tried to fool him. During the day, they sailed the ship slowly east toward Africa. At night, under the cover of darkness, they changed course and sailed quickly toward the northeastern United States. On August 29, *La Amistad* was seized by the US navy. The kidnapped Africans were taken to Connecticut, where they were arrested for mutiny.

Cinqué and the other captives went on trial in 1840. As their defence, they argued that they were free men who had been illegally kidnapped and imprisoned onboard *La Amistad*. Therefore, they had broken no laws by attempting to regain their freedom. In a landmark decision, the court agreed with them. The judge declared the Africans were indeed free men. The decision was appealed, but in 1841 it was upheld by the US Supreme Court.

Another mutiny took place onboard the *Creole* in 1841. The ship was on its way from Virginia to the auction blocks in New Orleans. Onboard were at least 135 enslaved Africans. One of them was a man named Madison Washington. He had escaped to Canada from a plantation in Virginia. But he was recaptured when he returned to Virginia to free his wife.

Washington led a group of 19 rebels aboard the *Creole*. They killed the captain and overpowered the crew. Then they took over the ship and steered it to the British port of Nassau in the Bahamas. By now, slavery was illegal throughout the British Empire, so all of the captives were set free.

REVIEW AND REFLECT

1. Working with a partner, create a graphic organizer outlining the importance of Triangular Trade and the relationship between Europe, Africa, the Caribbean, and the Americas.
2. Imagine you are an enslaved African onboard one of the ships during the Middle Passage. Write a journal entry or draw a sketch to describe your living conditions.

Oppression and Survival

Those who survived the Middle Passage to reach the Caribbean and the Americas were physically, emotionally, and psychologically scarred. Even after all they had endured, their ordeal was not over. Once they disembarked from the ships, many captives were sent to "seasoning" camps. The camps had one purpose: to break the will of the captives and wipe out their identities.

At the camps, people endured cruel punishments, even torture. Many died from the abuse. Others committed suicide. Some people's spirits were broken. But many others found ways to conform while keeping their dignity intact through their spirituality and their faith.

Sold

The degradation did not end with the seasoning camps. To ensure a quick sale, the traders gave their captives time to rest. They washed and shaved them. Then they rubbed their bodies with palm oil and other ointments to conceal evidence of diseases, wounds, and injuries. The traders were careful to cover up any scars from whippings—lash marks were a sign of rebelliousness, and would turn away potential buyers.

With their bodies tortured and their spirits crushed, the captives were sold into bondage. The healthiest ones were sold first in auctions. They were paraded one by one in front of buyers or displayed on platforms. Auctioneers sold each captive to the highest bidder.

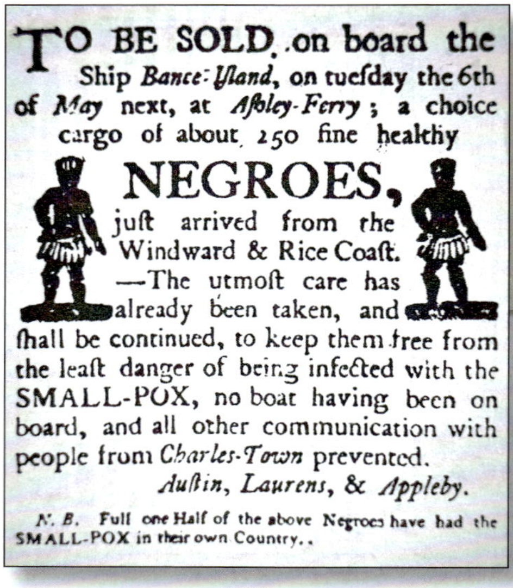
TO BE SOLD on board the Ship *Bance-Yland*, on tuesday the 6th of *May* next, at *Ashley-Ferry*; a choice cargo of about 250 fine healthy

NEGROES,

just arrived from the Windward & Rice Coast. —The utmost care has already been taken, and shall be continued, to keep them free from the least danger of being infected with the SMALL-POX, no boat having been on board, and all other communication with people from *Charles-Town* prevented.

Austin, Laurens, & Appleby.

N. B. Full one Half of the above Negroes have had the SMALL-POX in their own Country.

FIGURE 3.20 Advertisement for auctions

Auctions were advertised in advance in flyers, posters, and newspapers. The small print at the bottom of this ad guarantees that 50 percent of the captives have had smallpox.

Why do you think the traders would want to advertise this point?

FIGURE 3.21 An auction in Charleston, South Carolina

Healthy African captives were sold at auctions. Some auctions lasted for days while hundreds of human beings were traded or sold.

The sick, old, and injured Africans were sold in scrambles. These took place onboard ships or in land enclosures. The captives were herded onto the selling block with a fixed price on their heads. At an appointed time, the gates were thrown open. Buyers rushed in to grab as many Africans as they wanted to buy.

Whether the Africans were sold at auctions or scrambles, there was no regard for families. Mothers were separated from their children. Husbands were separated from their wives. Brothers and sisters were separated from their parents and siblings. Most people never saw their family members again.

In the colonies, the enslaved Africans were cut off from everything that was familiar to them. They had to learn a new language. They had to adapt to a different climate. They had to eat unfamiliar foods. They had to learn new work routines. But worst of all, they had to find a way to live without their freedom.

FIGURE 3.22 Plantation owners at auction

Buyers examined the captives to check their health. They poked their bodies, bent their limbs, and prodded their teeth. Sometimes they forced them to dance or strip naked.

Who do you think created this image? What makes you think so? What message does it convey?

On the Plantations

Most of the enslaved Africans worked on the sugar, coffee, cotton, and tobacco plantations scattered throughout the European colonies. They toiled in the fields or worked as domestic servants. Often they were worked to exhaustion. Sometimes they were worked to death. For the plantation owners, it was cheaper to buy more Africans than to give them food, water, medical care, and warm shelter. This indifference to basic human needs fuelled the trade in African peoples for centuries.

> I was immediately sent to work in the salt water with the rest of the slaves. . . . I was given a half barrel and a shovel, and had to stand up to my knees in the water from four o'clock in the morning until nine, when we were given some Indian corn boiled in water. . . . We were then called again to our tasks and worked through the heat of the day, the sun flaming on our heads like fire, and raising salt blisters in those parts which were not completely covered. Our feet and legs, from standing in the salt water for so many hours, soon became full of dreadful boils, which eat down in some cases to the very bone. . . . We came home at twelve, ate our corn soup . . . and went back to our employment till dark at night. We then shoveled up the salt in large heaps, and went down to the sea, where we washed the pickle from our limbs, and cleansed the barrels and shovels from the salt.
>
> Mary Prince, *The History of Mary Prince, A West Indian Slave, As Related by Herself*, 1831

On the plantations, many Africans found small ways to resist. They worked slowly or faked illness. They committed small acts of sabotage. They negotiated for more free time or permission to marry or attend religious services. Some ran away using complex escape routes. Many people made it. Many others did not.

The people kept the spirit of freedom alive during their captivity. They held onto their cultural identities through art, religion, and music. They danced to music inspired by dreams of freedom. They sang work songs and religious spirituals. They held secret religious services to bolster their faith. They spoke in coded languages as they planned their escapes. These expressions of struggle and resistance were proof that the people refused to accept their bondage.

While enslaved Africans in the colonies had many things in common, their lives differed in many ways, too. You will learn more about life in the colonies in Chapters 5 and 6.

REVIEW AND REFLECT

1. Read the following excerpt from the *New York Daily Tribune* published in 1859:

   > The slaves remained at the race-course, some of them for more than a week. . . . [They] were examined with as little consideration as if they had been brutes indeed; the buyers pulling their mouths open, pinching their limbs to find out how muscular they were, walking them up and down to detect any signs of lameness. . . .
   >
   > And so the Great Sale went on for two long days, during which time there were sold 429 men, women, and children. . . . The total amount of the sale foots up $303 850 [about US$6.7 million today].
   >
   > "Slave Auction, 1859," *The New York Daily Tribune*, March 9, 1859

   What does this excerpt tell you about the trade in African peoples?

2. How did enslaved Africans resist their captivity and strengthen their spirits?

EXPRESSIONS

CARNIVAL!

Carnival is an annual celebration of life found in many countries around the world. It blends art, theatre, music, and folklore into one great party!

The European origins of Carnival began hundreds of years ago in Italy. As Catholics, the Italians were not allowed to eat meat during Lent. So they called their celebration *carnevale*—meaning "to put away the meat." The practice of celebrating Carnival spread to other Catholic countries in Europe, such as France, Spain, and Portugal. When these countries set up their colonies in the Caribbean and Latin America, they brought their Carnival celebrations with them.

In the colonies, though, the enslaved Africans were forbidden from taking part in the Europeans' Carnival celebrations. So they created their own based on ancient African traditions such as the *egungun* (spirits of the ancestors) and the *n'golo* (dance of the zebras). African music, drums, and dancing transformed the European version of Carnival into the international celebrations we know today.

The original Caribbean Carnival began in Trinidad and Tobago around 1785. Enslaved Africans dressed in costumes and masks designed to bring good fortune and scare away angry spirits. Carnival became a way for people to express their power as individuals and to celebrate their rich cultural traditions.

After slavery was abolished, Blacks in the Caribbean were free to expand their Carnival celebrations. People paraded through the streets singing songs, playing drums, and dancing to an African beat. They reenacted scenes of *Cannes Brulées* (Burning Cane), which had its roots in slavery. When fire broke out in the fields, workers from surrounding plantations were rounded up and driven to the scene. Drivers cracked their whips, shouting at the workers to harvest the cane before it burnt to the ground. *Cannes Brulées* came to be known as *Canboulay* in Carnival. People carried lighted torches and danced in the streets mocking the White planters.

(a) (b) (c)

FIGURE 3.23 Carnival characters

Carnival created characters like
(a) *Jab Molassie*, a frightening painted devil;
(b) *Dame Lorraine*, a mockery of European plantation women; and
(c) *Fancy Indian*, an elaborately costumed indigenous character.

Today, Carnival is Trinidad and Tobago's main tourist attraction. But it is celebrated throughout the Caribbean on islands such as St. Vincent and the Grenadines, Barbados, the Bahamas, Jamaica, Grenada, Dominica, Haiti, Cuba, St. Thomas, and St. Marten. Most Carnivals mark a celebration of freedom of the day slavery ended.

The mass immigration of Blacks from the Caribbean to North America and Europe since the 1960s has spread Carnival celebrations around the world. There are major Carnivals in places like New York, Miami, and London. One of the biggest Carnival celebrations takes place right here in Canada. Toronto hosts the Caribana festival every August. People from around the world come to join in the celebrations in the largest Caribbean Carnival in North America. The highlight of the event is the parade. Over 1 million people line the route in this high-energy celebration of Caribbean heritage and culture.

Find Out More

Do some research to find out about a Carnival celebration in Canada or another country. Present your findings in a photo collage with captions.

FIGURE 3.24
Toronto's Caribana

Costumes and masks are created using feathers, sequins, beads, shells, fabrics, and glitter. It requires a great deal of creativity, energy, time, and patience to create these lavish masks and costumes.

Abolition

The transatlantic trade in African peoples and the practice of slavery in the Caribbean and the Americas lasted for centuries. In time, however, a number of factors led the imperial powers of Europe to abolish the horrific trade in African peoples.

Struggle and Resistance

Many enslaved Africans resisted their captivity in whatever small ways they could. Their ultimate acts of resistance, however, were violent rebellions. Most took place on the large plantations of Brazil and the Caribbean where enslaved Africans outnumbered Europeans. Almost all of these rebellions were crushed by authorities. Yet on one Caribbean island a great revolution took place. You will learn about the Haitian Revolution and other Caribbean rebellions in Chapter 6.

The Abolitionists

Building a case for the abolition of slavery took centuries of resistance, rebellion, and moral persuasion. By the late 18th century, however, the abolitionist movement was gaining strength. In Britain, the London Committee to Abolish the Slave Trade was founded in 1783. Motivated by religion and the new ideas of the **Enlightenment**, religious leaders, social reformers, artists, writers, politicians, and former enslaved Africans joined together to fight for an end to slavery. They set out to raise public awareness of the immorality and cruelty of the trade in African peoples. They promoted the autobiographies of former enslaved Africans like Olaudah Equiano and Mary Prince. They publicly displayed the tools of torture used to subdue African peoples. To dispel the historical European notion of African peoples as "primitive" and "savage," they drew attention to the sophisticated artifacts produced in many African cultures.

Enlightenment
a philosophical movement in Europe in the 18th century in which reason and the rights of the individual were emphasized over traditional institutions, customs, and morals

FIGURE 3.25 Stamps honouring British abolitionists

These leading abolitionists were honoured on the 200th anniversary of the abolition of trade in African peoples in 2007. From left to right: British MP William Wilberforce; former enslaved worker Olaudah Equiano; social reformer Granville Sharp; abolitionist crusader Thomas Clarkson; poet and writer Hannah Moore; and composer, actor, and writer Ignatius Sancho.

In 1807, the abolitionists persuaded the British Parliament to pass the *Abolition of the Slave Trade Act.* This banned trade in African peoples throughout the British Empire. It did not ban slavery itself, though. British sea captains who violated the law faced fines for every captive found onboard their ships. The United States passed a similar law in 1808. Other countries followed, including the Netherlands (1814) and Spain (1820). These laws set the legal framework for the decision in the *La Amistad* case in 1840 you read about earlier in this chapter.

To enforce the new law, the British Royal Navy formed the West African anti-slavery squadron. Its role was to intercept trading ships and free any captives found onboard. Unfortunately, the trading ships were often able to outrun the British naval ships. The squadron's success rate was low. Estimates suggest they caught only 10 percent of all ships trading in African peoples.

FIGURE 3.26
The British attack a slavery ship off the west coast of Africa, 1892

Records show that between 1807 and 1860, the West African anti-slavery squadron captured 1600 ships and freed 150 000 enslaved Africans. But this was only a small percentage of the ships making the Middle Passage.

Economic Factors

Rebels and abolitionists were not the only factors in ending slavery. Important economic and political factors came into play, too. By the mid-1800s there were a growing number of large sugar plantations. Better production methods increased sugar production. Together, these factors created a sugar surplus. Market prices dropped, but the cost of buying enslaved Africans and quashing rebellions did not. After hundreds of years, profits from the trade in African peoples and the system of slavery were dwindling.

At the same time, the Industrial Revolution brought profound changes to farming, mining, manufacturing, and transportation. The new industrialists realized they could earn more money exploiting cheap sources of labour at home in the mines and factories than on the colonial plantations. The new domestic labour force also created a market for the goods they manufactured. It made more economic sense to leave Africans in Africa. They could produce raw materials needed for the new industries at home. They could also be markets for the new manufactured goods.

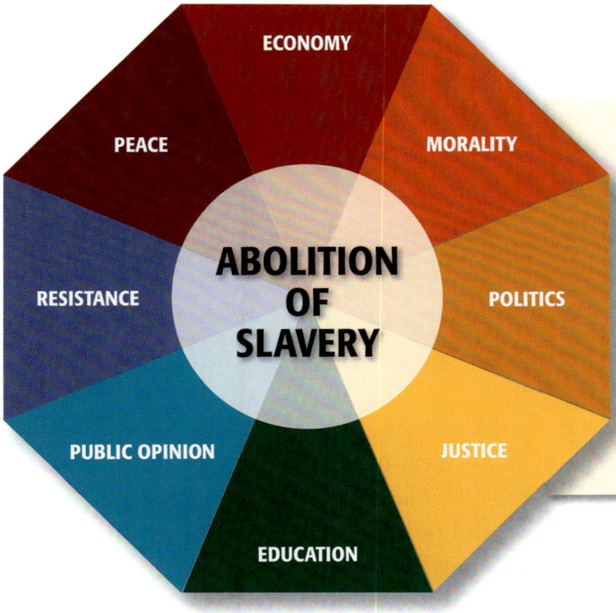

FIGURE 3.27
Factors leading to the abolition of slavery, 1833

This diagram highlights the multiple causes that led to the abolition of slavery.

Slavery Abolished

In 1833, Britain passed the *Slavery Abolishment Act*. It made slavery illegal throughout the British Empire. Britain urged other countries to do the same. France ended slavery in 1848. Portugal banned the practice in 1858, although it required former enslaved Africans to fulfill a 20-year apprenticeship that was, in reality, another form of slavery. Slavery was abolished in the United States in 1865 following the four-year Civil War between the North and South. You will learn more about slavery in the United States and the abolition of slavery there in Chapter 5.

REVIEW AND REFLECT

1. Write a one-page newspaper article describing the mutiny onboard *La Amistad* and explaining the importance of the court decisions in this case.
2. Begin a timeline showing the key events leading up to the abolition of slavery described in this chapter. You will have the opportunity to add to this timeline in Chapters 5 and 6.

A Lasting Legacy

The transatlantic trade in African peoples lasted almost 500 years. It affected the lives of millions of people on four continents. It changed the course of world history. It strengthened the power and wealth of the countries of Europe and North America. The trade in humans replaced trade in Africa's natural resources. Africa's own production of these resources collapsed. Innovation was impossible during this period of terror. As you will learn in Chapter 4, it set the stage for a new colonial relationship between Africa and Europe—one that would affect Africa even more profoundly than the trade in African peoples.

The Impact on Africa

Trade had a profound impact on West Africa from the outset. Eventually, its impact extended to the southern tip of Africa and around the Cape of Good Hope, where it overlapped with the East African trade.

The transatlantic trade in African peoples created conflict among Africans themselves. Rulers battled one another in their quest to supply European traders with African captives. Acquiring guns became essential for survival. Neighbours became mortal enemies. African villages, towns, and peoples were destroyed by European-fostered wars. New political divisions emerged that created a deep and lasting distrust of political and economic elites, which would make it impossible to unite people against the colonial conquests that were to follow in the 19th century.

Warfare and the trade in African peoples disrupted economic development, too. The abduction of millions of young Africans devastated the African population and robbed Africa of millions of workers in their prime. The importing of European textiles and other manufactured goods wiped out many local industries. Local rulers and traders traded away gold, silver, ivory, and other valuable resources for firearms, alcohol, clothing, and trinkets. In the process, they hindered the development of local economies. They caused some economies to collapse altogether. Africa's economic growth and development were stunted by the trade in African peoples.

The Impact on African Peoples

The transatlantic trade in African peoples strengthened attitudes of racism, prejudice, and discrimination against Africans and their descendants. It created a common perception that enslaved Africans were not human beings, but simply property that could be bought and sold. After slavery was abolished, many White people continued to believe in the myth that the White race was superior to the Black race. As you will discover later in this book, they would treat African peoples accordingly for many decades to come.

Despite attempts to suppress and even eliminate African cultures, however, enslaved Africans held on to their rich traditions. They spread these traditions throughout the Americas and the Caribbean through their stories, art, music, dance, and religion. The passing down of these traditions is a testament to the endurance and perseverance of African peoples.

The Search for Roots

Many people of African heritage were inspired by Alex Haley's novel *Roots*, published in 1976, to begin looking into their own African roots. Since then, many descendants of enslaved Africans have travelled to Africa to learn about their ancestral homeland. New technologies and sources of information allow people to learn more about the histories of African peoples. Their stories are uncovered through oral histories, **genealogical** research, and DNA analyses. All of this information is helping people whose ancestors survived the Middle Passage to gain a stronger sense of their identity and strengthen their pride in their heritage.

genealogical
concerning the line of descent traced continuously from an ancestor

FIGURE 3.28 Michaëlle Jean

Governor General Michaëlle Jean is the descendant of enslaved Africans. Her grandparents were forced into slavery on the Caribbean island of Haiti. Jean and her family later fled the island to escape the dictatorship of François Duvalier. They settled in Montreal, where Jean built a career as a journalist and an advocate for the rights of women. In 2005, she became the first Governor General of Canada of African heritage.

IDEAS

PSYCHOLOGICAL SLAVERY

Europeans justified the trade in and enslavement of African peoples with their belief that Africans were an inferior race. They based this belief on the physical differences between Whites and Blacks and on Christian ideas about good and evil:

White = goodness, light, and purity

Black = evil, darkness, and fear

Therefore, being White was good. Being Black was bad.

This racist misconception infiltrated the daily lives of Black people for hundreds of years. It allowed White people to take total control over the lives of Black people. White owners separated Black families. They took Black children away from their mothers and fathers. They created social divisions among enslaved Africans. Lighter-skinned Blacks became domestic servants in White households. Darker-skinned Blacks were forced into the backbreaking labour of the plantation fields. The physical brutality of slavery created a psychological shock for enslaved Africans. They lived in constant fear of extreme violence, even death. The lack of freedom to make even the smallest decisions for themselves hurt their self-reliance and independence.

Even after the abolition of slavery, the White majority continued to control the Black minority. Most enslaved Africans were uneducated. They knew only what their White owners wanted them to know. After slavery was abolished, Black children were allowed to attend school. But the information they received was distorted and unbalanced. They were taught only what White society wanted them to know. They learned about White history, culture, and values. They learned nothing about Black society or about Africa, their roots, or their heritage. Black children were taught that "White was right." Education did little to free their minds.

Today, many African scholars believe that these physical, social, and psychological controls have trapped the descendants of enslaved Africans in a form of psychological slavery. They believe the misconceptions about race are so deeply ingrained in the collective psyche of Black people that it has made their quest for equality and justice an even greater challenge.

Think It Through

How can people of African heritage emancipate themselves from psychological slavery? Explain your ideas.

Emancipate yourselves from mental slavery, None but ourselves can free our minds.

– Bob Marley, *Redemption Song*, Kingston, Jamaica: Tuff Gong/Island, 1980

FIGURE 3.29 Bob Marley

These lyrics are from a song written by reggae artist Bob Marley about 150 years after the abolition of slavery. They recall the words of Jamaican activist Marcus Garvey. Garvey believed that the shackles of slavery had an invisible grip on the descendants of enslaved Africans. He believed it was time for Blacks to "free their minds" from hundreds of years of mistreatment, abuse, and oppression.

The Question of Compensation

Many descendants of enslaved Africans have demanded compensation for the death and destruction caused by the transatlantic trade in African peoples. In Europe, many people want the European nations involved in the trade to pay off the debts of African nations. They argue that slavery played a big part in the economic problems in Africa today. Therefore, they believe those powers that gained the most from trade in African peoples have an obligation to eliminate African debt.

In the United States, many people focus on the promise made to enslaved Africans when they gained their freedom after the Civil War. They were promised "40 acres [16 hectares] and a mule." But the government never kept its promise. Now many Black Americans are demanding that the United States make amends. They have held rallies demanding compensation. Some groups have filed lawsuits against companies that profited from slavery.

Many people argue, however, that compensation is not realistic. They would settle for a formal apology from the United States and the colonial powers of Europe for their involvement in the trade in African peoples. They believe that acknowledging this gross violation of human rights will help to address deeply rooted inequalities in Western societies. Yet, as of 2009, the United States and the countries of Europe that benefited from the trade in African peoples had successfully resisted pressure to issue such an apology.

REVIEW AND REFLECT

1. What impact did the trade in African peoples have on Africa?
2. How did slavery contribute to racism and discrimination against African peoples?
3. In what ways are the ancestors of enslaved Africans building a sense of pride and identity? Discuss your ideas with your classmates.

The Historian's Craft

THE WRITTEN RECORD

As a student of history, you know that many of the historian's primary sources are found in written records. In this book, written records range from proclamations, acts, and other official documents to the voices of ordinary people expressed in their own words. All of these pieces of primary evidence help you to learn more about the past. As you do, however, you need to evaluate the evidence.

LOOKING FOR MEANING

When you analyze a written document, you should read through it once for general understanding. For example, when you read the words of Mary Prince on page 98, you gained an understanding of what her working conditions were like. But you should really read a document a second and even a third time. Then you will get an idea about the person's feelings. For example, if you were to reread Mary Prince's words, you will likely realize that she had an incredible will to live despite the hardships she endured.

As a historian, when you analyze a document, you must identify the central ideas and the evidence or examples that support it. For example, if you were to read Olaudah Equiano's description of slavery auctions on page 87, you would see that his central idea is that enslaved Africans were treated as commodities, not as human beings. The supporting evidence is the phrase "we were all pent up together, like so many sheep in a fold" and the reference to enslaved peoples as "parcels."

ASSESSING FOR DEPENDABILITY

After analyzing a document for meaning, as a historian you still have more work to do! First, you determine how valid and reliable the document is. Then you check for point of view and bias on the part of the document's author. To do this, you need to ask a few questions:

- Is the document complete? If not, what is missing?
- How does this affect the work?
- Did the author participate in the event or was he or she only a witness?
- If the author was a participant, what role did he or she play?
- Is the author knowledgeable about the subject? Is he or she an authority?
- Is there evidence of bias? Does the author favour one side over another?
- Is there evidence of prejudice, discrimination, or racism?

If the answer to any of these questions is "yes," then you must decide how dependable this source of evidence is in presenting an accurate picture of the past.

Even if you determine that a source of evidence is biased, it does not mean that you have to discard it altogether. It means that you have to use your skills as a historian to weigh the author's words carefully. Documents that are biased, or even racist, can be valid sources of information. They reveal to us what life was like—for better or for worse—in other places and times.

TRY IT!

Choose one of the pieces of primary written evidence in this chapter. Read it carefully and write down the central idea contained in the document. What evidence supports this central idea?

STUDY HALL

KNOWLEDGE & UNDERSTANDING

1. How did the Europeans try to break the will and spirit of the African people they enslaved?
2. In a chart, list the ways in which African peoples suffered during the Middle Passage under the headings "Physically," "Psychologically," and "Emotionally."
3. Create a graphic organizer highlighting all those involved in the trade in African peoples—the Africans, the Portuguese, the Spanish, the Dutch, the French, and the British. Explain why each group was involved, how they were involved, and how significant you think their role was in the overall trade.

THINKING

4. What impact do you think the loss of millions of young African men and women had on the social and economic life of African cultures? Explain your response.
5. Do you think that Africa and/or the descendants of enslaved Africans should be compensated for the past? Write a persuasive argument expressing your point of view.

APPLICATION & COMMUNICATION

6. Draw a map showing some of the modern cities that were once part of the Triangular Trade route. In a legend, identify the most important industries for these cities today.
7. Place yourself in the role of the leader of a secret group of enslaved Africans meeting to discuss escaping to freedom. Write a song to convince the others to join in the escape.
8. Write a blog explaining the significance of the *La Amistad* case and its impact in the 19th century.
9. Imagine you have escaped from slavery. Create a poster in support of the abolitionist movement.
10. Do some research into an art form that was created by enslaved Africans, such as jazz, swing dancing, banjos, spirituals, or choral music. Present your findings in a presentation that explains its origins and its impact on modern culture.
11. Prepare a role-play or debate in which the key stakeholders discuss the idea of compensation for the descendants of enslaved Africans in the United States.

CHAPTER

4 Africa and the Age of Imperialism

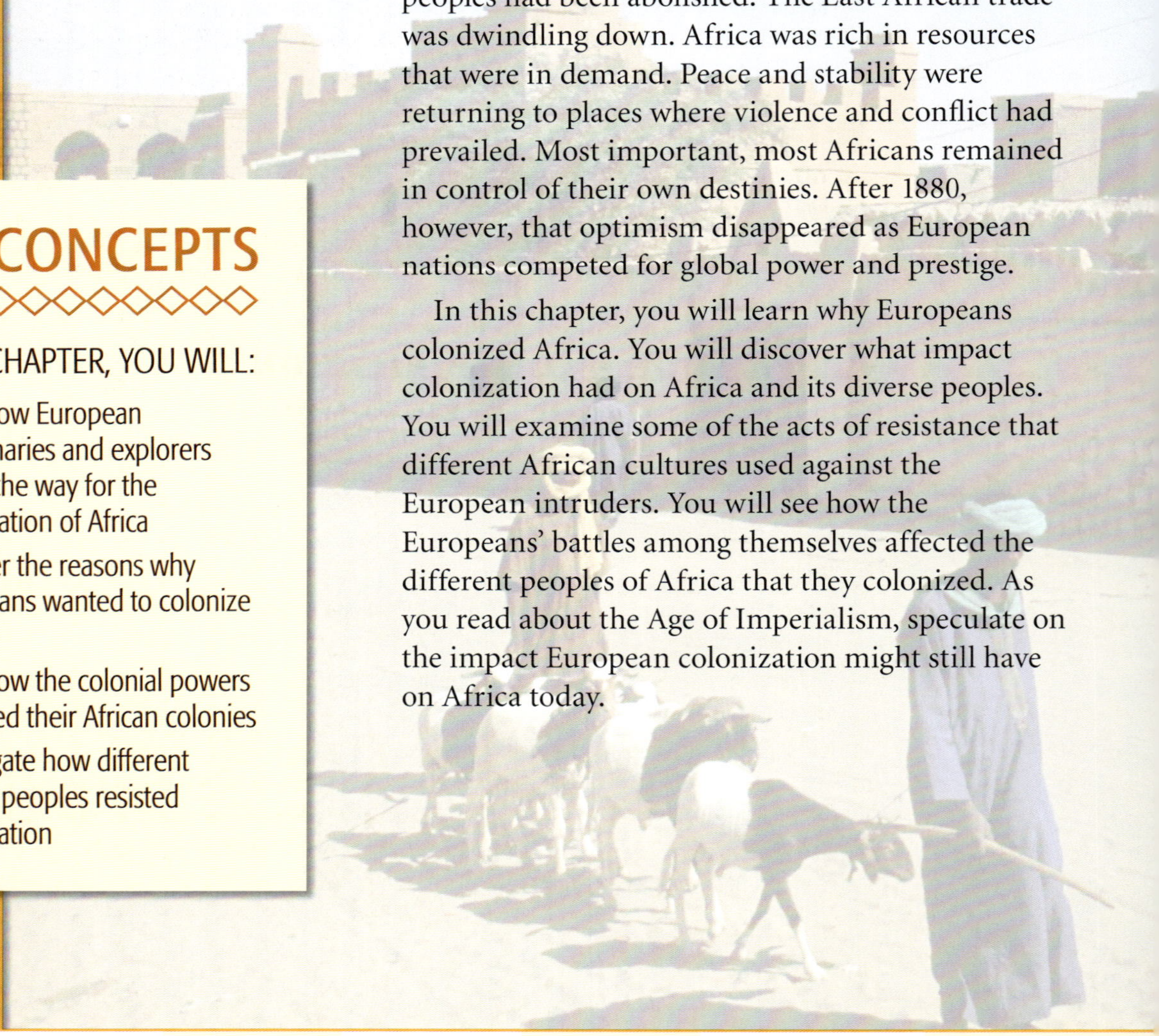

A People's Story

In 1880, the people of Africa had reason to be optimistic. The transatlantic trade in African peoples had been abolished. The East African trade was dwindling down. Africa was rich in resources that were in demand. Peace and stability were returning to places where violence and conflict had prevailed. Most important, most Africans remained in control of their own destinies. After 1880, however, that optimism disappeared as European nations competed for global power and prestige.

In this chapter, you will learn why Europeans colonized Africa. You will discover what impact colonization had on Africa and its diverse peoples. You will examine some of the acts of resistance that different African cultures used against the European intruders. You will see how the Europeans' battles among themselves affected the different peoples of Africa that they colonized. As you read about the Age of Imperialism, speculate on the impact European colonization might still have on Africa today.

KEY CONCEPTS

IN THIS CHAPTER, YOU WILL:

- learn how European missionaries and explorers paved the way for the colonization of Africa
- discover the reasons why Europeans wanted to colonize Africa
- learn how the colonial powers exploited their African colonies
- investigate how different African peoples resisted colonization

Missionaries begin converting Africans to Christianity; Europeans begin exploring Africa	Afrikaners' Great Trek begins	Liberia declared independent	The Scramble for Africa begins	Berlin Conference sets rules of colonization	Europeans stake claims in Africa
CE 1800s	1835	1847	1879	1884–85	1879–1914

Image Analysis

FIGURE 4.1 *The Rhodes Colossus*, published in the British magazine *Punch*, 1892

Political cartoonists had their own messages about colonial expansion in Africa. What is the message in this cartoon depicting Cecil Rhodes, the wealthy owner of the British South Africa Company?

What do you see in this image? How does it reveal the Europeans' view of themselves and their role in the world in the late 19th century—that is, how did they want the world to perceive them? How do you think the people of Africa might have responded to this image?

›pian resistance defeats Italy	South African War between Britain and the Afrikaners	The Asante launch their final act of resistance	The Nama/Herero rebellions quashed	The Congo Free State turned over to Belgium	First World War begins	German colonies divided among Britain, France, and Belgium
1896	1899–1901	1900	1907	1908	1914	1918

The "Dark Continent"

In the 1800s, Europeans knew little about Africa. During the trade in African peoples, few Europeans ventured beyond their trading posts on the Atlantic Ocean. As a result, they thought of Africa as a mysterious and uncivilized place—a "dark continent." The Europeans used this idea to justify their mission to bring "progress" and "civilization" to Africa.

The Europeans' view of their role in the world was reflected in the poem "The White Man's Burden" by Rudyard Kipling. It called for the "civilized" people of Europe to teach people of other races how to live and act like Europeans. In the spirit of this "burden," the powers of Europe set out to impose their religion on the people of Africa and to exploit Africa's resources for European gain.

Spreading the Faith

Christian evangelicals
a religious group that believes people should change their moral values and repent their sins and that promotes social reform and missionary work

Some of the Christian missionaries who went to Africa in the 19th century were members of a group of **Christian evangelicals** from Britain, the United States, and other countries. They had campaigned for the abolition of slavery. Now they wanted to spread Christian moral values around the world.

In Africa, the missionaries mistakenly believed that non-Muslims had no religious beliefs of their own. They set out to convert African peoples to Christianity. African cultures passed down their histories through the stories they told. They had no written languages. So the missionaries created written scripts for African languages. Then they translated the Bible and taught the people how to read.

polygamy
being married to more than one spouse at the same time

puritanical
a strict religious moral behaviour, especially one that opposes pleasure

The missionaries wanted to "civilize" Africans by having them adopt European ways. They taught them the things they thought they should know. They tried to persuade them to abandon traditional practices, such as nudity and **polygamy**, because these customs offended their **puritanical** Christian values.

FIGURE 4.2 A missionary school in Liberia

Liberia was established as a settlement in 1822 for former enslaved Africans from the United States. In 1847, it became an independent state. Those who settled in Liberia brought their Christian faith with them. They established a missionary school there.

What details do you see in this photograph? What impact do you think these schools might have had on African peoples?

Some Africans converted to Christianity, but many others rebelled against the missionaries. They questioned how a religion that preached fairness and equality could support a system that placed power and leadership exclusively in the hands of White people. Many African Christians were ready to become leaders themselves. But the missionaries were unwilling to loosen their hold on power.

In response, many Africans broke away from the Western missions. They created their own independent churches, with African leaders. Many of these churches blended the teachings of the Bible with traditional African beliefs. They acknowledged the value of African cultures and institutions.

FIGURE 4.3 Mutesa I

Many African rulers used the missionaries to their own advantage. Mutesa I of Buganda invited Christian missionaries to his court. He also invited Muslim traders. His reasons had nothing to do with religion. Mutesa courted both Christians and Muslims to strengthen his position against his enemies.

The Quest for Fame and Fortune

While missionaries were spreading Christian faith, European explorers were learning about the African interior. Some were motivated by curiosity. They wanted to learn about the natural world and about African cultures. Most had another motive, though: fame and fortune.

FIGURE 4.4 René Caillié (1799–1838); below, Timbuktu today

The *Societé de Géographie* in Paris offered a reward to the first European to reach the legendary city of Timbuktu—and live to tell about it! A French explorer named René Caillié took up the challenge. Disguised as an Arab, he arrived in Timbuktu in August 1828. But when he got there he found no hint of the city's fabled reputation for gold. Instead, he found a poor little village. Many Europeans refused to believe Caillié when he told them that Timbuktu was not the city it once was. Today, nothing remains of the grand palace built by Mansa Musa. But the mosque he built still stands as a memorial to the great civilization that once thrived there.

The explorers were searching for rivers that would lead them to Africa's natural treasures. Expeditions often lasted for years. During this time, African peoples guided the explorers. They showed them the trade routes. They acted as interpreters and translators. They organized the caravans and managed the pack animals. They taught the explorers how to survive in the rainforests, deserts, and mountains. The European explorers could not have succeeded—or even survived—without the Africans.

FIGURE 4.5 David Livingstone (1813–1873); below, Lake Tanganyika today

Dr. David Livingstone was both a missionary and an explorer. He explored the Zambezi River and Lake Tanganyika and located Lake Malawi and Victoria Falls. In 1866, he began a seven-year search for the source of the Nile. He was joined by two Africans, Abdullah Susi and James Chuma. Livingstone died in 1873 without finding the source of the Nile. Susi and Chuma carried his body to Zanzibar so that it could be returned to Britain for burial.

Today, places like Lake Tanganyika lure modern-day explorers and adventurers from around the world.

By the 1870s, a new generation of explorers ventured into Africa. They were better armed than any of the explorers who had gone before them. They played an active role in the Europeans' colonial conquest of Africa. One of these explorers was Henry M. Stanley. One of his first encounters with African peoples led to a horrible misunderstanding. The accounts on page 116 reveal two very different expectations when Stanley met African Chief Mojimba in 1878.

We saw a great fleet of canoes hovering about in the middle of the stream. The canoe men, standing up, gave a loud shout when they saw us and blew their horns louder than ever. . . . We had sufficient time to take a view of the mighty force bearing down on us and to count the number of the war vessels. There were 54 of them! A monster canoe led the way, with two rows of upstanding paddles, 40 men on a side, their bodies bending and swaying in unison as with a swelling barbarous chorus they drove her down toward us.

The monster canoe aimed straight for my boat, as though it would run us down; . . . when nearly opposite, the warriors above the manned prow let fly their spears. . . . But every sound was soon lost in the ripping, crackling musketry. . . . Our blood was up now. It was a murderous world, and we felt for the first time that we hated the filthy, vulturous ghouls who inhabited it.

Henry M. Stanley, *Through the Dark Continent*, 1878, in *Social Studies Review*, Fall 2004

When we heard that the man with the white flesh was journeying down the Lualaba, we were open-mouthed with astonishment. . . . We will prepare a feast, I ordered, we will go to meet our brother and escort him into the village with rejoicing!

We donned our ceremonial garb. We assembled the great canoes. . . . We swept forward, my canoe leading, the others following, with songs of joy and with dancing to meet the first white man our eyes had beheld, and to do him honour.

But as we drew near his canoes there were loud reports, bang! bang! and fire-staves spat bits of iron at us. We were paralyzed with fright. . . . Several of my men plunged into the water. . . . Some screamed dreadfully, others were silent—they were dead, and blood flowed from little holes in their bodies. . . . That was no brother. That was the worst enemy our country had ever seen.

Chief Mojimba describing his reaction to seeing Stanley, as recorded by Father Frässle, a Catholic missionary, in *Social Studies Review*, Fall 2004

FIGURE 4.6 Top, Henry M. Stanley (1841–1904); bottom, the Congo today

As an explorer, Stanley is credited with opening up the Congo for trade. As you will discover later in this chapter, his reputation was tarnished by the role he played in the oppression of African peoples in the Congo Free State. The Congo's natural beauty stands in stark contrast to its oppressive political history.

REVIEW AND REFLECT

1. The British writer Rudyard Kipling wrote the following lines in his poem "The White Man's Burden" in 1899:

    Take up the white man's burden–
    Send out the best ye breed–
    Go bind your sons to exile,
    To serve your captives' need;
    To wait in heavy harness,
    On fluttered folk and wild–
    Your new-caught sullen peoples,
    Half devil and half child.

    How do these lines express Europeans' attitude toward African peoples?

2. Why did evangelical missionaries want to convert Africans to Christianity?

3. What evidence of bias is there in the accounts by Stanley and Mojimba? What are the positive and negative connotations of the words each person uses? How do you think these contributed to the misunderstanding between Stanley and Mojimba?

On the Eve of Colonial Occupation

The explorers proved that Africa was a treasure house of rich natural resources. They had found rivers that could be used to gain access to these resources. At the same time, the Industrial Revolution had transformed European economies. Markets were needed to sell the goods being produced in the new mills and factories. European business leaders were eager to exploit Africa's resources and its people. They urged their governments to intervene in Africa's affairs.

Economics was not the only factor driving the forces of European **imperialism**, however. The French Revolution in 1789 had unleashed the powerful force of **nationalism**. By the 19th century, nationalist fever was spreading throughout Europe. This new national pride fuelled the competition for global power and prestige. By 1880, acquiring colonies in Africa was much more than a means of spreading Christianity and accumulating wealth. It was a matter of national pride and honour.

I contend that we are the first race in the world, and that the more of the world we inhabit the better it is for the human race.

British imperialist Cecil Rhodes, "Confession of Faith," 1877

imperialism
the expansion of a country's political and economic influence through the seizure of new territory and/or the imposition of its values, beliefs, and culture on other peoples

nationalism
a patriotic feeling toward one's country

FIGURE 4.7 Africa, 1880

During the trade in African peoples, Europeans in Africa remained primarily in coastal areas. But in the final decades of the 19th century the continent was quickly divided into a patchwork of European colonies.

What impact do you think this would have on Africa and its people?

The Scramble for Africa

The Scramble for Africa began in earnest in 1879. As the powers of Europe staked their claims in Africa, they were often competing for the same territory. The German chancellor, Otto von Bismarck, invited Western leaders to Berlin in November 1884 to settle their territorial disputes.

The negotiations lasted for months. In February 1885, the leaders agreed to the terms of the *Berlin Act*. This deal sealed the fate of Africa—even though no African leaders had been invited to the talks.

FIGURE 4.8 The Berlin Conference, 1884–1885

Fourteen countries attended the Berlin Conference. The countries with the most at stake, however, were the four that controlled most of colonial Africa at the time: France, Germany, Britain, and Portugal.

How do you think this influenced the terms of the *Berlin Act*?

The Berlin Conference set up rules for carving up Africa into European possessions. The process of colonization was to be carried out in three stages.

STAGE 1
SIGNING TREATIES

The colonial powers asked African rulers to recognize them as their people's protectors. To seal the deal, rulers marked an "X" on a document. The colonial agents deceived the African leaders, though. Since few could read European languages, they could not understand the real meaning of the treaties. They thought they were signing treaties of friendship. They did not know they were giving up their independence and control of their land.

STAGE 2
DEFINING TERRITORIAL BOUNDARIES

The colonial powers created territorial boundaries without consulting local rulers. They had no regard for traditional boundaries that took into account shared languages and cultures. They divided over 175 religious, language, and cultural groups and separated families, clans, cultures, and nations. Many groups were merged with others they had little in common with. Some were forced to live alongside their long-standing enemies.

STAGE 3
ACCEPTING COLONIAL RULE

The colonial powers had to control the people in their colonies. Most colonies were governed by just a few Europeans. They used a "divide and conquer" strategy. They asked certain local groups to help them run the colony. They granted them privileges other groups did not have. This earned their loyalty, but it created resentment among other groups. Colonial rulers used military force against all those who resisted them.

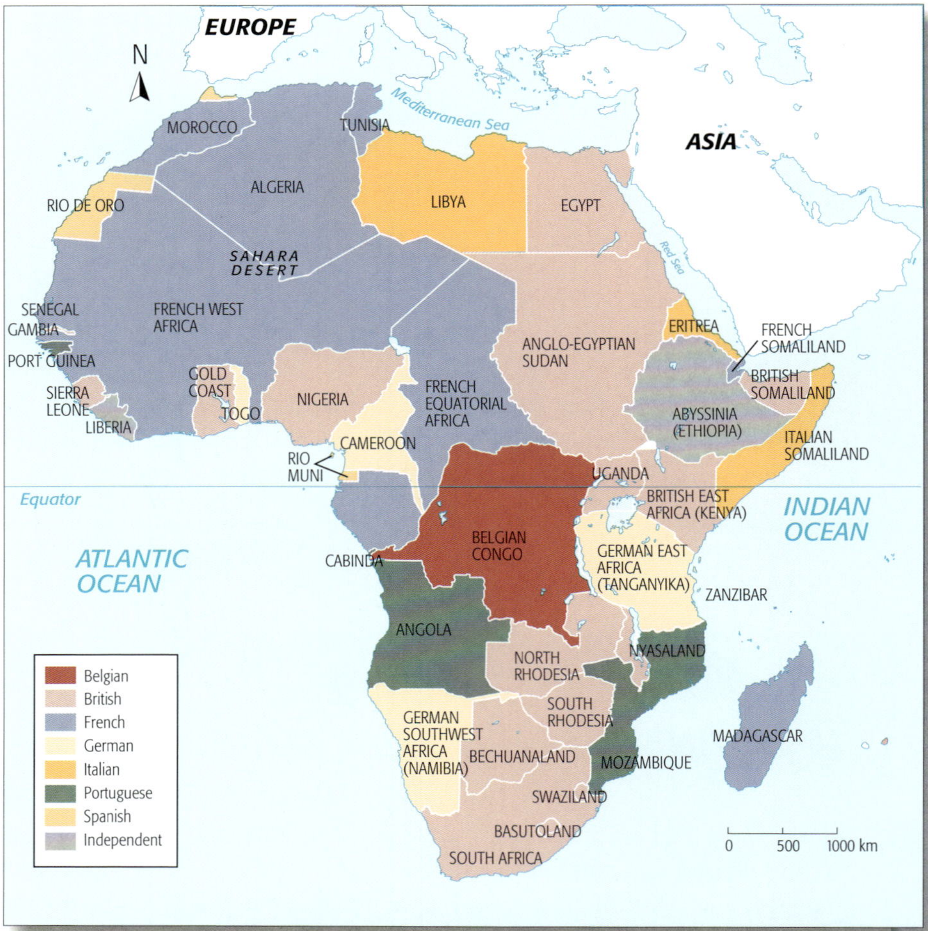

FIGURE 4.9 Africa, 1914

After the Berlin Conference, the Europeans rushed to stake their claims in Africa. Never in the history of Africa had so much change taken place within such a short period of time. By 1910, the Europeans ruled almost all the continent.

Which European country had the most colonies? Which had the greatest amount of territory? Which two African countries did not become colonies?

Building the Colonies

Europe's colonial powers established two types of colonies: *colonies of settlement* and *colonies of exploitation*. Colonies of settlement, such as Kenya and Rhodesia, provided land for European settlers. Colonies of exploitation, such as Nigeria and the Congo, exploited natural resources using cheap African labour. They opened up trade by creating African markets for European goods. Most colonies in Africa were colonies of exploitation.

FIGURE 4.10
"The Devilfish in Egyptian Waters," an American cartoon, 1882

The character in the centre is John Bull, the national personification of England popularly used by British illustrators and writers.

What does this cartoon suggest about Britain's role in Africa and around the world?

GOVERNING THE COLONIES

The Europeans created two forms of colonial government: *direct rule* and *indirect rule.*

DIRECT RULE	INDIRECT RULE
Direct rule was based on the European misconception that African peoples were incapable of governing themselves. It cast aside traditional African ways of governing. African leaders were replaced by colonial governors, who followed orders from their home countries. It was a **paternalistic** system in which Europeans believed they had to teach Africans the "proper" way to live—that is, the European way. France, Portugal, Germany, and Belgium favoured direct rule in their colonies. They wanted to **assimilate** local peoples and impose their beliefs and values on them.	Under indirect rule, colonial governors and their advisers made laws for the colony. Local African rulers who were loyal to the governor kept some of their traditional authority. Their power was limited, though. They appointed local councillors, but they did not influence government decisions. Britain practised indirect rule throughout its empire. It was a practical form of government. By the late 1800s, Britain had colonized a third of Africa. There were not enough officials or soldiers to rule the colonies without the help of local leaders. Indirect rule also created the illusion of independence. This helped to limit African resistance.

paternalistic
a policy or practice of treating or governing people by providing for their needs without giving them rights and responsibilities

assimilate
to absorb a group of people into one's culture

MAKING A PROFIT

The Europeans had a common goal: to make their colonies self-sufficient and profitable.

Farming was a traditional activity in many African societies. In Egypt and West Africa, local farmers had built strong export economies. When the Europeans arrived, they wanted local farmers to produce even more crops for export. In some colonies, the Europeans set production targets. Exports earned foreign currency. Foreign currency could buy imported goods from Europe.

Most colonies specialized in one or two crops. When those crops failed or there was a slump in market prices, it hurt the entire economy. The emphasis on exporting crops also meant that many colonies did not have enough food to feed their own people. As a result, they became dependent on food imported from Europe.

Mining played an important role in colonial economies. Many parts of Africa had rich deposits of valuable minerals, such as gold, diamonds, and copper. European investors bankrolled mining operations. All the profits went to them. The dangerous and back-breaking labour was supplied by poorly paid Africans.

The Europeans invested in roads, railways, and harbours. These were needed to transport raw materials for export and imported manufactured goods from Europe. The railways also helped colonial governments maintain control by transporting troops and police quickly to trouble spots.

To finance the colonies and ensure a regular supply of labour, the colonial governments imposed taxes on local people. The taxes had to be paid in cash. The only way Africans could earn cash was to work for the Europeans. Taxation became the motor that made colonial economies run.

The Impact of Colonial Rule

The arrival of European colonists created rapid social, political, and economic change in Africa. Before colonial rule, most Africans lived in rural areas. As colonial cities grew, some people moved there hoping for a better life. Other people were forced to move to cities to find work so that they could pay their taxes. Some people became migrant workers who left home for long periods to work in the mines and on the plantations. As a result, the tradition of close-knit villages began to crumble.

FIGURE 4.11
Loot from the royal palace at Benin City

Europeans had a devastating impact on African cultural history. In 1896, these British soldiers raided the royal palace in Benin. They stole over 3000 priceless cultural artifacts. Today, these symbols of Benin culture and civilization are in the British Museum in London. The people of Benin are demanding they be returned to them.

Who do you think created this photograph? Who was the intended audience? What attitudes does this photograph reveal?

As the colonies developed, the Europeans set up banking systems. They introduced their own currencies. These currencies reduced the value of traditional African forms of currency. But the Europeans continued to pay African workers in their traditional currencies. This meant they were being paid even lower wages. But the Africans had to pay their taxes in European currencies.

A revolution in firearms technology helped the Europeans maintain their hold over their colonies. In the past, African spears, arrows, and knives had been effective weapons against inefficient European muskets. But the Europeans gained the military advantage in 1885 with the invention of the first modern machine gun, the Maxim gun.

FIGURE 4.12
A demonstration of a Maxim gun

"Whatever happens we have got, the Maxim gun and they have not!"

What impact do you think advanced technology would have had on the relationship between the colonists and African peoples?

The colonists introduced Western education. Their schools condemned African cultures and way of life. Children were taught that their traditions and beliefs were primitive. They learned about European history. But they were taught nothing about their own histories. They were encouraged to wear European clothing and adopt European ways.

Colonialism led to the breakdown of traditional patterns of life in Africa. In just a few decades, colonialism had a more profound impact on Africa than the hundreds of years of trade in human lives.

REVIEW AND REFLECT

1. In your own words, explain the importance of each of the following to the colonial occupation of Africa:
   - the Industrial Revolution
   - imperialism
   - nationalism
   - the *Berlin Act*
2. Why do you think African rulers were not invited to attend the Berlin Conference? How did the conference pave the way for the Scramble for Africa? Do you think the Europeans were justified in their actions? Discuss your ideas using a think-pair-share strategy.
3. At the Berlin Conference, the British prime minister, Lord Salisbury, remarked, "We have been giving away mountains and rivers and lakes to each other, unhindered by the small impediment that we never knew exactly where they were." How would you explain his statement? What impact do you think it had as the Europeans divided the African continent? Discuss your ideas with a partner.
4. What attitude did most Europeans have toward the African peoples they ruled? How did this affect the kinds of governments the Europeans established in their colonies? Explain your response in a concept web.

IDEAS

THE LEGACY OF COLONIALISM

Today, most of the nations of Africa have been free from colonial rule for decades. Yet many of these independent nations are struggling economically and, in some cases, politically. This raises a critical question: *What is the legacy of colonialism?*

It is impossible to predict what Africa would be like today had colonial rule never taken place. Some Western historians argue that African countries lacked the social and economic structure to develop into modern states on their own. African nationalists dismiss this argument, pointing out that other countries, such as Japan and China, became major world economies without the "benefit" of colonial rule.

> **If [African nations] had not become European possessions, the majority would probably have remained very much as they were.**
>
> D.K. Fieldhouse, historian, Cambridge University, in Tunde Obadina, "The Myth of Neo-Colonialism," *African Business & Economy*

> **It is not true that Africa couldn't have developed without colonialism. If it were true, then there is something wrong with the rest of the world which developed without it.**
>
> Moshood Abiola, Nigerian politician, in Tunde Obadina, "The Myth of Neo-Colonialism," *African Business & Economy*

Read the following arguments defending and criticizing colonial rule.

DEFENDERS OF COLONIALISM	CRITICS OF COLONIALISM
The overall effect of colonialism was positive: ◆ it ended slavery ◆ it reduced the economic gap between Africa and Europe ◆ it brought formal education and modern medicine to Africa ◆ it developed agricultural exports and introduced new industries ◆ it built a foundation for economic growth and development ◆ it united former warring nations in modern nation-states that are better able to survive in an increasingly global world ◆ Africa's own inadequacies made colonization necessary ◆ the fact that many African nations today face great challenges suggests that the colonial powers withdrew too soon	The overall effect of colonialism was negative: ◆ colonial rule left Africans poorer than they were before ◆ colonial powers exploited African peoples and resources, which limited Africa's ability to develop ◆ colonialism created economic systems that were dependent on Europe to meet Africa's needs ◆ the countries of Europe created a trading system that discriminated against African nations ◆ by redrawing the map of Africa, colonialism created cultural conflicts that destabilized the continent ◆ by replacing African political systems with alien models, colonialism laid the seeds of current political instability

Think It Through

Think about the arguments on both sides of the legacy of colonialism. Decide which side you agree with. Then, in your own words, write either a defence or criticism of the legacy of colonialism.

African Resistance

alliance
a union for a common purpose

Different African peoples had different responses to colonialism. Some African rulers submitted to the European invaders. Some did so because they knew it was futile to resist. Others needed protection from their African enemies. Some African rulers agreed to form **alliances** with Europeans. They believed they were securing their nation's future. Some used these alliances to expand their own influence. Others allied with Europeans in exchange for protection.

In almost every part of Africa, however, there were brave leaders who led their people to resist the European invasion. When they failed, it was not because of a lack of courage or commitment. It was because, at that moment in history, they faced enemies who benefited from superior weapons and technology and vast new sources of wealth. Many Africans who gave their lives in the resistance are remembered today as heroes. In this section, you can read a few of the many remarkable stories of resistance that took place all across Africa.

The Congo Free State: The Fight for Human Rights

From his first journeys, the explorer Henry Stanley realized the great commercial potential of the Congo River basin. In 1877, he emerged from the rainforest near the mouth of the Congo after tracing the river to its source. When he returned to England, Stanley urged Britain to claim the vast Congo territory. He had plans to build a road and a railway into the interior, dotted with trading posts along the way. But Stanley could not convince either the government or any British financiers to back him.

At the Berlin Conference, King Leopold II of Belgium was granted control of the Congo River basin. He promised to end the trade in African peoples. As "proof" of his mission, he named the territory the Congo Free State. He then claimed the Congo—not for his country but for himself.

FIGURE 4.13 King Leopold of Belgium (1835–1909)

King Leopold II controlled the lives of over 30 million people in the Congo Free State—even though he himself never set foot there!

Leopold hired Henry Stanley to survey his territory. He leased huge tracts of land to private companies to exploit the natural resources, especially wild rubber from the rubber trees in the rainforest. In return, the companies promised to build roads and railways and to share their profits with the king.

It was a rewarding partnership for the rubber companies and the king. Both made tremendous amounts of money. For the people of the Congo, though, it was a very different story. Company agents forced local villagers to harvest the rubber. They cut off their hands if they failed to collect enough. They destroyed local crops so that the people starved. They worked the villagers to exhaustion—sometimes even to death. They murdered people on a daily basis. Millions of Congolese died at their hands. Desperate to escape, many people fled into the forests. They lost their homes and possessions. Most faced almost certain death from starvation.

In time, the Congolese began to fight back. They gathered weapons to rebel against their oppressors. Their resistance focused attention on the crimes being committed in the Congo. Missionaries told stories of the **atrocities** they witnessed. Journalists alerted the public to the horrific acts being committed in the Congo.

atrocity
an appalling act or condition, especially of extreme cruelty

The negative publicity created a public backlash against Leopold. In 1908, he was forced to turn over the Congo Free State to the Belgian government. Some historians have called this the first successful human rights campaign of the 20th century. But as you will discover in later chapters, the people of the Belgian Congo would face many more challenges.

North West Africa: A Clash of Imperial Ambitions

Samori Touré was a Muslim who ruled the Mandika Empire in North West Africa. By the time the Scramble for Africa began, he had built a politically stable and commercially strong kingdom. Then the French began to aggressively expand into the area in the 1880s. They launched their first attack against the Mandika in 1882. Although Touré and his army successfully defended the kingdom, they also learned about the power of European firearms. In 1885, Touré offered to place his kingdom under British protection. Britain was not interested in a

FIGURE 4.14 Samori Touré (1830–1900)

Touré built a disciplined army of 30 000 to 35 000 soldiers. He organized them into European-style platoons and companies.

confrontation with France. But it agreed to sell Touré large numbers of modern European weapons.

Throughout the 1880s and 1890s, the Mandika army fought intermittently with French forces as they pushed deeper into the kingdom. The French forced Touré to sign a number of treaties turning over much of his territory. He was forced to move further and further east. By 1898, however, Touré faced a concentrated assault from French forces. He could defend his kingdom no longer. He was captured in 1898 and exiled to Gabon.

West Africa: The Asante Wars

Few African peoples fought harder against colonialism than the Asante. The Asante were a brave and aggressive people who lived in the rainforests of West Africa. During the 19th century, the Asante repeatedly rebelled against British rule. The British financed their battles with the Asante with the assets they obtained from seizing the Asante's gold mines and with the taxes they forced them to pay.

FIGURE 4.15 King Nana Prempeh I

In 1891, the Asante king, Prempeh I, took a diplomatic approach in his relations with the British. He turned down their initial offer of protection and tried to negotiate a deal. But in 1895, Britain invaded Asante lands. The king was forced into exile in the Seychelles Islands in the Indian Ocean.

In 1895, the British launched what they hoped would be their final attempt to subdue the Asante. A large British force invaded the Asante's remaining land. After 100 years of resistance, the Asante empire was on the verge of collapse. Britain claimed the last of the Asante's land as its **protectorate**.

protectorate
a relationship of protection and partial control assumed by one power over another

In 1900, the British governor met with Asante leaders. He demanded that the traditional symbol of the Asante's independence, the Golden Stool, be turned over to him. The Asante men sat in silence. Afterwards, the Queen Mother, Yaa Asantewaa, called the men cowards. She challenged them to stand up to the British. Then she led the Asante in their final act of resistance in March 1900.

FIGURE 4.16 Asante men with a ceremonial staff displaying the Golden Stool

The Golden Stool is so sacred that no one has ever actually sat in it. The Asante are sworn to defend it. Although the British defeated the Asante, the Asante proclaimed victory because they had fought to defend the stool, and they had.

For months, the Asante attacked the British mission at Kumasi. Britain brought in 1400 reinforcements to regain control. The final battle between the British and the Asante took place on September 30, 1900. Yaa Asantewaa was the last rebel to be captured. Like the king, she was forced into exile in the Seychelles. As they finally defeated the Asante, Britain proclaimed the Gold Coast its colony.

South West Africa: The Nama/Herero Resistance

One of the great tragedies in African resistance was in South West Africa. In 1884, Germany proclaimed the area that is now Namibia as its protectorate. German settlers moved in. They took over the grazing lands of many local Herero and Nama cattle farmers. They introduced their own laws and imposed taxes.

In the late 1890s, a disease imported by Europeans wiped out much of the Herero and Nama's cattle stocks. The colonists lent the Africans money. But soon the people were deeply in debt. They could not pay back their loans, so the colonists seized the few cattle they had left. Now the traditional lifestyles of the Herero and the Nama were destroyed.

The Africans were desperate to regain their livelihood. Toward the end of 1903, the Nama chief, Hendrik Witbooi, led his people in a war of anti-colonial resistance against the Germans. A few months later, the leader of the Herero, Samuel Maherero, called upon his people to rise up and join the fight against the Germans, too.

FIGURE 4.17 Nama Chief Hendrik Witbooi (1825–1905)

Witbooi, commemorated here on Namibia's currency, was a fierce opponent of the Germans. He was killed during the revolt against colonial rule in 1905.

Over the course of a few days, the Herero destroyed German homes and farms. They killed 100 German settlers and 13 German soldiers. Germany responded by sending in 10 000 heavily armed troops. Their commander had just one game plan for war—to win at any cost! He ordered the execution of all Herero and Nama men who were captured. The women and children were to be exiled into the desert wilderness.

The uprising lasted for three years. By the time the Germans quashed the rebellion in 1907, much of the Herero and Nama populations had been wiped out. Half of the Nama population was dead; only 10 000 people were left. Only 15 000 Herero remained out of a population that had once numbered 80 000. Many people have called this the first **genocide** of the 20th century.

genocide
the mass murder of human beings, particularly of a race, nation, or culture

FIGURE 4.18
A group of Herero survivors

The Herero were driven into the Omaheke Desert. The Germans sealed off the watering holes. Then they built a fence so that the people could not return. The Herero died of starvation, thirst, or disease. Those who remained in the colony were forced to work in labour camps. Many people died there from starvation, disease, or exhaustion.

Ethiopia: Resistance Succeeds

One country successfully resisted European occupation during the Scramble for Africa: Ethiopia. In the 1880s, Italy was competing with Britain and France for colonies in eastern Africa. In 1885, Italy had annexed the port of Massawa in Eritrea on the Red Sea. This raised fears in neighbouring Ethiopia that the Italians had designs on their country, too. Ethiopia's emperor, Menelik II, wanted to ensure that his country maintained its **sovereignty**, so he signed a treaty with Italy in May 1889.

sovereignty
the absolute independence of a community or nation

But the Italians had deceived Menelik. In the Italian version of the treaty, they had added a clause that gave Italy the exclusive right to advise Ethiopia on foreign affairs. In effect, it made Ethiopia an Italian protectorate. When Menelik II discovered the Italians' trickery, he asserted Ethiopia's independence through diplomatic means. He invited representatives from other European powers to meet with him. In 1893, he rejected the treaty altogether.

The Italians were determined to gain control of Ethiopia. In 1895, they declared war on the ancient nation and launched an invasion from Eritrea. Menelik called upon his people to rise up against the invaders. Thousands of Ethiopians marched off to defend their country armed with African spears and machetes as well as European guns and cannons.

The Ethiopian forces moved swiftly north toward the Eritrean border. Along the way, they fought—and won—several skirmishes with Italian troops. Then, with a force of 17 000 soldiers, the Italians launched a surprise attack at Adwa on March 1, 1896. They were met by an Ethiopian force of over 100 000. Heavy fighting lasted throughout the day. By nightfall, Ethiopia, the strongest power in Africa, had defeated Italy, the weakest colonial power in Europe.

The defeat was a major blow for Italy's colonial ambitions in Africa. In October 1896, Italy signed the Treaty of Addis Ababa, which recognized "absolute and without reserve the independence of the Ethiopian Empire." The defeat of the Italians was the greatest victory in African resistance to colonial rule. Ethiopia's resistance was a source of pride and inspiration for all Africans.

FIGURE 4.19 An illustration of Menelik II

A European artist created this impression of Emperor Menelik.

How does it compare with the photograph in Figure 4.20?

REVIEW AND REFLECT

Create a graphic organizer summarizing African resistance in the Congo, North West Africa, South West Africa, and Ethiopia under the following headings: Who Was Involved; How They Resisted; The Final Outcome. Then share your results with a partner.

ORIGINALS

MENELIK II (1844–1913)

During the Scramble for Africa, the ancient country of Ethiopia preserved its independence largely because of one man: Menelik II. Menelik was crowned emperor of Ethiopia in 1889. According to legend, he was descended from the Queen of Sheba, who ruled Ethiopia in the 10th century CE, and Israel's King Solomon.

When Menelik came to the throne, Ethiopia was loosely united. Local rulers showed little loyalty to the emperor. But Menelik moved quickly to consolidate his power and bring these rulers under control. He built a new capital at Addis Ababa and set up a strong central government there. Gradually, he built a sense of national unity among the people of Ethiopia.

Menelik II was a shrewd leader. As he watched the powers of Europe sweep across the continent claiming African lands as their own, he prepared to defend his country. He took advantage of the rivalries among the nations of Europe to obtain modern weapons. He notified the rulers of Europe that he would not sit by and wait for a European invasion.

> **I have no intention at all of being an indifferent spectator, if the distant Powers hold the idea of dividing up Africa, Ethiopia having been for the past fourteen centuries, an island of Christians in a sea of pagans.**
>
> Menelik II, in a letter to Britain's Queen Victoria, April 1891, in "The Colonial Challenge: Africa Under Foreign Domination, 1880–1935," *the UNESCO Courier*, May 1984

FIGURE 4.20 Emperor Menelik II

After the Italian invasion, Menelik arranged for inaccurate maps of the country to fall into enemy hands. He sent spies to the Italian camps to plant misleading information. He used the stockpile of weapons he had acquired from the Europeans in his successful showdown with Italy.

The victory of the Ethiopian forces in the battle of Adwa greatly enhanced Menelik's international reputation. Foreign ambassadors and advisers were eager to visit the ancient kingdom. In his quest to modernize his country, Menelik embraced new technology. He invited foreigners to share their expertise. He built a railway between Djibouti and Addis Ababa. He introduced telephone and postal services. He built modern bridges and telegraph lines. He built the first bank, hotel, and hospital. He introduced a modern education system. The changes Menelik brought about were unprecedented in Ethiopian history.

In 1906, Menelik suffered the first of a series of paralyzing strokes. Power passed to his wife until his death in 1913. For his many achievements, he was remembered by his people as the "King of Kings."

Think It Through

What is the significance of Menelik standing up to the powers of Europe? Explain your response in an opinion paragraph.

Competition and Conflict

The Africans in southern Africa were caught in the European competition for control of the southern tip of the continent. At first, this competition was limited to the opportunities created by trade between West Africa and India. In 1652, the Dutch established the Dutch East India Company at Cape Colony as a supply station and naval base. In 1795, the British seized the colony from the Dutch. They occupied it until 1803 before abandoning it to engage in war in Europe. Britain regained control of Cape Colony in 1806. At the time, 20 000 Dutch settlers lived there. Soon, though, British settlers began to dominate local politics. They passed laws the Dutch settlers opposed, including ending the trade in African peoples.

The Dutch (known today as *Afrikaners*) resented the British intrusion in their lives. They also faced conflicts with neighbouring African peoples. Beginning in 1835, the Afrikaners gathered their possessions in covered wagons and headed north. Between 1835 and 1843, 10 000 to 12 000 Afrikaners embarked on the Great Trek. They were looking to settle on lands where they could live their lives their way.

FIGURE 4.21 Southern Africa, 1850s

The Afrikaners left a huge social impact wherever they settled. They believed Europeans were racially superior to Africans. They kept their communities separate from those of local African peoples. They denied Africans any rights. This policy of racial **segregation** would have a long-lasting impact on the indigenous peoples of southern Africa.

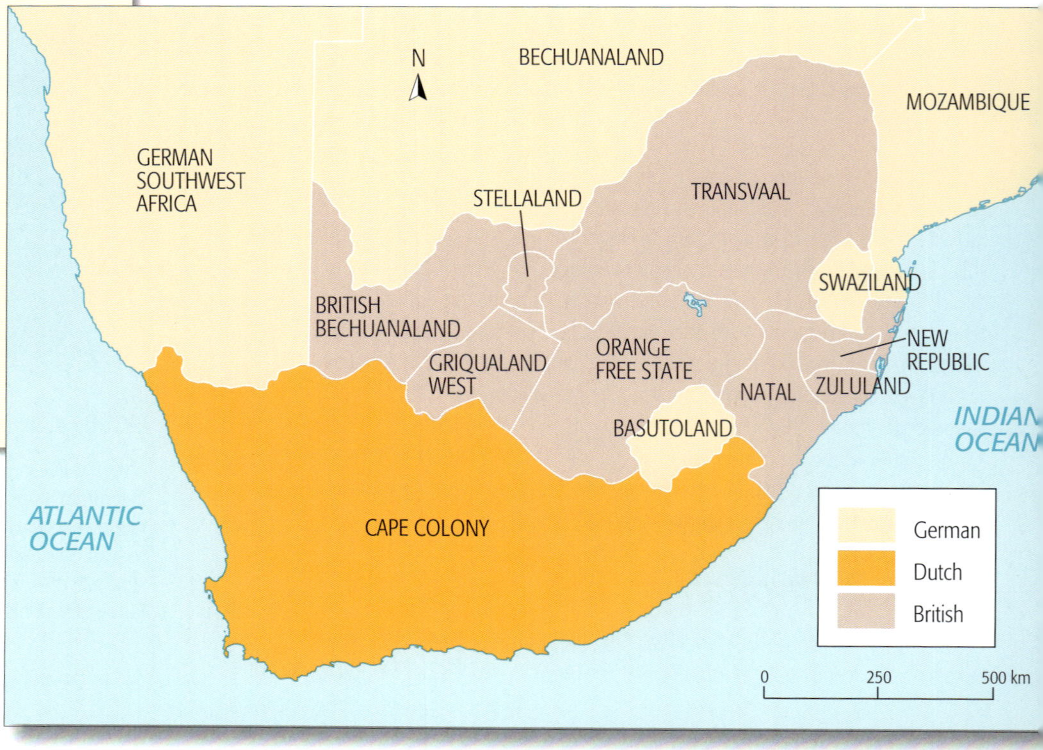

segregation
the separation or isolation of a race, class, or culture through enforced residence in a restricted area or by other discriminatory social barriers

Afrikaner Resettlement

The Afrikaners from Cape Colony arrived on the western border of Basutoland (present-day Lesotho). They claimed the land as their own. They set up two independent republics: the Orange Free State in 1852 and the Republic of Transvaal in 1854. But the Afrikaners were not welcomed by the local Sotho people who already lived there. For the next 30 years the two sides clashed over land. In a war in 1858, the Sotho defeated the Afrikaners. But in another battle in 1865, they lost much of their land to the newcomers. The Sotho chief, Moshoeshoe, was desperate to preserve what remained of his kingdom. So in 1868 he placed his land under British protection.

Raising the Stakes

In the 1860s and 1870s, huge new deposits of diamonds and gold were discovered in southern Africa. The lure of great wealth from these resources raised the stakes for the Europeans. British settlers became locked in a battle with the Afrikaners for control of southern Africa. Their competition had a dramatic impact on both Europeans and the Sotho and Zulu peoples who lived in the region.

THE ZULU WAR

With the vast resources of diamonds and gold at stake, Britain was determined to extend its control over southern Africa. The Zulus were the most powerful force in the region. When the British claimed the coastal area of Natal, they wanted to limit the influence of the Afrikaners. So they allied themselves with the Zulus. But when the British annexed the Afrikaner territory of Transvaal in 1877, they inherited the border disputes between the Afrikaners and the Zulus. Now, instead of supporting the Zulus, Britain wanted to destroy them.

In December 1878, Britain issued a set of demands to the Zulu chief, King Cetshwayo. When the king failed to respond, British troops gathered along the frontier of Zululand on January 22, 1879. The British advanced to Isandlwana and set up a base camp. In a surprise attack, they were surrounded by more than 10 000 Zulu soldiers. The British were overwhelmed. In a stunning defeat, more than half the British force was killed.

> The Zulus were tall, strong, fierce warriors, who knew neither fear nor mercy. . . . Their weapons were stabbing ***assegais*** and shields, throwing spears, **knobkerries**, and a few firearms ranging from muskets to modern rifles. They charged their British opponents at an effortless pace, half trot, half jog, banging their *assegais* against their shields, hissing between their teeth and shouting Cetewayo's war cry: "Usutu! Usutu! Usutu!"
>
> Edwardo Zinna, *Out of Africa*, London: Edward Arnold, 1898

assegais
a light spear with a short shaft and long blade for close combat, used by the Bantu peoples of southern Africa

knobkerry
a short wooden club with a heavy knob on one end

FIGURE 4.22 A painting by C.E. Fripp of the Battle of Isandlwana, January 22, 1879

The British army at Isandlwana was a mix of British and African soldiers. African soldiers were recruited for colonial forces because they were familiar with local land, language, and culture. In the Battle of Isandlwana, approximately 450 African soldiers were killed along with 850 British soldiers.

Shocked by their devastating defeat, the British took time to regroup. In late March, they returned to the battlefield with reinforcements. For the next few months, they fought a tough campaign against the Zulus. But they managed to score key victories, with the help of the first continuous-fire machine gun, the Gatling gun.

By summer, British troops were advancing toward the Zulu capital of Ulundi. In August 1879, the last battle of the Zulu wars was fought. Britain defeated the Zulus. The Zulu kingdom was now in ruins, its king in exile. Britain divided the Zulu kingdom among 13 pro-British African chiefs. In 1887, Britain proclaimed the former Zulu territory a British colony.

THE SOUTH AFRICAN WAR

Two centuries of conflict between the British and the Afrikaners led to the first Boer War in 1880–81. The Afrikaners battled the British to regain the Transvaal's independence. The tensions grew deeper following the discovery of massive amounts of gold in the Afrikaner republic of Transvaal in 1886. The discoveries gave the Transvaal the potential to be the richest and most powerful nation in southern Africa. The British were determined to seize the gold mines for themselves. The Afrikaners were equally determined to retain control. In 1899, the long-standing tensions erupted into war.

The second Boer War, or South African War, was considered a "White Man's War." It was a brutal battle between a force of 450 000 British and African troops and 52 000 Afrikaner soldiers. During the long period of colonial rule in southern Africa, history focused on the British and the Afrikaners. Little attention was paid to the Africans' stories of neglect, suffering, and death.

FIGURE 4.23 Canadians in the South African War

Canadian troops were drawn into the South African War because Canada was part of the British Empire. The war was controversial in Canada. Many English Canadians supported Britain's fight against the Afrikaners. But most French Canadians and many immigrants questioned why Canada should fight in a foreign war halfway around the world.

At least 50 000 Africans fought with the British against the Afrikaners. Thousands died in battle or were executed by Afrikaner forces. Most of these unsung soldiers were buried and forgotten in unmarked graves.

While Britain's **scorched earth** policy destroyed the farms of many Afrikaners, it destroyed the farms of many African families, too. Thousands lost their land and homes. More than 116 000 displaced Afrikaner women and children were interned in the world's first concentration camps. At least 115 000 African women and children were imprisoned in separate camps. The captives were used as forced labour for the British forces. They grew food to feed British soldiers. But they were denied enough food to feed themselves. Almost 28 000 Afrikaners and 20 000 Africans starved to death or died from diseases in the concentration camps.

scorched earth
a military strategy in which anything that might be useful to the enemy is destroyed, including food supplies, shelter, transportation and communication facilities, and industries

The South African War ended in May 1902 with a British victory. Many Africans hoped the British would give them greater political equality. After all, they had sided with the British and had served in their army.

Yet Britain's priority was to reconcile with the Afrikaners. They wanted to protect their interests in southern Africa. They agreed to let the Afrikaners discriminate against Africans by denying them the right to vote in their territories of the Transvaal and the Orange Free State. This planted the seeds of racial discrimination against Africans. By the time the Afrikaners gained self-government in 1907, the British themselves supported the exclusion of Africans from political and social life in southern Africa. This widespread racial discrimination would dominate the new Republic of South Africa for decades to come.

EXPRESSIONS

PROTEST AND RESISTANCE

Imagine what it would be like to be told that you are inferior because of your race. Imagine having to carry a pass when you travel outside your own town. Imagine being arrested or beaten by the police for no reason. Imagine being denied the right to go to school or to see a doctor. Imagine that you have no rights at all. You are not allowed to vote, so you have no way of changing things. This is what life was like for Africans under **apartheid**, the South African government's official policy of racial discrimination.

The seeds of apartheid were planted at the end of the South African War. By the end of the First World War, these seeds had taken root. The war had created great economic and social hardship. Many White Africans were afraid that the segregated worlds in which they lived were about to collide. They called for the complete separation of the races in all aspects of life—social, political, economic, and legal. Segregation was practised in most South African communities. It became official government policy in 1948. It remained a bitter fact of life for Black South Africans until 1994.

Many Black South Africans refused to accept this oppression without a fight. Some expressed their discontent in rousing speeches. Others incited violence and riots. Some expressed their resistance through the arts.

Herbert Dhlomo was one of the major Black writers in South Africa. In the 1920s and 1930s, he campaigned for the rights of Black South Africans. He published articles in the *Umteteli wa Bantu* newspaper aimed at influencing White liberals to support the rights of Black South Africans. He also wrote patriotic poems protesting political oppression.

How can you rest content so near the hells
Of poverty where Moloch fiercely dwells;
Where children die of hunger and neglect.
While city Fathers boast suburbs select;
Where minds disease and dead to Love make gains
Through drunkards, widows, waifs and worker's pains . . .

Herbert Dhlomo, "On Munro Bridge, Johannesburg"

Peter Henry Abrahams was another influential Black writer in the resistance movement. His book *Mine Boy* (1946) depicted the dehumanizing effects of racial segregation in South Africa. The story centres around a young man named Xuma who migrates from the country to Johannesburg to work in the gold mines. In the city, Xuma is quickly awakened to the realities of a society in which the colour of his skin determines everything.

A policeman was only ten yards [9 m] away and he was coming straight at Xuma. Xuma waited. He had done nothing. He had just stood there watching. The policeman came nearer. He raised his stick and brought it down with force. It missed Xuma's head and struck his left shoulder. Pain shot through his body.

"I have done nothing," he said and grabbed the policeman's arm before he could hit again.

"Let go! Bastard!" the policeman shouted and kicked out.

Xuma felt pain shooting up his leg.

Peter Henry Abrahams, *Mine Boy*, London: Heinemann Books, 1989

For Xuma, Johannesburg, the so-called city of gold, was a city of despair. His vision of a raceless society is shattered by the realities of life as a Black South African in a White regime. *Mine Boy* is considered the first modern novel of Black South Africa.

By the 1960s, there was a literary revival among Black writers who had long been silenced by repression. The Soweto poets defined a new political consciousness among Black South Africans. They reaffirmed Black cultural values and reclaimed Black identities. Their poetic messages raised Black consciousness and racial pride.

apartheid
an official policy of racial segregation involving political, social, legal, and economic discrimination against non-Whites

i am the man you will never defeat
i will be the one to plague you
your children are cursed
if you walk this earth, where i too walk
and you tear my clothes and reach for my flesh
and you tear my flesh to reach my blood
and you spill my blood to reach my bones
and you smash my bones and hope for my soul
...
i am the man you will never defeat
i will be your shadow, to be with you always
and one day
when the sun rises
the shadows will move.

Mongane Serote, "No Baby Must Weep," 1975, in Michael Chapman, ed., *Soweto Poetry: Literary Perspectives*, The University of Kwa-Zulu Natal, 2007

Throughout the years of apartheid, Black South Africans resisted the oppression and violence that were forced upon them. After apartheid was finally dismantled in 1990, Black South Africans wanted to move forward into the future, but they did not want to forget the lessons of the past. In 2001, the Apartheid Museum was opened in Johannesburg. The museum's exhibits provide a window into the dark days of apartheid and honour the many ways in which Black South Africans resisted the forces of oppression.

Think It Through

Think about something that you think is unjust in the world today. Write a poem or short story or draw an illustration to present your point of view.

FIGURE 4.24 The Apartheid Museum, South Africa

In this room, 131 nooses, representing all of the political prisoners who were executed during the apartheid regime, hang from the ceiling as a stark reminder of the dehumanizing effects of that era.

How does this exhibit make you feel? How powerful is its message?

The First World War

For all the tense competition for territory in Africa, no two European imperial powers came to blows in Africa—until the First World War. The British fired the first shots in Africa in Togo in 1914. Thereafter, Africans were relentlessly dragged into the conflict as the two sides—the Central Powers led by Germany and the Triple Alliance that included Britain and France—sought to occupy their enemies' colonies.

The war's impact was felt throughout the continent. The need for raw materials to feed the people of Europe and to stock European factories placed unprecedented demands on the people of Africa. Young men were forced into service in the army or as labourers. Subsistence farmers and herders were forced to turn over their crops and livestock. The Europeans' quest for food often left little or nothing for the Africans themselves.

FIGURE 4.25 French Senegalese troops on the Western Front

All colonial governments requisitioned African men to serve in European armies. France was especially aggressive in recruiting African soldiers for duty in Europe. France needed to make up for the devastating losses it had suffered on the Western Front. More than 30 000 African soldiers were killed in Europe.

When the war was over in 1918, Germany was defeated. Britain, France, and Belgium became trustees of Germany's former colonies, overseen by the newly formed **League of Nations**. However, the victorious European nations still maintained power in their own colonies in Africa.

League of Nations
an international organization formed in 1920 to promote international peace and cooperation

For many Africans, the war left feelings of bitterness, anger, and resentment toward their colonial rulers. African soldiers who fought alongside Europeans realized that the Europeans were no different than anyone else. They had their strengths and weaknesses. There were both heroes and cowards among them. This realization gave many young Africans the courage and determination not only to question their colonial rulers, but to challenge them as well.

After the war, Africans expected to be rewarded for their service and sacrifice. They believed they had earned the right to more equitable lives. But colonial rulers offered no hope for change. The Africans' disappointment contributed to a growing postwar discontent with colonial occupation. As you will discover in Chapter 7, a new generation of Africans was about to emerge, one that would lead the fight for independence for their peoples. One of their biggest challenges would be to unite populations divided by language, religion, and culture.

REVIEW AND REFLECT

1. What impact do you think the Afrikaners' Great Trek had on local African peoples? Discuss your ideas with a partner.
2. Why was the South African War traditionally considered a "White Man's War"? Do you think this is an accurate description? Explain your response.
3. Do you think colonial governments should have compensated Africans for their contributions during the First World War? Working in small groups, generate possible responses to this question. Record your ideas in a chart. Then discuss and debate all ideas as a class.

The Historian's Craft

INTERPRETING VISUAL EVIDENCE

Visual primary sources are windows into the past. They show you the way people dressed, how they lived, and what things were important to them at a given time and place. Like written primary sources, visual sources of evidence must be analyzed for reliability, perspective, and bias. Remember, you are seeing only what the artist or photographer wants you to see, so you need to interpret the work carefully to construct a picture of the past.

LOOKING FOR MEANING

Your first task is to identify the subject and the action taking place. Then you need to think about what the evidence tells you. Think about your overall first impression. What is your first impression of the political cartoon on British imperialism in Figure 4.10 on page 121? You can see that the cartoon depicts Britain as an octopus with its tentacles spread around the world. Now think about the cartoon's message. It is a powerful statement about the imperial ambitions of Britain during the late 19th century.

Now look at the photograph in Figure 4.11 on page 123. What is your first impression? It shows a group of confident Europeans showing off a treasure trove of African cultural artifacts. If you look more closely, you can see that the stolen treasures reveal that the people of Benin had distinct religious beliefs and cultural traditions and valuable commodities, such as ivory. You might conclude that Benin was a prosperous kingdom.

LOOKING MORE DEEPLY

Once you have a first impression, you need to examine the evidence more closely. Look at the cartoon in Figure 4.10 again. John Bull appears as a well-fed merchant. This symbolizes the prosperity that empire building brought to the British economy. You might speculate that imperialism was not just about trade and wealth. It was about military might. Britain's dominance as a naval power depended on its naval bases around the world. The octopus wants to keep these in its grasp.

Now look at the photograph in Figure 4.11 again. Notice the composition. The British soldiers are framed in the centre, posed above their loot. This suggests that they believed they were superior to African peoples. It shows that they had little respect for their rights and possessions. The man in the centre has his arms crossed, suggesting both physical strength and self-satisfaction. The man to his left holds a sheaf of papers—perhaps an inventory of the stolen treasures to show how Britain has brought organization to Africa. The photograph reflects the European attitudes of superiority that prevailed in the late 19th century.

ASK YOURSELF

Here are a few questions to ask yourself when you analyze visual evidence.

- What is the message? Is it positive or negative?
- What is the purpose of the message?
- Who is the intended audience?
- Do any visual techniques affect the accuracy of the image?
- Do I know of any evidence that conflicts with this message?

TRY IT!

Using the questions above, analyze one piece of visual evidence from this chapter. What does the image tell you? From whose perspective was it created? What bias might it have?

STUDY HALL

KNOWLEDGE & UNDERSTANDING

1. Complete a graphic organizer similar to the one below listing the effects of colonization under the headings Methods of Control, Social Effects, Economic Effects, and Political Consequences on African Culture.

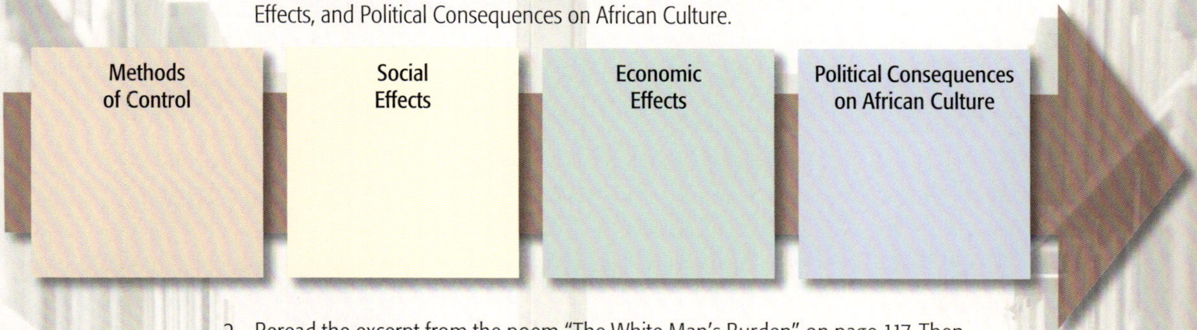

2. Reread the excerpt from the poem "The White Man's Burden" on page 117. Then write a response to the poem that disagrees with Kipling's position.

THINKING

3. What factors do you think cause some nations to feel superior to others? Do you think that there is ever a justification for colonization? Discuss your ideas in a think-pair-share strategy.
4. Reread the quotations from the explorer Henry Stanley and King Mojimba on page 116. Why do you think Stanley misunderstood the king's welcome? How might their encounter have been different if he had understood that the king was there to greet him?

APPLICATION & COMMUNICATION

5. How would you feel if missionaries from another country came to your community to try to convert you to their religion? Write a message or speech that you would deliver to them expressing your views about their mission.
6. Write a 30-second television news report describing the encounter between Stanley and Mojimba.
7. Create a political cartoon expressing your opinion about the Scramble for Africa.
8. Do research to find out about another African community or nation that resisted colonization during the Scramble for Africa. Present your findings in an oral or written report.
9. Research the effects of colonialism on First Nations in Canada. Then compare your findings with the effects of colonialism on African peoples in a comparison organizer.

UNIT 3

Toward Freedom

TABLE OF CONTENTS

Nelson Mandela addresses a crowd after apartheid is lifted in South Africa

The story of Nelson Mandela, a former political prisoner who became the leader of a new and liberated South Africa, reflects the quest for freedom by people throughout the African diaspora.

CHAPTER

5 Oppression and Resistance: Canada and the United States

KEY CONCEPTS

IN THIS CHAPTER, YOU WILL:

- examine the causes and outcomes of the American Revolution and its impact on Black Americans
- investigate why Black Loyalists and Black refugees immigrated to Canada
- analyze the implications of the American Civil War and its aftermath
- identify the problems Black settlers faced coming to Canada
- evaluate the role of the Underground Railroad in freeing enslaved Black people
- look at the impact of urbanization on Black culture
- learn about the struggle for civil rights in the United States and Canada

A People's Story

At different times in history, Canada has offered refuge to Black Americans fleeing oppression in the United States. Yet Canada is not without its own history of oppression. Slavery existed in both the United States and Canada. Even after slavery was abolished in the British Empire, Blacks who came to Canada faced racism and discrimination.

In this chapter, you will have the opportunity to learn more about slavery and the Black experience in both Canada and the United States. You will see the role that slavery played in New France and British North America. You will discover why slavery was so entrenched in American society, particularly in the South, and investigate the circumstances under which Black Americans immigrated to Canada. You will learn how Black Americans and Black Canadians have responded to the challenges before them. As you read, think about the effect that slavery has had on culture. Think about the reasons why one group of people may feel compelled to oppress others. Reflect on the morality of racism, prejudice, and discrimination, and the impact that these have on modern societies.

Black Loyalists come to British North America	Black refugees from War of 1812 migrate to Canada	Peak of the Underground Railroad	American Civil War	The Emancipation Proclamation frees enslaved Blacks in the Southern United States	14th Amendm passed in t United Stat
1776–1783	1812	1830–1865	1861–1865	1863	1865

Image Analysis

FIGURE 5.1 *What Does Freedom Mean to You?*, 2008

This painting by contemporary artist Joy Martyr-André shows different ways that freedom can be interpreted. As you will learn in this chapter, Blacks in Canada and the United States had a long, hard journey to freedom, and the freedom they gained often had its own hardship and challenges.

What do the shackles in this image represent? What do the words on this painting reveal about how freedom is gained and what challenges may arise from this state of being?

oloured omen's founded Montreal	*Immigration Act* of Canada passed	Viola Desmond of Halifax fights segregation in Canadian courts	The Montgomery bus boycott in Alabama	Little Rock Nine and school desegregation in Arkansas	Halifax tears down Africville	American *Civil Rights Act* passed	American Black Power movement	Barack Obama is elected president of the United States
902	1910	1946	1955	1957	1961	1964	1960s	2008

Black Chattel Slavery

Black chattel slavery dates back to the early 1600s in both Canada and the United States. In Britain's Thirteen Colonies, the first enslaved Africans arrived in 1619 to work on the tobacco plantations of Virginia. By the late 1600s, there were 28 000 enslaved Africans in the Thirteen Colonies. However, that number skyrocketed between 1700 and 1775, when at least 255 000 people were captured and kidnapped from their African homelands and enslaved in the United States. Enslaved Africans were most often delivered to ports in the heart of the American South. There they were sold into slavery as field workers on the plantations and domestic servants on the colonial estates.

As you learned in Chapter 3, Britain's and France's involvement in the transatlantic trade in African peoples extended into the New France and British North America colonies. Originally, slavery involved Aboriginal peoples in New France. But as the trade in African peoples expanded in the 1600s, the Europeans turned to enslaved Africans as a source of labour in the fur trade and in the fishing, mining, and forestry industries. Following the Seven Years' War (1756–1763) between Britain and France, France was forced to surrender New France to Britain. Under the terms of surrender, Britain agreed to allow slavery to continue in New France.

To increase the colony's English-speaking population, Britain offered the people in its New England colony large plots of land if they relocated to New France. The new settlers brought their enslaved workers with them. As a result, there was a steady increase in the population of enslaved Africans.

FIGURE 5.2 Selling enslaved Africans at auction

The public auctions you read about in Chapter 3 demonstrate how enslaved Africans were bought and sold as property in the same way that livestock was sold.

What did these auctions reveal about the attitude of White colonists toward Africans?

Black Chattel Slavery Life in the Americas

FIGURE 5.3
The cotton gin

The invention of the cotton gin in 1793 transformed the cotton industry. It is slow and painstaking work to pick out the seeds from cotton balls by hand. The cotton gin extracted the seeds and cleaned and combed the cotton fibres. This made it much faster to process cotton.

The invention of the cotton gin revolutionized cotton production in the United States. With the help of federal soldiers, the colonists displaced Native Americans from their traditional lands. Then they used enslaved Africans to prepare the land for cotton production. Five years after Eli Whitney's invention, cotton production in the United States had tripled. The growth of the cotton industry helped spread slavery throughout the South.

Enslaved Blacks worked year-round. The men cleared forests and chopped the wood. They planted the crops and brought in the harvest. The women worked in the fields and tended to the gardens. They took care of the livestock and butchered them when they were ready for the dinner table. Working conditions were brutal, sometimes unbearable. Men, women, and children died from sheer exhaustion or from severe malnutrition or disease.

Some men and women were spared the back-breaking work of the plantation fields and worked in their owners' homes as domestic servants. The men did carpentry work, shoed the horses, ran errands, and drove the carriages. The women washed, ironed, cooked, baked, and cared for the children of their owners.

Many Black females also had to endure being forced into sexual activity by White males. Black men were powerless to help as their siblings, daughters, and wives were sexually abused.

Black Chattel Slavery Life in British North America

Canada's climate is very different from the climate of much of the United States. As a result, the lifestyles of enslaved Africans in British North America were different, too. The growing season was much shorter. During the colder months, enslaved peoples worked as domestic servants in the homes of their owners. If the owners had enough servants or wanted to make extra money, they rented enslaved workers to hotels, taverns, and other businesses.

Although their lifestyles differed in some respects, their treatment was no less inhumane. Enslaved Africans in Britain's North American colonies were cruelly treated and physically abused. Enslaved African women here also faced sexual abuse by White males.

Resistance

As you learned in Chapter 3, enslaved Africans resisted their status and treatment in a variety of ways. Sometimes they faked illnesses, destroyed tools, sabotaged their owners' homes, played dumb, and worked slowly to frustrate their owners. You can read about one famous act of resistance in the feature on page 152.

Many enslaved Africans in both the Americas and British North America ran away. In the Americas and British North America, some were running from the brutality of their lives. In the southern states, some were searching for loved ones who had been sold to another plantation. In those states, women sometimes ran away for short periods of time. They wanted to show their resistance to their enslavement. But they did not want to run away permanently and leave their children behind.

In many cases, owners placed ads for runaways in newspapers and offered rewards for their return. Here is an example of an ad for a missing slave:

> **Ran away from her master, John Rock on Monday the 18th day of August last; a Negroe Girl named Thursday ... Whosoever may harbour said Negroe Girl, or encourage her to stay away from her said Master, may depend on being persecuted the Law shall directs. And whosoever may be so kind as to take her up and send her home to her said Master, shall be paid all Costs and Charges, together with TWO DOLLARS Reward for their Trouble.**
>
> John Rock, Halifax, September 1, 1772, *Nova Scotia Gazette and Weekly Chronicle*

Those who were caught and returned to their plantations faced harsh punishment to discourage them, or anyone else, from trying to escape again.

FIGURE 5.4 Enslaved Africans being branded (above); personalized branding irons

Plantation owners used cruel and brutal punishments to force the Africans to obey. Those who resisted or tried to escape were whipped, dismembered, **castrated**, and even killed. The owners branded the Africans with their own personal initials, too.

What belief do you think the owners were expressing by branding their initials on other human beings?

castrate
to remove a man's reproductive organs, making him unable to have children

ORIGINALS

MARIE-JOSEPH ANGÉLIQUE

One night in April 1734, a fire spread through the city of Montreal. No one was killed but 46 buildings were burned to the ground. Montrealers believed that 29-year-old Marie-Joseph Angélique, an enslaved domestic servant who worked for Madame Thérèse de Francheville, and her lover, Claude Thibault, a White indentured servant who also worked for de Francheville, set the fire before trying to escape to freedom. Thibault fled the scene and was never seen again. But Angélique was captured and tried for arson.

Throughout her trial, Angélique insisted she was innocent. Twenty prosecution witnesses described her as disobedient and disrespectful. Yet none could claim they had seen her set the fire. Then a young child took the stand and claimed she had seen Angélique do it. Angélique was convicted of arson and imprisoned to await execution.

FIGURE 5.5 *Portrait of Angélique*

In New France, people could be prosecuted based on rumours alone.

In what ways could enslaved people like Angélique avoid rumours about their lives?

On June 21st—the day Angélique was to die—the judge visited her in prison and threatened to torture her if she didn't confess. Unable to exact a confession, the judge ordered the torture to begin. Her torturer—himself a Black man—crushed her legs using barbaric tools from the Middle Ages. In horrible pain, Angélique broke down and confessed. But the torture continued until she begged the men to hang her to end her suffering.

> **Let me die, monsieur. No one advised me. No one helped me set the fire....You are killing me. ... I did it by myself. ... Hang me. ... I said it was I who did it ... with a small stove. No one told me to do it, monsieur, a bad thought came to me.**
>
> Marie-Joseph Angélique, June 21, 1734

After her confession, Angélique was paraded through the charred streets of Montreal in a garbage cart. She was forced to wear a white chemise bearing the word *incendiare*—arsonist—and made to carry a burning torch as a symbol of her crime. Onlookers screamed and spat at Angélique as she passed by. When she reached the charred remains of the de Francheville home, she was hanged. Her dead body dangled from the gallows for two hours before it was finally cut down and placed on a funeral pyre.

No one knows for sure whether Angélique set the blaze. The prosecution never produced any concrete evidence to prove her guilt. Today, some scholars believe she did set the fire as an act of resistance against her enslavement. Not everyone agrees, though. Some people think Angélique was a scapegoat who was sentenced to death because her skin was black. While it may be impossible to know the truth, today Angélique's story has become symbolic of Black resistance in Canada.

Think It Through

Write the script for a memorial plaque about the life and death of Marie-Joseph Angélique.

Free Blacks

Although most Blacks in the Thirteen Colonies were enslaved, some Blacks were free. Some had arrived in the colonies as indentured servants before slavery. They had been freed after completing their contracts. Their children were free, too. Sometimes owners freed enslaved Blacks at their discretion. But as slavery gained a stronghold, White colonists, particularly those in the South, viewed free Blacks as a threat. They brought in laws that made it almost impossible for enslaved Blacks to gain their freedom, except under extraordinary circumstances.

For the Blacks who were free, their freedom was severely restricted. Throughout the colonies, there were racist policies designed to limit the power of Blacks. They could not own businesses or property. They could not live in White neighbourhoods. They could not work in certain occupations. In some places, they faced the prospect of being sold into slavery if they were convicted of even a minor offence. Many Black men opted to escape to the high seas. Many Black women found sanctuary working as domestic servants and as seamstresses.

REVIEW AND REFLECT

1. How important do you think the invention of the cotton gin was for the colonies of the American South? Why did this invention increase trade in African peoples?
2. In what ways was slavery different in British North America from in the United States?
3. How did enslaved Africans resist their captivity?
4. Why do you think the White colonists considered the free Blacks to be a threat to them?

Migrations to Canada in the 1700s

Even while White colonists in the Americas oppressed thousands of Blacks, they themselves complained about being oppressed by Britain. The colonists resented the taxes they were forced to pay. They were frustrated by restrictions that prevented them from expanding their territories. Many of the colonists wanted freedom from British rule. Their demands for independence led to the American Revolution, which began in 1775. This event led to the eventual migration of many Blacks to Canada.

Fighting for the British

Although the American Revolutionary War between 1776 and 1783 was fought over American independence, it affected the lives of many Black Americans. In 1775, the governor of Virginia, Lord Dunmore, issued a proclamation calling for all able-bodied men to come to Britain's defence of the colony. The offer extended to the American rebels' enslaved Black workers. They were promised freedom in exchange for their military service.

To become British soldiers and gain their freedom, enslaved Blacks first had to find a way to escape from their owners. Many owners inflicted cruel public beatings on their enslaved workers to deter them from even thinking about escape. But even for those who were not intimidated by such acts of cruelty, fleeing was not an easy decision. They were afraid their owners would retaliate against their family and friends. They were willing to risk death themselves, but they would not have those they left behind tortured because of their actions.

Many enslaved Blacks still made the decision to flee. Most ran away under cover of darkness so that their owners would not know they were gone until morning. By then, they would be far away. Once they reached British military bases, they would be safe.

Dunmore's proclamation was hugely successful. Within weeks, hundreds of Black men had joined his army. His proclamation was the first mass **emancipation** of enslaved peoples in American history.

emancipation
the act of setting someone free

FIGURE 5.6
Detail from *The Death of Major Pierson*, 1782–1784

This painting shows a Black soldier fighting in the American Revolutionary War. Lord Dunmore called this regiment of freed Blacks the Royal Ethiopian Regiment. Black soldiers had "Liberty to Slaves" embroidered on their uniforms.

What effect do you think these words had on the soldiers who wore them?

Fighting for the Patriots

The American patriots were fighting for freedom. Many free Blacks believed they would offer liberty to Blacks who were still enslaved, so they volunteered to join the rebel forces. But the relationship between American freedom and American slavery was deeply conflicted. Many patriot leaders refused to allow Blacks to join their units.

FIGURE 5.7
James Armistead (1745–1830)

In spite of the patriots' racism against Black soldiers, there were many who played important roles in the rebels' victory. James Armistead was an enslaved Black man from Virginia. He was one of the war's most successful spies. Posing as a runaway behind British lines, he gathered important information about their military strategies. In return, he was granted his freedom in 1786.

The Black Loyalists

When the American rebels gained the upper hand in the war, thousands of Loyalists, Black and White, fled north to British North America. Most of the Black Loyalists went to the Atlantic colonies, in particular Nova Scotia, an area that includes modern-day Nova Scotia as well as New Brunswick and Prince Edward Island. They were promised freedom and plots of land equal to those given to White Loyalists—either a small town lot and 20 hectares of farmland or 80 hectares of farmland in the country. Most of the Black Loyalists received the town lots. But few received the plots of farmland. Those who did had to wait a long time and, in some cases, petition the government to get them. When they did, the land was in remote locations that were not good for farming. The soil was poor and covered with rocks and was almost impossible to cultivate.

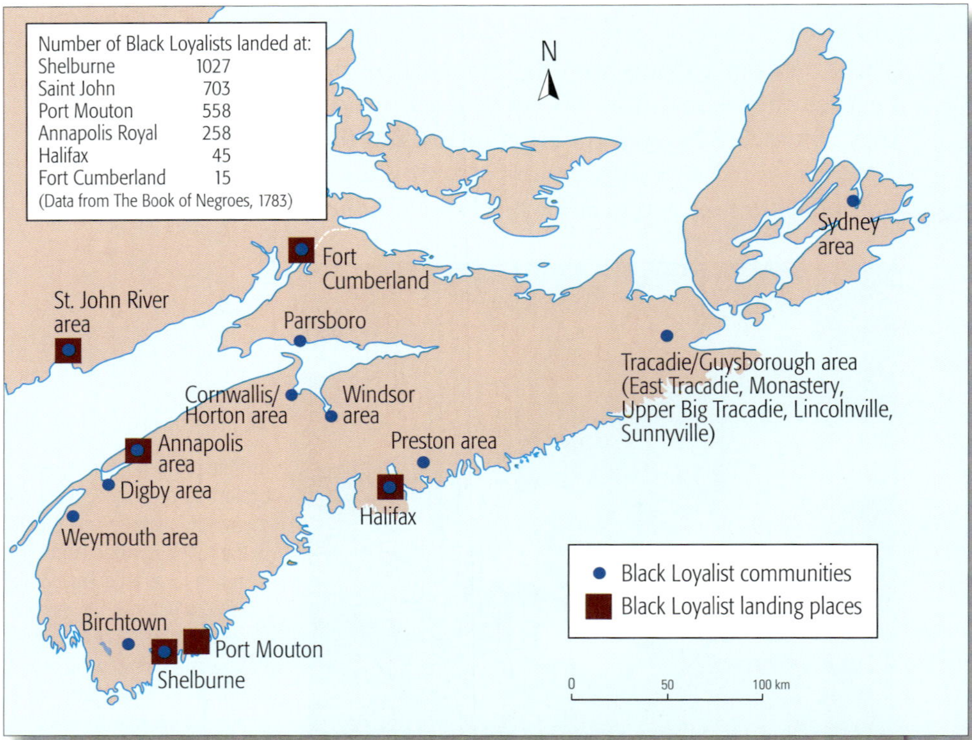

FIGURE 5.8 Black Loyalist settlements in Nova Scotia

The largest free Black settlement in Nova Scotia was Birchtown, founded in 1783. At its peak, between 1500 and 2000 Blacks lived there. This made it the largest community of free Blacks outside of Africa. Today, Birchtown, Shelbourne County, is home to the Black Heritage Loyalist Society.

Unable to farm for a living, the Black Loyalists faced poverty and starvation. To survive, some used their skills to practise a trade such as shoemaking or piloting boats. Others became indentured servants or domestic workers. They were exploited by their White employers. They were forced to perform back-breaking labour. They were tricked into signing long-term work contracts. Sometimes the White employers sold their Black workers back into slavery in the United States and the Caribbean. Although it was against the law, many people found ways to smuggle Black captives onto ships bound for foreign shores.

In 1791, an English abolitionist company offered the Black Loyalists the opportunity to settle in Sierra Leone, a free Black colony in Africa. Nearly 1200 Blacks accepted and set sail for Africa on January 15, 1792 to begin new lives. But those who stayed behind persevered and built strong and vibrant communities in Atlantic Canada.

REVIEW AND REFLECT

1. How did the American Revolution affect the lives of enslaved Blacks?
2. How did the British use slavery and the desire for freedom to benefit their own military agenda?
3. Why was British North America a desirable place for Black Americans?
4. What challenges did Black Loyalists and refugees face when they arrived in British North America?

After the Revolution

The American Revolution had been fought for freedom and equality. After the war, many White Americans saw the conflict between freedom and slavery. Abolitionists began campaigning for the abolition of slavery. But the federal government knew it would face fierce resistance from the southern states, where slavery was the foundation of the economy. The federal government was unwilling to take a stand. So they decided to let the states decide for themselves whether to abolish slavery. Maryland, Virginia, and North Carolina allowed owners to free their enslaved workers at their own discretion. By 1790, there were more than 25 000 free Blacks living in these states. But the lower southern states continued to import African labour. As a result, after the American Revolution the enslaved population in these states continued to grow.

In 1808, the United States joined other nations in discontinuing the trade in African peoples. But in the southern United States, slavery continued to flourish. In 1830, 86 percent of the 3.6 million Black Americans were enslaved. They still held on to their dreams of freedom. They worked during what little spare time they had to earn money to buy their freedom. Others hoped that good behaviour and loyal service would lead to their eventual freedom.

At the same time, many Black Americans resisted through escape and rebellion. Often their escape route led them to Canada, where in 1793 John Graves Simcoe had passed a law that would gradually eliminate slavery in Upper Canada. This law did nothing to help people who were already enslaved in Canada. They remained in slavery until their deaths. However, the law did have an impact on the total number of enslaved peoples in Canada. By 1809, that number had plummeted by 75 percent. The rest were finally declared freed on August 1, 1834 when, as you learned in Chapter 3, the *Slavery Abolishment Act* came into effect throughout the British Empire.

FIGURE 5.9
Heading north to freedom

As slavery in British North America tapered off, the British colonies became a refuge for former enslaved peoples from the United States. In the first half of the 19th century, thousands of enslaved Blacks from the American South escaped north to the British colonies.

What types of dangers do you think they faced as they made their way north?

The Underground Railroad

Quakers
a Christian religious society dating back to 17th-century England

By the early 1800s, freed Blacks were working with White abolitionists, including a society of **Quakers** and various Native Americans, to create the Underground Railroad. This was a network of people working secretly to help enslaved Blacks from the American South escape to freedom. The escapees travelled secretly at night. By day, they hid in safe houses, barns, and lofts. Some spiritual songs, like the popular "Swing Low, Sweet Chariot," besides offering a sense of community and comfort, hid coded messages. On the surface, the song was about being delivered from suffering into the next life. But it was also a code to announce the approach of conductors on the Underground Railroad.

SWING LOW, SWEET CHARIOT

Swing low, sweet chariot,
Coming for to carry me home.
Swing low, sweet chariot,
Coming for to carry me home.

I looked over Jordan, and what did I see,
Coming for to carry me home?
A band of angels coming after me,
Coming for to carry me home.

If you get there before I do,
Coming for to carry me home,
Tell all my friends I'm coming too,
Coming for to carry me home.

FIGURE 5.10 Routes of the Underground Railroad

The Underground Railroad was perhaps the greatest protest action against slavery in American history. Enslaved Black Americans followed many different routes on their secret journeys to freedom.

Trace the routes on this map. Where were the escapees headed? Why would they have chosen these destinations?

HARRIET TUBMAN

Many of the conductors who led the escapees were fugitives themselves, including Harriet Tubman, perhaps the most famous conductor of all.

Harriet Tubman was born in Maryland, one of 11 children. Her parents were both enslaved. As a child, she worked in her owner's house. She married John Tubman in 1844. In 1849, her owner died. Tubman was afraid she might be sold into slavery in the Deep South, where the living conditions for enslaved people were far worse than they were in Maryland. She escaped to Pennsylvania, a free state. From there, she began making secret trips to free members of her family. In Philadelphia, she became involved with the abolitionists in the Underground Railroad. She became its most successful conductor. She made 19 trips to the American South between 1850 and 1860 and guided more than 300 Black men, women, and children to freedom.

FIGURE 5.11 Harriet Tubman (1820–1913)

Harriet Tubman freed her entire family, including her aging parents. US authorities offered huge rewards for the capture of Tubman and her charges. Her bravery and passion for freedom earned her the nickname "Moses" in reference to the biblical Moses, who, as written in the book of Exodus, led the Jewish people out of slavery in Egypt to freedom.

Between 1830 and 1865, the Underground Railroad reached its peak. It successfully confronted slavery without resorting to violence through the cooperative effort of a loosely organized group of people of different cultures and religions. At least 100 000 Blacks escaped via the Underground

Railroad. The secrecy of the Railroad's mission meant that much of the evidence of their work was hidden or destroyed to protect those involved. There is evidence of the contributions made by people like Harriet Tubman. But the identities of many others who played vital roles in the Underground Railroad will forever remain a mystery.

FIGURE 5.12
Mary Shadd Cary (1823–1893)

Mary Shadd Cary was an outspoken abolitionist originally from Delaware. She eventually settled in Windsor, where she was committed to helping Black Americans who escaped via the Underground Railroad to build new lives. She founded the *Provincial Freeman*, a newspaper that promoted the abolitionist cause. Eventually, Cary returned to the United States, where she earned a law degree—the first Black woman to do so.

The War of 1812

Black American immigration to Canada also occurred during the War of 1812 between Britain and the United States. In April 1814, the commander of the British navy made an offer: any resident of the United States who reported to a British ship or military station and volunteered to fight on the British side would be transported to any British colony free of charge after the war. While the offer was open to all, it was primarily aimed at Black Americans. Many accepted Britain's offer. By the end of the war, more than 3500 enslaved Blacks had gained their freedom fighting for Britain.

Over 2000 freed Black Americans settled in British North America. Some of them were granted land. But most received the same empty promises of good farmland the Black Loyalists had received after the American Revolution. After years of disappointment and hardship, Blacks in the community of Preston, Nova Scotia filed a petition demanding that the government act on its promises.

Rather than eke out a living in small towns and villages, in the 1840s eight families decided to build their own community in the north end of Halifax. They bought three lots of land and founded the Campbell Road Settlement, later called Africville. Africville eventually grew to a population of 400. You will learn about the fate of this independent community later in this chapter.

FIGURE 5.13
Africville, circa 1969

The people of Africville were industrious and independent. They built their own church, school, and community centre.

Rebellion

Rather than fleeing to Canada or other free states, many enslaved Blacks rebelled to gain their freedom. Black fugitives and refugees set up communities in the swamplands of North Carolina, Virginia, Georgia, and Louisiana. They armed themselves with weapons they had kept during the American Revolution. They survived by stealing from local plantations and fighting off raids by state militia. Others executed violent rebellions that frightened and terrorized plantation owners.

On August 21, 1831, Nat Turner, an enslaved Black man in Virginia, began what would become the largest rebellion against slavery in the South. With the aid of a few trusted Blacks, he killed his owner and his family. Then the rebels travelled from house to house, freeing enslaved Blacks and killing any Whites they encountered. Within 48 hours, over 3000 state militia had suppressed the revolt, but not before the rebels had killed 57 Whites. Nat Turner was executed on November 11, 1831. His body was dismembered by authorities as a reminder of the consequences of rebellion.

FIGURE 5.14
Nat Turner preaches religion

Nat Turner believed that God had chosen him to lead a mass rebellion.

Why might other enslaved Blacks have felt compelled to follow his leadership?

The Struggle for Abolition in the United States

The abolitionist movement that began in Britain in the late 18th century spread to the United States. Black Americans joined forces with a growing group of White Americans to demand an end to centuries of oppression. White abolitionists like William Lloyd Garrison published newspapers like *The Liberator* to urge the abolition of slavery. Free Blacks published their own newspapers such as Samuel Cornish's *The Rights of All*, and *The North Star*, created by William Nell, Martin Delany, and Frederick Douglass.

In 1845, Douglass's book about his own life of enslavement, the *Narrative of the Life of Frederick Douglass, an American Slave*, turned the spotlight on the cruelties of slavery. In 1850, *The Narrative of Sojourner Truth*, the biography of Sojourner Truth, a woman born into slavery in New York, captured national attention. Harriet Beecher Stowe's bestselling novel *Uncle Tom's Cabin* was published in 1851. The book forced many Northerners to wake up to the cruel injustices of slavery. Despite this new awareness, slavery continued with the passing of a new law.

THE FUGITIVE SLAVE LAW

The Fugitive Slave Law of 1850 brought thousands more Black Americans to the British colonies. The law stated that anyone who escaped from slavery would be returned to their owners if captured, even if they were caught in free territories. This meant that all Black Americans, regardless of their status or where they lived, were in danger of being forced back into slavery.

To ensure their freedom, many free Blacks from the northern United States sought refuge in British North America. Many came to Ontario. They settled in communities such as Buxton, Elgin, Toronto, and Owen Sound. They owned their own property. They built their own churches, schools, and businesses. They studied law, medicine, and theology. They worked as teachers, ministers, and skilled workers. For these Black Americans, Canada was the land of freedom.

A group of free Blacks in California also decided to abandon the United States and move north. Although California was a free state, the new law did not allow Blacks to testify in court against Whites who might claim they were fugitives. Believing their safety and freedom were at risk, close to 600 Black Americans abandoned California for Vancouver Island in 1858. The majority settled in Victoria. Others went to Salt Spring Island and the mainland.

In Victoria, the Black Americans became an integral part of the city's booming economy. Leaders in Victoria's Black community, such as Joshua Howard, Peter Lester, and Mifflin Gibbs, became successful politicians, lawyers, and businesspeople. Blacks opened their own businesses as barbers, tailors, bakers, seamstresses, and carpenters.

FIGURE 5.15 Victoria Pioneer Rifle Company, circa early 1860s

A Black militia unit called the Victoria Pioneer Rifle Company (also known as the African Rifles) was formed in 1861. It was the first and only organized security force in Victoria, British Columbia until it was disbanded in 1865.

REVIEW AND REFLECT

1. Why was the American federal government reluctant to abolish slavery?
2. Reread the lyrics to "Swing Low, Sweet Chariot" on page 158. What words suggest it is a song about escaping slavery? What words suggest it is an expression of religious faith?
3. To many, Nat Turner is a hero in the Black resistance. To some, he is a controversial figure. Which side do you agree with? Give reasons for your response.
4. Why did many free Blacks move to Canada from the United States after the passing of the Fugitive Slave Law?

The Civil War and Its Aftermath

By 1860, political tensions between North and South had reached the breaking point. During the federal election, there were heated debates over the extension of slavery. An Illinois politician named Abraham Lincoln was elected president of the United States. He was not an abolitionist. But he believed that slavery had to be destroyed before it destroyed the American Union.

To protest Lincoln's election, on December 20, 1860, South Carolina **seceded** from the United States. Six other states followed. They formed the Confederate States of America, which eventually incorporated 11 states (Alabama, Arkansas, Florida, Georgia, Louisiana, Mississippi, North Carolina, South Carolina, Tennessee, Texas, and Virginia). In its new constitution, the Confederate States guaranteed the continuation of slavery and the rights of individual states. They urged the American government to allow them to exist in peace. But in the North, the people demanded that the American Union be preserved. The stage was set for civil war.

secede
to formally withdraw from an alliance or union

The Emancipation Proclamation

During the first year, the Union army had limited success against the Confederate States. Lincoln decided it was time to take bold action. On January 1, 1863, he issued the Emancipation Proclamation, which held the promise of freedom for the 3 million enslaved Blacks living in the South.

> **Now, therefore I, Abraham Lincoln, President of the United States . . . order and declare that all persons held as slaves within said designated States, and parts of States, are, and henceforward shall be free; and that the Executive Government of the United States, including the military and naval authorities thereof, will recognize and maintain the freedom of said persons.**

US President Abraham Lincoln, The Emancipation Proclamation, January 1, 1863

FIGURE 5.16 Blacks in the Union army

The Emancipation Proclamation gave hope to millions of enslaved Blacks: freedom was theirs if the Union army could defeat the Confederates. Almost 200 000 joined the Union army to fight for their freedom.

Southern leaders denounced Lincoln for his proclamation. Abolitionists and Black American leaders praised him. However, the proclamation fuelled racism among many Northerners. They supported the civil war as a means of reuniting the country. But they were less willing to fight a war now that its mission was to free enslaved Blacks. As the war dragged on, these racial tensions mounted. Many Whites directed their anger at Blacks. **Lynch mobs** roamed the streets looking for Black victims.

lynch mob
a gang that seizes people and puts them to death, especially by hanging, for alleged offences, immediately and without a legal trial

Reconstruction

By 1864, a tide of Union victories left little doubt that the North would win and the Union would be restored. When the war was over, it left a nation transformed. Slavery was finally abolished on December 18, 1865. Then the period known as Reconstruction began. To be readmitted to the Union, the Confederate States had to draft new constitutions guaranteeing the right to vote to former enslaved Black males. Then the federal government began the task of helping Black Americans make the transition into a free society.

THE FREEDMEN'S BUREAU

With the end of slavery, the plantation economy collapsed. Many former enslaved Blacks found themselves free, but with no means of support and no place to live. The Freedmen's Bureau was created to help Black people find jobs and housing. It supported over 3000 schools across the South where former enslaved Blacks could get a basic education. It worked to reunite Black families torn apart by slavery. There were frequent acts of resistance from White Southerners who wanted to preserve their power. Federal troops were sent in to maintain law and order.

THE BLACK CODES

The southern states did not accept the abolition of slavery willingly. Most southern states passed laws known as the Black Codes. These restricted the working rights of Blacks, prevented former enslaved Blacks from owning land, and prohibited interracial marriages.

In response, Congress passed the 14th Amendment to the Constitution in 1866. It ensured that states could not deny Blacks their civil rights, including the right to own property and the right to sue in court. In 1869, Congress passed the 15th Amendment. It declared that no male citizen could be prevented from voting because of race. It gave the federal government the right to intervene in elections to ensure that Blacks were not prohibited from voting. In time, the states found ways around these amendments. They denied former enslaved Blacks the right to vote. One method used to keep Black Americans from the ballot box was the "grandfather clause." A man could vote only if his grandfather had voted. Poll taxes, literacy tests, voting fraud, intimidation, and violence were other ways of denying Blacks the right to vote.

SHARECROPPING

Many freed Blacks hoped to receive a portion of the land they had worked when they were enslaved. Then they could become independent farmers. But it soon became clear that the government had no plans to distribute land taken from former plantation owners. Few Blacks could afford to buy land on their own. Some worked on the plantations that remained for cash wages or a share of the profits. Others became sharecroppers: a family received a plot of land and they were free to cultivate it in exchange for paying part of their harvest to the landowner.

Rather than being a way of earning a living, though, sharecropping became another form of bondage. The families could not leave their plot of land until the harvest had been paid. They often borrowed seed and supplies on credit from the landowners, which was payable against the next year's crop. As a result, the sharecroppers were indebted to the landowners, while the landowners had a cheap source of labour that was financially dependent on them.

THE KU KLUX KLAN

Some southern Whites took their hatred to extremes. In 1866, a group of Confederate army veterans founded the Ku Klux Klan (KKK). This secret organization assaulted and murdered Blacks in campaigns of violence and terror across the South. Blacks formed militias to defend themselves against the Klan's brutality. But after the government stripped the militias of their weapons, Black communities were left unprotected and vulnerable. After federal troops withdrew from the southern states in 1877, Blacks lost their last line of protection.

FIGURE 5.17
The Ku Klux Klan

Members of the Klan wore hoods to disguise their identities.

Why do you think KKK members wanted to disguise who they were?

Blacks Return to the United States

The end of the American Civil War in 1865 led many Blacks to return to the United States from Canada to reunite with their families or to find jobs. They didn't feel there was any advantage to staying in Canada, which had its own forms of racism and segregation. Black citizens of Canada had few rights. They were forced to live in their own communities. Most of these communities did not receive the same services White communities did. Many Black children were forced to attend segregated schools that were not as well equipped as the schools White children

FIGURE 5.18 Students at King St. School in Amherstburg, Ontario, ca. 1890

Many Black Americans wanted the chance for an education. They thought their children would be free to attend public schools in Canada. But the Ontario *Common Schools Act* of 1851 led to the creation of segregated Black schools, particularly in towns west of Toronto. Black parents protested the schools in petitions and meetings.

Why might this situation have motivated some Black Americans to return to the United States?

attended. Few Black students had the opportunity to attend university, so as adults they often ended up working in low-paying jobs. In Nova Scotia, the discrimination could be seen in the way Halifax treated the community of Africville.

AFRICVILLE

In Nova Scotia, the community of Africville was poorly treated by the city of Halifax. It became the dumping ground for unwanted facilities other Halifax neighbourhoods rejected. In 1853, the city built a prison there. In 1870, it built a hospital specializing in infectious diseases. In 1905, it built a dump and an incinerator. Over time, pollution-producing industries such as a tar factory and a fertilizer plant opened on the outskirts of the community. The heavy smoke and unpleasant odours from these factories drifted across Africville every day.

The residents of Africville were mistreated in other ways. They paid their taxes to the city of Halifax, but they received little in return. In 1960, they still had no running water, no roads, and no electricity. Finally, in 1961 the city decided to tear down Africville as part of an **urban renewal** plan.

urban renewal
the process of rejuvenating poor, rundown districts of a city through redevelopment

FIGURE 5.19 Africville ceremony, 2002

Many Black Canadians honour Africville as a symbol of Black determination and pride. Here, Ruth Johnson, a former Africville resident, left, and former Heritage Minister Sheila Copps participate in a ceremony to declare Africville's location a National Historic Site.

expropriate
to take away property from its owner

public housing
government-owned housing rented to low-wage earners

Africville was **expropriated** by the city. The homes and businesses the families of Africville had nurtured for over 100 years were confiscated. Each household received only $500 for the loss of their homes and businesses. Garbage trucks were sent in to move the people's belongings. More than 400 people were uprooted and their homes demolished. By 1970, all of the buildings had been destroyed. The majority of these people were moved into **public housing**.

REVIEW AND REFLECT

1. Add key events from pages 165 to 170 to your abolition of slavery timeline from Chapter 3. If you don't have an existing timeline, begin a new timeline based on the events in these sections. You will have another opportunity to add to the timeline in Chapter 6.
2. In your own words, explain the significance of the Civil War in ending slavery in the United States.
3. In a T-chart like the one shown below, list the pros and cons of Reconstruction.

Pros of Reconstruction	Cons of Reconstruction

4. Imagine that you are a long-time resident in Africville who has just been informed that you have to move out. Write a letter to the editor expressing your thoughts about moving, and about the fate of Africville.

Black America and Canada at the Turn of the 20th Century

Although all Black Americans had gained their freedom after the Civil War, it was a different kind of freedom from other Americans. The Supreme Court ruled that it was illegal for states to pass laws that discriminated against Blacks. But private business and industry were still free to make their own decisions. Many refused to serve Blacks. In 1896, the Supreme Court ruled that states had the right to provide separate public facilities and services for Blacks and Whites. This applied to washrooms, schools, drinking fountains, and seats on public buses. Officially, these facilities and services were supposed to be "separate but equal." In reality, though, they were anything but. These laws ensured that Blacks received the poorest services and the worst facilities. The laws were called "Jim Crow" laws after a popular song and dance routine performed at minstrel shows by a White American entertainer who coloured his face black and mimicked Black people.

No such laws existed in Canada, but the racial segregation that was common in the 19th century continued into the early 20th century. This segregation affected most aspects of Black Canadians' lives. For example, they were prevented from joining trade unions, working in stores, or renting a room in a hotel.

Racial segregation extended to sports as well. Black Canadians were barred from playing in White hockey leagues. In the Maritimes, Blacks formed their own league. Teams in the Coloured Hockey League played on frozen ponds using hockey sticks crafted by Black woodworkers. Money was tight, but families saved to buy their sons hockey skates. At the end of the season, there were playoffs to decide the annual championship. There was a modest trophy and the title "Coloured Hockey Champions of the Maritimes."

FIGURE 5.20 The Halifax Eurekas of the Coloured Hockey League

The Coloured Hockey League operated from 1900 to 1920. After that, the number of teams dwindled until the league faded out in 1928. In time, Black Canadian hockey players integrated into White teams.

Immigration to Canada at the Turn of the Century

Despite segregation in Canada, there were still Blacks from the United States who were willing to come to Canada at the turn of the century. In 1898, Clifford Sifton, the Minister of the Interior, offered free land to immigrants who were willing to settle in the West. Many Black settlers came from the American Midwest to settle on the Canadian prairies.

This Black migration continued after Oklahoma became an official American state in 1907. Many Blacks who lived there wanted to escape the new discriminatory laws and practices that had been made legal by the government. They also wanted to escape the terrorism of the Ku Klux Klan. These free Black populations had owned significant amounts of land and saved their money so that they could move to Canada. The descendants of Black families, such as the Mayes, Proctors, Robinsons, and Browers, can still be found on the Canadian prairies today.

FIGURE 5.21 Bobby Crump family from Oklahoma, circa 1911

Over 1000 Black settlers came to the Prairies between 1905 and 1911. Some of them preferred to live and work in urban areas. In Edmonton in 1910, the Board of Trade stated that "We want settlers that will assimilate with the Canadian people and in the negro we have a settler that will never do that."

Why do you think some Edmontonians were reluctant to welcome Black immigrants?

Black migration slowed down significantly when the 1910 *Immigration Act* of Canada was passed. Section 38 prohibited "entry of immigrants belonging to any race deemed unsuited for the climate or requirements of Canada." Many government officials supported and repeated this falsehood, effectively trying to keep Black people out of Canada. In 1911, border officials were instructed to reject Blacks based on their medical exams. They offered immigration doctors bonuses for turning Blacks away. Blacks would not enter Canada in significant numbers again until the 1960s.

IDEAS

BLACK STEREOTYPES

Fixed images of Black Americans were based on oversimplified and misunderstood ideas about people's behaviour and appearance. In earlier chapters, you discovered some of the stereotypical ideas Europeans had about Africa and its people. In the United States, a new set of stereotypes emerged both during and after slavery. These stereotypes limited people's ideas about what it meant to be Black—not only for White Americans but for Black Americans as well.

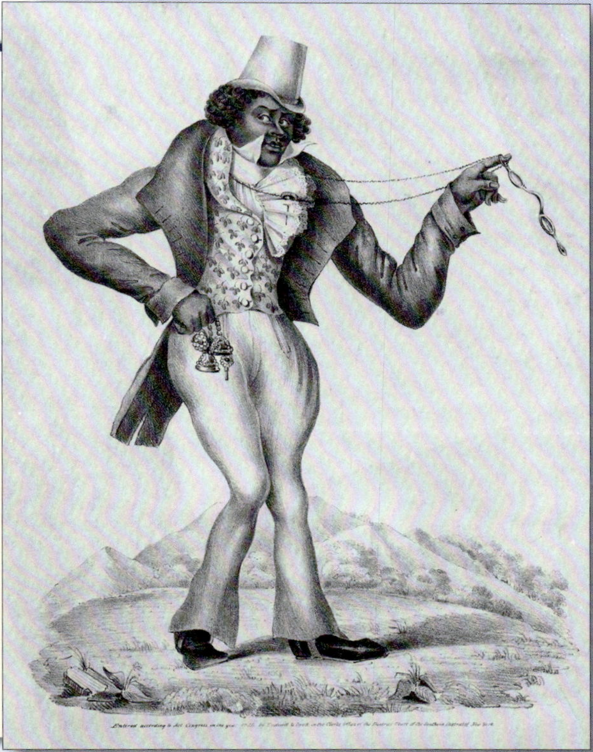

FIGURE 5.22 The coon caricature

The coon caricature is one of the most offensive of all Black stereotypes. "Coon" is an abbreviation of *raccoon*. Its use during the period of slavery reflected the attitude of white people toward Blacks, whom they saw as less than human. Owners interpreted enslaved men's resistance to slavery—sabotaging tools, faking illnesses, and working slowly—as stupidity rather than resistance. Therefore, the coon caricature was depicted as a slow, lazy, dimwitted Black man, a buffoon who was afraid of his own shadow.

FIGURE 5.23 Uncle Tom

Uncle Tom was a character in the anti-slavery novel *Uncle Tom's Cabin*. He is pictured here with Little Eva, another character from the novel. The caricature of Tom is a gentle, always smiling, wide-eyed servant who is hard-working and eager to please his owners. He never rebels or tries to run away. Despite Uncle Tom's willingness to please, he is eventually beaten to death. The terms "Tom" and "Uncle Tom" are still used by some people today to describe Black Americans who are subservient to Whites at the expense of themselves or others in the Black community.

FIGURE 5.24 Mammy

Another common stereotype is Mammy—the happy, fat, maternal Black woman. For much of the 20th century, this was a common racial caricature. Like Uncle Tom, Mammy was a content and faithful worker, dedicated to her White employers. The Mammy stereotype suggested that Black women were only suitable for domestic work. You may have seen the face of one famous Mammy, Aunt Jemima. A woman from Nova Scotia named Dorothy Paris was hired to play Aunt Jemima. The image on the left was synonymous with pancakes for much of the 20th century. Modern packaging on Aunt Jemima pancakes now emphasizes the product.

FIGURE 5.25 "Gangsta rappers"

Modern racial stereotypes of Blacks reflect the intimidating "gangsta rapper." These modern Black stereotypes reflect the lifestyles of inner-city youth. Some Black youth act out these stereotypes as a form of rebellion against the inequalities in American society. While these stereotypes may not have a direct connection to slavery, they still perpetuate ideas about Blacks that are discouraging and limiting.

Think It Through

Look at the modern package of Aunt Jemima waffles. Do you think the image of Aunt Jemima is still stereotypical? Give reasons for your response.

Black American Leadership

Without government support and protection, Black Americans had to find their own way to fight stereotypes and racist policies to survive. Two leaders of this struggle were Booker T. Washington and W.E.B. Du Bois.

Booker T. Washington rose up from slavery and illiteracy in Virginia to become a respected educator. After slavery was abolished, he enrolled in a school for freed Blacks. After graduation, he opened a Black school in Alabama. Washington took a non-threatening approach to Black issues. He told Black Americans not to expect racial equality right away. He encouraged them to remain in the South and take part in Reconstruction.

William Du Bois was born and raised in New England. He was of mixed race, which exposed him to prejudice and discrimination as a youth. But it did not prepare him for the extreme racism he encountered when he attended university in the South. Du Bois eventually went to Harvard, where he became the first Black American to earn a PhD. He went on to become a founding member of the National Association for the Advancement of Colored People (NAACP) and an editor of its magazine, *The Crisis*. Du Bois believed Blacks should demand immediate equality and that the best way to achieve this was through education.

FIGURE 5.26 Booker T. Washington (1856–1915)

Booker T. Washington was known as the "Great Accommodator." **How did his nickname reflect his actions?**

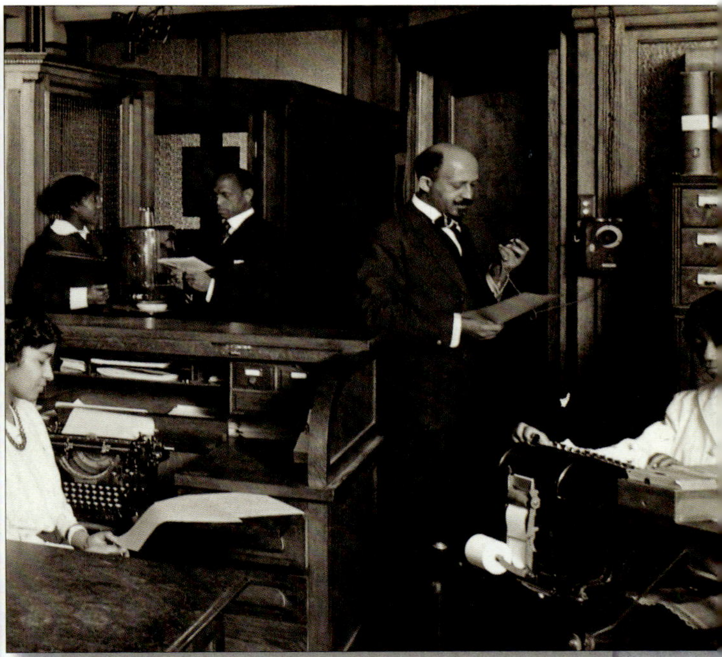

FIGURE 5.27 William Du Bois (1868–1963)

William Du Bois is shown here working in the *Crisis* office. The magazine had a large readership among Blacks as well as White sympathizers.

REVIEW AND REFLECT

1. What was the purpose of the Jim Crow laws? What effect did they have?
2. What did Canada's immigration policies in 1910 and 1911 reveal about public attitudes toward Blacks?
3. Create a graphic organizer similar to the one shown below to compare the backgrounds of Booker T. Washington and William Du Bois and their approaches to the struggle for equal rights.

	Booker T. Washington	William Du Bois
Background		
Approach		

Urbanization and Black Pride

A variety of circumstances in both the United States and Canada led to the Black population moving to urban centres. In the United States, approximately 7 million Black Americans left the southern states and moved north between 1910 and 1970. This movement was known as the Great Migration. Black Americans were looking to escape racism and the terrorism of the Ku Klux Klan and to find work for themselves and better education for their children. They migrated to large cities like New York, Philadelphia, Detroit, Chicago, and Cincinnati, as well as to smaller centres like Toledo, Omaha, Dayton, and Albany.

In Canada, many Black men and women also made their way to cities. In fact, by the 1920s, most Black Canadians could be found living in urban centres. Most of these people moved to cities in search of employment.

The Great Migration

The Great Migration created the first large, urban Black communities in the northern United States. The cultures of many modern northern cities were forged in the aftermath of this massive influx of Black Southerners.

Although many northern workers resented the newcomers, the Black immigrants made significant gains in employment. Many became skilled workers in the auto, steel, shipbuilding, and meatpacking industries. Educated migrants worked in such fields as education, business, law, and politics. The migration marked the transition for many Black Americans from lifestyles as rural farmers to urban workers.

Although it was often more subtle, the newcomers faced discrimination in the North, too. Black Americans competed with other cultural groups for housing. Many cities passed laws that kept Blacks out of White neighbourhoods. As a result, Black Americans were confined to their own neighbourhoods. They created Black cities within the larger cities of the North. The largest of these was Harlem in upper Manhattan in New York City. More than 200 000 Black Americans moved into a neighbourhood that had been virtually all White only 15 years earlier. In Black communities, racial pride and consciousness in Black culture began to emerge. The showcase for this emerging Black culture was Harlem.

FIGURE 5.28 Harlem today

Harlem is the historic capital of Black American culture. But, like many communities, Harlem is changing. Redevelopment threatens to wipe out affordable housing and family businesses. Many people believe these changes are destroying Harlem's unique character.

How might redevelopment change Harlem?

EXPRESSIONS

FIGURE 5.29 Zora Neale Hurston (1891–1960)

Black authors wrote ground-breaking novels, such as Hurston's *Their Eyes Were Watching God* (1937). It gave a voice to Black women and the issues they faced in the early 20th century.

THE HARLEM RENAISSANCE

As Black Americans moved out of the rural South and into the cities of the industrial North, they brought Black American culture with them—the music, songs, dances, and stories of their African roots. With racism and discrimination all around them, the arts were one of the few avenues for Black Americans to express pride in their culture and heritage.

In the 1920s and 1930s, this pride found an outlet in the Harlem Renaissance. This artistic and intellectual movement was the spiritual coming of age for Black America. Through music, dance, literature, theatre, and cabaret, Black Americans celebrated their culture. Through the arts, they achieved the recognition and respect they could not attain through politics.

Black-owned magazines and newspapers flourished. They allowed Black Americans freedom of expression. Publications such as *Opportunity* and *The Crisis* launched the literary careers of Black writers such as James Weldon Johnson, Countee Cullen, and Zora Neale Hurston. Works like Alain Locke's anthology *The New Negro: An Interpretation* helped define the new Black identity. Poets like Langston Hughes declared their pride in being Black, often in ways that made many White readers uncomfortable.

> **We younger Negro artists now intend to express our individual dark-skinned selves without fear or shame. If white people are pleased we are glad. If they aren't, it doesn't matter. We know we are beautiful. And ugly too.**
>
> Langston Hughes, 1926

The Harlem Renaissance also produced critically acclaimed artists, actors, musicians, and singers. Paul Robeson was a multitalented actor, athlete, author, singer, scholar, and political activist. The musician Duke Ellington was considered one of the greatest jazz composers of all time. Louis Armstrong and his trumpet revolutionized the music world. The unique and soulful singing voice of Billie Holiday made her a superstar, while the exotic dancing of Josephine Baker earned her international fame.

Like so much of American society, the Harlem Renaissance faded during the hard times of the Great Depression in the 1930s. But its legacy changed the dynamics of Black American arts and literature. It led to greater social and political consciousness and paved the way for future generations of Black artists and writers. The richness of the Harlem Renaissance is still felt in American culture today.

Think It Through

How do you think the Harlem Renaissance changed the way the world saw Black America?

FIGURE 5.30 *Into Bondage*, 1936

Aaron Douglas was among the prominent Black artists in the circle of the Harlem Renaissance. He wanted people to understand the spiritual identity of Black America.

What do you think the message is in this painting?

Urban Black Canadians

In Canada, Montreal became an attractive place for many Black Canadians. Black men came to the Canadian Pacific Railway's headquarters in Montreal to be employed as railway car porters. Though they had to endure the patronization of White passengers, within their own communities Black porters were highly respected. Their wages were lower than White railway workers but they made more money than many other Black workers. They saved their money to buy cars and houses or to send their children to university. They built strong Black communities in Montreal and other railway centres of Canada, such as Halifax, Toronto, Winnipeg, Calgary, and Vancouver. You will learn more about the Black porters in Chapter 8.

FIGURE 5.31 A porter assists passengers on the Canadian Pacific Railway, 1925

Black railway porters travelled thousands of kilometres on trips that could last up to six days. They took trip after trip with no vacations. Throughout their journeys, they catered to their patrons day and night.

How do you think this work affected the porters and their families?

Many single Black men from the United States also came to Montreal during the summer months to work at any one of the city's four race tracks. When prohibition laws banning the sale of alcohol were passed in the United States, many of the American summer workers chose to remain in Montreal and open nightclubs or run gambling and prostitution rings. Montreal's entertainment industry began to boom, and the city became known for its nightlife and jazz music. The world-renowned jazz pianist Oscar Peterson was one legendary figure in the storied history of Montreal's Black community.

COMMUNITY ORGANIZATIONS

A new-found sense of pride and empowerment was taking shape in Black Canadian communities across Canada. Twelve different chapters of the Universal Negro Improvement Association (UNIA) were created in cities like Montreal and Toronto and in communities in Nova Scotia. The UNIA's leader, Marcus Garvey, preached a message of African pride, power, and independence. You will learn more about Marcus Garvey in Chapter 6.

The strength of the newly urbanized Black community could also be found through the activities of the women. The Coloured Women's Club of Montreal was founded in 1902. It was the first Black women's group in Canada. It was started by a group of Black American women whose husbands worked as porters. Blacks were excluded from the many charitable organizations that had emerged in Canada's cities to help Canadians adapt to the new industrial era. So the working Black women of Montreal formed their own social group to help the poor in their community.

In 1907, the Coloured Women's Club helped create Montreal's oldest Black church, the Union United Church. It provided the church with furniture, carpeting, and linens. The women of the club worked to end the social and political exclusion of Blacks in Montreal.

FIGURE 5.32 Coloured Women's Club, 2002

Over the years, the women in this club volunteered in local hospitals. They counselled young mothers. They gave shelter to the homeless and they bought cemetery plots so that the poor could be buried with dignity. The Coloured Women's Club continues its work to this day.

The Two World Wars

When it became evident that Canada would be fighting in the First World War, which began in 1914, many Black Canadians took it as an opportunity to show their national pride and dedication by supporting the war effort. At first, a few local regiments allowed Blacks to enlist, but this was short-lived. Though an official statement made by the Canadian government had declared that racial discrimination would not be tolerated or practised by the armed forces, Blacks found themselves being repeatedly turned away.

On July 5, 1916, permission was given to form a predominantly Black battalion with White commanders. Blacks from across Canada and some from the United States joined the No. 2 Construction Battalion, with its headquarters in Nova Scotia. Initially, the Battalion left by ship from Halifax to dig trenches, build bridges, and repair roads for soldiers training in England. Soon, though, they joined the Canadian Forestry Corps in France, where their primary task was to provide lumber for trenches and railways. A few of these men were eventually allowed to join the fighting units. They fought courageously, as did Black Canadian men who had been allowed to join fighting battalions earlier in the war. On the home front, Black Canadian women raised money for the Patriotic Fund, formed organizations such as the Universal Black Cross Nurses in Vancouver, and volunteered in hospitals.

When the United States entered the First World War in 1917 under the slogan "Make the World Safe for Democracy," many Black Americans questioned fighting to make the world safe for democracy when they were denied democracy at home. Blacks were not allowed to serve in the marines, the coast guard, or the air force. In the navy, they could only work in the mess halls. Even so, over 400 000 Black men

FIGURE 5.33
Two members of the No. 2 Construction Battalion

Five hundred men from Nova Scotia joined the 600-member No. 2 Construction Battalion. Nova Scotia contributed more men to the battalion than all the other provinces combined. Though few of these men served in battles, they often worked close to the battlefields and were at risk from gunfire, mustard gas, and work accidents.

enlisted in the army. They served in segregated units. Often they were sent on the most dangerous missions. A higher percentage of Black soldiers lost their lives than White soldiers: 14.4 percent of Blacks compared with 6.3 percent of Whites. Many Black soldiers believed they would be rewarded for their sacrifices when the war was over. But it was not to be. During the Allied victory march through Paris, the US army denied Black soldiers the right to take part, even though Black soldiers from European armies marched alongside their White comrades.

THE SECOND WORLD WAR

By the time the Second World War began, in 1939, restrictions against Blacks in the military had eased. Black citizens served in all branches of the military and on all fronts of the war in the United States and Canada. As they had in the First World War, Black American soldiers recognized the contradiction in fighting for freedom when they were denied freedom at home. As the war unfolded, they insisted on the full rights of citizenship. They were willing to fight for their country. But this time they demanded something in return.

FIGURE 5.34 Workers in an airplane factory

During the Second World War, Black women played an important role in the war effort in Canada and the United States. They worked long hours as riveters in airplane factories such as the one pictured, and faced dangerous conditions in munitions factories.

REVIEW AND REFLECT

1. How did the cultures of northern US cities change as a result of Black migration?
2. How did the activities of urbanized Black women in Canada reflect their communities' new-found pride?
3. Why do you think Black Americans and Canadians enlisted in the military during the First and Second World Wars?

The Civil Rights Movement

After battling overseas, Blacks in Canada and America continued their fight for civil rights. In the 1940s, the NAACP won several legal victories that gradually led to the collapse of the Jim Crow laws in the United States. One of the most significant was *Brown v. Board of Education* of Topeka, Kansas. In 1951, Thurgood Marshall, a lawyer for the NAACP (and later the first Black justice on the US Supreme Court) argued that school segregation violated the 14th Amendment of the Constitution. In a landmark decision, the US Supreme Court agreed. It declared that the principle of "separate but equal" had no place in the school system. This victory laid the foundation for the desegregation of all public facilities in the American South.

The Montgomery Bus Boycott

A year and a half after the *Brown* ruling, the fight for civil rights entered a new phase. On December 1, 1955, a Black seamstress named Rosa Parks boarded a bus in Montgomery, Alabama on her way home from work. She sat in the section designated for Blacks. As the bus filled up, the driver asked Parks and three others to give up their seats to White passengers. When Parks refused, she was removed from the bus and arrested. For her act of defiance, she was fined $10 plus $4 in court fees.

> I did not get on the bus to get arrested; I got on the bus to go home. . . . I had no idea that history was being made. I was just tired of giving in. Somehow, I felt that what I did was right by standing up to that bus driver. I did not think about the consequences.
>
> Rosa Parks, 1955

What seems like a simple act of civil disobedience today was a courageous act of defiance in 1950s Alabama. In refusing to give up her seat, Parks placed herself in physical danger. Her actions set a powerful force in motion as the Black citizens of Montgomery mounted a successful boycott of the bus system. It turned the national spotlight on Dr. Martin Luther King Jr., a charismatic new leader in the civil rights movement. Despite efforts to break it, the boycott lasted more than a year.

The issue of bus segregation was taken all the way to the US Supreme Court. On November 13, 1956, the Court ruled that segregation on buses was unconstitutional. The boycott officially ended on December 21. Its success proved that non-violent protest could be effective in bringing about change.

The Little Rock Nine

In Arkansas in 1957, the Little Rock school board announced its plans to comply with the *Brown* ruling. But they encountered widespread opposition to school integration among Whites. Even the governor opposed the idea, claiming it was too dangerous for Black students.

Nine students—the Little Rock Nine—were chosen as the first Black students to attend Central High School in Little Rock. Angry White mobs demonstrated in front of the school and prevented the students from entering. A judge ordered that the Black students be allowed to enter the school. But the governor refused to enforce the court order. Another attempt by the students to enter the school under police escort failed.

The standoff in Little Rock captured international attention. The US president, Dwight Eisenhower, sent in federal troops. The Little Rock Nine were finally able to attend school. Over the next decade, schools across the South continued to resist integration. By 1965, more than 75 percent of Southern schools remained segregated.

Dr. Martin Luther King Jr.

Dr. Martin Luther King Jr. had arrived in Montgomery the year before the bus boycott to become pastor of the Dexter Avenue Baptist church. After playing a leading role in the boycott, he organized the Southern Christian Leadership Council (SCLC) as a means of fighting segregation. King advocated non-violence and civil disobedience in the battle against racism in the United States. He urged Black Americans to break the Jim Crow laws through boycotts, sit-ins, and marches.

FIGURE 5.35
Dr. Martin Luther King Jr. (1929–1968)

King put a face to the civil rights movement. His captivating speeches drew national attention. With King as their leader, many Black Americans began to believe they could achieve equality in their lifetime.

Why do you think King also inspired many Whites to fight segregation?

In 1963, US President John F. Kennedy introduced a new civil rights bill. The bill faced widespread opposition in Congress. In response, King and other civil rights leaders organized the March on Washington for Jobs and Freedom. On August 28, 1963, a crowd of over 250 000 Americans listened to King deliver his speech "I Have a Dream."

> I have a dream that one day this nation will rise up and live out the true meaning of its creed: "We hold these truths to be self-evident, that all men are created equal."
>
> Dr. Martin Luther King Jr., Washington, DC, August 28, 1963

King's influence helped pass the *Civil Rights Act* in 1964. The following year, King was awarded the Nobel Peace Prize. He launched the Poor People's Campaign and continued his fight for civil rights. On April 3, 1968, King spoke in Memphis, Tennessee to striking public works employees. His words were hauntingly prophetic.

> I've been to the mountaintop. And I've seen the promised land. I may not get there with you. But I want you to know that we, as a people, will get to the promised land.
>
> Dr. Martin Luther King Jr., Memphis, Tennessee, April 3, 1968

The next day, April 4, 1968, Martin Luther King's eloquent voice was silenced forever by an assassin's bullet.

The Civil Rights Movement in Canada

Canada has a long history of ethnic and colour prejudice that prevented specific groups of people from enjoying the same rights and privileges as others. Blacks were among the minority groups that were regularly denied housing, land grants, or service at restaurants, hotels, and even hospitals across the country. Like their American counterparts, Black Canadians refused to accept second-class status. They demanded the same rights and privileges as other Canadians.

Fighting against the type of racism practised in Canada was not an easy task. Since there were no laws like the Jim Crow laws in the United States, whenever Black Canadians voiced complaints to the highest levels of government, they were asked by skeptical White politicians to prove that racism existed. When incidents of colour prejudice and discrimination were taken to court, cases were often dismissed on the grounds that business owners were within their rights to refuse service to anyone they chose.

THE FIGHT FOR CIVIL RIGHTS IN NOVA SCOTIA

The fight for civil rights in Canada sometimes led to legal action in the courts. One of the most prominent civil rights cases played out in Nova Scotia in 1946. Viola Desmond was dragged out of a movie theatre in the small town of New Glasgow. She had bought a ticket and sat in the main floor section of the theatre. But theatre policy required Blacks to sit in the balcony. When Desmond refused to move, she was arrested. She spent the night in the town jail. No one told her her rights. No one represented her in court the next day. Desmond was found guilty and sentenced to 30 days in jail or a $20 fine. She paid the fine, but decided to challenge the verdict in the Supreme Court of Nova Scotia.

FIGURE 5.36 Viola Desmond (1914–1965)

Viola Desmond came from a prosperous Halifax family. At the time of her arrest, she was a 32-year-old entrepreneur who owned a successful hair salon in the city. With her brave act of defiance, Desmond became a leader in the civil rights movement in Canada.

How would you compare Desmond's act of defiance with that of Rosa Parks in Alabama? In what ways were their actions similar? In what ways were they different?

A prominent civil rights activist in Nova Scotia, Dr. Carrie Best, took up Viola Desmond's cause. Best founded Nova Scotia's first Black newspaper, the *Clarion*, in 1946. When she heard about Desmond's case, she used the *Clarion* to rally public support. Best and Desmond were joined by the co-founder of the Nova Scotia Association for the Advancement of Coloured People (NSAACP), Pearleen Oliver, in raising money for Desmond's appeal. In spite of their efforts, however, the Supreme Court unanimously upheld the earlier decision.

Best, Desmond, Oliver, and the NSAACP continued to organize Blacks to lobby the government to repeal the province's segregation laws. After a vigorous campaign, the Nova Scotia government finally backed down and repealed its discriminatory policies in 1954—more than a year before Rosa Parks and the Montgomery bus boycott spearheaded the civil rights movement in the United States.

> **This meant something to our people. Neither before or since has there been such an aggressive effort to obtain rights. The people arose as one and with one voice. Much of the positive action that has since taken place stemmed from this.**
>
> Dr. William Pearly Oliver, co-founder of the NSAACP, in "Women and Minorities," www.citizenvoices.gg.ca

FIGURE 5.37 Dr. Carrie Best (1903–2001)

Carrie Best grew up in the Black Loyalist community of Little Tracadie, Nova Scotia. A strong and independent social activist, she campaigned tirelessly for the civil rights movement in Canada. She used the *Clarion* to publish her investigative reports into discrimination and human rights violations in Nova Scotia. Viewed in the historical context of the day, Best's achievements were truly remarkable. Like all Black Canadians, she faced intense discrimination and segregation. Yet she successfully challenged the status quo and gave Blacks in Nova Scotia a strong and clear voice.

The Growth of Political Activism in Canada

In spite of the setbacks, Black Canadians stepped up the fight against racism. A number of new civil rights groups emerged across the country. The Canadian Negro Women's Association (CNWA) was formed to fight for the rights of Black women in the workforce. In Ontario, the National Unity Association (NUA) pressured the provincial government to pass laws prohibiting discrimination in housing and employment. The Negro Citizenship Association (NCA) lobbied the federal government to open up immigration to people from all countries. The efforts of these groups had a lasting impact on Canadian society and literally changed the face of a nation.

Black Power

In the 1960s, many Black Americans were frustrated by the slow pace of political and social change. Inspired by the independence movements in the colonial countries of Africa, many young Black Americans embraced a more militant approach to their quest for civil rights. New movements emerged that promoted violent resistance. Young Black Americans talked about self-determination and the creation of an independent Black state. They promoted Black self-worth and self-esteem. Many Black Americans began to openly promote their African heritage. They gave themselves and their children African names. They wore traditional African clothing. They adopted an uplifted fist as their symbol of Black unity. Black pride changed the way Black Americans viewed themselves and how they demanded others view them.

The Black Power movement sought cooperation and unity among Blacks, both within the United States and around the world. Many powerful and influential Black leaders rose to the top of the Black Power movement. Among them were Malcolm X, Stokely Carmichael, and Angela Davis.

FIGURE 5.38 Malcolm X (1925–1965)

Malcolm X (born Malcolm Little) was a Black Muslim minister. A charismatic speaker, he embraced the Black Power movement and advocated Black separatism and independence. For many years, he was a member of the **Nation of Islam**. But he broke with that group and founded the Organization of Afro-American Unity in 1964. In 1965, Malcolm X was assassinated by a small group of Black Muslims in Harlem. To his detractors, Malcolm X was a radical who preached racial hatred and violence. To his supporters, he was a courageous advocate for the rights of Black Americans who boldly indicted White America for its crimes against his people.

Nation of Islam
a Black Islamic organi
founded around 1930
became prominent ur
the influence of Malco
its members are know
Black Muslims

FIGURE 5.39 Stokely Carmichael (1941–1998)

Stokely Carmichael was born and raised in Trinidad and Tobago before coming to the United States at the age of 11. While attending university, he joined a group known as the Freedom Riders. They travelled through the Deep South challenging racial segregation at bus terminals. Carmichael admired Martin Luther King. But he believed that his cautious approach to civil rights was outdated and ineffective. Carmichael did not back away from controversy. His cries of "Black Power" at rallies unsettled White authorities and made him a target of FBI investigations.

FIGURE 5.40 Angela Davis (1944–)

Born in Birmingham, Alabama, Angela Davis was exposed to the painful effects of racism at an early age. She was a community activist and socialist philosopher as well as an influential thinker and writer in the women's movement. She gained national notoriety when she was arrested and charged with conspiracy, kidnapping, and homicide in the murder of a California judge. Davis was acquitted of all charges, but her trial made her a heroine in the Black Power movement. She became a university professor and an activist for the rights of Blacks and women.

Into the New Millennium

In the closing decades of the 20th century and the opening decade of the 21st century, Black Americans and Black Canadians gained greater power and influence in society. While racism and discrimination have persisted, many obstacles have fallen. Though most Black men and women are average citizens who have aspired to and achieved their goals without fanfare, several have risen to positions of prominence in all walks of life. As you discovered in the Introduction to this book, many Black Americans believe they may finally have reached Dr. Martin Luther King's "promised land" when, in November 2008, Barack Obama was the first Black American to be elected president of the United States.

REVIEW AND REFLECT

1. Martin Luther King sought equality through civil disobedience and non-violence. Malcolm X advocated the use of violence where necessary. Which philosophy do you think is more effective? Give reasons for your response.
2. Why was it difficult for Black citizens in Canada to challenge segregation through the court system?
3. In what ways do you think the Black Power movement encouraged Black Americans to take pride in their African heritage?
4. Reread the Introduction on pages x–xi. Then create a timeline on the civil rights movement, culminating with the inauguration of Barack Obama as the 44th president of the United States on January 20, 2009.

The Historian's Craft

THINKING LIKE A HISTORIAN

As a student you may sometimes feel that historical information is overwhelming—there are too many facts, too many dates, and too many people. Historians make sense of the great mass of information by identifying key concepts, important facts and dates, and significant people. You can make better sense of the contents of this book—and of history generally—if you think like a historian.

KEY CONCEPTS

As you study history, keep in mind some of the big ideas or key concepts that historians use as they do their research, organize their findings, and make sense of history. For example, in this chapter, you can recognize the concept "cause and effect" in the impact of the Civil War on the lives of enslaved Black Americans. Some other key concepts that are evident in this chapter are:

- conflict and change
- patterns in history
- transformations in history
- stereotyping
- cultural renaissance

IMPORTANT FACTS AND DATES

Some people think that being a good history student means being good at memorizing facts and dates. Yet even professional historians don't know all the facts and dates. They use reference books like this text to check specific information. Historians do understand, however, what makes facts and dates important. Facts are important when they:

- illustrate key concepts
- mark a turning point in history
- are tied to the "end of" or the "beginning of" a period in history
- symbolize the spirit of the age

When it comes to dates in history, remember this general rule: having a sense of time (for example, the century or decade) and a sense of chronology (the order of events) is more important than knowing isolated dates. Having a sense of time and chronology provides you with a scaffold for organizing the important facts in history. Here are some ways to categorize dates and time:

- turning points (e.g., Emancipation Proclamation, January 1, 1863)
- decades (e.g., Reconstruction, 1860s and 1870s)
- pre and post periods (e.g., pre-Civil War and post-Civil War)
- periods of migration (e.g., the Great Migration)
- times (e.g., colonial times, modern times)
- official dates (e.g., Martin Luther King Day: US holiday on the third Monday in January)

SIGNIFICANT PEOPLE

How do historians identify the significant people from the millions who have taken part in history? They highlight the people who are associated with the key concepts and the important facts and dates referred to above. Sometimes these people are well-known figures named in many history resources—like Mary Shadd Cary or Nat Turner. Sometimes they are lesser-known people who have also had an impact on history—like the unnamed enslaved Africans who escaped on the Underground Railroad or the Canadian railway porters. These significant people remind us that history is based not just on concepts, facts, and dates, but also on the stories of real people.

TRY IT!

From one section of this chapter, pick out a fact that marks a historic turning point. From another section, identify an important date. From a third section, select a significant person. Support your selections.

STUDY HALL

KNOWLEDGE/UNDERSTANDING

1. Lincoln believed that to defeat the Confederate States he needed to emancipate enslaved Blacks in those states. Why do you think this was so?
2. Create a web diagram to show why the Black Loyalists and Black soldiers from the War of 1812 immigrated to Canada.
3. In recent years, the popular Black American entertainer Bill Cosby has suggested that Black Americans need to take control of their own destinies and take advantage of their civil rights to advance and prosper in the United States. Discuss this idea as a class.

THINKING

4. Create a cause-and-effect organizer about the American Revolution with particular emphasis on its impact on Black people.
5. Evaluate the impact the Underground Railroad had on the African diaspora (both enslaved and free Blacks) in the United States and Canada.
6. Choose one Black community or settlement that was founded in Canada in the 1800s, research its history, and create a visual display that explains its history.
7. Create a political cartoon to demonstrate your understanding of the situation in Africville in Halifax.

APPLICATION & COMMUNICATION

8. Write a poem expressing the fears, hopes, and aspirations of Black settlers who came to Canada.
9. Investigate the experiences of Black members of the Canadian military during either the First World War or the Second World War. Take on the role of one of these people and write a diary entry describing your experience.
10. Another leader in the Black Power movement was Huey Newton, co-founder of the Black Panthers. Investigate Huey Newton and the Black Panthers and write a paragraph discussing whether or not you think their actions were effective in promoting their cause. Be sure to include reasons to support your opinion.
11. Revisit your analysis of Figure 5.1 on page 147.
    a. Taking into account what you have read in this chapter, do you agree with your original interpretation of this image? Why or why not?
    b. Create two phrases about freedom that you would add to the painting to reflect what you have read.

CHAPTER 6

Oppression and Resistance: The Caribbean and Latin America

KEY CONCEPTS

IN THIS CHAPTER, YOU WILL:

- identify the colonial and imperial systems that caused slavery
- examine how enslavement was used to shape the world economically, socially, and politically over time
- assess and evaluate the key factors that led to the conflict, oppression, and liberation of enslaved Blacks
- discover how enslaved Blacks maintained their spiritual and cultural identities
- consider the ways in which Blacks resisted their enslavement
- learn how Blacks in the Caribbean became empowered and gained independence from their colonial rulers
- consider the impact of African cultures on cultural and social traditions in the Caribbean and in Latin America

A People's Story

From 1492 until the second half of the 19th century, the Caribbean and Central and South America experienced a profound transformation. The original inhabitants of these lands—the Caribs, the Arawaks, the Lucayans, the Aztecs, the Incas, and many others—were almost wiped out by Europeans, killed either through conflict or by disease. The Europeans were eager to exploit the lands they had conquered in their competition for global power and prestige. But in order to build prosperous colonies, they needed cheap labour. Just as they did in many places in North America, they solved their labour problems by stealing Africans from their homelands.

In this chapter, you will learn about slavery in the Caribbean and Latin America. You will discover what prompted the Europeans to bring enslaved Africans to these lands. You will learn how the enslaved Africans fought against their oppression in places like Jamaica, Haiti, Barbados, and Brazil. You will follow the path they took, first to freedom and then to independence. As you read, think about what it would be like to be denied your freedom. Think about what circumstances allow one group of people to hold power over another. Then reflect on the impact that colonialism and slavery had on the African diaspora.

1518	1500s	1655	1731	1791	1796	1804	1810–1860
Spain begins conquest of Central and South America	Sugarcane revolution in the Caribbean	Britain seizes Jamaica from Spain	First Maroon War in Jamaica	Haitian Revolution begins	Trelawney Maroons exiled to Nova Scotia	Haiti declares independence	Slavery abolished in Spanish Latin America

Image Analysis

FIGURE 6.1
Harvesting sugarcane

Harvesting and refining sugarcane was a lot of work. Juice was extracted by crushing the sugarcane. Then the juice was boiled until the liquid evaporated, leaving only the sugar crystals. The European colonists in the Caribbean needed workers to produce the sugar. They had all but wiped out the local populations through conflict or exposure to diseases. So they brought in enslaved Africans from West Africa.

What does this image tell you about labour requirements on the sugar plantations? How would this affect the trade in African peoples?

Bussa's surrection in Barbados	Sam Sharpe's Rebellion in Jamaica	Slavery abolished in the British Empire	Slavery abolished in Brazil	Labour strikes and riots rock the Caribbean	Blacks in the Caribbean begin forming labour unions	Caribbean colonies join global independence movement
1816	1831	1834	1888	1917–1930s	1920s	1960s

The Sugarcane Revolution: Slavery in the Caribbean

As you discovered in Chapter 3, Europeans first occupied territories in the Caribbean and the Americas in their quest for gold and silver. By the middle of the 1500s, however, they were eager to cultivate another valuable resource: sugarcane.

In northern Europe, people used sugar to sweeten tea, coffee, cocoa, jam, candy, and other foods. But sugar was in scarce supply. As the population of Europe expanded, only the wealthy could afford to import sugar produced in the Mediterranean. But in the Caribbean, the Europeans found a subtropical climate and arable land that were ideal for growing sugarcane. So they began to transform their island colonies into sugar-producing machines.

During the sugarcane revolution, a fierce competition developed among the powers of Europe to control the sugar trade. The French set up sugar plantations on their colonies of Martinique, Guadeloupe, and Saint-Domingue (Haiti). The Dutch colonists in Curaçao and the Danish colonists in St. Croix built sugarcane plantations, too. But the leading player in the sugarcane revolution was Britain. In 1655, the British seized the island of Jamaica from Spain. By the middle of the 1700s, the most successful colonies in the Caribbean were British, and Jamaica was the jewel in the crown. It was Britain's richest and most valuable colony in the Caribbean.

FIGURE 6.2 European colonies in the Caribbean, 1700

The Caribbean is a collection of thousands of islands and cays lying between North and South America. After Christopher Columbus landed on the island of Hispaniola in 1492, Europeans began colonizing these lands. As this map of colonial territories in the Caribbean and Central America shows, Spain controlled most of the territory in 1700. But Britain, France, and the Netherlands refused to recognize Spain's claim of ownership of the Caribbean region. As they challenged Spain's domination, the Caribbean colonies changed hands many times.

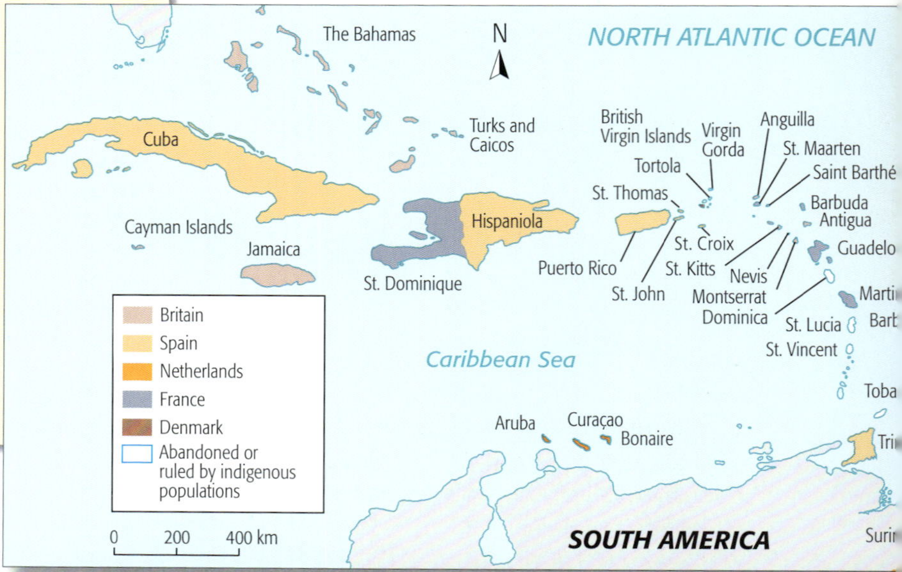

Work Gangs

Producing sugar required endless hours of back-breaking labour by hundreds of workers. As the demand for sugar reached its peak in the 1700s, the sugarcane planters began to import thousands of enslaved Africans to work on the plantations. The backbone of the plantation economy was the enslaved field workers. These were the lowest ranking Blacks on the plantations.

The field workers were divided into gangs of 100 or more based on their age and physical ability. The strongest men and women made up the first gang. They had to do the hardest and most physically demanding work. They cleared trees and shrubs from the land, planted the crop, and harvested the sugarcane. The second gang was made up of boys and girls between the ages of 12 and 18, elderly men and women, and new mothers. They did lighter fieldwork, such as tying the harvested canes together and loading them onto carts bound for the sugar mills. The third gang was made up of children between the ages of 6 and 10. They pulled weeds from the fields and spread manure.

The workday began for everyone at five in the morning. It lasted well into the evening. The gangs worked 18 hours a day, six days a week, all year long—sometimes more during the harvest.

FIGURE 6.3 Montpelier Plantation, Jamaica, 1821

In the early 1800s, enslaved Africans made up more than 90 percent of Jamaica's population. Over 60 percent lived on huge plantations like this one. These plantations had anywhere from 100 to 400 workers. The highest ranking workers on the sugar plantations were the domestic servants who worked in the owners' houses. Plantation owners promoted these differences in social status between field workers and domestic servants to create divisions among the people they enslaved.

Living Conditions

Living conditions varied throughout the Caribbean, but some things were common in almost all plantations. The goal of all plantation owners was to make as much money as possible. So they refused to provide their enslaved workers with even the bare necessities of life. The workers were left to take care of themselves in their limited time off. They grew their own food in small gardens. They used coarse cloth to make basic clothing. They were not given any shoes, so they worked barefoot. They had only straw and mud to build small huts to live in.

The poor living conditions made many women infertile. Those who became pregnant often gave birth to stillborn babies. Among the babies born alive, three out of four died before the age of five. Many children who survived were stolen from their mothers and sold into slavery.

The deplorable living conditions affected the adults, too. Many died from malnutrition and disease. Their deaths were of little consequence to the planters, though. They could always buy more people from Africa to work their plantations.

> **Some of the Africans in my country kept slaves, which they take in war, or for debt; but those which they kept are well, and good care taken of them, and treated well. . . .**
>
> **But I may safely say that all the poverty and misery that any of the inhabitants of Africa meet among themselves is far inferior to those inhospitable regions of misery which they meet with in the West Indies where their hard-hearted overseers have neither regard to the laws of God, nor the life of their fellow-men.**
>
> Ottobah Cugoano, *Narrative of the Enslavement of a Native of Africa*, 1787

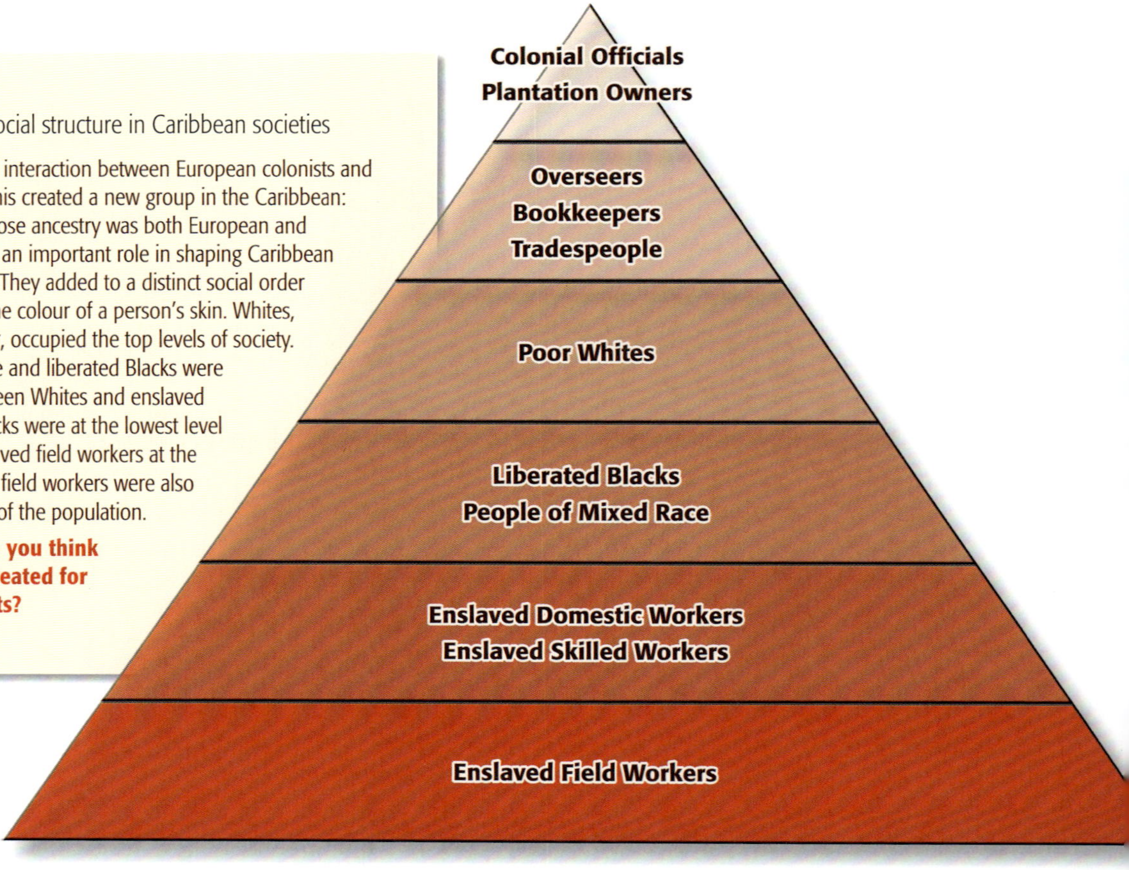

FIGURE 6.4 The social structure in Caribbean societies

Slavery led to sexual interaction between European colonists and enslaved Africans. This created a new group in the Caribbean: people of colour whose ancestry was both European and African. They played an important role in shaping Caribbean identity and culture. They added to a distinct social order that was based on the colour of a person's skin. Whites, whether rich or poor, occupied the top levels of society. People of mixed race and liberated Blacks were sandwiched in between Whites and enslaved Blacks. Enslaved Blacks were at the lowest level of society, with enslaved field workers at the very bottom. Yet the field workers were also the largest segment of the population.

What concerns do you think this might have created for the White colonists?

Maintaining Their Identities

Keeping their traditions and customs alive helped the enslaved Africans maintain their identities. Women played a key role in passing down their heritage. They told African stories and folktales. They passed down their traditional religious beliefs. They raised their children with traditional values so they would know who they were and where they came from.

Music was a major part of their lives. The enslaved Blacks sang songs in the fields to regulate their work pace. They made African instruments, such as drums, tambourines, flutes, banjos, and shakers, to play along with their songs and dances. They created unique languages and dialects that blended African and European words. These allowed Blacks to communicate in ways White people could not understand. They used these languages and dialects to plan their escapes and rebellions.

REVIEW AND REFLECT

1. What impact did the sugarcane revolution have on slavery in the Caribbean?
2. Why was it important for the enslaved Africans to maintain their identities?
3. Is your cultural identity important to you? Explain your answer in a written paragraph.

Resistance, Rebellion, and Emancipation in the Caribbean

Europeans in the Caribbean colonies lived in constant fear of violent rebellions by the people they enslaved. On most plantations, the owners and their families were outnumbered 10 to 1 by enslaved Blacks. On the largest estates, the ratio was as high as 50 to 1. Colonial governments gave planters absolute authority over the lives of their enslaved workers. The enslaved Africans had no rights and no say in even the most personal aspects of their lives. Day after day they endured humiliation and punishment designed to break their spirit and destroy their will to fight for their freedom.

Resistance

Yet enslaved Blacks refused to break under the will of their owners. Thousands escaped, hiding out in remote places. A few passed themselves off as Blacks who had been freed by their owners. They took jobs in towns or worked onboard ships.

Those who stayed behind on the plantations found ways to resist their enslavement. They worked slowly, pretending to be stupid or lazy. They broke tools and equipment and committed other acts of sabotage. Those who learned to read and write the European languages of the colonists taught their friends and families to read and write, too. They used these skills to forge documents that allowed them to travel freely outside the plantations.

For some, life on the plantation was not worth living, so they took their own lives. But thousands more fought back, using violent resistance to break free of their oppressors.

WOMEN'S RESISTANCE

Women played a huge part in resisting slavery. They refused to accept their fate without a fight. They deliberately did their work poorly. Sometimes they refused to work at all. They faked illnesses. They stole equipment. They harassed their overseers. In return, they were verbally abused or physically punished. But this did not stop them. Many plantation owners declared that the women were more difficult to manage and more troublesome than the men.

> **These injustices have been met with resistance. We have heard about an uprising in the Virgin Islands in which two women severed their own hands in protest. Also, women are more vocal in their opposition to slavery, as they are less likely to be flogged by their masters because of the masters' interests in maintaining healthy women for breeding. . . . They are becoming a strong voice, although every uprising has been defeated.**
>
> C. Beltray, British colonist and abolitionist in Barbados, "Multiple Perspectives on Slavery: An Eighteenth Century English Colloquium," University of Michigan, 2002

Rebellion

The first successful insurrection in the Caribbean took place on the island of St. John on November 1, 1733. A group of enslaved Africans defeated the Danish colonial army. After seizing control of the tiny island, the rebels raised their own flag in defiance of the Danes. Neighbouring European colonies rushed in troops to reinforce the Danish forces. After six months, the colonial forces managed to overpower the rebels. But the uprising was the first clear sign that the oppression of slavery would not go unopposed by the enslaved Africans.

> **If any man should buy another man and compel him to his service and slavery without any agreement of that man to serve him, the enslaver is a robber and a defrauder of that man every day. Wherefore it is as much the duty of a man who is robbed in that manner to get out of the hands of his enslaver as it is for any honest community of men to get out of the hands of rogues and villains.**
>
> Ottobah Cugoano, *Narrative of the Enslavement of a Native of Africa*, 1787

THE JAMAICAN MAROONS

When the British invaded the Spanish colony of Jamaica in 1655, the Spaniards fled. They left behind thousands of enslaved West Africans. Many escaped to the hilly mountainous interior of the island rather than be re-enslaved by the British. The fugitives were skilled trackers and hunters who knew how to survive in the rainforests. They remained holed up in the rugged mountains of Jamaica. This natural fortress protected them from repeated raids by British soldiers.

Over time, the Maroons came to control large areas of the Jamaican interior. From there, they swept down from the hills to raid the plantations. They damaged property. They stole food, tools, and weapons. They helped other enslaved Blacks escape. By the 1720s, they posed a serious threat to the British.

In 1731, Britain's battles with the Maroons turned into the First Maroon War. It lasted off and on for eight years. Unable to defeat the Maroons, the British reached an agreement with them in 1739–40. They promised the Maroons farmland and freedom. They could remain in their five main settlements of Accompong, Trelawny Town, Moore Town, Scots Hall, and Nanny Town under the leadership of their own chiefs, with British supervisors. In exchange, the Maroons had to agree not to help any more runaways. Instead, they were paid small bounties to hunt them down.

For a time, the threat from the Maroons subsided. But the Trelawny Town Maroons thought the British had tricked them. The land they had been given was rocky and not good for farming. In 1795, they rebelled once again in the Second Maroon War. In 1796, the British decided to rid the colony of its "problem" by deporting approximately 600 of the Trelawney Maroons to Nova Scotia.

FIGURE 6.5 Nanny of the Maroons

Nanny was one of the most powerful captains in the Maroons. She was an enslaved African from the Asante nation in West Africa. She had a fierce fighting spirit and was particularly clever at making plans to free enslaved Blacks. Little is known of Nanny from written records. As a result, her story is part myth, part folklore, and part legacy. In 1994, Nanny was honoured on Jamaica's currency.

In Halifax, the colonial governor was impressed by the Maroons. He offered them work building the new fortifications at the Citadel. But after their first winter in Nova Scotia, the Maroons became disillusioned. They found it hard to adjust to farming in a northern climate. They did not want to convert to Christianity. Colonial officials began to see the Maroons as a threat to peace and order. After four troubled years, in 1800 the British arranged for the Maroons to leave Nova Scotia to join the Black Loyalists in Sierra Leone.

FIGURE 6.6 *Leonard Parkinson, a captain of the Maroons*, 1796

Written records of the Maroons in Nova Scotia are scarce. But one document from 1812 describes them as good workers who valued their own community and culture.

Rebellion Spreads

The persistence of the Maroons inspired other rebellions across the Caribbean. Some were planned in advance. Others were spontaneous reactions to specific situations, such as sexual assaults or extreme cruelty. Every colony in the Caribbean experienced these rebel uprisings. Some would have a lasting impact on the future of slavery in the Caribbean.

THE HAITIAN REVOLUTION

In 1791, almost 500 000 enslaved Africans in the French colony of Saint-Domingue on the island of Hispaniola rose up against 25 000 French colonists. They were motivated by the ideals of the Enlightenment and inspired by the **French Revolution** two years earlier. The enslaved workers of Saint-Domingue were called upon to overthrow their oppressors in a powerful speech by a Black priest named Dutty Boukman.

French Revolution the overthrow of the French monarchy between 1789 and 1799 that united various groups in French society against the established order

> The Good Lord who created the sun which gives us light from above, who rouses the sea and makes the thunder roar—listen well, all of you—this god, hidden in the clouds, watches us. He sees all that the white man does. The god of the white man calls him to commit crimes; our god asks only good works of us. But this god who is so good orders revenge! He will direct our hands; he will aid us. Throw away the image of the god of the whites who thirsts for our tears and listen to the voices of liberty which speaks in the hearts of all of us.
>
> Dutty Boukman, "The Voice of Liberty," 1791

Colonial officials arrested Boukman and beheaded him for inciting rebellion. But they could not stop the rebels' momentum. An enslaved African named Toussaint L'Ouverture stepped in to lead the rebels. Although he was enslaved, L'Ouverture learned to read and write. He was inspired by the French literature published during the Enlightenment. He demanded the same freedom for enslaved Blacks that the people of France had demanded for themselves during the French Revolution.

FIGURE 6.7
The Haitian Revolution

For 12 years, thousands of enslaved Africans fought in a rebel army to overthrow the government of the French colony.

The rebels' cause was a daunting one. Saint-Domingue was the richest colony in the world. France was determined to quash the rebellion, but it was distracted by wars in Europe. It managed to send 44 000 troops to the colony to fight the rebels. But they were no match for the enslaved peoples of Saint-Domingue, who were driven by a passion for freedom—and a desire for revenge! The rebels burned the plantations to the ground. They attacked any French colonists and soldiers they found. After years of struggle, the rebels were victorious. On January 1, 1804, Saint-Domingue declared itself the independent state of Haiti.

The success of the Haitian rebels ignited unrest throughout the Caribbean. Threats of rebellion were everywhere. Some uprisings involved just a few people. Many others, however, involved hundreds and sometimes thousands of enslaved Blacks. They launched major uprisings in places like Tobago in 1801, Trinidad in 1805, Barbados in 1816, Antigua in 1831, and the Bahamas in 1832. Plantation owners began building shelters where they could hide if their enslaved workers revolted. Waves of fearful colonists fled to Europe and the United States. The Europeans knew they were sitting on a powder keg. It was only a matter of time before it would explode.

BUSSA'S INSURRECTION

In the 1600s, enslaved Blacks in Barbados staged three unsuccessful rebellions:

- in 1649, workers on two plantations rebelled against a lack of food; the uprising was quickly put down
- in 1675, after three years of planning, an island-wide rebellion was quashed when one of the enslaved Blacks leaked details about the plot; over 100 Blacks were arrested and tortured; 40 were executed
- in 1692, in another island-wide rebellion, over 200 Blacks were arrested; 90 were executed

Afterward, the frequent presence of British military ships bringing supplies to the island kept rebellions in Barbados simmering in the background. By the early 1800s, however, the enslaved Blacks of the tiny British colony were inspired by the Haitian Revolution and the anti-slavery debates taking place in Britain. Their desire for freedom sparked the Easter Rebellion, also known as Bussa's Insurrection, after its African-born leader, a mysterious man named Bussa.

Bussa's Insurrection on April 14, 1816 was the first large-scale rebellion in the British Caribbean. It was not a spontaneous uprising. It was a carefully planned, organized, and executed rebellion by enslaved Blacks on a number of Barbadian plantations. Between 500 and 1000 Black men and women were killed in the fighting. More than 140 were arrested and executed. More than 120 others were exiled from the colony.

FIGURE 6.8
Bussa (?–1816)

Mystery surrounds the life of Bussa. Little is known about him before he emerged as the leader of the Easter Rebellion in Barbados. Born a free man in Africa, he was captured and brought to Barbados in the late 18th century. He is celebrated in the collective memories of Barbadians as the man who struck a blow for freedom.

The uprising frightened officials in London. They insisted that the Barbadian colonists introduce reforms to reduce the risk of further uprisings. Reluctantly, the colonial plantation owners agreed to certain "rights" for enslaved workers:

- the right to own property
- the right to testify in court
- the right to pay reduced **manumission** fees

manumission
the act of setting a person free from slavery or bondage

The events in Barbados advanced the crusade for freedom. In Britain, abolitionists stepped up their campaign to abolish slavery.

SAM SHARPE'S REBELLION

Another great challenge to slavery in the British colonies took place in December 1831, again in Jamaica. A Baptist preacher named Samuel Sharpe launched a general strike on December 27. Unlike many enslaved Blacks, Sharpe could read and write English. He read many of the anti-slavery pamphlets published by the abolitionists in Britain. He spread the word to his followers and persuaded them not to return to work until slavery was abolished. But when the signal to start the strike was sounded, it exploded into a full-scale rebellion. More than 60 000 enslaved Blacks joined the fight. They had no weapons, so they burned down the sugar-cane fields and the great houses of the plantations.

The rebellion raged on until it was finally overpowered by British forces in early January 1832. For weeks, British soldiers hunted down fugitive rebels on the run. Hundreds were captured. Many were killed on sight. More than 300 others were arrested and executed, including Sam Sharpe, who was hanged for organizing the strike. Although the rebellion failed, it sent a clear message to Britain: slavery could not be maintained much longer in the British Caribbean.

Emancipation

The cost of putting down the rebellions and repairing the damage they left in their wake was taking a huge toll on the finances of the colonies. Back in Europe, news of the rebellions focused attention on the injustices of slavery. As you learned in Chapter 3, people began demanding that their governments end the inhumane practice. With a sense of urgency, Britain passed the *Emancipation Act* and formally abolished slavery on August 1, 1834. In the years that followed, the other European powers abolished slavery in their colonies, too.

REVIEW AND REFLECT

1. How did literacy empower enslaved Blacks?
2. Why were the Maroons so threatening to the British in Jamaica?
3. Why was the Haitian Revolution so significant?
4. Add key events from this section to your abolition of slavery timeline from Chapter 3. If you do not have an existing timeline, begin a new timeline based on the events in this section.
5. Discuss your predictions for the future of the enslaved Africans following the abolition of slavery.

Life in the Caribbean After Slavery

When Britain agreed to abolish slavery throughout its empire, it did so in a roundabout way. The British government wanted the planters to have workers to keep the plantations going. So they created an apprenticeship system. All enslaved Blacks over the age of six had to work as apprentices on the plantations for six years. Three-quarters of each day was spent working for the plantation owners—without pay. In exchange, workers received food, clothing, shelter, and medical care. In their spare time, they could work for wages if they wanted to. It was a degree of freedom, but with strings attached.

Indentured Workers

To help ease their labour shortages, the planters hired indentured workers from India and Asia. Most had contracts to work for five years on the plantations. In return, they received wages, food, shelter, health care, and passage back home. Life on the plantations was not any easier for the indentured workers than it was for the Blacks. But there was one critical difference: the indentured workers received wages whereas the Black apprentices did not. This created tensions between the two groups.

With the arrival of workers from India and Asia, Whites became an even smaller minority in the Caribbean. To ensure that the Black apprentices and indentured workers did not join forces and rise up against them, the colonists exploited the tensions between the two groups. The planters encouraged indentured workers to look down on Black workers. They reinforced stereotypes of Blacks as lazy, backward, and uncivilized. This helped to ensure that freed Blacks remained solidly entrenched at the bottom of the social order.

In time, however, tensions between the two sides eased. The different cultures began to intermarry. This created new populations of people of mixed heritage on the Caribbean islands. Blacks, Indians, and Asians influenced each other's lives in language, dialect, food, music, and religion. The impact of these interactions is an integral part of Caribbean life today.

Social Conflict

After the abolition of slavery, social conflict between Blacks and Whites was inevitable. Blacks were determined to fight for the rights and privileges of citizenship. Whites were equally determined to maintain their grip on power and their control over Blacks. The Europeans had to find a way to justify taking over foreign lands and subjecting African peoples to the inhumanity of slavery. They did so by fostering the myth that

Europeans were superior to all other people on earth and that their institutions were the symbol of order, discipline, success, and achievement. They entrenched this idea by granting certain rights and privileges to Europeans while denying them to Blacks and mulattos. This led many people to believe that their own cultures, customs, traditions, and religions were inferior. Some tried to imitate the colonists' lifestyle, values, and views, but they could never do so successfully because of their differences. As a result, many people experienced a loss of identity.

Resistance Through Culture

Just as the Jim Crow laws segregated Blacks in the United States, there was also cultural oppression in the Caribbean. Despite attempts to repress them, Blacks refused to be denied their culture and traditions. Music, religion, and education became a means of expressing their heritage.

MUSIC

Calypso can be traced back to the 17th century when the first enslaved Africans were brought to Trinidad to work on the sugar plantations. They were forbidden from speaking to one another as they worked the fields. So they began to sing songs like the ones they knew in West Africa as a means of communicating. Early calypso music was sung in a French

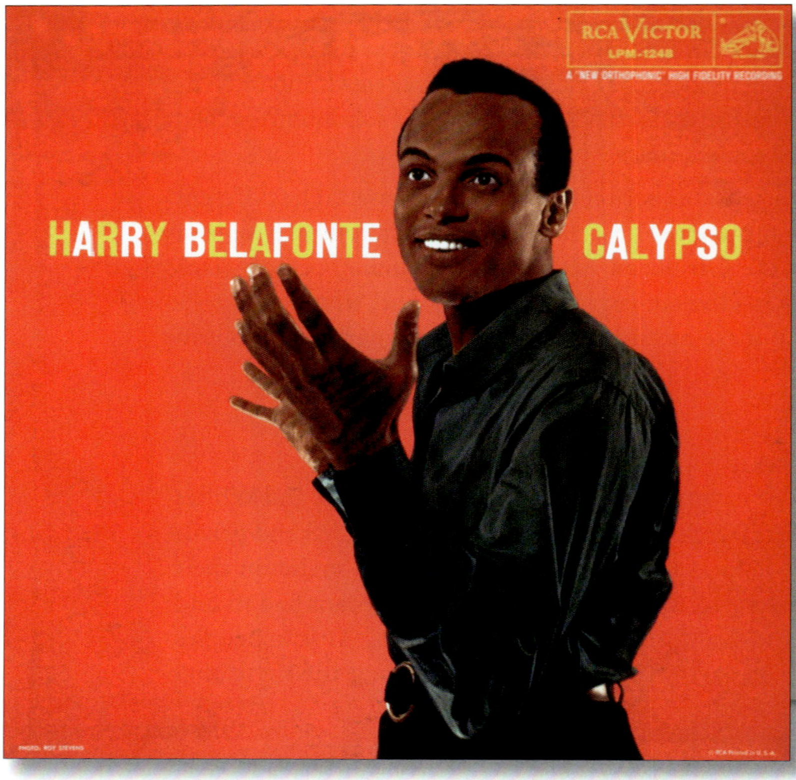

FIGURE 6.9
Harry Belafonte (1927–)

Harry Belafonte is an American musician, actor, and social activist of Jamaican heritage. In the 1950s and 1960s, he popularized calypso music with such hits as the "Banana Boat Song" with its famous lyric "Day-O." His album *Calypso* (1956) was the first recording by a single artist to sell over 1 million copies in the United States. Dubbed the "King of Calypso," Belafonte's music launched a national calypso craze!

dialect. It allowed the enslaved Africans to secretly ridicule their plantation owners. It was another form of resistance against the oppression of slavery.

After slavery was abolished, calypso music reflected Black Trinidadians' struggle against colonialism. The song lyrics became more political as people sang about discrimination and oppression. Colonial authorities tried to restrict calypso performances, but the music's popularity could not be repressed. Calypso gave Black Trinidadians the opportunity to express their emotions. In time, this expression of resistance against oppression spread throughout the Caribbean.

Today, calypso remains a powerful force of communication and commentary. It helps shape the thoughts and feelings of diverse audiences in concerts, carnivals, and festivals throughout the Caribbean and around the world.

RELIGION

Missionaries first brought Christianity to the Caribbean islands during the days of slavery. They attempted to convert African peoples to Christianity. Some accepted the missionaries' efforts. Others ignored them. Many blended Christian ideas with their own African beliefs and values. Through religion, Blacks expressed their sorrows and celebrated their joys.

Religion gave Black people the opportunity to be leaders in their communities, free from the constraints of White authority. Charismatic religious leaders shaped the intellectual and political ideas of their congregations. They provided the people with moral and psychological support. They helped them gain the confidence to fight for their rights through **grassroots** organizations.

After slavery was abolished, Christianity remained the dominant religion in the Caribbean. But now the doors were open to religious diversity, too. Different peoples of the Caribbean developed a vibrant variety of faiths. For many Caribbean peoples, it was possible to be a Christian and also practise other forms of religious expression, such as **voodoo**, **revivalism**, and **Santeria**. The indentured workers from India and Asia also brought their religions with them. In places like Trinidad and Tobago, a growing number of islanders practised the Hindu and Muslim faiths.

grassroots
efforts involving ordinary people working at a fundamental level

voodoo
a religion practised primarily in the Caribbean, particularly in Haiti, that involves witchcraft and ancestor worship

revivalism
religious fervour that leads to a spiritual awakening

Santeria
an African-based religion similar to voodoo that combines the worship of Yoruban gods with the worship of Roman Catholic saints

EDUCATION

During slavery, Europeans believed that teaching enslaved Blacks to read and write would empower them to resist authority. After the abolition of slavery, Europeans used education to maintain cultural and psychological control over Blacks. Although Blacks were allowed to attend school, their lessons were filled with propaganda. They were taught nothing about their own heritage. In fact, they were led to believe that Blacks had no history at all. Instead, they learned about European history. It was a strategy designed to promote the myth of European superiority.

Blacks knew that education was the way to move up in Caribbean societies. Many Black students earned scholarships to universities. Some of them returned to the school system as principals and teachers. Others pursued further education abroad in Europe and North America. When they returned to the islands, they demanded equality and democracy—ideas that the colonists had repressed among Blacks for hundreds of years.

As more Blacks gained an education, many Black Caribbean writers rose to prominence. They published works condemning the injustices of colonialism, discrimination, and racism. They wrote poems that explored their cultural identities. They created novels with colourful characters that reflected their islands and cultures. Writers like Nobel Prize-winning poet and essayist Derek Walcott (1930–) from St. Lucia, essayist Aimé Césaire (1913–2008) from Martinique, poet Kamau Brathwaite (1930–) from Barbados, and folklorist Louise Bennett Coverley (1919–2006) from Jamaica presented the Black Caribbean experience to the world.

COLONIZATION IN REVERSE

Wat a joyful news, miss Mattie,
I feel like me heart gwine burs
Jamaica people colonizin
Englan in Reverse

By de hundred, by de tousan
From country and from town
By de ship-load, by de plane load
Jamaica is Englan boun.

Dem a pour out a Jamaica,
Everybody future plan
Is fe get a big-time job
An settle in de mother lan.

What an islan! What a people!
Man an woman, old an young
Jus a pack dem bag an baggage
An turn history upside dung!

Excerpt from "Colonization in Reverse" by Louise Bennett Coverley

FIGURE 6.10 Louise Bennett Coverley

Louise Bennett Coverley—affectionately called "Miss Lou"—challenged the fact that Jamaican children were taught in formal English since the majority of Jamaicans did not speak or understand it. She wrote in the dialect of Jamaican English to express the Jamaicans' uniqueness as a people. When she died in Toronto in July 2006, she was mourned by her followers around the world.

REVIEW AND REFLECT

1. Why do you think the Europeans tried to justify colonialism and slavery? Explain your response.
2. Listen to a recording of Harry Belafonte's "Banana Boat Song." How would you describe the music? Why do you think it was so appealing?
3. Read Louise Bennett Coverley's poem "Colonization in Reverse." What is the poem's message? Why do you think it was important to write in the dialect of Jamaican English?

From Occupation to Independence in the Caribbean

By the end of the 19th century, Blacks in the Caribbean islands still did not have the right to vote. Nor were they represented in colonial governments. As a result, Blacks joined together to create their own self-help movements. The only political tools they had were strikes and riots. Between 1917 and 1919, frustrated Black workers staged a series of labour strikes and riots in Jamaica, Trinidad, and other Caribbean islands. They were protesting unemployment, low wages, and poor working conditions. At first, these protests were unorganized. Then Black leaders formed trade unions to fight for the rights and interests of Black workers.

In the 1920s and 1930s, labour unions were formed throughout the Caribbean. Despite their efforts, however, the majority of Blacks still lived in poverty. Jobs that paid a living wage were scarce. Elementary schools for Black students were overcrowded. Secondary schools were too expensive for most Black families. Food shortages led to unhealthy diets and malnutrition. Weakened bodies made it harder to fight diseases. A shortage of hospitals, doctors, and medicines led to high death rates among Black infants and children. In the 1930s, the hopelessness and frustration that had been building for more than half a century exploded as more riots rocked Jamaica, Trinidad, Barbados, St. Kitts, and other Caribbean islands. The colonial governments transported troops from Europe to quash the uprisings.

Political Activism

Pan-Caribbean
countries in the Caribbean that are connected politically, historically, or culturally

Labour union leaders realized the only way to create change was to gain political power. They turned their unions into political parties to fight for the rights of Blacks on a larger scale. They were supported by Black veterans of the First World War who had been given pensions and land in Caribbean territories when the war ended. The discrimination these soldiers had faced in European armies left them critical of colonial policies. They formed the heart of a **Pan-Caribbean** movement determined to fight for political reforms and to bring self-government to the islands. They laid the groundwork for the generation of politicians who would dismantle colonialism in the Caribbean in the 1960s.

The threat to the status quo posed by the social and political unrest caught the attention of homeland governments. In 1940, Britain, for example, passed the *Colonial Development Welfare Act.* It earmarked £1 million a year for 18 years to improve living conditions for Blacks in its Caribbean colonies. Britain extended the right to vote to all adults over the age of 21 and introduced political changes that allowed for limited self-government.

universal suffrage
the right to vote for all adults

In Jamaica, Norman Manley, a lawyer of mixed race, and his cousin, Alexander Bustamante, campaigned for and won **universal suffrage** and a new constitution in 1944. Other British colonies soon followed. In most colonies, political parties relied on the support of the labour unions to gain power in their governments. After the Second World War, colonial governments began giving benefits to workers. As the unions flourished, real wages began to steadily increase.

Decolonization

In the aftermath of the Second World War, three main factors contributed to the global phenomenon of decolonization. The first was the colonies' determination to gain their independence. This determination joined forces with the people's growing resistance to racial discrimination. At the same time, the colonial powers of Europe were distracted by other international affairs.

In addition, during the war the Allies had made promises of independence to the African colonial forces that played such an important role in the Allied victory. In the Caribbean, Blacks and mulattos joined the fight taking place in the colonies of Africa in a global campaign for decolonization and independence.

The West Indies Federation

By the 1950s, the power of the old colonial guards was weakening. For the Europeans, the cost of maintaining the colonies was beginning to exceed the financial benefits. The people of Black and mixed heritage in the Caribbean now formed the middle class. They were emerging as a powerful political force. In 1958, Britain agreed to allow a degree of self-government in its Caribbean colonies through the creation of the West Indies Federation. The goal was to unite the territories under one government that would eventually be fully independent.

FIGURE 6.11 The flag of the West Indies Federation

The design on the flag of the West Indies Federation represents the sun shining down on the waves of the Caribbean. The federation consisted of 10 island territories: Jamaica, Trinidad and Tobago, Barbados, Grenada, St. Kitts–Nevis–Anguilla, Antigua and Barbuda, St. Lucia, St. Vincent and the Grenadines, Dominica, and Montserrat.

YEAR	COUNTRY
1804	Haiti (Fr)
1844	Dominican Republic (Sp)
1898	Cuba (Sp)
1962	Trinidad and Tobago (Br)
	Jamaica (Br)
1966	Barbados (Br)
	Guyana (Br)
1973	The Bahamas (Br)
1975	Suriname (the Netherlands)
1974	Grenada (Br)
1978	Dominica (Br)
1979	St. Lucia (Br)
	St. Vincent and the Grenadines (Br)
1981	Belize (Br)
	Antigua and Barbuda (Br)
1983	St. Kitts and Nevis (Br)
1985	Aruba (a member state of the Netherlands)
2008	Curaçao and Saint Marten (autonomous territories of the Netherlands)

FIGURE 6.12
Timeline of Caribbean independence

As of 2009, several Caribbean islands remained under European rule. The United Nations has called for all non-self-governing territories to achieve home rule by 2010.

But the West Indies Federation was doomed from the start. It had little popular support among Caribbean political leaders. The two largest members, Jamaica and Trinidad and Tobago, could not agree on political representation. Trinidad and Tobago had revenue from its oil and natural gas reserves. It wanted political representation to be based on financial contributions to the federation. Jamaica, on the other hand, had a larger population. It wanted political representation to be based on population. By 1961, the federation was on the verge of collapse. Jamaica opted out. Not wanting to have sole financial responsibility for the remaining eight small, poor islands in the federation, Trinidad and Tobago withdrew as well.

Independence

With the collapse of the West Indies Federation, Britain began negotiating independence for many of its Caribbean colonies. In 1962, Norman Manley led the team that negotiated Jamaican independence. That same year, a Trinidadian-born Black man named Eric Williams won independence for Trinidad and Tobago. In 1973, the Bahamas gained independence under the leadership of Lyndon Pindling. In Antigua and Barbuda, a Black labour activist named Vere Bird guided his island homeland to independence in 1981. All across the Caribbean, island colonies became independent nations. By 2009, only a handful of islands remained under foreign control.

REVIEW AND REFLECT

1. To what extent did life improve for Blacks in the Caribbean following the abolition of slavery?
2. Some countries, like Britain and the United States, have said they will not comply with the UN's demand that all non-self-governing territories achieve their independence by 2010. Why do you think they would defy the UN? Should they be forced to comply? Explain your response.
3. Imagine you are living in a territory that is controlled by a foreign power. Write a letter to the leader of that foreign power demanding self-government.

ORIGINALS

MARCUS GARVEY (1887–1940)

Marcus Garvey was a Black nationalist who promoted Pan-Africanism—that is, the return of Blacks around the world to Africa. Born in Jamaica in 1887, he rose from relative obscurity to lead the largest global Black movement in history.

After travelling to Central and South America and to London, England, Garvey founded the Universal Negro Improvement Association (UNIA) in Kingston, Jamaica in 1914. The organization promoted Black pride. It called upon Blacks around the world to return to Africa and reclaim their homeland from European colonists.

> The Universal Negro Improvement Association stands for human rights, not only for Negroes, but for all races. The Universal Negro Improvement Association believes in the rights of not only the black race but the white race, the yellow race, and the brown race. . . . In view of the fact that the black man of Africa has contributed as much to the world as the white man of Europe, and the brown and yellow man of Asia, we of the Universal Negro Improvement Association demand that the white, yellow and brown races give to the black man his place in the civilization of the world. We ask for nothing more than the rights of 400 000 000 Negroes. We are not seeking . . . to destroy or disrupt the society or the government of other races, but we are determined that 400 000 000 of us shall unite ourselves to free our motherland from the grasp of the invader. . . . We are looking toward political freedom on the continent of Africa, the land of our fathers.

Marcus Garvey, "Aims and Objectives of UNIA"

In 1916, Garvey left Jamaica to settle in Harlem and open an American chapter of the UNIA. He promoted Pan-Africanism in electrifying speeches that helped the UNIA raise money to open Black-owned and operated businesses. In 1919, Garvey launched a steamship company called the Black Star Line to promote trade and commerce among Black communities around the world. Garvey envisioned the Black Star Line as the linchpin in a global Black economy.

FIGURE 6.13 Marcus Garvey (1887–1940)

In 1920, Marcus Garvey held an international convention on the rights of Blacks in New York City. During the convention, he issued the Declaration of the Rights of the Negro Peoples of the World and was elected Provisional President of Africa.

FIGURE 6.14 Parade of the Universal Negro Improvement Association, August 31, 1930

Black Americans demonstrated their support for Garvey's Universal Negro Improvement Association in an annual parade through the streets of Harlem.

But the Black Star Line was ill-fated from the start. Garvey bought old ships in desperate need of repair at inflated prices. A series of mishaps, combined with poor management, caused the shipping line to quickly turn into a financial disaster. By the time the company folded in 1922, the losses were estimated at $1.25 million. Then Garvey was arrested on charges of mail fraud stemming from the sale of Black Star Line stock. In 1923, he was found guilty and sentenced to five years in prison.

Despite the problems with the Black Star Line, it was a powerful symbol to Blacks everywhere. It was the first shipping company ever owned and operated by Blacks. It served as a recruitment tool for the UNIA and made Garvey a hero among working-class Blacks. But he was criticized by Black leaders such as W.E.B. Du Bois. Du Bois believed that Garvey's campaign to return all Blacks to Africa undermined efforts to win civil rights for Blacks in the United States.

The US government was suspicious of Garvey, too. It constantly monitored his activities. When Garvey's prison sentence was commuted in 1927, the United States deported Garvey to Jamaica. In his homeland, he founded Jamaica's first modern political party, the People's Political Party (PPP), in 1929. The PPP focused on workers' rights, education, and aid to the poor.

In 1935, Garvey moved to London, where he continued his work with the UNIA. In 1938, he set up the School of African Philosophy in Toronto to train UNIA leaders. In the years before his death, Garvey's health was failing. He died in London of a stroke on June 10, 1940 while reading his own obituary, published prematurely in the newspaper. In 1964, his body was returned to Jamaica, where he was declared the country's first national hero.

Marcus Garvey's memory lives on. Many schools, universities, highways, and buildings in the Caribbean, Africa, Europe, and North America are named in his honour.

Think It Through

Why do you think the Black Star Line was a powerful symbol for Blacks? Give reasons for your response.

Slavery in Spanish Latin America

In 1502, Spain began shipping hundreds of Spanish-born Blacks it had captured in West Africa to work in the gold and silver mines of its South American colonies. This marked the beginning of the European conquest of what is now Latin America. Within a century, the Europeans had all but wiped out the indigenous populations through conflict and the introduction of diseases. To offset the loss of local peoples, they turned to Africa as a source of enslaved labour. Between 1519 and 1870, more than 5 million Africans were stolen from their homeland to work in Latin America.

FIGURE 6.15
Latin American colonies

For centuries, Spain and Portugal had vast colonial empires throughout Central and South America. Spain occupied all of what are now Mexico and the countries of Central America. It also occupied much of the western half of South America, including the countries that are now Venezuela, Colombia, Ecuador, Peru, Bolivia, Paraguay, Uruguay, Chile, and Argentina. Portugal occupied the vast colony of Brazil. The Europeans seized control of the land and its people. They granted huge tracts of land to wealthy Europeans, who grew even wealthier through slavery.

Europeans in Latin America used enslaved Africans in every conceivable way. At first, they used them as soldiers in their battles with indigenous peoples. Then they used them to work in the dangerous gold and silver mines and on the labour-intensive plantations. Africans became the foundation of slavery economies in many parts of South and Central America for more than 400 years.

FIGURE 6.16 Diego Rivera's mural *Colonial Domination*

This image shows enslaved West Africans being brought to the Americas by the Spaniards.

There are many symbols included in this painting. Which symbols can you identify? What do they mean?

Most of the enslaved Africans worked on plantations that produced sugar, coffee, cotton, tobacco, and rice. Yet, with the exception of Brazil, slavery was less important to the colonies of Latin America than it was to the Caribbean colonies. Whereas 47 percent of enslaved Africans went to the Caribbean and 38 percent to Brazil, only 6 percent went to the mainland colonies of Latin America.

Social Structure

Most of the enslaved Blacks in Latin America worked in domestic service or as plantation workers. The social structure was three-tiered. At the top were Europeans. In the middle were people of mixed heritage. At the bottom were enslaved Africans and indigenous peoples. The rights and privileges of each group varied from place to place. Areas with the greatest demand for enslaved workers, such as Brazil, imposed the harshest restrictions and punishments. In other places, such as the interior of Venezuela and Argentina, social restrictions were more relaxed and Blacks had greater mobility.

In Latin America, enslaved blacks could buy their freedom through a time-purchase plan called *coartación*. The majority of enslaved Blacks who purchased their freedom were female domestics. When they became free, their children became free, too. Sometimes White men who fathered the children of enslaved Black women granted freedom to those children.

Yet enslaved Africans were not the only Blacks in Latin America. Many free or semi-free Blacks came to the colonies with European colonists. By the 19th century, for example, the free Black population in what is now Panama, Colombia, Venezuela, and Ecuador was over 400 000, while the number of enslaved Blacks was just 20 000.

The Abolition of Slavery

Spain's position as a world power began to slip away in the 19th century. It could not hold on to its colonies in the Caribbean or Latin America. As a result, these colonies gained independence more than 100 years before other European colonies. Between 1810 and 1826, Spain's colonies fought for independence. They promised to abolish slavery once they achieved their goals. In 1821, Venezuela abolished slavery and freed all enslaved Blacks who had fought for independence in the rebel armies. Gradually, all enslaved Blacks were granted their freedom until the last enslaved Black in Venezuela was freed in 1854. A similar process took place in Argentina, beginning in 1813 and ending in 1861. By the middle of the 19th century, one by one, the Spanish colonies of Latin America had abolished slavery.

After the Abolition of Slavery

After slavery was abolished, the new governments of Latin America compensated the former plantation owners for the loss of their enslaved workers. But there was no compensation for the freed Blacks. They did not have the money or skills to compete with the new wave of immigration that flowed into many parts of Latin America. As a result, they were left to do menial labour. They remained firmly entrenched at the lowest social and economic levels.

In much of Latin America, such as Mexico, Peru, Bolivia, Chile, Argentina, and Ecuador, Blacks made up less than 1 percent of the population. They experienced the negative effects of racism and discrimination from the White elite. Whites throughout Latin America refused to accept multicultural societies. In the 19th century, many of the newly independent countries prohibited Black immigration. As a result, as the populations of Latin American countries expanded, the Black populations became overwhelmingly outnumbered.

Blacks in Latin America Today

For centuries, people of European, African, Asian, and indigenous descent have intermarried in Latin America. The result is a complex social hierarchy that is influenced by many factors. But a strong African influence is evident in the music, dance, literature, religions, and dialects of Latin American culture. Whether they came as enslaved workers or free immigrants, Africans brought a variety of their own cultural influences to Latin America.

FIGURE 6.17 Dancing the *candombe*

The vibrant rhythms and melodies that Blacks brought with them from Africa have had a strong influence on Latin American music. The *candombe* is an important element in many African celebrations throughout Latin America today.

What other music are you familiar with that has been influenced by African culture?

REVIEW AND REFLECT

1. How were women instrumental in bringing freedom to enslaved Africans in Latin America?
2. Explain why Latin America has such a complex social structure today.

Slavery in Portuguese Brazil

As you discovered in Chapter 3, the Portuguese initiated the trade in West and Central African peoples in the 15th century. Over the next 400 years, they transported more than 3.6 million of the estimated 12 million enslaved Africans to one destination: Brazil. Portugal's huge South American colony was the single largest exploiter of enslaved Africans in the Americas and the Caribbean.

Period	1500–1700	1701–1760	1761–1829	1830–1855
Numbers	510 000	958 000	1 720 000	618 000

Instituto Brasileiro de Geografia e Estatística

FIGURE 6.18 Number of enslaved Africans transported to Brazil, 1500–1855

The flow of enslaved Africans began relatively slowly. But it skyrocketed in the 18th century as the Portuguese exploited the colony's resources.

At first, the majority of the captives came from West and Central Africa. But by the late 18th century, almost all of Africa was threatened by the trade in African peoples as the Portuguese expanded their supply zone to southern and East Africa.

On the Sugar Plantations

In Brazil, the colonists grew rich on the backs of millions of enslaved Africans. In the 17th century, more than half a million Africans were imported to work on the labour-intensive sugarcane plantations. The working conditions were beyond imagination. The plantation owners literally worked the Africans to death. Most did not survive more than a few years. Their deaths were of little consequence to the plantation owners. It was cheaper to buy more Africans than to provide the basic necessities of life to those they already had.

For a time, this massive amount of free labour helped Brazil's sugarcane plantations keep their prices for refined sugar low. But in the late 1600s, competition from the new sugar plantations in the Caribbean led to sagging sugar prices on world markets. Brazil's sugar exports plummeted. The Portuguese began searching for other resources to maintain their colony.

FIGURE 6.19 A sugar plantation in Brazil

During the colonial era, slavery was the backbone of the Brazilian economy. Without the wealth produced by the work of enslaved Africans, the Portuguese would have had to abandon their colony.

In the Gold Mines

The discovery of gold at the turn of the 17th century refocused the Brazilian economy. It sparked the first gold rush in the Americas as thousands of colonists raced to the rugged mountains north of Rio de Janeiro, eager to make their fortunes in gold.

The gold rush caused Brazil's volume of trade in enslaved Africans to skyrocket. Between 1700 and 1720, more than 292 000 enslaved Africans came ashore at Brazilian ports. Over the next 20 years, another 312 000 Africans were seized from their homelands and forced to make the Middle Passage to work in Brazil's gold mines. But even then Brazil's trade in African peoples had not reached its peak. Between 1741 and 1760, another 354 000 enslaved Africans were imported to Portugal's South American colony.

The mining took place deep in the interior of Brazil. The ruthless Portuguese men who oversaw the mining operations were a law unto themselves. They drove the enslaved Africans mercilessly, ensuring that their lives were nasty, brutish, and short.

FIGURE 6.20 Public whipping in Brazil, 1620 (left); iron mask for punishing slaves, Brazil, 1817–18

Many enslaved Africans tried to escape from their captors. Those who failed were brutally punished. They were tied to posts in public squares and flogged. They were forced to wear painful restraints designed to make it almost impossible to flee again.

RESISTANCE

The enslaved miners resisted the brutality of their lives. Many smuggled gold, which they used to buy their freedom. Thousands more escaped. They hid out in remote settlements called *quilombos*. In the *quilombos*, the people built self-sufficient communities. They grew their own crops and hunted local game. They traded with one another. Occasionally they taunted the colonists by raiding their plantations.

Many *quilombos* modelled their communities after the West African kingdoms of their homeland. They spoke their own languages and practised their cultural traditions. In the 1600s, one *quilombo* called Palmares in the northeastern mountains of Brazil grew into a settlement of 30 000 people. For close to 100 years, Palmares was a centre of resistance. The people fought off repeated attempts to destroy their community. But in 1694 they were finally overpowered by colonial forces.

FIGURE 6.21 A *quilombo* today

Slavery was abolished in Brazil in 1888. Yet today remnants of the *quilombos* remain scattered throughout the country's dense rainforests and remote mountains. No one knows for sure how many *quilombos* there are. Estimates range from about 1100 to more than 3000. Their isolation has ensured the people's cultural survival. But it has also contributed to their extreme poverty. Today, the Brazilian government is working to resolve land issues and improve the quality of life for people living in the *quilombos*.

On the Coffee Plantations

Coffee was introduced as a crop in Brazil in the early 18th century. At first, coffee was produced only for local consumption. But when world coffee prices soared in the late 1820s and early 1830s, Brazil acted quickly to cash in on its ability to produce coffee as an export crop.

Like the sugar plantations, the coffee plantations needed a huge supply of cheap labour. Africa continued to be the source of enslaved workers. In the first half of the 19th century, Brazil imported 1.5 million Africans to work the coffee plantations. Like all those who went before them, the enslaved Africans endured a harsh life. Beatings, even murders, occurred on a regular basis. The plantation owners faced no consequences for their actions. The Africans who died were simply buried on the plantations. No one questioned how they met their fate.

The cruelty the plantation owners inflicted on the people they enslaved meant that the owners always had to be on their guard. The enslaved Africans embraced any opportunity to retaliate. Some rebelled openly and killed their owners. Others looked for more subtle ways to free themselves. They planted deadly scorpions in the plantation owners' boots. They ground up glass and mixed it into their owners' cornmeal. Constant fear was the price that Whites paid for a society based on violence and oppression.

FIGURE 6.22 Enslaved workers on a Brazilian coffee plantation

Slavery in Brazil produced a way of life that was similar to the large plantations of the American Deep South. Eventually, the owners of the coffee plantations became some of the richest people in Brazil.

XPRESSIONS

APOEIRA: THE DANGEROUS DANCE

ivity could not stifle the cultural creativity of the ved Africans. Throughout the colonies, they found to keep their art and culture alive. The unique game poeira (ka-pu'ej-re) first emerged in Brazil over 400 ago. This form of martial arts blends self-defence music, dance, acrobatics, and theatrics.

o one knows for sure how Capoeira got started in . Its roots, though, lie in West Africa. The game's ments contain elements of West African traditions, as the *sanga*, or sword dance, and the *n'golo*, or e of the zebras. Enslaved West Africans from places ngola and the Congo brought these traditions to and incorporated them in the Capoeira.

or years, Capoeiristas had to practise their art in t. Brazilian authorities banned the game because were afraid it promoted violent resistance. Police ed down hard on anyone who played it. As a result, e 1920s Capoeira had almost disappeared from the ts of Brazil.

n the 1930s, a famous Capoeirista, Mestre Bimba, inced the government that Capoeira was a valuable of Brazilian culture. The ban was lifted and Bimba ed a teaching academy. He wanted to make sure Capoeira would never be banned again. He created w form of the game called Capoeira Regional that ved a strict set of rules.

oday, two forms of Capoeira, Capoeira de Angola Capoeria Regional, are taught in schools and uni- ties throughout Brazil. Angola is a slower, more lated, and expressive game. Regional is faster and aggressive. Since the 1970s, both forms of Capoeira gained popularity around the world, including here anada. There are academies across the country e Canadians of all cultures can learn the intricate f Capoeira.

d Out More

nline to find photographs and videos of the game ipoeira. After viewing the images, make a list of the and qualities you think are necessary to become a essful Capoeirista.

FIGURE 6.23
A game of Capoeira

Some people think enslaved Africans created the Capoeira as part of a plan to gain their freedom. The elements of self-defence were disguised in traditional West African dances and rituals. The plantation owners never knew their captives were strengthening their bodies and minds to fight for their freedom!

FIGURE 6.24 A modern game of Capoeira Regional

Players form a *roda*, or circle. In the middle of the circle, two fighters play the *jogo*, or game. Around the circle, the other players play music, sing, chant, and clap. Capoeira looks like a beautiful dance. The players are in constant motion, combining a flurry of kicks with acrobatic flips. The music determines the nature of the fight. Slow music creates a slow and deliberate game. Fast music creates a true battle that only the most cunning players can win!

Slavery's Last Gasp

By the 1830s, the Brazilians were under pressure from the British to abolish slavery. In 1831, Brazil made it illegal to import enslaved Africans. But authorities did little to enforce the law. Still, the Brazilians knew that the trade in African peoples was about to end. They took advantage of the time they had left to increase the number of enslaved Africans they imported. But as British ships from the anti-slavery squadron began capturing their ships at sea, the Brazilian government was forced to ban the trade in 1850. Even so, slavery continued in Brazil as more than 2 million Africans remained in bondage.

Brazil maintained slavery longer than any other colony or country. Faced with mounting international pressure, however, Brazil finally phased out the oppressive practice. In 1871, the Brazilian government passed a law that freed all children born to enslaved Blacks. Then in May 1888, Brazil finally liberated all remaining enslaved Blacks.

FIGURE 6.25
The many faces of Brazil

Brazilian society today is a mixture of vitality, diversity, and creativity The blending of multiple cultures has created a unique and vibrant society.

How would you compare this with Canadian society?

The Emergence of a Multicultural Society

Freedom did little to improve the economic lives of Blacks in Brazil. The coffee planters refused to hire them as paid workers. Instead, they hired European immigrants from Italy. At the same time, Germans and Poles came to Brazil to farm. In the early 20th century, Brazil's racial mix became even more diverse with the arrival of Japanese and Middle Eastern immigrants.

In time, all of these groups intermingled and intermarried. This created a population of many different degrees of colour and physical characteristics. Today, 85 percent of Brazilians have some African ancestry. Yet discrimination still exists in Brazilian society. It is a subtle discrimination, hidden behind unwritten rules and unspoken attitudes. The darkness of people's skin still determines where they stand in the social order.

REVIEW AND REFLECT

Use a Venn diagram to compare and contrast slavery in the plantations of the American South, the Caribbean, and Brazil.

IDEAS

MIXED-RACE IDENTITIES

As you discovered in Chapter 1, science has proven that the idea the world is divided into a handful of different races is false. But even though science may not recognize race, society does. The term *race* continues to be used to classify and categorize people by their physical characteristics, particularly the colour of their skin.

Today, Canada is a country in which people of many different backgrounds live together. As a result, cultural and racial lines are becoming blurred as the number of mixed marriages increases, producing children of mixed race. These children cannot fit neatly into a single classification. Many embrace both sides of their heritage. Others are drawn to one heritage over another. As people of mixed heritage explore their own identities, they challenge our ideas about the Canadian identity.

Racial identity is about how you see yourself, about how you construct a sense of belonging, community, awareness, and allegiance.

Lawrence Hill, *Black Berry, Sweet Juice: On Being Black and White in Canada*, Toronto: HarperCollins, 2001

Until 1967, there were laws in the United States banning interracial marriages. Though Canada did not impose such legal barriers, Canadians were not always accepting of interracial marriages. But our views are changing. In 2007, 92 percent of Canadians approved of interracial marriages. According to Statistics Canada, mixed-race relationships are on the rise. The 2006 census showed that the number of married couples of mixed race has increased by more than a third since 2001. Experts predict that interracial marriages will double in the next 15 to 20 years as Canadian society becomes increasingly diverse.

One of the problems many people will face in the 21st century will be the question of identity. As our society becomes more diverse, it will be more difficult to answer the questions "Who am I? Where did I come from?"

I was raised in two different cultures. I have my father, who is African American, and my mom, who is Asian, specifically Thai. I had to understand and appreciate more than just one way of looking at things. . . . I was probably raised more in the Asian tradition because my father was working and my mom, who was at home more, was the disciplinarian.

Being Black is looked at differently. And in this country [the United States] I'm looked at as being Black. When I go to Thailand, I'm considered Thai. It's very interesting. . . . I don't know why it is, but it just is.

Tiger Woods, "Tiger Woods Actually Talking About Race," Mixed Media Watch, May 25, 2005

FIGURE 6.26
Tiger Woods, his daughter Sam Alexis, his mother Kultida, and his wife Elin

Golfing legend Tiger Woods is of mixed race. He raised a lot of controversy when he described himself as "Cablinasian." He used the term to reflect his Caucasian, Black, Native American, and Asian heritage. Many people thought he was denying his Black heritage.

How does the quotation from Tiger Woods reflect the conflict children of mixed heritage may feel?

Think It Through

Write your autobiography. Include the things you remember about your past and the traditions your family has. Think about how your past reflects your personal identity.

The Historian's Craft

THINKING CREATIVELY

Historians work systematically and critically as they research and write about history. They must use their imaginations to challenge existing thinking and to bring history alive.

BEYOND EXISTING THINKING

Sometimes historians cannot think creatively because they are trapped by the limitations of past thinking. But it is possible to break through these limitations by rejecting old ideas and traditional ways of thinking. In the past, historians focused on the role of men in shaping history. In this chapter, that thinking would have focused only on the role of enslaved Black men in the rebellions against slavery. Today, historians are more inclusive. They recognize the important contributions of women and minorities throughout history. And so, in this chapter, you learned not only about the role of enslaved Black men, you learned about the role of Black women in the uprisings against slavery, too.

Another way to challenge existing thinking is to speculate about what *might* have happened and to think about why it did not. For example, what if Bussa's Insurrection had succeeded? What impact might this have had on the abolition of slavery? Such speculation helps you gain a deeper understanding of why history unfolded the way it did.

Another way to move beyond existing thinking is to imagine impossible meetings. For example, what exchange might have taken place in a meeting between Sam Sharpe and Marcus Garvey? By re-enacting impossible historical meetings, you can learn a great deal about people and their perspectives. It might even lead to other creative ways to study history!

PUT YOURSELF IN THEIR SHOES

Another way to think creatively is to *empathize*—that is, to put yourself in the shoes of someone who was there. Empathy is not the same as *sympathy*. When you sympathize with someone, you imagine what a person felt like in a certain situation and you identify with that person. When you empathize, you use evidence to help you understand the motives and reasons behind a person's thoughts or actions. For example, you might put yourself in the shoes of an enslaved African who worked in a gang in Barbados.

When you use empathy, history comes alive and becomes more meaningful. But there are some pitfalls to watch out for. You must avoid fantasies about the past and make sure you are dealing with historical accuracy. Though you try to allow yourself to feel the person's experience, you have to keep in mind that you bring your own modern outlook to the exercise, too.

Here are some tips for empathizing with historical figures:

- Review your general knowledge of the period.
- Reconstruct the personal context of the figure—that is, his or her class, age, ethnicity, gender, and beliefs.
- Find the similarities and differences between your own experiences and those of the person with whom you are empathizing.
- Reflect on the person. Was he or she typical of the times? What things are universal in this person's experience? What things are unique?

TRY IT!

1. Choose one of the unsuccessful rebellions discussed in this chapter and ask yourself, "What if this uprising had succeeded?" Then re-examine why it did not succeed.
2. Choose one historical figure in this chapter and write an "in their shoes" report that empathizes with this person.

STUDY HALL

KNOWLEDGE & UNDERSTANDING

1. Why did slavery exist for so long before it was finally challenged and abolished?
2. In a graphic organizer, identify the ways in which enslaved Blacks maintained their identities through music, religion, and sports.
3. Create a political cartoon depicting slavery in Brazil.
4. To what extent did governments in the Caribbean and Latin America help freed Blacks integrate into their societies after the abolition of slavery?

THINKING

5. Imagine you are an enslaved Black worker on a plantation or mine in Brazil or the Caribbean. How might you plan a resistance movement or rebellion? Write a journal entry outlining your plans to work with others to change your conditions.
6. What responsibilities do you think governments have to eliminate racism and discrimination? Explain your point of view in an opinion paragraph.

APPLICATION & COMMUNICATION

7. Find examples of literature written by Black writers from the Caribbean. Select one work, read it, and write a review.
8. Choose one European colony in the Caribbean or Latin America and conduct further research into slavery there. Then prepare a visual display or an oral presentation to present your findings to the class.
9. Systemic racism prevented Blacks in Brazil from gaining economic advantage. To what extent do you think systemic racism exists in Canada today? Do some research to find information to support your ideas.
10. Write a song, rap, or poem against racism in today's society.

CHAPTER 7

The Fight for African Independence

KEY CONCEPTS

IN THIS CHAPTER, YOU WILL:

- examine African resistance to colonial rule between the First and Second World Wars
- discover how the Second World War contributed to the rise of African independence movements
- examine how Cold War rivalries influenced events in Africa
- explore the fight for independence in the African colonies
- learn about the Africans who led the fight for independence and the strategies they used
- look at the challenges faced by newly independent African states: despotism, ethnic violence, and poverty
- identify the goals and achievements of the Pan-African movement

A People's Story

European imperialism in Africa in the 19th century was short-lived. The Africans who led the fight for independence came of age during the time between the world wars, a period when colonial rule reached its high point. The decades following the Second World War saw dozens of former colonies become independent states. With few exceptions, they achieved independence by peaceful means. But independence was often followed by internal conflicts that caused suffering, despair, and death for millions of people. At the same time, economic development in these newly independent states was slow and the majority of Africans remained poor.

In this chapter, you will have the opportunity to think about the ways the following major players in Africa viewed events: colonial rulers, African leaders, White settlers, the African people, and Western leaders. As you read, think about why colonial powers decided to give up their colonies and if the reasons were the same from one colony to the next. Consider why so many newly independent African states experienced internal conflicts and economic hardship. Then reflect on the challenges those nations faced on the road to democracy.

1919	1921	1922	1923	1935	1942
Delegates attend first meeting of the Pan-African Congress	Simon Kimbangu establishes independent Christian Church in the Belgian Congo	Britain declares Egypt's independence but maintains an army there	African National Congress formed in South Africa	Italy invades Ethiopia	Hitler's Afrika Korp[s] fight the British at th[e] Battle of El Alamei[n]

Image Analysis

FIGURE 7.1 Advertising poster: *The Battle of Algiers*

This image is a poster from *The Battle of Algiers*, a film from the 1960s that depicts events from the war of independence between Algeria and France. The film caused controversy in France because it showed both sides committing and being victims of brutal acts. The colour red, which symbolizes freedom, is one of the colours used on the Algerian flag. The central scene is from the film, which was shot in black and white to make viewers feel like they were watching a documentary of actual events.

How might the following have reacted to the images on this poster: (a) colonial rulers in Africa (b) other Africans seeking independence from European rule?

rrender of German d Italian troops in North Africa	The Brazzaville Conference	Pan-African Federation established	African colonies become independent states	Suez Crisis	First Conference of Independent States	Founding of the Organization of African Unity	Apartheid ends in South Africa
1943	1944	1946	1951–1980	1956	1958	1963	1994

Colonial Rule During the Inter-War Period

During the two decades of peace following the First World War, European powers invested heavily in their African colonies. While colonial officials might have stated that their actions were improving the lives of Africans, the underlying purpose of African colonies was clear: to benefit Europeans by providing opportunities for settlement, investment, and trade. As you learned in Chapter 4, Europeans wanted to harvest Africa's natural resources, build or expand roads and railways, and use Africans as a cheap labour force. Africans were told that their traditions and practices were inferior and had to give way to a European system that was superior. This attitude and the actions that came with it led to resentment and growing resistance among Africans.

African Resistance to Colonial Rule

Africans responded to the unpopular policies of colonial governments by mounting increasing resistance to colonial rule between the First and Second World Wars. Opposition took different forms, but it did not yet involve large-scale efforts to achieve political independence. That would come later.

Rebellion: In the late 1920s, uprisings in French Equatorial Africa involving the Baya and other African peoples were put down at the cost of tens of thousands of lives.

Labour unrest: Despite colonial laws prohibiting labour unions, African miners and railway workers in several parts of Africa took part in a number of strikes to protest unfair taxes, low pay, and dangerous working conditions.

Growth of Islam: In West Africa, large numbers of Africans converted to Islam because it accepted traditional practices, such as polygamy, and offered education free of Christian missionary influence. Colonial officials generally left the Islamic population alone because they often used local Muslim rulers called *emirs* to enforce colonial rules and policies. The expansion of Islam during this time can be viewed partly as an expression of growing African frustration toward colonial rule.

FIGURE 7.2 Young men on their way to initiation school

In sub-Saharan Africa, young boys and girls went to initiation schools where they received religious and moral instruction. One of the reasons Africans were drawn to Islam was because it accepted these schools, which still exist today.

The Kimbanguist Movement: In 1921, Simon Kimbangu, a former Baptist missionary, founded an independent Christian Church in the Belgian Congo. His inspired preaching and reputation for performing miraculous cures drew thousands of followers. When the Kimbanguist movement took on a nationalistic, anti-European tone, Belgian authorities arrested him. Kimbangu was sentenced to 120 lashes and life imprisonment. Elsewhere in Africa, such as South Africa, independent Christian churches grew in influence.

Resistance to racial segregation in South Africa: As you learned in Chapter 4, racist policies were widespread in South Africa for most of the 20th century. South Africans resisted these policies in several ways. In 1912, representatives from several regional African associations met under the leadership of Pixley ka Isaka Seme and formed a national political organization called the South African Native National Congress. Renamed the African National Congress (ANC) in 1923, this group relied on peaceful means such as petitions and political gatherings to persuade the South African government to abandon racist laws designed to keep Blacks and other dark-skinned peoples separate from Whites. Despite, or perhaps because of, its cautious tactics, the South African government paid them no heed, but the ANC's efforts did prepare the way for more effective action, as you will discover later in this chapter.

FIGURE 7.3 Members of the South African Native National Congress

This group included a businessman, a clergyman, a newspaper owner, and a school principal. They went to England in 1914 to protest a law in South Africa called the *Native Land Act* (1913), which created reserves for Blacks and prohibited sales of land between Blacks and Whites.

During this period, South African Blacks also resisted racist policies by holding rallies, going on strike, and forming unions such as the Industrial and Commercial Workers Union. The police used violent tactics to break up rallies and strikes and thousands of workers were fired for participating in protests or job actions.

PAN-AFRICANISM AND ANTI-COLONIALISM

Pan-Africanism is the belief that Africans possess a common identity and should work together to achieve common goals. In 1900, Henry Sylvester Williams, a lawyer from Trinidad, organized the first Pan-African Congress. It was held in London, England. Those who attended praised the accomplishments of African civilization. They spoke about the need to uphold and protect African dignity. They demanded that Africans have access to good education.

Other meetings followed. The renowned African-American scholar W.E.B. Du Bois organized four congresses: in Paris (1919); in London, Paris, and Brussels (1921); in London and Lisbon (1923); and in New York (1927). The attendees were often sponsored by labour organizations. Their demands included self-government for Africans, an end to White minority rule, the economic development of Africa for the benefit of Africans, and an end to lynch law in the United States.

FIGURE 7.4 Attendees of the 1921 Pan-African Congress in Brussels, Belgium

People from Africa, the Caribbean, Europe, and the United States attended these meetings. Notice that Whites were among those who attended.

Why do you think Brussels, London, and Paris were chosen as meeting places in 1921?

REVIEW AND REFLECT

1. What factors led to the growth of Islam in some parts of Africa?
2. Why do you think the initial tactics used by the African National Congress to resist apartheid were ineffective?
3. Did the Pan-African Congresses focus only on problems facing Blacks in Africa? Explain.

Africa in the Second World War

Italy's invasion of the independent African state of Ethiopia in 1935 marked the failure of international collective security pledged by the League of Nations. The invasion set the stage for the Second World War. This war was to have a lasting effect on Africa, opening the door to nationalist struggles for independence in the European colonies.

The Invasion of Ethiopia

Italy's invasion of Ethiopia, ordered by the **dictator** Benito Mussolini in 1935, was the latest phase of an Italian effort to create a colonial empire in North Africa. This new attack was launched from the Italian colonies of Eritrea and Somaliland. Italian forces soon captured most of the country and Ethiopia's ruler, Emperor Haile Selassie, fled into exile. In June 1936, Selassie appealed to his fellow members in the League of Nations for direct military action to counter the Italian attack, but received no response.

dictator
a leader who holds absolute power over a people

FIGURE 7.5 Emperor Haile Selassie addressing the League of Nations, June 6, 1936

During his speech, Haile Selassie warned that other countries "may suffer the same fate as Ethiopia."

Why do you think countries like Great Britain and France did not immediately intervene against Italy?

Finally, in 1940, after Italy declared war against Britain, the British acted to stop Italian aggression in North Africa. They organized a large army made up of colonial troops from Nigeria, the Gold Coast, and Sierra Leone, and volunteer forces from Kenya, Rhodesia, and South Africa. By May 1941, Italian forces had been defeated in Ethiopia, and were on the run in Libya. The situation in Libya changed dramatically in early 1941 after Adolf Hitler, dictator of Germany, ordered the Afrika Korps to North Africa to assist the Italians. This force was commanded by the German general Erwin Rommel.

The Battle for North Africa

During 1942, North Africa was witness to two major military campaigns waged over vast distances. First, Rommel's Afrika Korps advanced east from Tripoli in Libya into Egypt, falling just short of its objective, the Suez Canal. Its capture would have cut Britain off from its supply line to the Middle East and Asia. Then, at the Battle of El Alamein in October, British forces under General Montgomery counterattacked and began advancing west. In 1943, in Tunisia, the British met up with American forces advancing east from Morocco and Algeria, and **Free French forces** advancing north from Chad. In May 1943, all German and Italian troops remaining in Africa surrendered. The fight for North Africa left much of the region devastated. War left towns and villages in ruins and thousands of civilians dead or homeless.

Free French forces
French resistance soldiers who continued the war against Germany following the fall of France in 1940

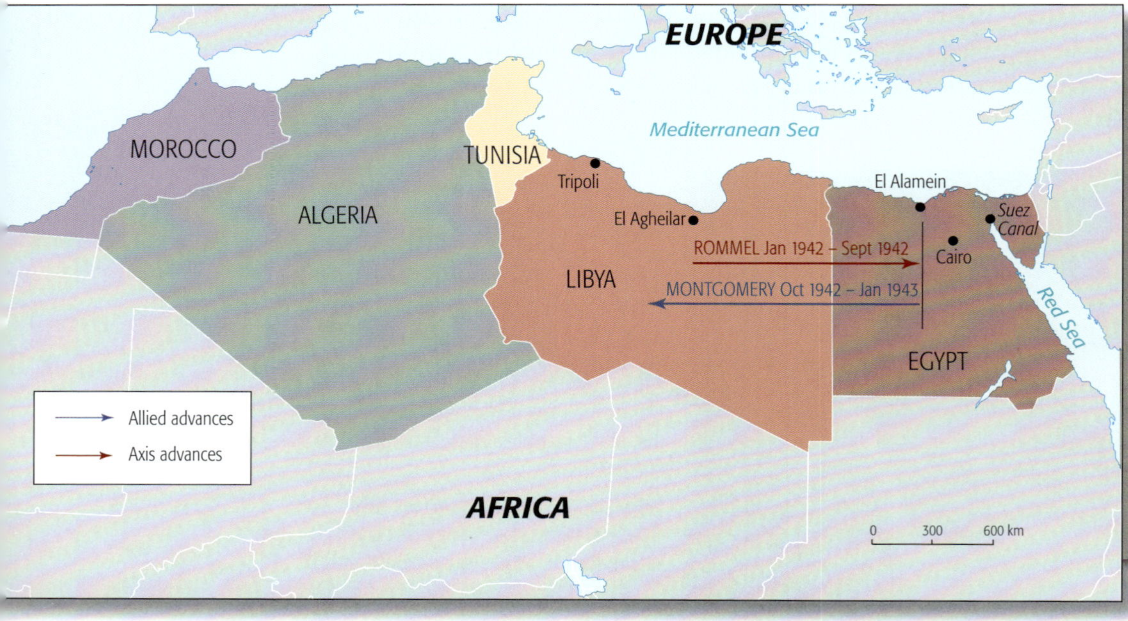

FIGURE 7.6 Major North Africa military campaigns, 1941–42

The Axis forces (Italy and Germany) wanted to take control of countries in North Africa.

Why was it important for the Allied forces (which included Britain, France, and the United States) to defend these countries?

FIGURE 7.7 General Rommel (left), commander of the Afrika Korps

Rommel's victories in Africa made him famous around the world and earned him the title of "The Desert Fox." Even those who fought against him recognized the German general as a great military strategist.

Impact of the War

How did the war affect Africa generally? In this section, you will examine two areas: battles fought on African soil, including the contributions of African troops, and economic development.

BATTLES

Just as in the First World War, African soldiers found themselves fighting battles inside and outside Africa to protect the interests of European imperial powers. African troops fought and died in Ethiopia and in North Africa. They fought and died defending France. They took part in the Allied invasion of Sicily and Italy in 1943. And they joined in the fight against the Japanese in Burma and other areas of Southeast Asia. In all, 200 000 African soldiers fought with British and French forces during the Second World War.

FIGURE 7.8 Sengalese soldiers land in sourthern France, 1944

While the British tended to rely on volunteers, the French favoured **conscription** to meet troop demands.

conscription
required service in the armed forces

ECONOMIC DEVELOPMENT

During the war, demand for Africa's traditional exports such as gold, tin, copper, palm oil, groundnuts, and cotton increased. When the rubber plantations of southeast Asia fell into Japanese hands, there was a revival of the rubber industry in the Congo. South Africa, in particular, witnessed a rapid expansion in manufacturing clothing, chemicals, and machinery. To assist economic growth, colonial governments invested heavily in new **infrastructure**, particularly airfields and port facilities. They promoted exports and set up systems of price controls to keep prices low. This meant that despite strong economic growth, most African farmers and farm labourers continued to struggle financially. Also, while employment opportunities increased in Africa's towns and cities, so many Africans sought work there that unemployment remained high and wages stayed low.

infrastructure
a state's physical assets such as roads, bridges, dams, power grids, and pipelines

REVIEW AND REFLECT

1. Describe how the League of Nations failed Ethiopia.
2. In a graphic organizer, show the ways that Africans contributed to the war effort.
3. Why were many African farmers and labourers continuing to struggle despite the economic growth during the Second World War?

Aftermath

The Second World War altered the way Africans viewed themselves and the colonial system in Africa. The war also produced major shifts in the distribution of global power. These changes were to have a strong effect on the course of events in Africa in the postwar period.

A New Consciousness

Africans, especially the educated elite, were generally knowledgeable about the events of the war. Their ideas and attitudes about the conflict were influenced by wartime **propaganda** channelled through radio broadcasts, film, and official publications, as well as by stories and editorials published in the growing number of African-owned newspapers. Africans began voicing their complaints about wartime measures placed on them by colonial officials. Tales of the exploits of African troops filled them with pride. At

propaganda
information spread to persuade people to adopt an attitude, accept something as fact, or change their behaviour in a particular way

the same time, the defeats of the British and French armies in the early stages of the war undermined the myth of European superiority and invincibility.

Many educated Africans were inspired by the idea of **national self-determination**. This was one of the founding principles of the League of Nations. League members accepted that colonial peoples had the right to form independent states but believed that they were not ready for this. The concept of self-determination was evident in the text of the Atlantic Charter, a statement of war aims declared by Prime Minister Winston Churchill of Great Britain and President Franklin Roosevelt of the United States in August 1941. The third clause of the Charter drew special attention:

national self-determination the right of a people of a defined territory to choose political independence

> [The President of the United States of America and the Prime Minister, Mr. Churchill, representing His Majesty's Government in the United Kingdom] respect the rights of all peoples to choose the form of government under which they will live; and they wish to see sovereign rights and self government restored to those who have been forcibly deprived of them.
>
> Atlantic Charter, August 1941

Churchill and Roosevelt were not thinking about African colonies when they drafted this statement, but by war's end, many Africans were demanding the same rights.

At the Fifth African Congress, held in Manchester, England in October 1945, 90 African delegates from England, the Caribbean, and Africa made the following declaration:

> We affirm the right of all colonial peoples to control their own destiny. All Colonies must be free from foreign imperialist control, whether political or economic.
>
> Declaration at the Fifth African Congress, October 1945

Four of those calling for the end of colonialism were future heads of state: Jomo Kenyatta of Kenya, Kwame Nkrumah of Ghana, Obafemi Awolowo of Nigeria, and Hastings Banda of Malawi. This event entrenched the leadership of the Pan-African movement in Africa. The economic situation also influenced the new consciousness. Though there was unemployment among unskilled labourers, colonial authorities were faced with shortages of skilled workers at all levels and the heavy burden of the war effort. As a result, they began promoting Africans into higher positions that traditionally had been reserved for Whites. To win African support for the Allied cause, they promised government reforms that would move colonies toward self-government. But few were willing to entertain full independence for colonies in the foreseeable future. They wanted to maintain Europe's economic domination of Africa. White settlers, for their part, were demanding more power so that they could keep the African majority in check.

IDEAS

BLACK HAIR

Sometimes I've wanted to get rid of the kink in my hair, and other times I've loved it and felt glad it was there.

Trey Anthony, playwright of *Da Kink in My Hair*

The new consciousness of Black people in the colonized nations of Africa and in North America was reflected in the way that Black people, especially Black women, styled their hair. Hair styles were a symbol of the struggle to create their own standards in a world dominated by European politics and Eurocentric notions of beauty. The styling of hair has always had an important social purpose in Africa. In the early 15th century the hairstyles of African peoples such as the Yoruba might signal their status in the community, age, marital status, religion, gender, or wealth. As well, African hairstyles have shown tremendous diversity in appearance and technique. In the late 1400s, European explorers observed that the hairstyles of Africans along the western coast of the continent included braids and patterns shaved into the scalp. African hairstyles also included the use of sinew, human hair, or vegetable fibre extensions to lengthen the hair. The people of the Ivory Coast would rub their hair with palm oil and

FIGURE 7.9 Senegalese women with beads in hair, 1900

African hairstyles included any combination of shells, flowers, beads, or strips of material woven into the hair.

charcoal to keep it black and to make it grow. Creating these hairstyles could take anywhere from several hours to several days. This represented important bonding time, especially for women.

When Africans were enslaved, their heads were often shaved by Whites who realized the importance of hair to their culture. Hairstyles of enslaved people were usually related to the work they did. Women who worked in the field wore head rags whereas men kept their hair short using animal shears. Those who worked closely with White people usually styled their hair more like White Europeans. This often meant straightening their hair.

Hair straightening has meant many things to the Black community. Straighter hair was associated with free-person status during the period of slavery. Later, Black women who were subjected to European beauty and fashion felt that straightening their hair was about being "modern." In 1905, Madame C.J. Walker invented a hair softener that helped Black women and men to straighten their hair more easily. This new product created jobs for Black Americans in the hairstyling industry who saw hair straightening as a way to revive their self-esteem. On the other hand, Black intellectuals like W.E.B. Du Bois, Booker T. Washington, and Marcus Garvey spoke out against hair straightening at the time because they felt that it was an act of shame and self-hatred. During the 1960s and '70s, the Black Power movement was concerned about the damaging psychological effects that European beauty standards had on Black women. Large Afros and natural hairstyles became more popular than ever, for both men and women who felt proud of their African heritage and who wanted to resist European standards of beauty.

More recently, scholars and women have argued that hair straightening is not an act of shame, but simply a way for Black women to try a new look or to present themselves for employment. At the same time, more Black women and men in the diaspora are also wearing Afros, braids, dreadlocks, and knots as hairstyles that express their beauty, boldness, rebellion, self-confidence, and spiritual consciousness.

Think It Through

In your own words, explain how hair styling has reflected the struggle for independence for Black people.

FIGURE 7.10 A variety of Black hairstyles

The variety of Black hairstyles reflects the variety of reasons that people choose them. These reasons may range from expressing pride in their heritage to expressing a personal sense of style.

BRAZZAVILLE CONFERENCE

In 1944, General Charles de Gaulle, leader of the Free French forces following the defeat and occupation of France by Germany in 1940, attended a conference in Brazzaville, the capital of French Equatorial Africa. De Gaulle recognized that France needed to improve its relations with its colonies in order to preserve the French colonial system. No African delegates attended the conference. The official declaration made at the end of the conference stated that:

- France's colonial empire would remain united
- a measure of local self-government would be established in each colony
- Africans who became citizens of French colonies would have the same rights as French citizens, including the right to vote in French parliamentary elections
- the indigenous populations would have the right to employment in public service positions in the colonies.

No mention was made of granting independence to the colonies. De Gaulle's goal was to keep France's African colonies part of a "Greater France." Africans would achieve their independence by becoming full citizens of this political community. De Gaulle's dream ran aground on the rocks of Africans' desire for self-determination.

FIGURE 7.11 General Charles de Gaulle at Brazzaville, 1943

De Gaulle's call for an improved relationship between France and its African colonies failed to satisfy the demands of African nationalists. **Why do you think this was?**

Shifts in Global Power

At the beginning of the war, several major powers dominated world politics—almost all were to be found in Europe. However, as a result of the terrible cost and destruction of the war, Europe lost its dominance. Two superpowers emerged that would control world affairs for the next several decades: the United States and the Soviet Union. These two nations had no colonies in Africa. Their main interest was to counter the threat each posed to the other. They began to compete for control and influence in all parts of the world, in a contest that became known as the Cold War. In Africa, Cold War strategy included efforts to develop close ties with newly independent former colonies in Africa and Asia.

THE SUEZ CANAL

The results of the shift in global power were clearly demonstrated in Egypt, one of the first African states to achieve independence. Before the Second World War, Britain's interest in Egypt stemmed mainly from the Suez Canal, which passed through its territory. In 1922, in the face of growing unrest in Egypt, Britain declared Egypt to be a self-governing constitutional monarchy headed by a sultan. In 1952, a military coup forced the ruling sultan to give up his power, but it wasn't until 1953 that Egypt became fully independent, under the leadership of socialist-leaning president General Gamal Abdul Nasser.

FIGURE 7.12 Egypt and the Suez Canal

Before 1956, the Suez Canal was owned by private European shareholders. It provided the British and French with a vital trade route to their colonies in East Africa and Asia.

Examine the map and suggest how the trade route would be altered if these nations could no longer access the Suez Canal.

nationalizing
transferring the ownership and control of a private business or property to the government

In 1956, Nasser enraged Britain and France by **nationalizing** the Suez Canal. British and French military forces seized the Canal Zone, while Israeli armies invaded and occupied the Sinai Peninsula, the area lying east of the canal. The United States and the Soviet Union condemned the seizure of the canal but could not agree on what action to take. The Soviet Union saw an opportunity to win friends among African anti-colonialists and threatened to intervene on Nasser's side. The United States, which was allied with Britain and France, feared that such an action might draw it into a direct military confrontation with the Soviets. That could trigger a third world war. President Dwight D. Eisenhower was furious with the British and French for not consulting him before acting.

In the end, Canadian diplomat Lester B. Pearson (later to be prime minister of Canada) proposed the idea of forming a United Nations peacekeeping force to occupy the Canal Zone while talks were held to find a peaceful solution. The United Nations accepted this plan and it was put into effect. The Suez Crisis was the first indication that Cold War rivalry between the United States and the Soviet Union could influence events in Africa.

FIGURE 7.13 Egyptian ships block the Suez Canal

Nasser deliberately blocked the entrance to the Suez Canal by ordering ships to be sunk there.

Why do you think he took this action?

REVIEW AND REFLECT

1. Why do you think that the Brazzaville Conference was not attended by any African delegates?
2. What was the impact of the Cold War on the events surrounding the Suez Canal?

African Independence

As you read earlier, Africa's population is made of numerous distinct groups divided by language, customs, religion, and historical experience. Until the 1900s, most people living on the African continent did not think of themselves as African, or even as belonging to a particular people.

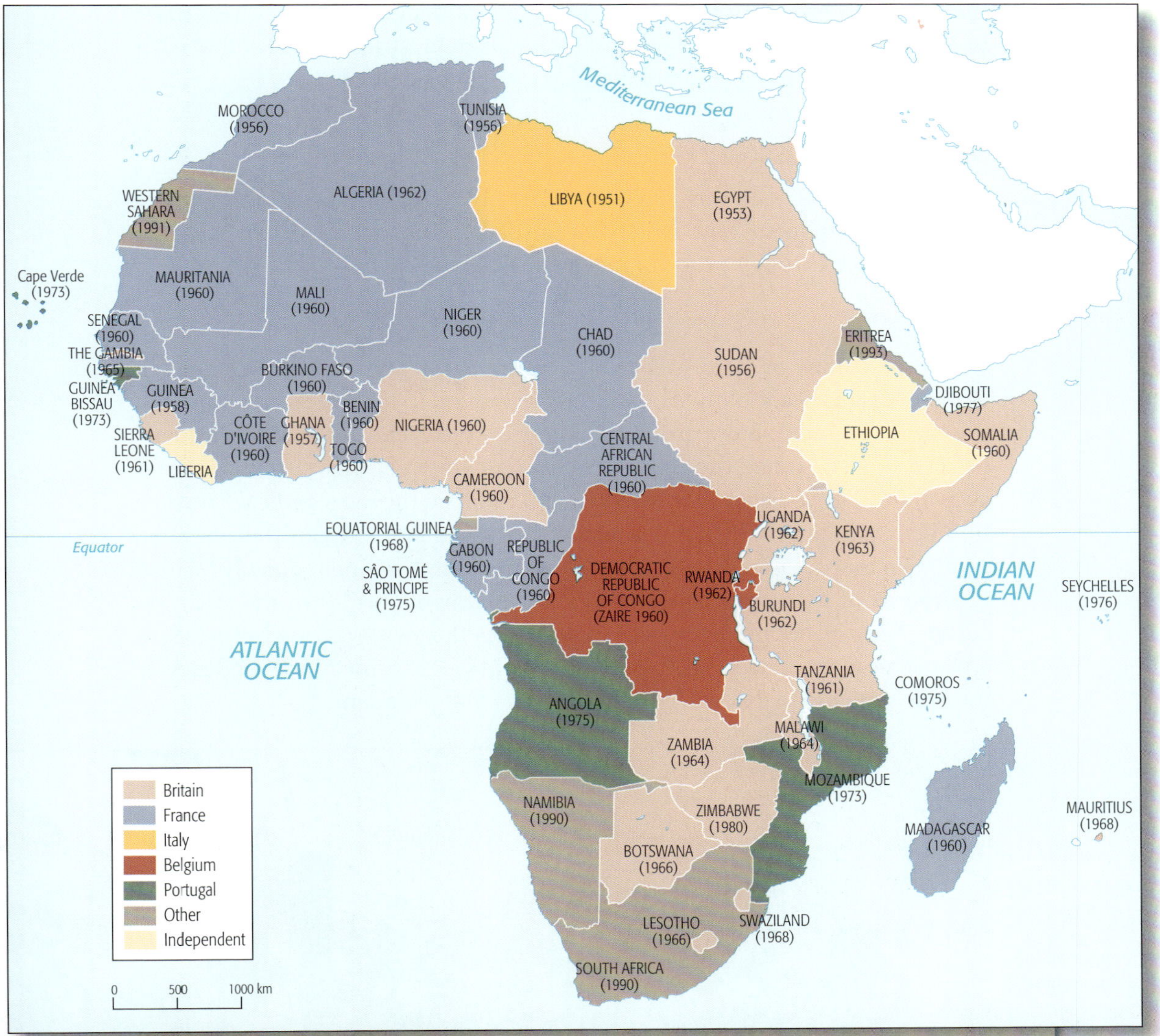

FIGURE 7.14 Africa after independence

This map shows the countries of Africa and their dates of independence from the colonial powers identified in the legend.

Compare this map to the one shown on page 120 in Chapter 4. Identify five differences between these two maps.

Africans identified themselves with their family, clan, or village. The one exception was religion, which blurred all divisions. Nationalist African leaders recognized that they could defeat European colonialism by uniting fellow Africans in the cause of national independence. The key was to foster a sense of unity and unique African national identity in each of the colonies. In November 1942, Winston Churchill, Britain's wartime prime minister, had said: "I have not become the King's first minister to preside over the **liquidation** of the British Empire." However the granting of independence to British India in August 1947, and the rising tide of nationalism in Africa, signalled that African demands for independence could no longer be denied.

liquidation
the taking apart of a business or a political organization

Non-Violent Resistance

African independence was achieved relatively peacefully in colonies where European settlement had made few inroads. One country that achieved independence through peaceful means was Ghana.

GHANA

It was the colony of Gold Coast that led the move toward independence in British West Africa. Colonial officials there wanted to take a gradual approach to self-government, but a group of Gold Coast lawyers and business leaders, formed in 1947, called the United Gold Coast Convention, pushed for faster action. In 1948, socialist Kwame Nkrumah founded the more radical Convention People's Party (CPP). A nationalist, but also a Pan-Africanist, he began a campaign to win immediate independence. A mass movement quickly formed in support of Nkrumah, and the CPP won clear majorities in the next two colony-wide elections. Nkrumah worked together with colonial officials to advance independence. Finally, in 1957, Gold Coast gained independence as the new state of Ghana, with Nkrumah as its first president.

FIGURE 7.15 Ghanaians celebrate 50th anniversary of independence, 2007

The star in the centre of the Ghanaian flag represents the country's freedom from colonialism while the colour red represents those who died or worked for independence. The other colours represent the country's minerals (gold) and vegetation (green).

ORIGINALS

KWAME NKRUMAH (1909–1972)

Kwame Nkrumah was born in 1909 in Nkroful, Gold Coast (now Ghana), and worked as an elementary school teacher before moving to the United States to study at Lincoln University in 1935. He spent ten years in the United States, where he was exposed to the ideas of Marcus Garvey and became heavily involved in the Pan-African movement, which was demanding freedom and independence for the colonies. Nkrumah left the United States for England where he helped organize the Fifth Pan-African Congress in Manchester in 1945.

In 1947, Nkrumah made the decision to return to Gold Coast to become secretary general of the United Gold Coast Convention (UGCC), a newly founded political party seeking independence through constitutional means. The UGCC was led by moderate intellectuals seeking independence "within the shortest possible time." After roughly 18 months, Nkrumah was expelled from the UGCC for being too radical. He formed his own party in 1949, which became the first mass political movement in Black Africa. The slogan of the Convention People's Party (CPP) was "Self-Government Now."

In 1950, Nkrumah began his "positive action campaign" designed to break the back of colonial order through widespread strikes and non-violent resistance. As a result of the campaign, Nkrumah was sentenced to three years in prison, which built up his hero status by turning him into a **martyr**. The following year, the CPP and Nkrumah swept Gold Coast's first general election. Nkrumah was released from prison and became the country's first prime minister in 1952. Five years later, Gold Coast won full independence as the Republic of Ghana. As Ghanaians celebrated their independence, Kwame Nkrumah addressed the crowd.

> We are going to see that we create our own African personality and identity. We again rededicate ourselves in the struggle to emancipate other countries in Africa; for our liberation is meaningless unless it is linked up with the total liberation of the African continent.
>
> Kwame Nkrumah, 1952

Within ten years, almost all African states were free from colonial rule. However, Nkrumah's long-term vision for Africa was never realized. He wanted newly independent African nations to create a powerful "United States of Africa" so that the continent could free itself from the West's economic stranglehold. "Divided, we are weak; united, Africa could become one of the greatest forces for good in the world," he explained in a 1961 speech. As time passed, Ghanaians became increasingly critical of their former hero as the economy spiralled downward and he began to restrict their freedoms. In 1964, Nkrumah banned opposition parties and declared himself president for life. Two years later, many Ghanaians celebrated after he was ousted by a military coup and forced into exile. He died in Romania in 1972 after a long battle with skin cancer.

FIGURE 7.16 Kwame Nkrumah

A political visionary, Nkrumah's views were formed by his experiences and studies in the United States, where he earned degrees in sociology, philosophy, and economics. He also studied theology and occasionally preached at Black churches in New York and Philadelphia.

Think It Through

How was Kwame Nkrumah important to the struggle for independence in Ghana? What brought about his eventual political downfall?

---

martyr
a person who suffers or dies for the sake of a moral principle or political cause

Violent Struggles

In colonies with large White settler populations, African demands for independence met strong, even violent, resistance. One of the countries that had a violent struggle for independence was Algeria.

ALGERIA

The Algerian War of Independence began in 1954 when Algerian insurgents belonging to the FLN (*Front de Libération Nationale*) launched an all-out war against the French. France was determined to hold on to Algeria to protect the rights of the two million French settlers who lived there, while the FLN was determined to make Algeria an independent, Islamic state. The fighting escalated as the French found themselves up against determined opponents, such as Ahmed Ben Bella, leader of the FLN. The fighting was ferocious and both sides committed terrible acts of violence. World opinion began to swing in favour of the Algerians. Ignoring the protests of the ***colons***, France agreed to negotiate Algeria's independence. Algeria became an independent nation in 1962.

colons
White colonists from France

FIGURE 7.17 Barricades in the streets of Algiers, capital of Algeria

In January 1960, Algerian nationalist leaders and civilians protested against French authorities by raising barricades in Algiers.

What do you think compelled so many people to take part in this protest?

FIGURE 7.18 French troops prepare for action in Algiers

Over time, France committed more than half a million troops to the struggle to hold on to Algieria. Despite impressive military victories, they failed to win the hearts and minds of native Algerians.

REVIEW AND REFLECT

1. What were the challenges facing Africans determined to end European colonialism?
2. Create a T-chart with the headings Ghana and Algeria to compare the ways Africans struggled for independence in these countries.

Politics in the Post-Colonial Period

The African leaders who ended European colonial rule were faced with a tough question: what should replace it? A few wanted Africans to unite politically and economically. By far the majority of African leaders wanted independent African states that retained colonial borders. Many of the features of political life that were evident in the post-colonial period could be traced to the legacy of colonial rule.

One-Party Rule

In preparation for independence, colonial authorities set up democratic, multi-party systems of government. The African political parties that formed tended to organize themselves by regional, religious, or ethnic interests rather than according to ideas about what *national* government policy should be. This development resulted from colonial boundaries that were drawn with little consideration for the needs of Africans. Colonial populations were deeply divided by language and culture. This produced distrust and political instability.

In response, most African countries soon became one-party states ruled by nationalist leaders who argued that one-party rule was necessary to maintain peace and economic progress. These leaders often abused their power. Government corruption spread and political opponents of those in power ended up dead, in prison, or in exile. However, there were a number of African states such as Tanzania where one-party rule functioned quite well for a time.

TANZANIA

Tanzania was formed when Tanganyika, under Julius Nyerere, took the lead in British East Africa in the fight for independence. A socialist and political moderate, the charismatic Nyerere had the advantage of being fluent in Kiswahili, the common language spoken in Tanganyika. This allowed him to foster a strong sense of unity and national identity among the ethnically diverse peoples of Tanganyika.

FIGURE 7.19 Prince Philip of Great Britain and Julius Nyerere

Julius Nyerere believed that "Violence is unnecessary and costly. Peace is the only way."

As you read on, consider how his actions reflected his words.

In 1954, Nyerere brought Tanganyikan nationalists together under the banner of TANU, the Tanganyika Africa National Union. Under his skillful leadership, TANU was able to attract support from the small community of White settlers. In 1961, Tanganyika became an independent republic under a non-racial constitution that did not give special rights to the Asian and White minorities. This was done over the objections of British colonial officials, who had been pressing for special status for these groups.

Three years after independence, Zanzibar, an island-state lying just off the coast of Africa, merged with Tanganyika to form Tanzania. Nyerere served as Tanzania's president from 1964 to 1985. He brought in a one-party system, arguing that it was necessary for the country's political and economic stability.

Military Regimes

Military coups became the most common way of changing national governments in Africa as the military seized power as an answer to government corruption and inefficiency. Military rule was often welcomed by the local population, and in several countries military leaders provided effective government. However, in others, they proved to be as corrupt and brutal as the civilian leaders they replaced. Generally, military leaders saw their rule as temporary and gave political authority back to civilian rulers when conditions seemed right. However, in several African countries military rule replaced civilian rule a number of times. Congo is just one of the African countries that has been ruled by a military regime.

DEMOCRATIC REPUBLIC OF THE CONGO

Following the Second World War, members of the small but influential Congolese middle class began pushing for independence. In 1959, in the face of a general breakdown in law and order, Belgium agreed to grant its colony full independence. However, it hoped to retain control by exercising power behind the scenes. In 1960, Patrice Lumumba, the socialist leader of the nationalist party, became prime minister of an independent Republic of Congo. Lumumba was a supporter of Pan-Africanism who wanted to establish a strong central government that enjoyed broad popular support.

In the weeks following independence, the political situation fell apart. In July 1960, elements of the Congolese army mutinied against their Belgian officers, and the diamond and copper-rich province of Katanga declared its independence. Belgium sent in paratroopers, supposedly to restore law and order, but in reality to protect Belgian business and financial interests. The United Nations Security Council followed up by organizing a peacekeeping force to help restore order. The UN force took control from the Belgian troops in all areas except Katanga. Katanga remained independent until early 1963, when the United Nations forced it to become part of the Congolese nation. On September 5, 1960, Lumumba was dismissed as prime minister and Joseph Mobutu, commander of the Congolese army, placed him under house arrest. He was executed by Congolese soldiers, allegedly in the presence of Belgian officers, on January 17, 1961.

In 1965, Mobutu seized power and established a one-party state. He renamed the country Zaire. Mobutu held power until 1997. The United States supported his regime—despite widespread corruption, serious violations of civil rights, and Mobutu's own looting of the national treasury—because he was viewed as an important Cold War ally in the fight against global communism. When he was overthrown in 1997, the country was renamed the Democratic Republic of the Congo (DRC).

In 1996, a year before Mobutu's departure, ethnic conflicts between two groups, the Tutsi and Hutu in Burundi and Rwanda, had spilled over into Zaire. A Tutsi army invaded the country to crush a Hutu army that had fled there. The invasion set off civil wars that killed more than three million Congolese and threatened the country's very survival. Uganda, Namibia, Angola, and Zimbabwe were all drawn into the conflict. A peace accord was reached in 2002, but as you will discover in Chapter 9, renewed violence in 2008 ignited the conflict once again.

FIGURE 7.20 General Sese Seko Mobutu

Mobutu used his position as commander in chief of the Congolese military to seize power. He ruled in the Democratic Republic of the Congo for more than 30 years.

Commitment to Existing Boundaries

Leaders of the newly independent African states were committed to preserving the boundaries set by Europe's imperial powers in the 19th century, no matter how artificial or arbitrary they were. They held to this in the face of regional forces that threatened to tear their countries apart. Efforts by ethnic minorities to break away were strongly resisted and sometimes resulted in destructive civil wars. This terrible scenario was played out in countries such as Nigeria.

NIGERIA

Nigeria was a colony with a large population divided by geography, religion, ethnicity, and political values. British colonial officials divided it into three districts. Progress toward independence was marked by sharp differences over how Nigeria should be governed, but in the end Nigerians opted for a federal system. This meant that, in addition to having a national government, Nigeria had three regional governments. The regions were divided along ethnic lines: the Northern Region (Hausa, Fulani), the Western Region (Yoruba), and the Eastern Region (Igbo). This arrangement proved to have serious flaws in the period after Nigeria became independent in 1960.

Nigeria's diversity bred disunity. In 1960, one of its territories—Southern Cameroon—voted to separate and join the Republic of Cameroon. A national election left the country politically divided, and in 1966 the military seized power. The military was to rule Nigeria on and off for the next 30 years. In 1967, the Eastern Region broke away, proclaiming itself the independent Republic of Biafra. The Nigerian army attacked Biafra, launching a terrible civil war that lasted 30 months.

FIGURE 7.21
Independence celebrations, Nigeria

Though most Nigerians celebrated their independence from colonial rule, in the years that followed Nigeria struggled to overcome political disunity.

EXPRESSIONS

20th-CENTURY AFRICAN LITERATURE

The experiences of Africans during the colonial and post-colonial era inspired literature from both Africa and the diaspora. In the early 1930s, African native (and future president of Senegal) Léopold Senghor, Guyanese native Léon-Gontran Damas, and Caribbean native Aimé Césaire met while living in France. They became the founders of a Black pride and literary movement called *Négritude*. They produced poems, essays, and other forms of literature that rejected colonization and expressed pride in African traditions. Though the movement had its critics, it exists to this day.

After the Second World War, African authors wrote about a variety of topics, including childhood memories, colonialism, independence of African nations, and apartheid. They also produced revised versions of African folktales. Authors such as Wolé Soyinka, Camara Laye, Ngugi wa Thiong'o, and Ben Okri wrote in English or French and became popular in North America and Europe. Ngugi wa Thiong'o and other writers also wrote in traditional African languages. After African nations became independent, some African writers wrote in exile, focusing on African dictatorships and on African dreams for the future.

One of the most well-known writers from Africa is Nigeria's Chinua Achebe. Born in 1930, Achebe has worked as a teacher, professor of English, and radio producer. His first novel, *Things Fall Apart*, was published in 1958. It describes pre-colonial life and the effects of colonialism in a traditional Ibo society. Through this novel and his other writing, Achebe strives to counteract the negative perceptions of African peoples—in the eyes of Europeans, and Africans themselves—displayed in English literary works such as Joseph Conrad's *Heart of Darkness*. Achebe described this "fundamental theme" as follows:

> **African people did not hear of culture for the first time from Europeans; that their societies were not mindless but frequently had a philosophy of great depth and value and beauty, that they had poetry and, above all, they had dignity. It is this dignity that African people all but lost during the colonial period, and it is this that they must now regain.**
>
> "The Role of the Writer in the New Nation," *Nigeria Magazine*, June 1964

Achebe's other novels include *A Man of the People*, which focuses on problems such as corruption in an African country after independence. He has also written essays and children's stories, and has received several literary honours.

FIGURE 7.22 Chinua Achebe poses with his novel *Things Fall Apart*, 1960

Things Fall Apart has been translated into more than 40 languages and is studied throughout the world. The book centres on the main character, Okonkwo, and how he reacts to colonialism. It also focuses on his relationship with the people in his village.

Despite the success of African male authors, there was a scarcity of published work by African women during colonial and early post-colonial times due to the state of girls' education and existing general sexism. Later in the century, a significant number of female writers emerged. Authors such as Juliana Makuchi and Tsitsi Dangarembga addressed the theme of gender roles in colonial and post-colonial African societies. Many female African writers continue to contribute to the massive body of African literature.

Contemporary African writers write about current events on the continent as well as African identity. African writers are important to Black culture because they provide a window into Africa. Furthermore, writers such as Chinua Achebe show the complexity of African societies, an understanding that is absent in many non-African texts related to African history and culture.

Think It Through

How does the work of writers such as Chinua Achebe help Africans and Europeans to recognize the depth of African culture?

Pan-African Efforts to End Colonialism

During the era of African independence movements, certain African leaders worked to unite Africans in a joint effort to end colonialism and give Africa a single, strong voice in world affairs. Beginning in April 1958, Ghanaian prime minister Kwame Nkrumah organized a series of conferences he hoped would lead to a united Africa. The first of these meetings, the Conference of Independent States, was held in Accra, Ghana. It was attended by delegates from Ghana, Ethiopia, Liberia, the United Arab Republic (a brief union of Egypt and Syria), Tunisia, Morocco, and Libya, as well as representatives of the National Liberation Front of Algeria.

This event paved the way for three future meetings (1958, 1960, and 1961) of a group called the All-African People's Conference. Representatives from 28 African colonies and independent states attended. They demanded immediate and unconditional independence for all African peoples, the end of racial discrimination, including apartheid, by White minorities in Africa, and resistance to **neo-colonialism**. Delegates also agreed that using violence to end colonial rule was justified in certain instances, such as "liquidating foreign military establishments."

neo-colonialism the continuation of foreign influence in the economic and political affairs of former colonies

In the end, these meetings did not accomplish Nkrumah's goal of a federation of African states united under a common government. Countries such as Ethiopia and Nigeria and many former French colonies strongly opposed political unification.

FIGURE 7.23 All-African People's Conference, 1958

Organizers hoped to move Africa toward political union.

What would be the advantages of such a union? What difficulties might prevent it?

THE ORGANIZATION OF AFRICAN UNITY

In 1963, Haile Selassie of Ethiopia helped engineer a compromise between countries that supported unification and those that did not, by hosting a conference in Addis Ababa. This meeting ended with the founding of the Organization of African Unity (OAU). The Charter of the OAU was signed by 32 independent African countries.

Under the three key principles of the Charter, member states would

- recognize the international borders existing in Africa at the time colonies gained independence
- follow a neutral position in world affairs to discourage neo-colonialism by external powers
- not interfere in the internal affairs of other member states

The non-interference rule had been criticized for allowing dictators such as Idi Amin of Uganda to trample on the rights of their people without fear of being punished by other African states. In January 1971, Colonel Idi Amin seized control of Uganda in a military coup. Amin remained in power for eight years, during which time he became famous for his ruthlessness. He fled into exile in 1979 after he commanded his army to attack Tanzanian territory, even though they faced certain defeat.

FIGURE 7.24 Idi Amin

Idi Amin expelled the Indian minority—80 000 people—that formed the backbone of Uganda's business and professional class. By one estimate, more than 300 000 Ugandans were killed during his rule.

Despite rulers like Idi Amin, however, the OAU did score a number of notable achievements. Its commitment to eliminating colonialism and neo-colonialism helped to complete the decolonization of Africa and end minority White rule in Angola, Mozambique, Zimbabwe, and South Africa. The Organization of African Unity functioned for 39 years before being replaced by the African Union in 2002. (See Chapter 9.)

South Africa: Road to Democratic Majority Rule

In 1931, the British Parliament passed the *Statute of Westminster*, granting independence to South Africa, Canada, and other self-governing dominions within the British Empire. But in South Africa, this landmark event did not translate into the rights of citizenship for all people. Instead, in 1948 it provided the White minority with the legal authority to adopt a racist policy known as apartheid.

REALITIES OF APARTHEID

In practice, apartheid meant that

- Four million Whites owned 87 percent of the land.
- Twenty million Blacks were stripped of their South African citizenship. They were assigned to homelands, or Bantustans, based on their tribal or ethnic origins. The plan was for these homelands to become self-governing states. Blacks were required by law to carry passes identifying their homeland.
- It was illegal for Blacks to marry or have sexual relations with Whites. Public places such as schools and parks were segregated.
- Blacks were taught in a separate school system that received far less government funding than the White system.
- Blacks could leave their homelands to work in White areas, but they were restricted to the lowest paying jobs. They were forbidden to join trade unions or practise skilled trades. Few could afford to bring their families with them. Their housing was substandard and their life expectancy was well below that of Whites.
- Blacks could not run for political office or even vote in elections.
- Government censorship of books and newspapers was widespread.
- Those who protested the apartheid system faced **house arrest**, imprisonment, torture, and death at the hands of the police and military.

house arrest
to be confined to one's home by court order

Apartheid's harsh measures provoked outrage and calls for action. A new generation of activists, such as Nelson Mandela and Oliver Tambo, persuaded the African National Congress to adopt more forceful tactics. In 1955, the ANC joined anti-apartheid groups of all nationalities to issue a "Freedom Charter." This document called for a unified South Africa under democratic majority rule.

> **South Africa belongs to all who live in it, Black and White, and . . . no government can justly claim authority unless it is based on the will of all the people.**
>
> **The rights of the people shall be the same, regardless of race, colour or sex.**
>
> African National Congress Freedom Charter, 1955

Soon after this, a dispute within the anti-apartheid movement led to the formation of the Pan-Africanist Congress. The PAC held to the Africanist view that only Blacks should participate in determining the destiny of South Africa.

Despite rejection of apartheid by the international community, and growing support for the ANC and other anti-apartheid groups, South African authorities continued their repressive measures, including banning membership in the ANC and PAC. Key events from the 1960s and 1970s are listed in the timeline below.

Police fire on a peaceful demonstration in Sharpeville. 69 people are killed and more than 180 are wounded.	ANC leaders are imprisoned for life after they are found guilty of authorizing armed attacks against the South African government.	Steven Biko, leader of the South African Student Organization (SASO), is murdered in prison.	Soweto uprising lasts for months and leaves hundreds dead.
1960	1963	1969	1976

FIGURE 7.25 South Africa timeline

Key events in the 1960s and 1970s included the Soweto uprising. These riots began when police fired on a peaceful demonstration at Soweto that included thousands of high school students.

The violence continued into the early 1980s. The Black townships of the eastern Cape descended into chaos as South African authorities turned Blacks against Blacks and used deadly force in an effort to end boycotts and demonstrations. The South African government established Black-run councils in the townships in an attempt to regain order, but these were attacked by Black militants as instruments of White oppression. Local security forces also encouraged Black migrant workers to attack the activists and their supporters. In 1986, the government placed the entire country under a state of emergency.

FIGURE 7.26 Anti-apartheid poster, 1977

Why do you think the image of a Black woman is used in this poster?

sanctions
penalties levelled against a government to punish it for breaking an international law or holding opposing principles

World opinion turned strongly against South Africa. **Sanctions** by international sports organizations barred South African athletes from participating in international tournaments and events such as the Olympics. Economic sanctions limited South Africa's access to strategic goods such as oil and weapons and hobbled its export trade. Cultural sanctions added to South Africa's isolation from the rest of the world.

In 1989, F.W. de Klerk became president of South Africa. A year into his term, de Klerk took the first steps toward ending apartheid by lifting the state of emergency, ending the ban on the ANC and other African nationalist parties, and freeing political leaders such as Nelson Mandela. Negotiations began on a new constitution that would enshrine racial equality and democratic majority rule. The apartheid system was dismantled. In April 1994, the ANC won a landslide victory in national elections held under the new constitution and Nelson Mandela was sworn in as president.

> We have fought for a democratic constitution since the 1880s. Ours has been a quest for a constitution freely adopted by the people of South Africa, reflecting their wishes and their aspirations. The struggle for democracy has never been a matter pursued by one race, class, religious community, or gender among South Africans. In honouring those who fought to see this day arrive, we honour the best sons and daughters of all our people. We can count amongst them Africans, Coloureds, Whites, Indians, Muslims, Christians, Hindus, Jews—all of them united by a common vision of a better life for the people of this country.

Nelson Mandela's inauguration address as President, Cape Town, May 9, 1994

FIGURE 7.27
Nelson Mandela

Nelson Mandela revisits the cell where he was confined for more than 25 years. He was one of the ANC leaders sentenced to life imprisonment in 1963. In 1993, he and de Klerk received the Nobel Peace Prize for their leadership in bringing about the end of apartheid. You will learn more about Nelson Mandela in Chapter 9.

With the end of apartheid in South Africa in 1994, the African continent was fully transformed. At the beginning of the 20th century, European imperial powers had held dominion over almost the entire continent. Now Africa was made up entirely of independent states. Independence restored the fundamental right of self-determination to Africans, but, as you will discover in Chapter 9, major challenges remained.

REVIEW AND REFLECT

1. Use a graphic organizer to compare the following three governments: Nyerere's one-party government; Congo's military regime; and Nigeria's federal government.
2. What was the impact of colonial rule in a newly independent Nigeria?
3. Why did the OAU feel that a neutral position in world affairs would discourage neo-colonialism by outside powers?
4. Why did President de Klerk decide to release Nelson Mandela and other African nationalist leaders from prison? Why Did Mandela recognize the contributions of all people who helped end apartheid?

The Historian's Craft

RESEARCHING AND ORGANIZING

In the first chapter, you read that the starting point for any research is curiosity about, and interest in, the topic. You also learned how to go a step further and develop an inquiry question or thesis. Once you develop your question or thesis, it is time to look for and record information that answers your inquiry question or supports your thesis.

RESEARCHING

When researching in libraries, look for up-to-date texts, journals, DVDs, and books produced by experts on the topic. When researching on the Internet, the sheer volume of material presents a challenge. Open access to the Internet means that anyone—expert or amateur—can prepare web pages. To identify accurate and reliable websites, ask yourself the following questions:

- Are the authors of the website identified? What qualifications do they have?
- Do the authors have a particular bias?
- Was the site created by a university, archive, or museum?
- Is it from a well-known online encyclopedia like Encarta or Britannica?

The information on a website is only as reliable as the individuals who create it. University, archive, museum, and commercial encyclopedia sites are prepared by experts, and their content is reviewed by editors.

RECORDING

As you research, record the author, title, and other bibliographical information of your sources. You need to reference your sources when you present your work.

Record your research findings. Make sure you note only the information that gives alternative answers to your inquiry question, or that relates to your thesis. Make note of important facts and dates that relate to your topic (see Historian's Craft, Chapter 5) and record the most effective evidence, including specific examples, statistics, and quotations. Quotations should be from historians who are experts on the topic and from people who played significant roles in the events.

ORGANIZING

Now it is time to organize your research findings. List the reasonable-alternative answers to your inquiry question and begin thinking about which alternatives best answer the question or support the thesis. Once you decide which answer you want to focus on, record the information that supports your thesis in chronological order or beginning with the strongest points. Organize the supporting evidence for your central idea so that you highlight the most persuasive and dramatic examples.

For major projects, you may find it valuable to organize your information under different fields of history: economic history, social history, cultural history, political history, military history, and diplomatic history. Taking the time to organize your findings as you do the research is an important step toward crafting an effective product.

TRY IT!

Choose one of the significant historical figures in this chapter (for example, Kwame Nkrumah, Julius Nyerere, Joseph Motubu). Locate and record five websites on the Internet that provide information about that person. Using the guidelines above, evaluate the websites for accuracy and reliability.

STUDY HALL

KNOWLEDGE & UNDERSTANDING

1. Do you believe the policies of the League of Nations supported anti-colonial movements? Explain.
2. To what degree did colonialism affect post-colonial governments? Document the ways that colonialism affected newly independent governmental policies.
3. Review all the information that you have read and studied on independence and democracy. In your opinion, how democratic were post-colonial African governments?

THINKING

4. Define apartheid in your own words. What reasons might the White minority have had for creating and enforcing apartheid laws?
5. Explain how the Cold War was a factor in European reluctance to grant independence to Africa.
6. Create a mind map starting with the heading "African post-colonial political trends."

APPLICATION & COMMUNICATION

7. Conduct research on the Organization of African Unity. What were some of the goals of the OAU? What obstacles did its members face in trying to implement their goals? Have these goals been successfully realized? How do these goals relate to the idea of Pan-Africanism?
8. Imagine you are the newly elected leader of a country that has just gained independence from colonialism. Write a brief, realistic speech to give to your people. Include the following topics:
   a. what the future holds for the country and its citizens
   b. promises for education, jobs, housing
   c. your expectations of the citizens
   d. the expected effects of the colonial heritage on your new country
9. Create a political poster that might have been displayed to encourage independence for an African country.
10. In a group of two or three students, research the events leading to independence, and the challenges following independence, in one of the following former European colonies:

    Britain: Kenya, Uganda, Sudan, Zimbabwe

    Belgium: Burundi, Rwanda

    Portugal: Angola, Mozambique

    Italy: Somalia, Eritrea

    Create an oral report presenting your findings to the class.

UNIT 4 Moving Forward

TABLE OF CONTENTS

Team Canada wins the 2003 World Hockey Championship

Anson Carter, who is of Barbadian heritage, scored the winning goal in overtime to give Team Canada its first win at the championship in five years.

CHAPTER 8

Black People in Canada Since the Second World War

KEY CONCEPTS

IN THIS CHAPTER, YOU WILL:

- compare and contrast Black communities in Canada and the impact of immigration
- examine the contributions and achievements of Black Canadians
- look at the traditions of Black churches as instruments for political, social, and educational leadership
- evaluate the concept of empowerment and investigate its impact
- demonstrate how community-based and grassroots organizations have developed over time
- analyze the challenges facing Black Canadians
- examine the concept of Africentricity
- analyze the portrayal of Black people in the media
- understand the role of Caribbean and African culture in Western culture

A People's Story

Black Canadians arrived in Canada at many different times. Some trace their roots here back hundreds of years to the days of the Black Loyalists. Others are in the process of gaining their Canadian citizenship. Since the Second World War, Black Canadians have come from many different places. Many came from the United States. During the 1950s, a few began coming from the Caribbean. Most Black Canadians have come to Canada in the last 40 years. At first, they came from the islands of the Caribbean. Then they began coming from the nations of Africa, too. Black immigrants have brought diverse backgrounds and histories with them. They have added a unique cultural dimension to Canada's social landscape.

In this chapter, you will have the opportunity to learn about the Black Canadian experiences in Canada since the Second World War. You will discover how Black Canadians fought for their civil and political rights. You will see how opening the doors of immigration changed the face of Canada. You will learn how different groups of Black immigrants have adapted to life in Canada and what challenges they face. As you read, think about the ways Canada has changed in the last 60 years and the roles that Black Canadians play in our society today. Then reflect on the ways in which Canada can become a more inclusive society.

1945	1955	1960	1962	1963	1967	
All-Black Brotherhood of Sleeping Car Porters formed	West Indian Domestic Scheme increases Caribbean immigration	*Bill of Rights Act* passed in Canada	Racial discrimination eliminated from immigration policy	Leonard Braithwaite first Black Canadian elected to provincial legislature	New immigration policy opens immigration from all countries	Cariba… found… in Toro…

Image Analysis

FIGURE 8.1 *Face of a Nation* by David Vasquez

David Vasquez is an artist of Dominican heritage now living in Toronto. His painting reflects his Caribbean background, infused with the African, Spanish, and native influences of the island.

What do you see in this image? What message does it convey to you?

rban Alliance Race Relations founded	February becomes Black History Month	Emergence of hip-hop culture	Lincoln Alexander becomes Ontario Lieutenant Governor	Jean Augustine becomes first Black female MP	Michaëlle Jean becomes first Black Governor General	First Africentric school opens in Toronto
1975	1976	1980s	1985	1993	2005	2009

Seeking Empowerment

In Chapter 5, you learned about the role Black Canadians played during the difficult years of the Second World War. Working alongside Whites in jobs across the country, hundreds of Black workers joined labour unions for the first time.

You also learned about the Black railway porters who worked on Canada's railways. After the war, the porters stood at the forefront of the fight for equal rights in Canada. They experienced the widespread racism in labour unions first-hand. They were barred from membership in the Order of Sleeping Car Conductors, a US-based union of White railway workers. So they took up their own cause.

In 1945, the Canadian branch of the US Brotherhood of Sleeping Car Porters (BSCP) organized the Black porters of the Canadian Pacific Railway (CPR) and the Northern Alberta Railway (NAR). In its first **collective agreement**, the union demanded—and received—higher wages, overtime and vacation pay, shorter working hours, and better working conditions. It was one of the greatest labour success stories in Canada in the first half of the 20th century.

collective agreement
a contract between labour and management for wages, benefits, and working conditions

I think the story of the porters is a story of the pain and the beauty of survival.

Clifton Ruggles, teacher, author, and artist, whose father was a sleeping car porter, in *Outsider Blues*, 1996

The BSCP extended its fight for equal rights beyond the railways. The union lobbied governments to ban discrimination in the workplace, housing, and public buildings. They went to court to fight job discrimination. In the 1960s, they won Black porters the right to move into other positions in Canada's railways.

FIGURE 8.2 Stanley G. Grizzle (1918–)

Stanley Grizzle was the son of Jamaican immigrants. His job as a porter led him to become a political activist in the BSCP and a leader in the fight for civil rights. Grizzle told his story in *My Name's Not George: The Story of the Brotherhood of Sleeping Car Porters in Canada*. The title refers to the practice of calling Black porters "George" regardless of their real names. "George" referred to George Pullman, the US inventor of the sleeping car. Calling the porters "George" was a degrading practice that had its roots in slavery, when enslaved Black people were named after their owners.

Throughout its struggle, the BSCP was supported by the Ladies' Auxiliary. The female relatives of Black porters raised funds for the union, collected dues, and organized meetings. A few Black women worked on the railways too, as maids, porters, and cleaners. But, like women in general in Canada in the middle of the 20th century, their interests were overshadowed by those of men.

The Road to Civil Rights

Despite the progress made by the Black porters, Blacks in Canada faced widespread racism and discrimination in the postwar years. In towns and cities across Canada, restaurants, bars, and movie theatres had separate sections for Black people. They were denied service in hotels, stores, barber shops, and other public facilities. In 1954, even the prime minister of Barbados, Grantly Adams, was denied a room in a Montreal hotel due to "regulations."

In the 1950s, however, new laws began to emerge that made discrimination illegal. The laws prevented anyone from denying services or work to any Canadian because of their race. In 1960, this quest for equality was achieved, at least in theory, with the passage of the *Bill of Rights Act*, which guaranteed equal rights for all Canadians. The Act committed the federal government to equality regardless of race, religion, colour, national origin, or gender. But provincial governments were not bound to enforce these rights and they were slow to take action to protect minorities.

The Global Rights Movement

In the 1960s, the fight for equality gained new momentum from the civil rights movement in the United States and the independence movements that were sweeping through European colonies in Africa and the Caribbean. The rights and interests of Black people all over the world emerged as a global issue. Black leaders in Canada joined their colleagues around the world in refusing to accept their status as second-class citizens. As Canada eased its immigration restrictions in the late 1960s, Black Canadians emerged as a powerful force for progress and change.

Community Activism

Many new organizations emerged to represent the interests of Black Canadians. Some were country-specific, such as the Jamaican-Canadian Association in Toronto and Kwacha House (taken from the nationalist slogan in Zambia, "Freedom Kwacha," meaning *a new dawn of freedom*) in Halifax. Other umbrella organizations, such as the Black Resources and Information Centre (BRIC), were formed to capture the diversity of the Black Canadian population. In 1978, Black activists Daniel Hill, Donna Hill, Wilson Brooks, and others co-founded the Ontario Black History Society, the first major public organization in Canada to focus on the history of Black Canadians. In 1983, the doors opened on the Black Cultural Centre outside Dartmouth, Nova Scotia, to give Black Canadians in the Maritimes the opportunity to explore their heritage in Canada and around the world.

In 1971, Black Olympian Harry Jerome was awarded the Order of Canada. In 1973, Kay Livingstone formed the first National Congress of Black Women. In 1975, the Urban Alliance on Race Relations was formed to fight discrimination on behalf of all racial communities.

Political Progress

Black Canadians made progress in the political arena, too. In 1963, Leonard Braithwaite became the first Black elected member of a provincial legislature, sitting as an MPP in the Ontario legislature. He helped amend the *Separate Schools Act* that ended segregation in Ontario schools. In 1968, Lincoln Alexander became the first Black Canadian to sit as an MP in the House of Commons. In 1985, he became the first Black Lieutenant Governor in Canada, holding that office in Ontario. In 1972, in British Columbia, Rosemary Brown became the first Black woman to be elected to a provincial legislature. In 1975, she ran for the leadership of the federal New Democratic Party (NDP) but lost on the fourth ballot. These political pioneers paved the way for Black Canadians to join the political process and take their place among Canada's political leaders.

FIGURE 8.3 Rosemary Brown (1930–2003)

Born in Jamaica, Rosemary Brown came to Canada in 1951. She studied at McGill University and the University of British Columbia before becoming a social worker. She was a tireless campaigner for equality for women and human rights. She also campaigned to eliminate sexism from textbooks and to prohibit discrimination based on gender or marital status. In 1996, Brown became an Officer of the Order of Canada.

REVIEW AND REFLECT

1. Describe the changes that the Brotherhood of Sleeping Car Porters was seeking.
2. Create a timeline documenting Black Canadian firsts in politics. Why are the contributions of Black Canadians important to our concepts of Canadian identity?

Black Canadians in Nova Scotia

The history of Blacks in Nova Scotia is long and deeply rooted. As you discovered in earlier chapters, Blacks have lived in the province since the days of the Loyalists. Later, these early settlers were joined by the Maroons from Jamaica and Black refugees from the United States during the War of 1812. Today, the descendants of these settlers form a distinct community in Nova Scotia that is unique in Black Canadian society. In this section, you have the opportunity to learn more about the Black community in Nova Scotia.

FIGURE 8.4 The Black Cultural Centre

To learn about the history of Black people in Nova Scotia, you can visit the Black Cultural Centre outside Dartmouth. The centre opened in 1983 to defend the culture and identity of the Black community. In addition to a museum and reference library, the centre offers educational workshops, lectures, theatrical productions, and concerts that reflect the province's Black heritage. The centre attracts visitors from around the world who are interested in exploring the Black history of Atlantic Canada.

FIGURE 8.5 Dr. Henry Bishop

Dr. Henry Bishop is the chief curator and director of the Black Cultural Centre as well as a noted author, artist, and African drummer. In 1996, he presented an original illustration to the Canadian embassy in Washington, DC entitled *Freedom Train to Canada* to commemorate the Underground Railroad. In 2000, Bishop became the first Black Nova Scotian to receive an honorary doctorate of fine arts from the Nova Scotia College of Art and Design.

Church and Religion

Church and religion have played an important role in Black communities in Nova Scotia. In the early days of settlement, Blacks were allowed to attend Anglican and Roman Catholic church services alongside Whites. But as the number of Black people attending these churches increased, Whites began to segregate them from their congregations. They forced the Blacks to sit in separate pews, in church balconies, and behind drawn curtains.

This systemic racism led Black people to break away from the established churches in the first half of the 19th century and form their own independent churches. Most were Baptist and Methodist, but they followed many other denominations too, including Anglicanism, Catholicism, and Pentecostalism. Blacks held positions of authority and leadership in their own churches. They were free to exchange their own ideas and express their own opinions.

Churches as institutions shaped Black culture, lifestyle, and values. They were the foundation of Black communities—safe places where people could interact with one another and offer mutual support in the fight for economic equality and social justice. The churches inspired people with stories of salvation and liberation and provided them with continuity from one generation to the next.

FIGURE 8.6
Cornwallis Street Baptist Church, Halifax

The African Baptist Church played a unique role in the development of Black communities in Nova Scotia. The first Baptist church, the Cornwallis Street Baptist Church in Halifax, was founded in 1832 by Reverend Richard Preston, a former enslaved Black. It was the founding church of the African United Baptist Association (AUBA). Today, the church remains a religious cornerstone for many people in Halifax's Black community.

THE IMPORTANCE OF SPIRITUALITY

For many Black people, faith is more than just a commitment to a religious institution. They embrace a deep and meaningful spirituality that connects them to a higher power. This spirituality has helped Black people cope with the racism, exploitation, and oppression they have experienced. Spirituality contributes to people's emotional and psychological well-being and serves as a buffer against racism.

RELIGION TODAY

Today, the church continues to play an important role in Black communities throughout Nova Scotia. Churches provide a forum for social activism where church members can speak out against injustice and inequality. Church leaders continue to speak on behalf of their communities with clear and strong voices as they work toward social progress and change.

Schools and Education

Nova Scotia has the longest history of Black education in Canada. Historically, Black schools were segregated from White schools. At White schools, students were taught advanced subjects such as geography, algebra, history, and grammar. At Black schools, though, students were taught only the basic skills of reading, writing, and arithmetic.

In 1954, after 150 years of segregation, and after a vigorous campaign by Black people demanding equal access to education, schools in Nova Scotia were integrated. But many schools in predominantly Black communities continued to have primarily Black students. They were taught a Eurocentric education, with no acknowledgement of their own culture or history. They learned little about the roles their ancestors had played in the history of Nova Scotia and Canada. The funding and services that schools in Black communities received were far less than what schools in other communities received. All these factors led to an inferior education, with the grades of many Black students falling below the grade averages of non-Blacks.

In 1968, a group of Black educators at Dalhousie University introduced a special education program aimed at high school dropouts in the Black community. The Transition Year Program offers a year-long training program to help Black and First Nations adults earn the qualifications for university.

FIGURE 8.7 The Regional Educators provincial spelling bee, Halifax, 2007

In 1969, the Black Educators Association (BEA) was formed to help Black communities develop strategies to gain equality in Nova Scotia's school system. The BEA sponsors spelling bees, education camps, and other events to promote education among Black youth. Eighty-eight Black Nova Scotian students took part in the 2007 spelling bee at Mount Saint Vincent University, including Brandon Skeete (left), Armond Fraser (centre), and Colton Smith.

After integration, racial tensions simmered in many schools in Nova Scotia. In 1989, these tensions finally boiled over at Cole Harbour High School in North Preston as racial slurs escalated into a physical confrontation between Black and White students. The faceoff sent racial tensions rippling throughout the community. The parents and students of North Preston launched their own political action group called the Preston Parents Student Association. They demanded an inquiry into the issue of racial discrimination in the school system and its impact on students.

The government refused to hold an inquiry. But racism in Nova Scotia schools became a high-profile media issue. A group of prominent Black educators, community leaders, and government members pressured the government to take action. In response, the Provincial Advisory Committee (which changed its name to the Black Learners Advisory Committee, or BLAC, in 1994) was formed in 1989.

The committee spent the next five years investigating the history and current status of Black education in Nova Scotia. In 1994, the committee's *Report on Education: Redressing Inequity—Empowering Black Learners* (commonly known as the *BLAC Report*) chronicled the crumbling state of Black education in the province. It stated that the struggle of Black Nova Scotians to obtain equality with other Nova Scotians in education, employment, and income was directly linked to being denied equal opportunities at school and in the workplace.

The *BLAC Report* outlined 46 recommendations to address racism in the Nova Scotia school system. It called on the province to invest more than $4 million in multiracial and anti-racist education policies and strategies.

PROVINCIAL GOVERNMENT INITIATIVES	◆ Council on African Canadian Education	– The Africentric Learning Institute to help Blacks build a positive identity and value their history and culture – The African Nova Scotian School Board Caucus to provide opportunities for Black representation on provincial school boards
	◆ African Canadian Services Division	– To develop, promote, and deliver programs, resources, and services to Black students
	◆ Representatives on	– Nova Scotia Museum Board – Nova Scotia Community College – Council on Higher Education – Apprenticeship Training Board – Nova Scotia Arts Council
SCHOOL BOARD INITIATIVES	◆ Race Relations Cross-Cultural Understanding/Human Rights	
	◆ Student Support Workers	
	◆ Monitoring Committees	
COMMUNITY INITIATIVES	◆ Black Educators Associations	
	◆ Regional Educators Programs	
	◆ Other community-based organization, including churches	

FIGURE 8.8 Black education initiatives in Nova Scotia

The Council on African Canadian Education oversees education initiatives at all levels in Nova Scotia.

BLACK EDUCATION INITIATIVES IN NOVA SCOTIA

One recommendation of the *BLAC Report* resulted in the creation, in 1996, of the African Canadian Services Division (ACSD) in Nova Scotia's Department of Education. ACSD promotes understanding of African Canadians and their history, heritage, culture, traditions, and contributions to society, recognizing their origins as Africans. It encompasses all levels of education, advising and guiding other divisions of the Public Schools Branch and the Department of Education of Nova Scotia about African Canadian education. ACSD also works with staff to address systemic racism and discrimination by helping to implement the Racial Equity Policy. It ensures that African Canadian students have greater access to postsecondary institutions. This involves financial support for students through a number of scholarships.

ACSD develops, promotes, and delivers programs, resources, and services for African Nova Scotian students. One of the services includes evaluating all public school program resources, emphasizing the inclusion of all races and cultures. Two courses have been developed: African Canadian Studies 11 and English 12: African Heritage Language Arts. These programs follow a thematic approach that focuses on:

- pre-colonial Africa
- slavery and resistance
- elements of the African diaspora
- reconstruction and renaissance
- the struggle for identity
- social and political change
- the journey toward empowerment and
- contemporary issues.

AFRICENTRIC EDUCATION

One of the recommendations of the *BLAC Report* was funding for Africentric education programs. In 2006, Mount Saint Vincent University in Halifax established the first Lifelong Learning Program in Canada on Africentric education. The goal of the program is to prepare Black youth to assume leadership roles in Black education in Nova Scotia. The first students to earn this Master's in Education degree graduated in October 2008.

> **This program was challenging, demanding, and personally rewarding. We were exposed to predominantly Black professors and professionals, and I could see myself in the material—I could relate and connect to it. It was very inspirational.**
>
> Tracey Thomas, graduate, Mount Saint Vincent University, "Mount's Africentric Education Program Makes History," October 16, 2008, Mount Saint Vincent University Media Centre

THE CULTURAL AWARENESS YOUTH GROUP

The Cultural Awareness Youth Group of Nova Scotia (CAYG) was formed in 1983. The organization fosters creativity, self-esteem, cultural pride, and academic excellence among Black youth in Halifax-Dartmouth high schools. Each high school has a CAYG chapter and is open to students from all races and cultures. The chapters plan activities to teach young people about Black culture. These range from presenting plays and films to holding debates and quizzes to planning community field trips. CAYG encourages Black students to explore their heritage and culture to develop a greater sense of identity and self-worth.

I remember my grade 7 history text had 380-odd pages, one and a half about us. We've done more than a page and a half.

Shingai Nyajeka, student narrator, *SPEAK IT! From the Heart of Black Nova Scotia, A User's Guide*, Halifax: The Black Educators Association of Nova Scotia, April 1995

FIGURE 8.9 Dr. Sylvia Hamilton

Dr. Sylvia Hamilton is an award-winning author and filmmaker. Her documentaries explore race and discrimination in Canada. They have brought the experiences of Black Nova Scotians into the mainstream of Canadian arts. Her film *SPEAK IT! From the Heart of Black Nova Scotia* explores the trials and triumphs facing a group of Black students at St. Patrick's High School as they open a new chapter of CAYG in a predominantly White community. In 2003, Hamilton won the Portia White Prize for excellence, innovation, and expression in the arts for her contribution to cultural life in Nova Scotia.

Business and Commerce

Black Nova Scotians have a long history of entrepreneurship. The first Black immigrants were blacksmiths, woodcarvers, and farmers, determined to build successful new lives in their new homeland. Their descendants maintained this determination to succeed in business. In the 1900s, many Blacks in Nova Scotia were shop owners and craft workers. Today, there are many successful Black businesses in the province. Since 1995, the Black Business Initiative (BBI) has created new initiatives to foster business opportunities for Blacks. The BBI helps Black business owners develop the essential skills they need to become successful entrepreneurs.

Today, many Black-owned businesses in Nova Scotia are experiencing unprecedented success. Some people attribute this success to the community spirit that exists among Blacks in Nova Scotia. Since the early days of immigration, Black Nova Scotians have developed a long history of working together to overcome the economic barriers they have faced.

That's a real high mark for us, the spirit of co-operation that runs through our community. It gives us a real business advantage—one that no one can take away from us.

Wayne Adams, journalist, business leader, and the first Black person elected to the Nova Scotia legislature, "Cultural Renaissance," *Nova Scotia—Come to Life*, 2008

BUSINESS OPPORTUNITIES FOR BLACK YOUTH

Within the Black Business Initiative, Business Is Jammin' (BIJ) focuses on Black youth. It encourages students to stay in school and to develop the skills and strategies they need to build successful business careers. BIJ organizes school presentations, conferences, and trade shows and provides an interactive website with games and links to educational, business, and youth organizations. To be eligible to take part in Business Is Jammin', you must be a self-motivated Black youth under the age of 30 with a proven interest in becoming a business entrepreneur.

Politics and Government

Historically, Black people in Nova Scotia have been under-represented in politics and government. Most experts attribute this lack of representation to systemic racism and cultural bias. Approximately 160 Blacks are employed in the provincial civil service. Most are women, working in administrative and clerical positions rather than management. The lack of Black people in the civil service has contributed to inequities in the provision of government services in health care, education, the legal system, and other areas. Black communities struggle to provide recreational and social programs for young people, families, and seniors.

To address these inequities, the Office of African Nova Scotian Affairs (OANSA) was created in 2003. Its goal is to open up dialogue between the provincial government and the Black community. OANSA provides Black people with a voice to express their concerns and a platform to address discrimination in education, employment, housing, the courts, and community development.

FIGURE 8.10
Nova Scotian Lieutenant Governor Mayann Francis

Blacks are beginning to gain greater recognition and representation in the provincial government. In 2006, Mayann Francis, the former executive director of the Nova Scotia Human Rights Commission, was the first Black person appointed lieutenant governor of Nova Scotia.

What impact do you think Mayann Francis's appointment will have on the Black community in Nova Scotia?

Environment and Empowerment

environmental racism intentionally locating hazardous waste dumps, landfills, incinerators, or other polluting industries near Black or First Nations communities

In Chapter 5, you learned how the community of Africville on the outskirts of Halifax was destroyed in the name of urban renewal. In 2006, the residents of another predominantly Black community, Lincolnville, launched a campaign to prevent a similar tragedy from happening in their community. The catalyst that prompted local residents to take action was a landfill site on the outskirts of Lincolnville. The Save Lincolnville Campaign claims that the municipal government is practising **environmental racism** by locating a toxic waste dump less than a kilometre from their community. The dump violates a 1992 recommendation by the provincial Human Rights Commission that no more landfill sites be located near Black or First Nations communities. The issue has created a growing awareness among many people in Nova Scotia about the underlying racism that still exists in Canada.

The dump accepts waste from 17 other municipalities in Nova Scotia. Lincolnville residents are concerned about the effects the landfill will have on their health. Although the health effects are unknown, residents believe their community has a higher than average rate of cancer. Residents of Lincolnville say they were targeted for this hazardous waste site because they are a small Black community with limited resources to fight back. They believe the landfill symbolizes the slow decline of Lincolnville brought on by government indifference and racist policies. Many residents are concerned that Lincolnville will disappear altogether, taking with it their cultural history and way of life.

> **Lincolnville is my home. It's been my home for 15 years and it's going to be my home for another 15 more—hopefully more than that. I learned from Lincolnville everything that I have. Everything is Lincolnville.**
>
> Cassandra Desmond, teenage resident of Lincolnville, "Race and Waste in Nova Scotia," *The Dominion*, December 7, 2006

FIGURE 8.11 Demonstrators protest Lincolnville landfill

In addition to local residents, the Save Lincolnville Campaign has attracted such supporters as the Halifax Coalition Against Poverty, Bound to Be Free, and the Dalhousie Black Law Students Association. Their concerns about environmental racism are shared by other Black communities in the province.

How effective do you think grassroots organizations are in bringing about change in their communities?

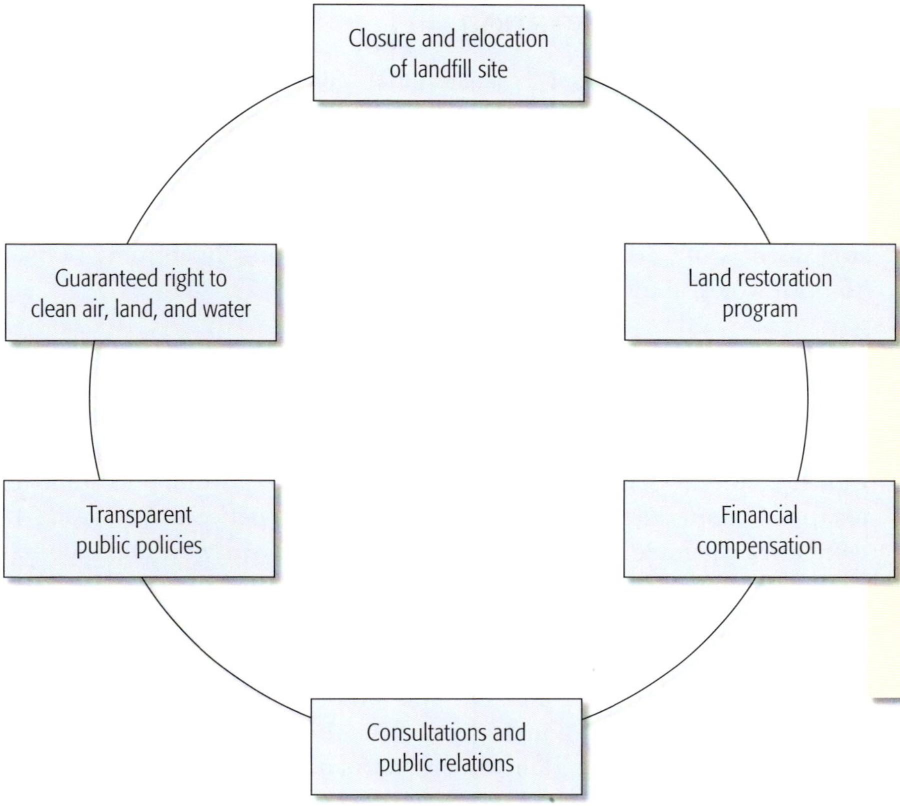

FIGURE 8.12 Demands of Concerned Citizens of Lincolnville

The grassroots organization known as the Concerned Citizens of Lincolnville is demanding that it get the same consideration and compensation as other communities facing similar circumstances have received in the past.

Over the years, marginalization, land misappropriation, and economic hardship have tested the strength of Black communities in Nova Scotia. However, the descendants of the original Black settlers have continued to thrive in the face of oppression and adversity. Many have become well-known and highly regarded artists, academics, politicians, and writers who speak out on behalf of the Black community and make important contributions to Black people's ongoing march toward equality.

REVIEW AND REFLECT

1. To what extent should the school curriculum be revised to include the histories and contributions of people from diverse cultures? Should specific criteria determine what is included in a revised curriculum? Explain your ideas.
2. In your opinion, how important are youth organizations like the Cultural Awareness Youth Group and Business Is Jammin'?
3. What incidents of discrimination are you aware of in Nova Scotia today? Prepare a newspaper report about one incident and what people are doing to take action.

Caribbean Immigration

After the postwar economic expansion that followed the Second World War, there was a great demand for unskilled workers. The *National Act* of 1948 was designed to attract cheap labour from the British colonies. Many Blacks from the Caribbean were looking for the chance to escape the poverty of the islands. They embraced the opportunity to build new lives in Canada. But in 1952, the government decided to stop the flow of Caribbean immigration by restricting the number of Black immigrants it would allow into Canada.

The West Indian Domestic Scheme

In 1955, the immigration doors opened slightly to allow Caribbean immigrants into the country. Between 1955 and 1960, the federal government sponsored the West Indian Domestic Scheme. It allowed select Caribbean women to come to Canada to work as domestics. Only healthy, single women between the ages of 18 and 35 with at least a grade 8 education qualified. After a year working as domestics, the women were given **landed immigrant** status. After five years they were allowed to apply for Canadian citizenship.

landed immigrant
a person who has relocated and changed his or her permanent residence to a country in which he or she is not a citizen

The plan originally allowed only 100 Caribbean women into the country each year. But when racial discrimination was removed from the Canadian *Immigration Act* in 1962, the number of immigrants from the Caribbean began to rise. By 1965, 2690 women, mostly from Jamaica and Barbados, had settled in Canada.

Opening the Immigration Doors

Before 1962, Canada's immigration policies restricted or prohibited non-Europeans from coming to Canada. As a result, by 1960 fewer than 11 000 Blacks from the Caribbean had immigrated to Canada—less than 1 percent of Canada's total number of immigrants.

Throughout the 1950s, however, political activists such as the Negro Citizenship Association (NCA) had fought against this discrimination. They lobbied the government to extend its definition of a British subject to include Blacks from Britain's Caribbean colonies. In 1962, their efforts paid off when Canada introduced new immigration rules based on education and job skills rather than country of origin. These changes opened the doors for non-White immigrants to come to Canada. However, Black Canadians were still not allowed to sponsor family members living in their homeland.

In 1967, the government implemented further changes to its immigration policy. A universal points system was introduced that eliminated discrimination from the selection process. The system awarded points to potential immigrants based on education, job skills, age, and ability to speak French or English. All those who earned enough points were eligible to apply to immigrate to Canada, regardless of their country of origin.

Authorities declared that the points system eliminated discrimination from immigration policies. But critics have argued that the system discriminates against women from developing countries, like many of those found in the Caribbean and Africa. They point out that in many of these countries women do not have the same access to education or the same job opportunities as men. Therefore, they cannot earn as many points and cannot qualify to enter Canada as independent immigrants.

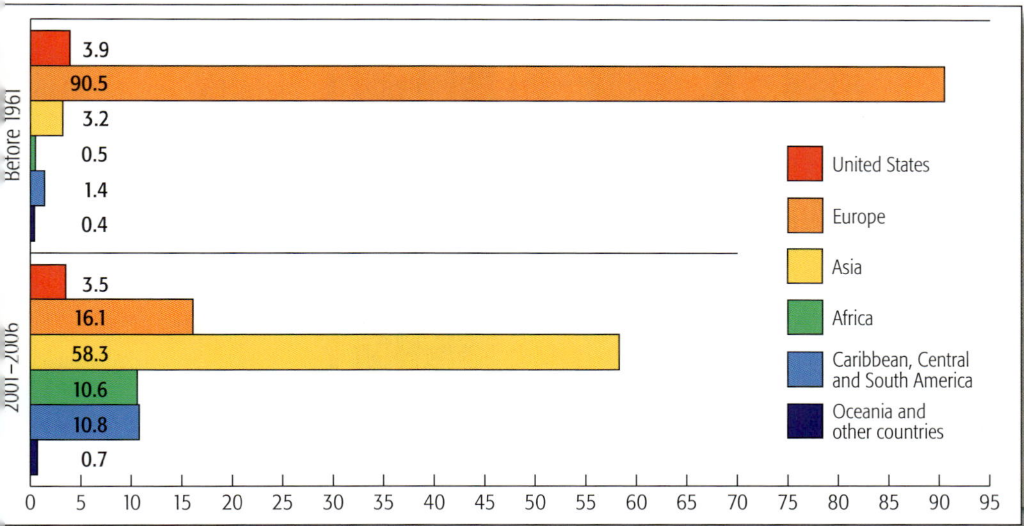

FIGURE 8.13 Place of birth of immigrants to Canada, before 1961 and from 2001 to 2006 (%)

This graph shows the places of origin of immigrants before Canada eased the restrictions on its immigration policies and since 2001.

What patterns can you identify?

English Caribbean Migration

The points system changed the face of Canadian immigration. Between 1967 and 1972, the number of immigrants from the Caribbean jumped to almost 70 000. That number continued to rise after the government added a family reunification clause to its immigration policy. This made it easier for immigrants from the Caribbean to bring their families to Canada.

Many Caribbean immigrants who were British subjects immigrated to Britain first. In the 1970s, however, growing racism and a poor economy led many of these immigrants to leave Britain and resettle in Canada. Since these "double-lap" immigrants came from Britain, they were not listed as Caribbean immigrants in the immigration records. It is estimated that between 10 000 and 15 000 Black immigrants have come to Canada via Britain.

The majority of Caribbean immigrants came from Jamaica. Between 1974 and 1989, almost 36 percent of Caribbean immigrants were Jamaicans. This figure rose to 40 percent by the early 1990s. Most Jamaicans came to Canada for the job opportunities. The majority settled in Toronto, with a few smaller communities in Hamilton, Montreal, and Ottawa. Immigrants from the English-speaking Caribbean have made a significant contribution to Canada's diverse cultural landscape. Today, the richness and vibrancy of Caribbean culture is reflected in cities across Canada.

FIGURE 8.14
A Caribbean restaurant in Toronto

Today, there are many Caribbean restaurants, grocery stores, bookstores, hair salons, and nightclubs all across the Greater Toronto Area (GTA). **How is the development of businesses like this one important to the identity of Caribbean Canadians?**

French Caribbean Immigration

Duvalier dictatorships the oppressive regimes of François Duvalier and his son Jean-Claude in Haiti between 1957 and 1986

political dissident someone who protests or disagrees with established political policies

Caribbean immigrants have not just come from English-speaking islands. Many immigrants have come from French-speaking islands, particularly Haiti. Haitian immigration began in the 1960s and 1970s as people fled the oppression of the **Duvalier dictatorships**. The first Haitian immigrants were professionals: doctors, lawyers, teachers, and **political dissidents**. (As you learned in Chapter 3, they included the family of the first Black Governor General of Canada, Michaëlle Jean.) Most of these immigrants settled in Quebec, where Canadians shared their French language and Roman Catholic religion. Since their professional qualifications filled a gap in the labour force, they were welcomed to the province.

After 1972, however, there was a dramatic change in both the number and the background of Haitian immigrants. This new group of immigrants was less educated. Many Quebeckers viewed them as cheap labour who would take away their jobs. This resentment led to racism and discrimination as the Haitians tried to integrate into Quebec society.

Today, more than 75 percent of Haitian immigrants say they have experienced discrimination. This has led to feelings of alienation. Leaders are mobilizing the 100 000-plus Haitians in Montreal to speak out on the issues that affect them and to take action to achieve equality.

FIGURE 8.15 *Haiti en scene* in Montreal, March 2008

Haitian-born Governor General Michaëlle Jean invited the troupe *Haiti en scene* from Port-au-Prince, Haiti to perform the rock opera *Starmania* in Montreal.

Do you think it is important for immigrants to maintain cultural connections to their homeland? Why or why not?

Remittances

Today, immigrants from all parts of the Caribbean maintain strong **transnational** connections to their island homes. Most immigrants are in weekly telephone contact with their families back home. Many return frequently to visit their families in the Caribbean. Almost half of all immigrants from the Caribbean send remittances in the form of money and gifts to contribute to their family's welfare. The money is sent to parents, grandparents, brothers, and sisters to be used for food, housing, school, and medical care. According to Statistics Canada, the amount of money these immigrants send home is based on three factors:

- their income
- their family obligations in Canada and abroad
- the level of poverty in their homeland—the poorer the country, the more money they send.

transnational involving more than one country

Remittances make a significant contribution to household incomes in the Caribbean. Average remittances total between $1000 and $1400 per family a year. In some countries, the total amount of remittances is greater than the revenue generated from their biggest exports.

REVIEW AND REFLECT

1. What were the "push" factors that led Black immigrants to leave the Caribbean to settle in Canada? What were the "pull" factors that drew immigrants from the Caribbean to Canada?
2. How did the screening process for potential immigrants to Canada change in the 1960s?
3. What were some of the challenges faced by Haitian immigrants who settled in Quebec?
4. What does the practice of sending remittances to the Caribbean suggest about the value of family to Caribbean Canadians?

African Immigration

By the beginning of the 21st century, almost half of all Black immigrants to Canada came from Africa, particularly Somalia, Ghana, Ethiopia, Egypt, South Africa, Morocco, Algeria, and Kenya. Africans come to Canada for three main reasons:

- to seek refuge from war or political corruption
- to study
- to settle and build new lives.

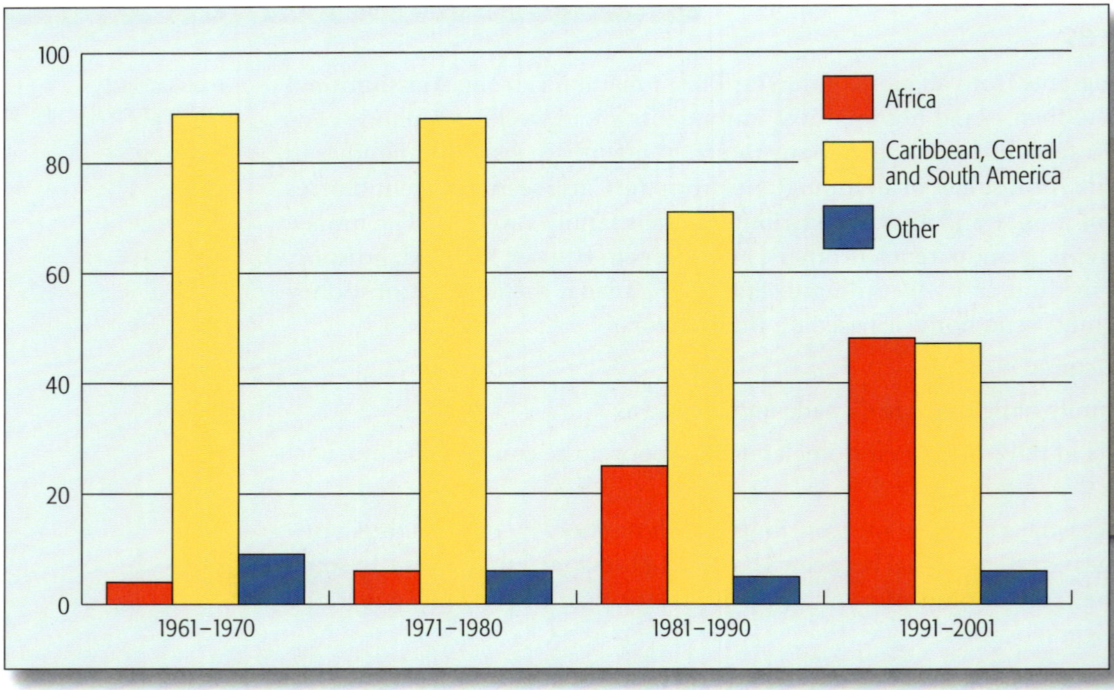

FIGURE 8.16 Black immigration trends since 1961

This graph shows the source of Black immigrants by decades since 1961. **What trends can you identify?**

Many Africans came to Canada to escape injustices and wars in their homeland—apartheid in South Africa, civil wars in Somalia and Ethiopia, and dictatorships in Uganda and Nigeria. Many of these immigrants experience **post-traumatic stress**, depression, or anxiety from witnessing atrocities in their homelands. Yet their strong family ties, their spirituality, and their eagerness to learn and work make these refugees resilient.

post-traumatic stress an anxiety disorder that develops after being exposed to a terrifying event or ordeal

Unlike other Black immigrants, African immigrants from war-torn countries cannot return home to visit their families. This makes it harder to maintain their customs, languages, and traditions and to instill a sense of their heritage in children who are born here.

Culture Shock

Many African immigrants settling in Canada experience culture shock. They find themselves in a society with different values from those they grew up with. In North America, people place the interests of the individual first. This is in sharp contrast to traditional African values, which emphasize the good of the community.

Immigrants from African countries like Ghana and Nigeria have a British heritage. They face challenges as they adjust to life in Canada, but their ability to speak English eases the transition. Immigrants from African countries like Somalia, where people speak Arabic or Somali, face greater difficulties. Many find it hard to communicate well in either of Canada's official languages.

Typically, Africans have large families. But a shortage of money often changes family dynamics. Many women who stayed home with their families in Africa find that they must work outside the home in Canada. Underemployment is another problem. Many African immigrants have some level of postsecondary education. But in Canada they cannot find work in their chosen fields. Their degrees and credentials are not recognized. They have no Canadian work experience. Sometimes their language skills limit their ability to work in certain fields. Many find themselves working in low-paying jobs for which they are overqualified.

> **We went through a lot fleeing Somalia. And when we got here, neither of my parents could get work in the professions they were trained for. They still can't.**
>
> Ali Farah, Somalian immigrant, *NOW Magazine*, February 23–March 1, 2006

African immigrants have to deal with Canadian misconceptions, too. Many people think all Black people are the same, regardless of where they come from. They do not understand that, like people of many different heritages, people of African heritage speak different languages, practise different religions, and have unique customs and traditions.

REVIEW AND REFLECT

1. Define *post-traumatic stress* in your own words. How do you think it might affect the integration of African immigrants into Canadian society?
2. List some of the challenges that Canadian culture presents for African immigrants. What kinds of support can African immigrants use to help them face these challenges?

ORIGINALS

K'NAAN (1978–)

K'naan was born Keinan Warsame. He is a poet and hip-hop artist who immigrated to Canada from Somalia in 1991. Unlike many hip-hop artists, K'naan refuses to glorify violence. He witnessed too much of it after civil war broke out in his homeland. Somalia was in a state of anarchy as warlords competed for power and control. K'naan lived in the war-torn capital of Mogadishu in one of the most dangerous neighbourhoods on the planet. Gangs armed with guns and other weapons roamed the streets. His neighbourhood was so dangerous and deadly it was called the River of Blood.

K'naan's father was an intellectual who had already been forced to flee Somalia. He settled in Harlem in New York City, where he worked as a cab driver. But he sent money home to his family, along with hip-hop and rap albums for his sons. Although K'naan could not speak a word of English, he taught himself to imitate the rhymes of his rap heroes.

Every day, K'naan's mother, Marian Mohamed, visited the American embassy, pleading for visas so that she and her two sons could flee the violence and go to the United States. She was finally granted the visas the day the US embassy closed its doors in Somalia. K'naan's family took the last flight out of Mogadishu before turf battles shut down the airport.

K'naan and his family lived in Harlem for a few months before moving to the community of Rexdale in Toronto. After he learned to speak English, K'naan began writing and performing his own music. It is a fusion of African rhythms and hip-hop rhymes, mixed with reggae, folk, and rock music. After K'naan signed a record deal, his music career took off.

In 2001, K'naan was invited to perform at the 50th anniversary of the United Nations Commission for Refugees in Geneva, Switzerland. In the middle of his performance, he stopped the band and rapped out a poem criticizing the United Nations for its failed relief mission in Somalia. The surprised crowd fell silent for a few seconds. Then they burst into applause, giving K'naan a standing ovation.

Today, K'naan travels the world campaigning to raise awareness about the issues facing Africa today. He performs at benefit concerts and works alongside other celebrity activists, such as Bob Geldof and Bono, who are fighting to end poverty in Africa.

FIGURE 8.17 K'naan

Rapper K'naan's poetic lyrics recount his own experiences in his homeland of Somalia and protest the violence and poverty that continue to ravage the country. At the same time, his music celebrates the beauty and dignity of Somalia and its people. In 2006, K'Naan's recording *The Dusty Foot Philosopher* won a Juno Award for Rap Recording of the Year. He released his second album, *Troubadour*, in 2009.

K'naan means the traveler; Warsame means one who carries the words of peace. Where I come from, you have to live up to your names.

K'naan, "Kicking Up Dust," CBC, June 30, 2005

Think It Through

Like Dr. Martin Luther King Jr., K'naan advocates positive action, not violence, to bring about social change. With a partner, create a dialogue that might have taken place if K'naan had had the opportunity to meet Dr. King.

Being Black in Canada Today

Many people believe that Canada is a tolerant country. They think that if racism ever existed here, it was wiped out long ago in our multicultural society. Many Canadians believe that everyone, regardless of their heritage, has an equal opportunity to succeed here. Yet this is not the reality for many Black people in Canada today. Although greater social, economic, and political opportunities have improved the quality of life for many Black Canadians, many challenges still remain. Racism and discrimination continue to hurt the vitality of Canada's Black community.

> **Racism is a wall which will only be broken down over time. You do the things you can yourself to create change. No one person can carry the weight of the world, we have to share the weight. I see it as a long protracted struggle—we all do our part. You break down one brick, two bricks, however many bricks you can in your lifetime, then you pass your chisel to somebody else and that person will keep on breaking it down. It won't happen all in one generation. It probably won't even happen in my lifetime.**
>
> Lennox Cadore, "Dismantling the Wall, Brick by Brick," *The Toronto Star*, February 21, 1999

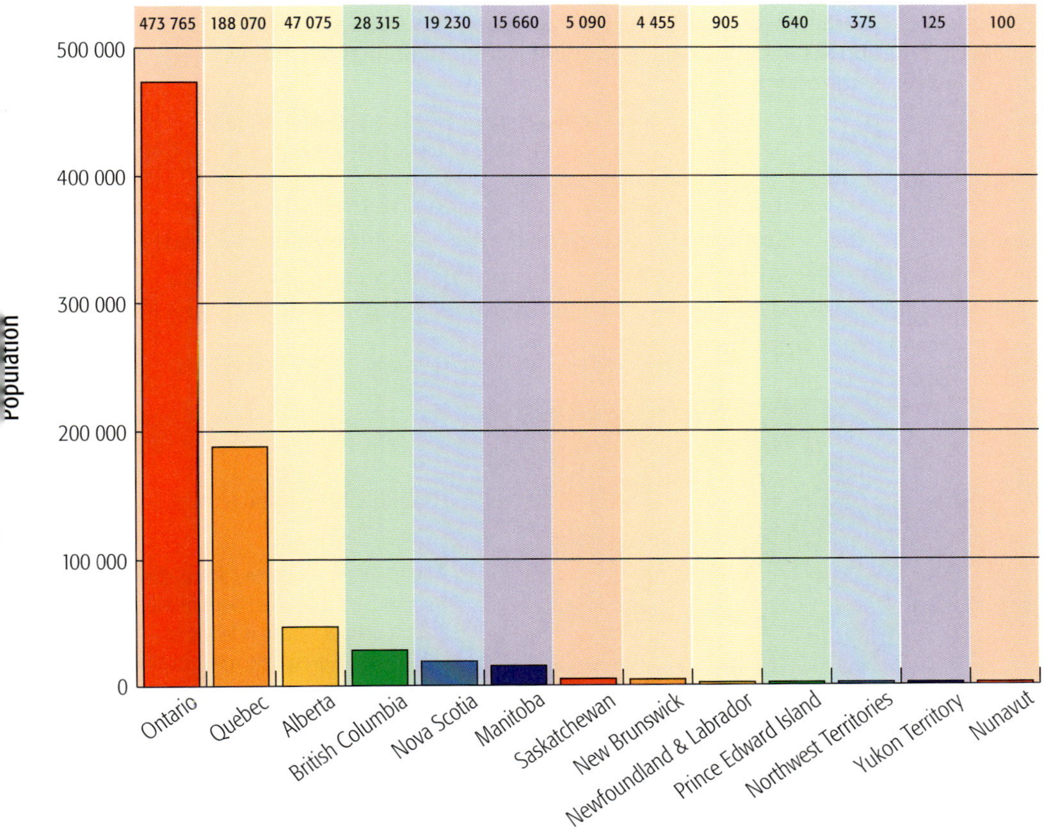

FIGURE 8.18
Black Canadian population, 2006

According to Statistics Canada, the Black population in Canada in 2006 was 783 795. Estimates predict there will be 1 million Black people living in Canada by 2017.

In which provinces do the majority of Black Canadians live? What factors do you think draw people to these provinces?

A Portrait of Black Canadians Today

- Black people are the third largest racially visible minority in Canada, after Chinese and South Asians.
- Nearly half of all Black people in Canada were born here, second only to Japanese among racially visible minorities.
- The Black population is younger than the overall population of Canada.
- Almost half of all Black Canadians live in Toronto, followed by Montreal and Ottawa.
- Canadian-born Black people are just as likely to have a university education as others born in Canada but they experience higher unemployment.
- On average, Black people earn less money than other Canadians and are less likely to be self-employed.

Statistics Canada, Anne Milan and Kelly Tran, "Blacks in Canada: A Long History," *Canadian Social Trends*, Spring 2004

Education

Black immigrants often face challenges when they enter the Canadian school system. Immigrants from countries that have experienced wars or natural disasters may not have had the opportunity to attend school.

> If your family has come from a refugee camp where they were worried about survival, about being murdered, about where the next meal was coming from, you bring a very different focus than a child whose family has been socialized into believing that books are important, education is important, that becoming a doctor or lawyer is important.
>
> Lee Gunderson, professor, University of British Columbia, "Toronto Schools Fail to Overcome Barriers," *The Toronto Star*, June 13, 2008

Youth from the Caribbean and Africa who went to school in their home countries may have difficulty adapting to Canadian schools. Teaching methods and learning strategies are often different in Canada from what they experienced back home. Students may also have language difficulties or problems understanding accents that are different from their own.

FIGURE 8.19 Black students at a Canadian school

A 2008 survey conducted across the Toronto District School Board revealed that the school system is failing to help students overcome roadblocks to their education. The report suggested that how well children do in school has a lot to do with their family background and whether they have experienced conflict or war.

Statistics indicate that Black school children born outside Canada show slower rates of progress and drop out of school at higher rates than the national average. They are over-represented in courses that lead directly to work and under-represented in courses that prepare students for college or university. Many students feel that teachers stereotype them as underachievers and do not respect or acknowledge their skills and abilities. They are often discouraged from pursuing careers in high-paying professions such as medicine, law, and engineering. Instead, they are persuaded to enter vocational or technical programs or are not offered any career guidance at all.

Black students are also adversely affected by the lack of role models in the school system. Though 12 percent of grade 9 to 12 students are Black, only 5 percent of their teachers are. There are even fewer Black role models in administrative positions. In colleges and universities, Blacks are even more under-represented. This is due in part to the fact that the credentials of many immigrants who received their teaching qualifications in their home countries are not recognized in Canada. In addition, the time and money needed to retrain often discourages immigrant teachers from applying for teaching positions in Canada. This lack of role models leaves many Black students feeling that the school environment is an unfriendly one that does not include them.

> **Most Black youth have a great deal of trouble seeing themselves reflected in the day-to-day power structure of their schools. . . . For Black students to stay in school, they have to be optimistic about having a shot at the good jobs—like the ones they see around them in schools.**
>
> Bairu Sium, teacher, Toronto District School Board, *NOW Magazine*, January 31–February 6, 2008

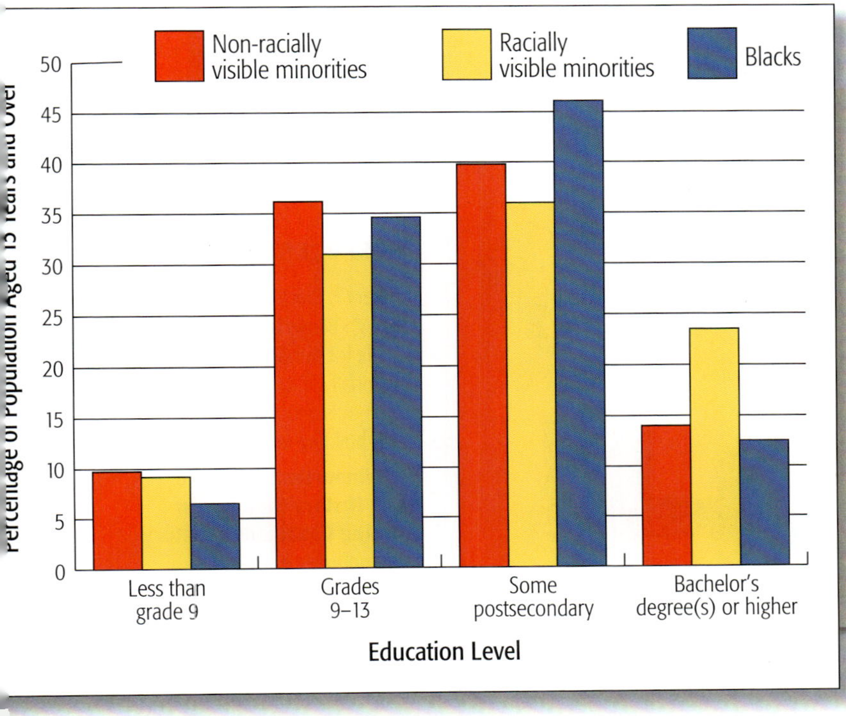

FIGURE 8.20 Level of education of Black Canadians, 2001

This graph shows the level of education achieved by Black Canadians. In Toronto, the majority of students are members of racially visible minorities. Yet 77 percent of their teachers are White and the curriculum they are taught is Eurocentric. Students are taught little about the contribution of Africans to world civilizations and societies. When Black issues are reflected in the curriculum, it is frequently from a negative perspective.

Do you think it is important for Black students to see themselves reflected in the curriculum? Explain your response.

To help Black students reach their full potential, Black educators and parents have formed committees in cities across Canada. They are encouraging school boards and ministries of education to promote academic excellence through school programs designed to meet the needs of Black students, particularly recent immigrants. They are urging ministries of education to review their curricula for bias and to reshape their courses to reflect the needs of Canada's diverse Black student population. They are asking school boards to offer more courses in Black studies, to hire more Black teachers, and to offer more after-school programs that promote Black culture and heritage. They are demanding more scholarships and other financial opportunities for Black students to help them afford postsecondary educations.

Black youth are playing their part, too. After graduating from colleges and universities, many young Black men and women are returning to their communities. Those who came to Canada as immigrants know the alienation and confusion their families faced as they settled into a foreign land. They have witnessed the frustration their parents experienced as they were refused jobs they were trained for in their homeland. They offer support to other young immigrants through school and community outreach programs. Other Black youth are working with Black Canadians who were born here to help them share in the opportunities Canada has to offer.

FIGURE 8.21 Black History Month

February is Black History Month. Although Blacks have been in Canada for hundreds of years, traditionally little has been taught in our schools about their contributions to the building of Canada.

How important do you think Black History Month is in teaching Canadians a history that includes everyone?

IDEAS

AFRICENTRIC SCHOOLS

In Canada, students of all backgrounds are taught that history, culture, science, and technology begins and ends with Europe and its colonies. Today, however, many Canadians believe that this Eurocentric approach to education is detrimental to all students because it excludes the views and contributions of other, non-European, cultures.

Within Canada's Black community, many people support the idea of teaching Black students from an *Africentric* point of view. Africentricity teaches Black students about the rich and diverse global contributions of Africans and Black Canadians as presented through Black content, images, and role models. It helps Black students understand their heritage and to see themselves through their own eyes rather than through the eyes of others.

In Toronto, the school board has applied the principle of Africentricity to the creation of an Africentric alternative school as one means of reducing a high school dropout rate of 40 percent among Black students. The school teaches the required curriculum, but lessons focus on the contributions of Africans and Black Canadians. So, for example, in grade 3, where the curriculum covers "early settlement in Upper Canada," students learn about the challenges faced by Black pioneers in Upper Canada.

The idea of an Africentric school drew many different opinions and prompted discussions across the country. Many Blacks in Nova Scotia began questioning whether an Africentric school should be opened in Halifax. Those who support the concept believe it is one way to keep Black students engaged in education. Others charge that it is a return to segregation. Still others believe that an Africentric school cannot address the diverse histories and interests of Black Canadians.

I believe there's nothing controversial about learning or developing the passion to learn or about offering to all what some take for granted as a matter of curriculum: an opportunity to learn about one's history and contributions; to read from authors that relate to one's experiences; to study events from a perspective that shapes positive self-esteem and offers a view of the world that honours their past, and encourages them to create a future—as trailblazers and as achievers.

Taryn Della, "Black-Focused School Doesn't Mean Student Segregation," *Halifax News Net*, March 13, 2008

FIGURE 8.22 Meeting of the Toronto District School Board, November 8, 2007

In January 2008, the Toronto District School Board voted in favour of an Africentric school for junior kindergarten to grade 5. The proposal called for greater emphasis on Black history and heritage and more Black teachers.

As a Canadian of Caribbean roots, I see this as a most saddening development for our education system. It is a regressive move, which seems to be embracing segregation. It will only promote a sense of inequality among our Black children, questioning why they have been singled out to attend these schools.

Anthony Moyston, "Voices: Black-Focused School," *The Toronto Star*, February 1, 2008

As soon as someone can define what exactly "Africentric" culture is, I will be happy. There is incredible cultural diversity within the Black community: Caribbean, West African, Somali, etc. It is insulting to lump them all together for purposes of social engineering. I guess there should also be "Asia-centric" or "Sino-centric" schools. They also have the right to reach their potential free of the tyranny of the majority, don't they?

Douglas Sweetlove, "Voices: Black-Focused School," *The Toronto Star*, February 1, 2008

Think It Through

What is your opinion about Africentric alternative schools? Express your ideas in a letter to the Minister of Education for your province.

Employment

Today, many middle-class Black Canadians occupy professional and managerial positions. Yet studies show that racial discrimination still plays a part in job opportunities for many Black Canadians. Black people report more cases of job discrimination or unfair treatment than other Canadians. Equal employment is the law in Canada, but many employers still do not adhere to this policy. They discriminate against Black applicants for a variety of reasons—for example, if they live in public housing or have emigrated from certain countries. And this discrimination is not just limited to the private sector. Black Canadians are also under-represented in all levels of government.

> **When you apply for a job you never say you're from the Park [Regent Park]. . . . You have to lie so they don't think you're a thug.**
>
> A young Black man in Toronto, *Colour of Poverty*, 2007

Often, the qualifications and experience of Black immigrants are not recognized by employers in Canada. These roadblocks hinder the ability of Black Canadians to climb the economic ladder. As a result, Black people are over-represented in low-paying jobs and under-represented in more secure, higher-paying occupations. Even if they work at the same jobs and have the same qualifications, Black Canadians typically earn less money than other Canadians.

Black Canadians have fewer opportunities for career advancement than other workers, too. They are almost absent from senior management and executive positions in businesses and industries across the country. Many people believe this is because there is a glass ceiling in the workplace—a plateau above which Black Canadians are unable to rise, regardless of their abilities or qualifications. To succeed, many Black employees must dress better, be more articulate, and act less aggressively to combat stereotypes that have lingered since the days of slavery and segregation.

In spite of discrimination in the workplace, however, many Black Canadian men and women have achieved success as **entrepreneurs**, professionals, **CEOs**, and business and community leaders. Through their achievements and contributions, they inspire young people to overcome society's barriers to achieve their goals.

entrepreneur
a person who organizes, operates, and assumes the risks of a business venture

CEO
chief executive officer—the executive responsible for the operations of a business

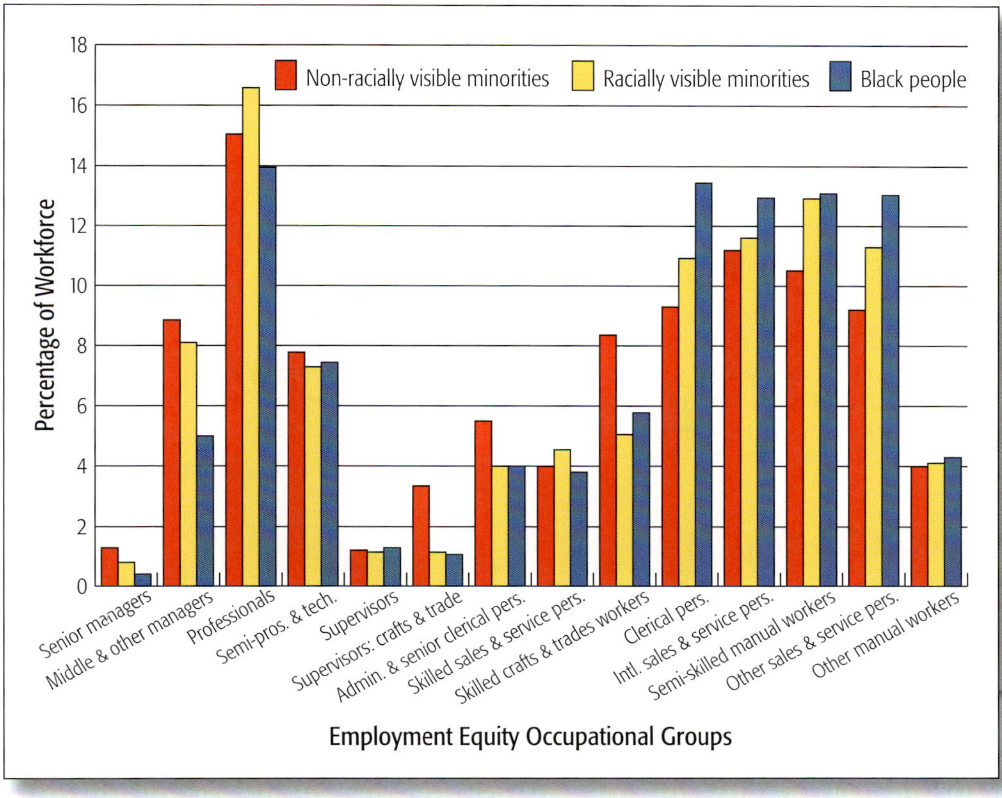

FIGURE 8.23 Percentage of Black people in the workforce, 2001

This graph shows the percentage of Black workers in the workforce compared with racially visible and non-racially visible minorities.

What patterns can you identify? What factors have contributed to these patterns?

Family Relationships

Marriage and family patterns among the descendants of early Black settlers largely reflect the **nuclear families** of mainstream Canadian society. But among immigrants there are some distinct patterns. There are many **transnational families** within the Black immigrant community. Some parents come to Canada to find work. They leave their children behind in the care of grandparents or other family members until they get established. Others come to Canada with the goal of eventually returning home after they retire. When they do, they leave behind their children and grandchildren.

nuclear family
a family unit consisting of a mother, a father, and their children

transnational family
a family whose members live in more than one country

Another distinct pattern among Black immigrants is the number of single-parent families. According to Statistics Canada, in 2006 almost 50 percent of all Black children aged 14 and under lived in single-parent homes led by women. While women in Canada on average earn 71 cents for every dollar men make, Black women earn just 64 cents. As a result, many families led by single mothers struggle to make ends meet. Many live in poverty.

Some social scientists link the poverty rate in the Black community to the absence of fathers in family households. Others believe that depicting Black fathers who are absent from the family home as irresponsible is a stereotype and that just because a father may be physically absent does not necessarily mean he does not provide financial support for his children. They argue that the real reason for higher levels of poverty in the Black community is **institutional racism**. They believe this affects the decisions young Black people make and keeps the cycle of poverty going.

institutional racism
a social pattern that imposes oppressive or negative conditions against a group based on race

> **Blacks . . . have been made to believe that living in a so-called "multicultural society" means that systemic racism doesn't play a significant role in the disproportionate degree of hardship that the Black community faces on a daily basis.**
>
> Black Youth Taking Action, 2008

Racial Profiling

racial profiling
any action that relies on stereotypes about race, colour ethnicity, ancestry, religion, or place of origin to single out a person for closer scrutiny rather than on reasonable suspicion

Racism and discrimination in Canada are evident in **racial profiling**. Many experts believe that Black people are consistently targeted by racial profiling. It exists on many levels. Sometimes it is open. Black Canadians may be stopped by police as they drive through their neighbourhoods. They may be searched more closely by airport security. They may be pulled aside for closer inspection at customs. They may be treated more harshly by the courts. They may face tougher discipline in school.

FIGURE 8.24
A political cartoon on racial profiling

This political cartoon makes a statement about racial profiling.

What is the message in this cartoon? How does the cartoon make you feel?

Sometimes, though, racial profiling is more subtle. Black Canadians may be viewed with suspicion in stores and restaurants. They may be watched more closely as people pass them on the street. It may not be in open view in government policies and laws. But it is there, lurking in the subconscious of Canadian society. Whether it is subtle or overt, racial profiling is proof that racism still exists in Canada today.

> **Being stopped and searched by the police . . . seems to be experienced by Black people as evidence that race still matters in Canadian society. That no matter how well you behave, how hard you try, being Black means that you will always be considered one of the "usual suspects."**
>
> Criminologist Scot Wortley, University of Toronto, "Racial Profiling," CBC *News Indepth*, May 26, 2005

FIGURE 8.25
Police stopping a Black driver

Most police forces do not keep race-based records of traffic stops. However, there is a deeply held perception that Black motorists are singled out by police. This idea was supported by the Kingston Pilot Project conducted between October 1, 2003 and September 30, 2004. It showed that Blacks were much more likely to be stopped by police than any other cultural group. Some Black Canadians call being pulled over by police for no apparent reason being guilty of "DWB"—Driving While Black.

There are many consequences of racial profiling. It leads to over-representation of racially visible minorities in the criminal justice system. It causes Black youth to mistrust the police and the legal system. It creates feelings of alienation. It builds stress in Black communities. It causes people to change their behaviour. It forces people to avoid certain situations. It creates negative views of Canadian society. But perhaps racial profiling's biggest impact is on a person's dignity, self-esteem, and self-worth.

FIGURE 8.26 A Black female RCMP officer

Experts believe that recruiting more racially visible minorities in law enforcement will help reduce racial profiling.

What other measures do you think authorities should take to reduce racial profiling?

REVIEW AND REFLECT

1. Look back at the graphs in Figures 8.20 and 8.23. What conclusions can you reach from the data presented in each graph? What connections can you make between the graphs? Discuss your ideas.
2. To what extent do you think institutional racism is responsible for the problems in many Black communities today? Discuss your ideas with a partner.

Culture and Identity

Many aspects of Black identity are shaped by the unique cultural expressions of Black communities. You have seen some of these expressions of Black culture at different times and in different places in the history of the African diaspora. Today, in Canada and around the world, one of the most popular expressions of Black culture is hip-hop culture.

Hip-Hop Culture

With roots in the *griots* of West Africa, hip hop began in Brooklyn and the Bronx in New York City in the 1970s. It grew out of street parties, where DJs such as Jamaican-born Kool Herc mixed passages from albums on turntables while rappers rapped out song lyrics over the beats. Known as the "godfather of hip hop," Kool Herc used rare records, and his partner Coke La Rock would speak or "rap" over music tracks, similar to the Jamaican technique of dubbing out the lyrics of a song. Other pioneering hip-hop artists were the Sugarhill Gang and Grandmaster Flash.

There are four general elements to hip-hop culture—the DJ (disk jockey), the MC (master of ceremonies), the breakers, and graffiti artists. MCs became part of the culture when DJs decided they needed announcers to act as masters of ceremony and attract crowds to their parties. Breakdancers displayed their physical prowess in gravity-defying dance moves that gave physical expression to hip-hop culture. Youthful artists scrawled graffiti "tags" on subway cars and other makeshift canvases to give visual expression to hip hop.

Hip hop spread to Canada when the country's first hip-hop radio show, "The Fantastic Voyage," began playing hip-hop music in 1982. The program was hosted by Canadian hip-hop pioneer DJ Ron Nelson. In the late 1980s, artists such as Michie Mee, Dream Warriors, and Maestro Fresh Wes rose to the forefront of the Canadian hip-hop scene. They paved the way for such artists as Choclair, Saukrates, and Rascalz today.

FIGURE 8.27
Breakdancing

Breakdancing involves many physically demanding moves, such as toprock (movement while standing up), downrock (movement while on the ground), and stalls (acrobatic pauses in movement). Functional fashion, such as flat-soled sneakers, baggy pants, and hats that help dancers spin on their heads, is an integral part of breakdancing.

FIGURE 8.28 Canadian rapper Kardinal Offishall

In Canada, the Toronto-based recording artist and producer Kardinal Offishall is at the forefront of the Canadian hip-hop scene. His mastery of the art form has gained him international attention and respect. He has recorded songs with artists such as Akon and Sean Paul and has toured with such international hip-hop stars as 50 Cent and Busta Rhymes.

Although rap began as a voice for a community that was not being heard, by the late 1990s it had emerged from hip-hop culture to become part of the commercial music scene. Hip-hop culture addresses issues that many young people face today, such as discrimination, relationships, and self-worth. For many young hip-hoppers, the culture provides an outlet for creative expression. Young people across the country are embracing hip-hop culture in recording studios and dance classes. They are expressing their own sense of style through colourful and creative hip-hop fashion such as baggy pants, oversized sports jerseys, and expensive sneakers. Today, hip-hop culture is a means of expression for an entire generation of young Canadians of many different backgrounds.

> **It used to be a Black thing and now it's an every thing. In inner cities and suburbs, in a country like Canada, there's a lot of immigration, and hip hop creates a multicultural space. Kids are attracted to it … because they can be comfortable being themselves.**
>
> Pablo Aravena, a Chilean Canadian, "The Suburbs Are Getting Hip (Hop)," *Montreal Gazette*, October 14, 2006

EXPRESSIONS

CANADIAN HIP HOP

Many American hip-hop artists are popular in Canada. But Canadian artists have struggled to gain acceptance and recognition south of the border. In 1988, Michie Mee became the first Canadian rapper to sign with an American recording company. But her debut album, *Jamaican Funk: Canadian Style*, received little airplay on US radio stations. Mee attributed the lack of airtime to resistance against the heavy reggae influence in her music.

Hip-hop artists had difficulty making significant breakthroughs in the Canadian music industry, too. Though hip hop flourished in the United States, it was rarely played on commercial airwaves in Canada before 1998. That year, the Vancouver-based band Rascalz collaborated with emerging rappers CheckMate, Kardinal Offishall, Thrust, and Choclair to produce *Northern Touch*. The song was a hit. It reached the top 10 in most major markets and was widely played on Canadian and international airwaves. Canadian hip hop was finally catapulted into the limelight.

> **This track is history in the making. You have all these cats from east to west on one track. It's Canada represented to the fullest, and it's a chance for us to show that we have a different agenda from the States.**
>
> Rascalz rapper Red 1, "Canadian Hiphop Gets the Northern Touch," *NOW Toronto*, June 4–10, 1998

By the late 1990s, Toronto's Flow 93.5 FM, the first Black-owned radio station in Canada, began showcasing Canadian hip hop. Other radio stations soon followed. Now, for the first time, Canadian hip-hop artists had airtime on a network of radio outlets across the country.

Think It Through

Write your own rap lyrics about something that is important to you. Present your work to the class.

FIGURE 8.29 Rascalz

Vancouver-based Rascalz made their debut in 1993 with their album *Really Livin*. The title track won the award for Best Rap Video at the MuchMusic Awards. Since then, their smart and edgy style has made Rascalz one of the major players in the world of Canadian hip hop.

The Role of Media in Racial Identity

What role do the media play in the identity of Black Canadians? Often expressions of Black culture are misrepresented in the media. These misrepresentations perpetuate negative stereotypes. Sometimes these stereotypes are reinforced overtly, as in the racially sterotyped character of Cleveland Brown in the animated television comedy series *Family Guy*. Other times the reinforcement is more subtle. But no matter how these stereotypes are presented, they influence the way young Black people see themselves. They shape their ideas about who they are—and about who they may become.

Many Black youth discover that the media have already defined who they are by the colour of their skin. As a group, they have been assigned certain traits and characteristics. When young people are steadily exposed to these stereotypes, they may begin to believe they are true. Often it discourages them from looking beyond the media images to find their true identities and reach their full potential.

FIGURE 8.30 President Barack Obama meets Governor General Michaëlle Jean in Ottawa, February 19, 2009

The meeting was a significant event in the history of North America. For the first time, the heads of state of Canada and the United States were Black.

What impact do you think positive media images like this can have on the way Black youth think about themselves and about their future?

Putting Race in Its Place

Today, many Black youth are taking action to eliminate racism, take back their identities, and improve the quality of life for Black Canadians, particularly for Black youth. In diverse communities across the country, Black youth groups, student associations, youth conferences, and action coalitions are working to make a difference. They are fighting the stereotypes, misrepresentations, and negative self-images about Black people that are presented almost daily in the media. They are focusing the spotlight on Black people who are dedicated to improving their communities to demonstrate that Black youth are a powerful force for positive change in Canada. They are encouraging young Blacks to stake a claim in their futures by taking part in the political process and voting for candidates of change in municipal, provincial, and federal elections. Across the country, Black youth are working to put race in its place.

FIGURE 8.31 Black Youth Taking Action

Black Youth Taking Action (BYTA) is a Toronto-based organization formed in 1997. Its original role was to organize tours of colleges and universities for Black students to encourage them to pursue postsecondary education. Today, members of BYTA learn leadership and organizational skills and how to promote the interests of Black youth. By tackling socioeconomic, educational, and criminal justice issues, the members of BYTA are working to improve the lives of Black youth in the Greater Toronto Area.

REVIEW AND REFLECT

1. a. In a graphic organizer, list the positive and negative effects that you feel hip-hop culture has on youth today.
   b. How has hip-hop culture affected youth in your community?
2. What actions can Black youth take to improve the quality of life for young Black people in Canada? What actions can you take?

The Historian's Craft

PRESENTING HISTORY

The traditional way of presenting history is the essay. You declare a thesis statement (for example, "Media portrayals of Black people promote stereotypes"), present supporting evidence, and draw a conclusion. Alternatively, you might pose a question of inquiry, such as "What explains the appeal of hip-hop music?" Then you present alternative answers and identify which ones best answer the question.

There are many other ways you can present your work. You have learned about some of these in earlier Historian's Craft features:

- analyzing visual evidence (for example, the political cartoon on racial profiling)
- identifying key turning points (for example, the role of Black people in Canadian politics)
- preparing a concept-focused organizer (for example, the causes and effects of Caribbean immigration)
- creating a video to dramatize an impossible meeting (for example, between K'naan and Dr. Martin Luther King Jr.)

ORAL PRESENTATIONS

Another way of presenting information is through an oral presentation (for example, on the role of Black porters in the fight for equal rights). When you make an oral presentation, ask yourself the following questions:

- What are the main points?
- How will I introduce them?
- Should I use visuals and statistics to support my arguments?
- How can I make a powerful conclusion?

DEBATES

Another way to demonstrate your understanding is through a debate. For example, you could debate whether there should be an Africentric school for Black students. When you take part in a debate, follow these guidelines:

- Gather relevant evidence to make your case.
- Ensure your evidence is credible and has impact. Include quotations from experts and statistics from reliable sources.
- Think about the points in your argument that your opponents will attack and be prepared to rebut their arguments.
- Outline the arguments that support the opposing side to help you prepare your rebuttal.
- Note any weak evidence or inconsistencies in your opponents' arguments and be prepared to counter them.
- Conclude your argument by restating your strongest point.

MAKING PRESENTATIONS PERSONAL

You may choose to present information in a way that reflects your personal interests. For example, you might present a biography of someone you admire. Or, if you are interested in music, you might relate the music of a Black artist to one of the themes in this chapter. Or perhaps you might follow the guidelines in The Historian's Craft in Chapter 5 to empathize with someone in this chapter.

TRY IT!

1. Prepare an essay outline on the ways in which the media influence Black identity in Canada. Write a thesis statement and list in point form the supporting evidence from this chapter. Then do more research to test your thesis.
2. Imagine you are presenting information on the impact of Caribbean culture on Canadian life today. What form of presentation would you choose? Why?

STUDY HALL

KNOWLEDGE & UNDERSTANDING

1. What lessons can we learn from the efforts of the Brotherhood of Sleeping Car Porters to fight for membership in the White porters' union? Discuss your ideas with a partner.
2. Why do you think Canada prohibited non-Europeans from coming to Canada in the first half of the 20th century? Do you think such restrictions could be enforced today? Give reasons for your response.
3. Explain the significance of the education statistics in Figure 8.25. What impact do you think a course such as this one might have in addressing the needs of Black students? Do you think building self-esteem can change these statistics? Explain your response.
4. How would you describe Canada's cultural identity? How does it differ from Caribbean and African cultural identities? Do you think this makes it hard for Caribbean and African immigrants to integrate into Canadian society? Explain your ideas. Discuss your ideas using a think-pair-share strategy.

THINKING

5. How do you think domestic workers were affected psychologically after they left their homelands to work as nannies in the homes of White families in Canada? What stereotypes do you think this created?
6. In what ways have the experiences of Black immigrants from the Caribbean in the 1950s influenced the contemporary Black Canadian identity?

APPLICATION & COMMUNICATION

7. Do some research into three organizations in your community dedicated to preserving Black culture. In a display or in PowerPoint, present images showing the work of each organization, with descriptions of their programs and how they preserve Black culture.
8. Create an immigration policy that you think is appropriate for Canada today. List at least 10 criteria you would use to assess immigrants applying to come to Canada. Try to make your document as equitable as possible.
9. In what ways can communities ease the transition of African immigrants who come to Canada from war-torn countries? Develop three programs and clearly explain how they can address the issues these immigrants face.
10. List the ways in which your community can realistically and effectively deal with the issues that face young people in Black communities.

CHAPTER

9 Africa Today

KEY CONCEPTS

IN THIS CHAPTER, YOU WILL:

- demonstrate an understanding of the diversity of Africa
- analyze how and why Western media shape and distort images of Africa
- examine the challenges facing Africa in the 21st century
- discover some of the many African-led initiatives working to meet these challenges
- consider the role of community-based groups and grassroots organizations in Africa
- examine economic development and the impact of globalization on Africa
- demonstrate an understanding of the consciousness of people of African descent throughout the diaspora

A People's Story

Africa is the second-largest continent in the world. It includes at least eight climates and enormous geographic diversity. There are 54 independent countries where more than 950 million people of diverse backgrounds, cultures, religions, customs, appearances, and ways of life live. Yet, despite the diversity and complexity of the continent, many countries in Africa share the same challenges: underdevelopment, poverty, environmental destruction, AIDS, wars and conflicts, corrupt governments, and human rights abuses. In some cases, nature is responsible for these problems. In too many other cases, though, it is humankind.

In this chapter, you will learn about the challenges many countries in Africa face in the 21st century. You will discover what progress the people of Africa are making as they work to build a better future for themselves. You will learn what individuals are doing to make a difference and how community action helps resolve many challenges. As you read, think about why these challenges exist and who is responsible for resolving them. Consider what development strategies will ensure that Africa experiences greater equality, freedom, and prosperity in the 21st century.

1994		1996	2000	2001	2002	2003	20
Genocide in Rwanda	Nelson Mandela elected president of South Africa	Wars begin in Democratic Republic of the Congo	UN adopts Millennium Development Goals for 2015	African Summit makes HIV/AIDS top priority	African Union replaces Organization of African States	Conflict in Darfur begins	China heavy in in A

Image Analysis

FIGURE 9.1 A rally for democracy, Ghana, 2009

Ghanaians rallied to support their newly elected president, John Atta Mills, at Independence Square in Accra on January 7, 2009. As he was sworn in as president, Atta Mills proclaimed "the dawn of a new era."

What message does the poster in this photograph convey? What impact do you think it had on people at the rally?

Johnson- f elected it of Liberia	Joint AU–UN peacekeepers deployed to Darfur	Floods and famines lead to fears over global warming	Election corruption in Zimbabwe	Renewed conflict in Democratic Republic of the Congo	Court rules against Niger for failing to protect against slavery	Ceasefire in Darfur	Democratic elections in Ghana

)06 2007 2008

Meeting the Goals of the New Millennium

In 2000, at the dawn of the new millennium, representatives of the world's nations met at the United Nations. They pledged to work together to find solutions by 2015 to the biggest global challenges facing the world.

POVERTY	EDUCATION	HEALTH	SUSTAINABLE DEVELOPMENT
1 Eradicate extreme poverty and hunger	**2** Achieve universal primary education	**5** Improve maternal health	**7** Ensure environmental sustainablility
4 Reduce child mortality	**3** Promote gender equality and empower women	**6** Combat HIV/AIDS, malaria, and other diseases	**8** Develop a global partnership for development

FIGURE 9.2 The Millennium Development Goals

The Millennium Development Goals (MDG) highlight the eight key challenges world leaders have pledged to resolve. They are numbered by priority.

Do you agree with these priorities? Why or why not?

By 2009, however, many international organizations had expressed concern that Africa was not on target to meet these goals by 2015. The MDG Africa Steering Committee disagreed. It identified the following strategies to support the millennium goals:

- launch an African Green Revolution to double agricultural output
- implement school feeding programs using locally grown foods
- invest in education to achieve gender equality and expand educational opportunities
- strengthen health-care systems to reduce child and maternal mortality rates
- provide family planning services
- fight infectious diseases such as HIV/AIDS by providing access to treatment
- implement national water supply and sanitation strategies
- invest in critical infrastructure (for example, water, transport, and power)
- strengthen statistical systems to monitor progress toward achieving the millennium goals.

Although the Africa Steering Committee acknowledged that these recommendations were ambitious, they believed their agenda was feasible. In the following sections, you will learn more about the challenges that Africa faces and about the progress being made in increasingly African-led initiatives across the continent.

DEAS

IE PORTRAYAL OF AFRICA IN WESTERN MEDIA

ıst people in North America know little about Africa, even though it is e to more than 950 million people. This is because Africa does not ve the same amount of media coverage that other parts of the world Vhen Africa is in the news, coverage leans toward stereotypes and mis-nation—Africa as poor, crowded, and uncivilized, overcome by disease, , despair, and disaster.

s you will discover in this chapter, Africa indeed faces many challenges. e are the stories that the Western media focus on—the internal conflicts, vars, genocides, and natural disasters. When there is positive coverage ica, the media usually highlight the "humanity" of Western aid workers are there to save Africa from itself. There is little effort to examine the of Africa's problems, to analyze the issues, or to show the positive s Africans themselves are doing to improve their own lives.

or . . . readers or viewers to be interested, news out f Africa must be negative. It must conform to the raditional stereotypes in its spotlight on grotesque nd sensational events. It must show misery, orruption, mismanagement, starvation, primitive urroundings, and . . . chaos and outright anarchy. . . .

We hear about famines and coups, but not the ejuvenation of its cities and the cultural vitality of its illage life . . . about oppression and massacres, but ot education, economic self-help, and political levelopment . . . about poaching and habitat estruction, but not ongoing active efforts at onservation, reforestation, and environmental wareness.

Most telling of all . . . news reports show outside vhite people helping black people. They never show lack people helping themselves.

Ezekiel Makunike, "Out of Africa: Western Media Stereotypes Shape Images," The Center for Media Literacy, 2007

Vhy is the media's news coverage of Africa so negative?

- Most media outlets do not station reporters in Africa full-time. Those that do usually have just one reporter for the entire continent.
- Most news stories about Africa are the product of *parachute journalism*. Foreign reporters drop into the continent to cover a story. They do not speak the local languages, so they cannot talk to the local people. Instead, they rely on government or embassy officials or other controlled sources of information.
- Coverage of news out of Africa is influenced by government policies. If Canadians are involved in Africa, newscasts may report it but they will likely focus on the Canadians rather than the Africans.
- What we see on television is driven by consumer demand. The news focuses on stories that attract the largest audiences because large audiences mean bigger advertising revenues.
- Most network and cable news organizations are run by White executives. They have little interest in African issues and are reluctant to devote resources to cover stories out of Africa.

Think It Through

Imagine that you are a news editor. Which of these two photographs would you publish? Give reasons for your answer.

FIGURE 9.3 Bill Clinton in Ethiopia, 2008

Former US president Bill Clinton met with villagers in the highlands of Ethiopia during a visit on behalf of the Clinton Foundation in August 2008.

FIGURE 9.4 African Union mediators broker a deal, February 2009

Djibril Bassole (seated left), the United Nations and African Union chief negotiator, meets with other African Union leaders to negotiate an end to the war in Darfur in Sudan.

Eliminating Poverty and Hunger

Poverty is the main cause of hunger. More than 40 percent of Africans live in extreme poverty. Most live in rural areas where more than 75 percent of poor households are small farmers.

People living in poverty experience chronic hunger, acute under-nutrition, malnutrition, and, at times, starvation. Hunger makes it impossible for people to obtain the vitamins and minerals they need to fight off diseases, to protect themselves from parasites, and to prevent diarrhea.

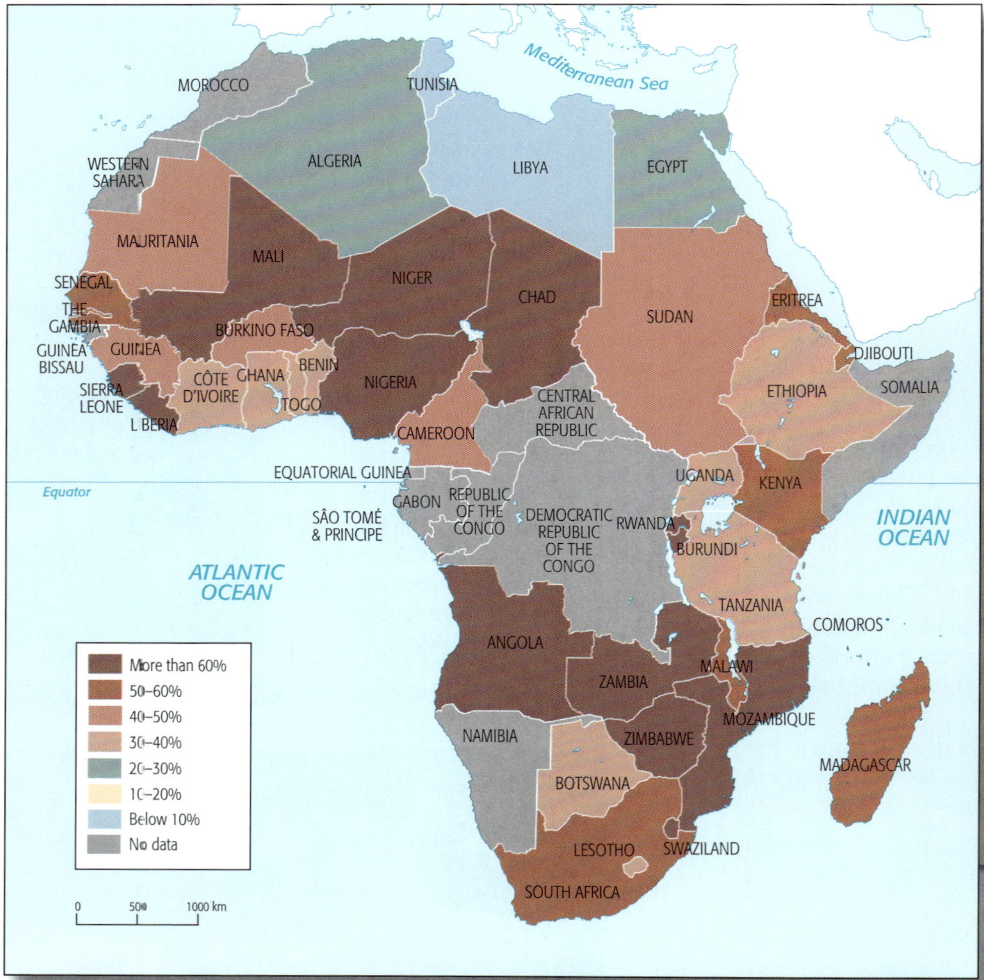

FIGURE 9.5
Percentage of population living below the national poverty line in Africa, 2008

This map shows the percentage of the population in countries in Africa who live below their country's national poverty line. The grey areas show countries where no data are available.

What patterns can you identify? Why do you think there are no data for some countries?

The key to eliminating hunger is to produce more food. Most small farmers in Africa are efficient. They use their limited resources wisely. Yet food production is unable to keep pace with Africa's rapid population growth. As a result, food consumption exceeds food production, sometimes by as much as 50 percent. There are many reasons why.

- After independence, increased urbanization and attempts to copy Western industrial development led to a growing dependence on imported food.
- Unreliable rainfall limits plant growth and can lead to drought. This reinforces the cycle of poverty and makes it difficult for farmers to make the transition from subsistence farming to small-scale commercial farming.
- Soils are often infertile, but most farmers cannot afford fertilizers.
- Many rural areas in African countries lack roads, bridges, and other infrastructure. This makes it difficult to transport crops to markets, and to store surplus food for use in drought years.
- Poor farmers have no access to credit to buy land and modern equipment to increase production.
- Inadequate laws to protect land ownership prevent investment in large agricultural enterprises.
- Government emphasis on cash crops, which raise funds to pay off foreign debts and to purchase imports, undermines food production.

Countries in North Africa have succeeded in reducing malnutrition among children under five. But conditions in sub-Saharan Africa have made it impossible to cut hunger in half by 2015. In the past 20 years, the number of poor people in the region has doubled to 300 million—more than 40 percent of the population.

INCREASING FOOD PRODUCTIVITY

Today, many countries are looking at ways to relieve chronic food shortages through long-term reconstruction programs. Grassroots farm organizations are taking control of their own destinies. They are developing communal farms, improving food production, and practising conservation. They are switching to hardier crops such as maize and millet that can be grown for local consumption, rather than producing crops for export. Farmers are refusing to be labelled as victims or to be told how to farm by relief agencies, financial institutions, and governments. They want to solve their food shortages using their own experiences, skills, and technologies.

FIGURE 9.6 A garden tended by a women's agricultural co-op

Women are responsible for 70 percent of farming in Africa. The demand for farmland among women today is growing. Many have formed agricultural co-ops to provide for their families and to sell surplus crops in local markets.

Children in Africa

FIGURE 9.7 Child mortality

Over 20 percent of children in Africa die before the age of five, most from preventable diseases. More than 30 000 children die each day. Nearly 2 million children under the age of 14 are HIV-positive. By 2008, however, the number of children being infected by HIV/AIDS was beginning to decline.

FIGURE 9.8 Orphans

War, AIDS, and famine have created a generation of children with no family members, no blood relatives, and no extended families. It is estimated that over 15 million African children have been orphaned by HIV/AIDS. This number is expected to reach 25 million by 2010.

FIGURE 9.9 School children

Before 2000, only 57 percent of African children attended primary school, but things are improving. In sub-Saharan Africa, enrollment in primary school jumped by 29 million children between 1999 and 2005. The ratio of girls to boys increased from 78 percent in 1991 to 87 percent in 2004.

HIV/AIDS

Sub-Saharan Africa has been affected by HIV/AIDS more than any place else on Earth. In 2008, an estimated 26 million men, women, and children in sub-Saharan Africa were infected with HIV—about 65 percent of the world's total. Since the AIDS epidemic began in the 1980s, an estimated 30 million Africans have died from the disease.

FIGURE 9.10 Estimated percent of adults in Africa who are HIV-positive, 2007

This map shows the distribution pattern of HIV in Africa. Over the next decade, countries like Botswana, Zimbabwe, and South Africa will lose close to 20 percent of their adult populations to AIDS. **What impact will this have on these countries?**

HIV/AIDS is transmitted primarily through unprotected sex and poor medical practices (for example, untested blood and unsterilized needles). But in sub-Saharan Africa, poverty, unemployment, rape, gender inequality, and a lack of education and health care contribute to the high rate of infection.

The impact of HIV/AIDS is devastating. It removes productive people from society in the prime of their lives. Life expectancy in sub-Saharan Africa has dropped to 47 years. Families are losing their income earners. Employers are losing their workers. Children are losing their parents. Orphans are being drawn into a life of crime and are being exploited in the sex trade. The toll on the health-care system is overwhelming. Medical professionals are dying of AIDS. The financial costs of fighting this **pandemic** are staggering.

pandemic
an epidemic spread over a large geographic area that affects vast numbers of people and challenges a society and its economy

WOMEN: THE FACE OF AIDS IN AFRICA

In Africa, women are disproportionately at risk of HIV/AIDS infection. Of all the women around the world infected with the disease, 75 percent are in Africa. One of the reasons for the high rate of infection is biological—the female reproductive system makes women more susceptible. But there are social and economic reasons, too. Migrant workers and truck drivers leave home for weeks or months at a time. On the road, many of these men have unprotected sex with women in the sex trade, many of whom have HIV/AIDS. When they return home, they pass on the disease to their wives. In places of conflict and war, girls and women contract the disease after being raped by soldiers who are infected.

The responsibility for caring for people with HIV/AIDS and for the orphans left behind by the disease also falls on women. They bear an enormous social and economic burden in their communities as they struggle to be both caregivers and providers. Increasingly, this burden is being shouldered by grandmothers who bury their daughters and then take responsibility for raising their children.

> **The state of the health of the women in the villages was ghastly. Household income was ransacked, and time once spent on walking to distant fields and growing a variety of foods had been given over to caring for the sick. AIDS leads to hunger; hunger exacerbates AIDS. It's a merciless interaction.**
>
> Stephen Lewis, director, the Stephen Lewis Foundation, *Race Against Time: Searching for Hope in AIDS-Ravaged Africa*, Toronto: Anansi, 2006, p. 134

FIGURE 9.11 Women helping women

Grandmothers in Africa are caring for millions of children orphaned by HIV and AIDS. In Canada, thousands of Canadian grandmothers have rallied to support the Stephen Lewis Foundation's Grandmothers to Grandmothers Campaign, which funds community-based projects in 15 African countries and provides African grandmothers with food, housing, grief counselling, and educational support for their grandchildren. The campaign has raised $4 million since it was launched in 2006.

MAKING PROGRESS

By 2009, there were signs that the epidemic was beginning to stabilize. Most countries have strategic plans and ongoing AIDS prevention programs that are helping them make progress in reversing the spread of the disease. However, the cost of drugs from Western pharmaceutical companies places vital medicines out of reach of many African countries. Yet, some countries have successfully negotiated the purchase of low-cost generic drugs. As a result, the number of HIV-infected people receiving medical treatment is slowly rising.

FESTUS MOGAE: BREAKING NEW GROUND

Botswana is one of the countries hardest hit by AIDS. More than 35 percent of its people are HIV-positive. As president of Botswana between 1998 and 2008, Festus Mogae pledged to stop the spread of HIV/AIDS by 2016. To reduce the stigma associated with the disease, Mogae had himself tested. Today, routine testing is an integral part of health care in Botswana. Much of Botswana's annual budget is invested in a ground-breaking program of universal access to free medicines to fight HIV/AIDS.

> **Prevention should be priority number one, priority number two, and priority number three.**
>
> Festus Mogae, "African News Round-up," *The Guardian*, August 8, 2008

FIGURE 9.12
Festus Mogae (1939–)

After leaving office in 2008, Festus Mogae continued his campaign against HIV/AIDS. He launched a new pan-African initiative designed to draw African leaders and AIDS support groups together in a renewed fight to create an HIV-free generation.

Meeting Environmental Challenges

Africa faces many environmental challenges. Some are the result of natural disasters. Many others are the result of disasters of the human kind.

CLIMATE CHANGE

greenhouse gas any of the gases in the atmosphere that absorb radiation and contribute to the warming of the Earth's atmosphere

One of the greatest environmental challenges Africa faces is the impact of global warming. Some scientists predict that rising temperatures in the Indian Ocean will result in a dramatic drop of 25 percent in rainfall by the end of the 21st century. Global warming is caused by the uncontrolled emission of **greenhouse gases** into the atmosphere. Africa contributes less than 3 percent of these emissions. Yet it may end up paying the greatest price for them. The resulting climate changes will lead to a host of environmental disasters, many of which are already under way.

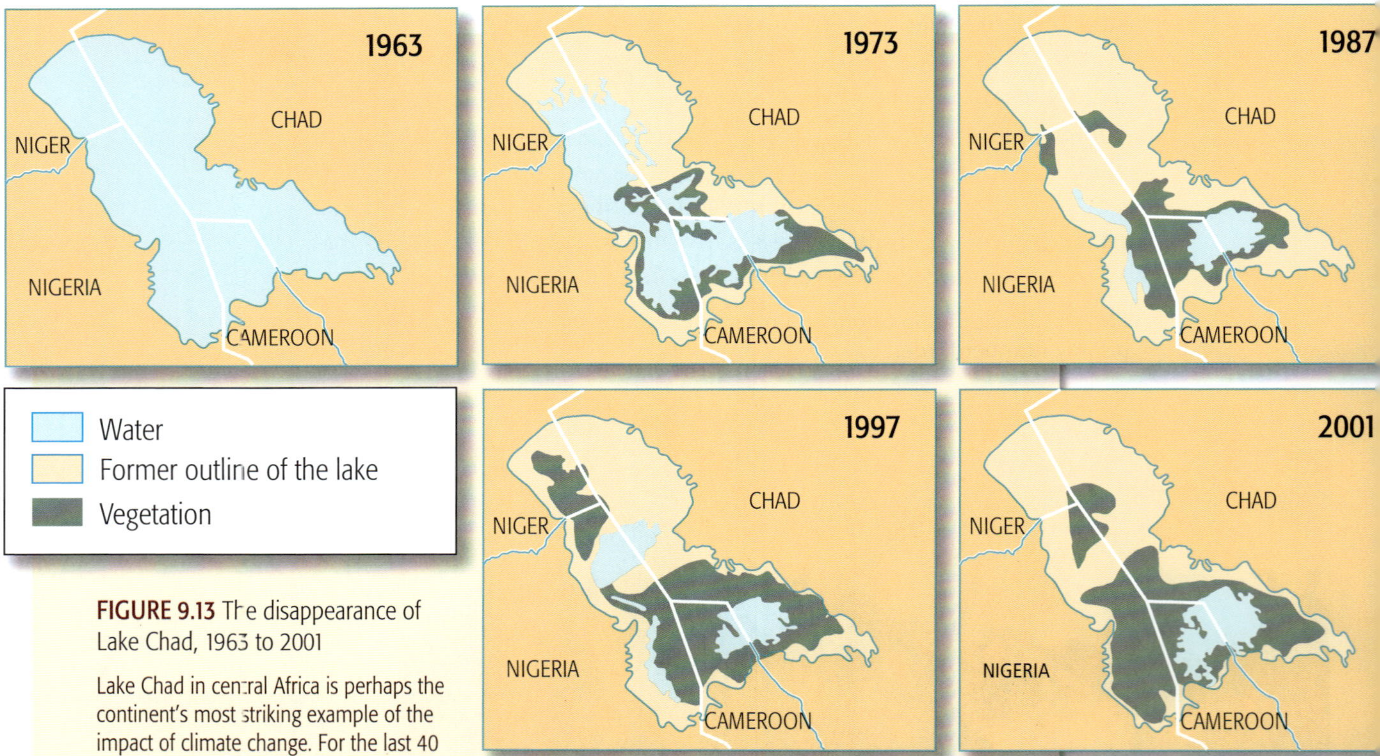

FIGURE 9.13 The disappearance of Lake Chad, 1963 to 2001

Lake Chad in central Africa is perhaps the continent's most striking example of the impact of climate change. For the last 40 years, the lake—once the third-largest inland body of water in Africa—has been shrinking. Some experts believe this is due to a decline in annual rainfall, global warming, and human activity such as irrigation. They warn that the lake could be nothing more than a pond in just two decades.

What impact do you think the shrinking of Lake Chad has had on the region?

The greatest impact of climate change is borne by the poor. Climate change can lead to drought, which reduces the amount of land available for farming and grazing. Millions of farmers and herders lose their crops and livestock. This in turn creates famine for untold numbers of rural poor, which in turn increases food insecurity and food prices.

Rising sea levels could permanently displace millions of people in low-lying areas and severely set back progress made toward economic development. Tropical storms and increased flooding may affect hundreds of millions of people living in poor housing and can contribute to the spread of diseases such as malaria and cholera. Changes to ocean currents could compromise coastal fisheries and further diminish the food supply.

A lack of drinkable water and firewood could lead to mass migrations of people and to more conflicts as people compete for rapidly vanishing resources.

POPULATION GROWTH AND THE ENVIRONMENT

A rapidly growing population is also contributing to Africa's environmental challenges. Today, more and more people are competing for essential but limited resources. Almost 90 percent of Africans need firewood for cooking. As a result, Africa's forests are being cleared at an alarming rate. Deforestation eliminates the natural vegetation. Deforestation and subsistence farming lead to rapid soil erosion, resulting in poor crop yields. When their habitat is lost, wildlife are threatened.

THE THREAT TO WILDLIFE

Loss of habitat is not the only threat to wildlife in Africa, though. Poachers slaughter rhinoceros for their horns, elephants for their tusks and feet, hippos for their teeth, and zebras, leopards, cheetahs, giraffes, snakes, and crocodiles for their skins. Rare species of monkeys, reptiles, and birds are captured for the growing trade in exotic animals. As a result, many species are threatened with extinction.

FIGURE 9.14 The bush meat trade

One of the greatest threats to wildlife is the illegal trade in **bush meat**. Bush meat, a traditional food among indigenous people in the rainforest, has grown into a highly profitable commercial industry. Many wildlife populations have declined by as much as 80 percent from this illegal trade. Today, bush meat is sold around the world, including in Canada.

bush meat
meat from the rainforest wildlife of Africa

PRESERVING THE ENVIRONMENT

Efforts to preserve the environment are often hampered by armed conflicts, corrupt governments, and limited financial resources. Today, however, there are many environmental groups all across Africa actively protesting projects and policies that damage the environment. They are conducting awareness campaigns to educate people about the harm being inflicted on Africa's delicate ecosystems. Governments are acting to preserve the environment through reforestation and other reconstructive programs.

SAVING KENYA'S FORESTS: DR. WANGARI MAATHAI

One activist in Kenya has played a key role in raising awareness of the need to preserve Africa's forests. Dr. Wangari Maathai founded the Green Belt Movement in 1977 to fight back against deforestation. Since then, she has inspired Kenyans to take charge of their environment by leading thousands of women across the country in planting 40 million trees to protect and restore the environment. Not only did the Green Belt Movement restore the forests, it helped meet the needs of women, too. Fast-growing trees blossomed with fruit and produced branches big enough to use as firewood.

FIGURE 9.15
Dr. Wangari Maathai (1940–)

Maathai is a strong advocate for human rights and democracy. She was imprisoned many times for demanding an end to government corruption. In 2002, she won a seat in the newly democratic parliament of Kenya and in 2004 was awarded the Nobel Prize for Peace.

REVIEW AND REFLECT

1. Do you believe that the Millennium Development Goals are realistic? What role can Canada play to be a part of its success? What role can you and your classmates play to contribute to its success? Use a think-pair-share strategy to discuss your ideas.
2. Why are women at the forefront in the fight against poverty and hunger?
3. Why are women in Africa so vulnerable to contracting HIV/AIDS? What can be done to reduce their risk of contracting the disease?
4. In a concept web, explain the connections between poverty and the environment.

Human Rights, Internal Conflicts, and Civil War

Since gaining independence, many countries in Africa have experienced political instability and internal conflict. Not everyone agrees on the root causes. Some attribute it to the effects of colonialism. As you discovered in Chapter 4, when the Europeans carved out their political boundaries in Africa, they didn't stop to consider long-standing cultural, linguistic, and religious rivalries. Common cultural groups were separated, while rival groups were forced to live together. New hostilities were created by the divide-and-rule policies of colonial governments. After independence, these tensions persisted as new political parties were formed along cultural and religious lines. This set the stage for political instability, one-party rule, internal conflict, and civil war.

Others believe the root causes of human rights abuses and armed conflicts are more complex. They argue that famine, social and economic inequality, political corruption and instability, the competition for natural resources, interference by foreign powers and **transnational corporations** (TNCs), and access to weapons have all played their part in human rights abuses and armed conflicts between and within countries in Africa. In this section, you will have the opportunity to examine the causes behind some of the more recent conflicts.

transnational corporation
an international corporation that operates in two or more countries

Genocide in Rwanda

In 1962, Burundi and Rwanda gained their independence. In the decades that followed, these former colonies were torn apart by violence between the **Tutsi** and the **Hutu**. Over the years, Hutu leaders in Rwanda successfully targeted the Tutsi, killing thousands and forcing millions into refugee camps in the neighbouring countries of Tanzania, Uganda, and the Democratic Republic of the Congo. The refugees demanded the right to return home, but the Hutu refused.

Tutsi
in traditional societies, the aristocratic or upper-class minority in Rwanda

Hutu
the larger class of peasants or commoners in Rwanda

In 1990, the Tutsi Rwandan Patriotic Front (RPF) invaded Rwanda from Uganda. This marked the beginning of a three-and-a-half year standoff between the RPF and the Hutu militia. The Hutu launched repeated attacks against the Tutsi, massacring thousands. By 1993, however, international leaders were pressuring the Hutu to share power with the RPF. Instead, the Hutu chose another option: to wipe out all Tutsi living in Rwanda.

The United Nations responded by sending in a small military mission led by Canadian Lieutenant-General Roméo Dallaire. Dallaire quickly realized that the situation in Rwanda was nearing catastrophic proportions. He pleaded for more troops. But for six months his calls for help went unanswered.

Then, on April 6, 1994, a private jet carrying the presidents of Rwanda and Burundi was shot down. The Hutu claimed the RPF was responsible. (Since the crash was never investigated, the truth has never been uncovered.) The death of the Rwandan president triggered one of the worst acts of genocide since the Second World War. Over the next 100 days, Hutu militias systematically slaughtered at least 800 000, and possibly as many as 1 million, Tutsi in Rwanda.

FIGURE 9.16 Canadian Lieutenant-General Roméo Dallaire

Two weeks into the genocide, the UN decided to slash Dallaire's peacekeeping unit from 4500 to 270 troops. Later it reversed its decision and promised additional soldiers. But in the end no reinforcements ever reached Rwanda. In *Shake Hands with the Devil: The Failure of Humanity in Rwanda*, Dallaire contends that hundreds of thousands of lives could have been saved if the UN had acted.

Civil War in the Democratic Republic of the Congo

Following the genocide in Rwanda, a Tutsi army invaded neighbouring Democratic Republic of the Congo (DRC) in 1996 to crush a Hutu army that had fled there. As you discovered in Chapter 7, the invasion sparked a civil war that devastated the region before a ceasefire was reached. In January 2008, however, the ceasefire collapsed, reigniting the conflict.

In August 2008, Tutsi rebels invaded the eastern portion of the DRC. Their leader claimed his forces were there to protect the minority Tutsi population from Hutu attacks. But also at stake were the valuable natural resources that the rival armies were using to finance their operations. The eastern part of the DRC contains 80 percent of the world's supply of coltan, which is used in making cellphones, laptop computers, pagers, and other electronic devices. Whoever controls the eastern DRC controls these valuable deposits.

In November 2008, renewed fighting broke out in the eastern DRC. The United Nations refugee agency braced for another 30 000 displaced people. Since 1996, an estimated 5 million people, mostly civilians, have died in the region, mainly from hunger and disease brought on by the conflict.

Crisis in Darfur

Since it gained independence in 1956, Sudan has faced long periods of turmoil between Arab Muslims in the north and Black Africans in the south. The most recent battleground is Sudan's western region of Darfur. In an age-old conflict between Arab herders and African farmers, the Sudanese army and Arab militias known as *Janjaweed* were pitted against African rebels after drought and desertification forced Arab herders to move into lands occupied by the African farmers. The Sudanese government sided with the *Janjaweed.* They supplied them with money and weapons to launch a scorched-earth campaign targeting civilian villages throughout western Sudan. The *Janjaweed* roamed Darfur at will, raping and murdering the people and looting and burning down their villages.

In 2003, rebels in Darfur countered with their own raids on government targets. The government responded with a campaign to drive out the local Black Sudanese and replace them with Arab settlers. The government described its policy as **ethnic cleansing**. The United States and other governments have described the killing of thousands of people as *genocide.* The crisis has spilled over into neighbouring Chad, which Sudan accuses of supporting the rebels in Darfur. In July 2008, the International Criminal Court accused the president of Sudan of war crimes. In November 2008, the president declared a ceasefire in Darfur and promised to disarm the *Janjaweed.* As of January 2009, however, peace still eluded the people of Sudan.

ethnic cleansing
creating an ethnically homogeneous region by using force or intimidation to remove people of a particular ethnic or religious group from a territory

FIGURE 9.17 Burning down villages in Darfur

The world vowed "never again" after the genocide in Rwanda. Yet in the conflict in Darfur, more than 450 000 people have died since 2003, and 2.5 million more have been driven from their homes. Many people have criticized the UN for once again failing to take action to end a terrible tragedy in Africa.

The Role of the United Nations

The United Nations operates peacekeeping missions throughout the world in an effort to maintain stability in places like Rwanda, Darfur, and the Democratic Republic of the Congo. It also sets up relief camps for the millions of people who are displaced by these conflicts. Figure 9.18 highlights the ongoing missions in Africa as of 2009.

Mission	Year	Location	Timeframe	Uniformed personnel	Contributing countries
UNAMID	2007	Darfur	2007–2008	10 461	31, including Canada; 19 African
MINURCAT	2007	Chad and Central African Republic	2007–2008	271	22, 9 African
UNMIS	2005	Sudan	2005–2009	9 930	62, including Canada; 17 African
UNOCI	2004	Cote D'Ivoire	2004–2009	9 153	41, 15 African
UNMIL	2003	Liberia	2003–2009	12 708	45, 13 African
MONUC	1999	Democratic Republic of the Congo	1999–2008	18 434	48, including Canada; 15 African

FIGURE 9.18 UN peacekeeping missions in Africa, 2009

As of 2009, there were six peacekeeping missions operating in Africa. Canada is involved in three of them. All missions are supported by troops from various countries in Africa.

Why do you think UN peacekeeping missions are not always able to resolve conflicts?

FIGURE 9.19 An orphan shelter in Sakali Refugee Camp in Darfur, 2008

Conflicts and wars in places like Darfur have created millions of **internally displaced persons** and **refugees**. Many of them are orphaned children whose parents have died as a result of the conflicts.

internally displaced person
someone who flees his or her home to take shelter in a safer part of the country

refugee
a person who flees his or her home by escaping to another country

REVIEW AND REFLECT

1. Why do human rights violations occur?
2. With a partner, review the events in the conflict between the Tutsi and the Hutu in Rwanda. Identify key points at which actions could have been taken to discourage further escalation of the conflict.
3. What are the challenges for each of the following during crises such as the ones described in this section? Discuss your ideas using a think-pair-share strategy.
   a. refugees and displaced persons
   b. countries that provide refuge
   c. relief agencies

ORIGINALS

FIGURE 9.20 Nelson Mandela

Nelson Mandela's given name is Rolihlahla. It means "to pull a branch of a tree" or, more informally, "troublemaker." Mandela was given his English name of Nelson by a school teacher.

NELSON MANDELA (1918–)

Nelson Rolihlahla Mandela was born in a village in eastern South Africa in July 1918. At 23, he moved to Johannesburg, where he earned a law degree and was drawn into politics. In 1944, Mandela joined other young members of the African National Congress (ANC) to form the African National Congress Youth League (ANCYL). They began the task of transforming the party into a more radical national movement, mobilizing millions of Blacks across South Africa to fight for freedom.

When the National Party introduced apartheid in 1948, the ANCYL responded by advocating strikes, boycotts, civil disobedience, and non-cooperation. In 1951, Mandela was elected president of the ANCYL. Throughout the 1950s, he was repeatedly banned, arrested, and imprisoned. He was branded a communist and a terrorist. In 1960, after the government outlawed the ANC, Mandela was forced underground, where he donned various disguises to evade capture.

In 1960, after police killed 69 anti-apartheid protestors at Sharpeville, Mandela became convinced that Blacks could not gain their freedom through peaceful means. The ANC began preparing for armed struggle. In 1962, Mandela left the country illegally to promote freedom and arrange for guerrilla training in Algeria. When he returned he was arrested. At his trial, Mandela defended himself, arguing that he had no duty to obey the laws of a government in which he was not represented. He was convicted and sentenced to five years in prison.

While in prison, Mandela was charged with sabotage. At that trial, he was convicted and sentenced to life in prison. His final statement to the court lasted for five hours. As he concluded, Mandela put down his papers and spoke to the judge directly:

> **During my lifetime I have dedicated myself to this struggle of the African people. I have fought against White domination, and I have fought against Black domination. I have cherished the ideal of a democratic and free society in which all persons live together in harmony and with equal opportunities. It is an ideal which I hope to live for and to achieve. But if needs be, it is an ideal for which I am prepared to die.**
>
> Nelson Mandela, June 12, 1964

Mandela, then aged 45, was imprisoned in the notorious Robben Island Prison off the coast of Cape Town. For the next 27 years, the international community pressured the South African government to end apartheid and free Nelson Mandela. In response, the government offered Mandela his freedom in exchange for renouncing violence. But Mandela refused.

Finally, in 1990, President F.W. de Klerk abolished apartheid. On February 11 Mandela was freed. The former political prisoner, now 72 years old, stood on the balcony of Cape Town's City Hall and addressed 50 000 cheering South Africans as millions of television viewers around the world watched history unfold.

Four years later, Mandela won South Africa's first democratic election. On May 19, 1994, he was inaugurated as his country's first Black president. The occasion was marked with the greatest celebrations South Africa had ever seen. Royalty, heads of state, and government leaders from 170 countries gathered in Pretoria to witness the culmination of Nelson Mandela's long journey.

Mandela served as president of South Africa until 1999. He then became his country's most famous ambassador, lending his voice to causes such as HIV/AIDS, poverty, and human rights. In 1993, Mandela won the Nobel Prize for Peace. At 85, he retired from political life.

Think It Through

Nelson Mandela is regarded by many as one of the greatest political leaders of all time. Do you agree with this assessment? Express your thoughts in an opinion paragraph.

An African Renaissance

When democracy finally came to South Africa in 1994, Nelson Mandela stated with optimism that the entire continent of Africa now stood on the threshold of a new era.

> We must face the matter squarely that where there is something wrong in how we govern ourselves, it must be said that the fault is not in our stars but in ourselves that we are ill-governed. We know that we have it in ourselves, as Africans, to change all this. We must assert our will to do so. We must say that there is no obstacle big enough to stop us from bringing about an African renaissance.
>
> Nelson Mandela, president of South Africa, at a meeting of the Organization of African Unity, June 1994

Many leading African politicians took up Mandela's call. They wanted to improve Africa's image in order to attract foreign investment and develop the African economy. In an African renaissance, one-party states and military dictatorships would no longer be tolerated. African leaders promoted multiparty democracies and new economic policies designed to attract investors and encourage capitalism.

The African Union

Part of this renaissance included plans to overhaul the discredited Organization of African Unity. As a result, in 2001 the OAU was replaced by the African Union (AU). In July 2002, the leaders of 53 African states gathered for the AU's first conference in Durban, South Africa. The AU launched the New Partnership for Africa's Development (NEPAD) with a mandate to accelerate African development. It was a time of celebration as the people of Africa looked toward a better future.

> This is a moment of hope for our continent and its peoples. The time has come that Africa must take its rightful place in global affairs. The time has come to end the marginalization of Africa. . . . Through our actions, let us proclaim to the world that this is a continent of democracy, a continent of democratic institutions and culture. Indeed, a continent of good governance, where the people participate and the rule of law is upheld.
>
> Thabo Mbeki, president of South Africa, at the first meeting of the African Union, Durban, South Africa, July 2002

To achieve greater unity and solidarity among African countries and peoples
To accelerate the political, social, and economic integration of Africa
To promote and defend common positions on issues of interest to Africa and its people
To promote peace, security, and stability
To promote democracy and good government
To promote cooperation to raise the standard of living of African peoples

FIGURE 9.21 Key objectives of the African Union

Unlike the OAU, the African Union was given the right to intervene in the internal affairs of a country—without that country's consent—to restore peace and stability and prevent war crimes, genocide, and crimes against humanity.

Source: *The Constitutive Act of the African Union*.

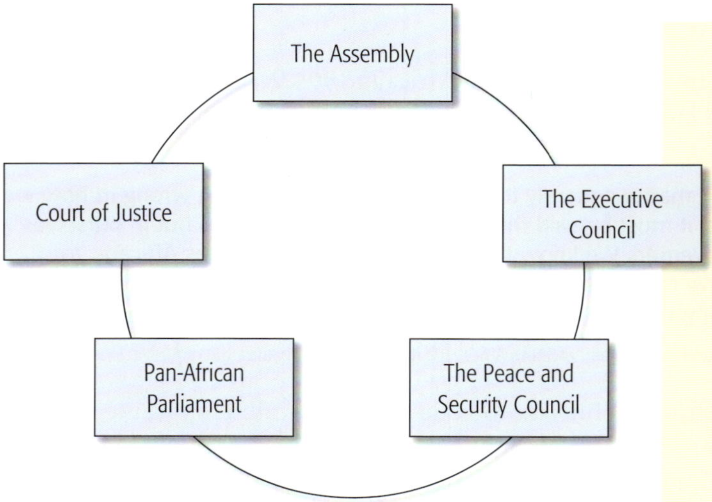

FIGURE 9.22
The main bodies of the African Union

The Assembly is made up of Africa's heads of state. The Executive Council carries out executive functions and is responsible to the Assembly. The Pan-African Parliament ensures that the people of Africa can participate in government.

THE AFRICAN STANDBY FORCE

One of the most important things to emerge from the new African Union is the creation of an African Standby Force (ASF), which will be ready in 2010. The ASF will intervene in hot spots across the continent to prevent them from exploding into major conflicts. Standby brigades of between 2000 and 3000 soldiers each will be stationed in five regions, ready to move in to defuse potential crises. All African countries have agreed to participate in the ASF. The African Standby Force will give the people of Africa the means to resolve their own conflicts.

Freedom and Democracy

For many years following the independence movements in Africa, most countries experienced one-party rule, military dictatorships, and authoritarian regimes. In recent years, however, there has been a growing trend toward greater freedom and democracy. Each year, many countries take steps toward greater respect for the rule of law, human rights, gender equality, the rights of minorities, political opposition, and freedom of speech and the press. In 2008, Freedom House, an organization that promotes political rights and civil liberties around the world, identified 11 countries in Africa as "free" and another 23 as "partly free."

> There is a saying among my people in Ghana: One head alone is not enough to decide.
>
> I often think of that when I hear people say that democracy is alien to Africa, or that Africans are "not ready" for democracy. In reality, African communities from the village upwards have traditionally decided their course through free discussions, carefully weighing different points of view until consensus is reached. So Africans have much to learn from their own traditions, and something to teach others, about the true meaning and spirit of democracy.

Kofi Annan, former Secretary-General of the United Nations, *The International Herald Tribune*, December 5, 2000

FIGURE 9.23 Freedom in Africa, 2008

Freedom House produced this map in 2008, showing the countries in Africa that are free, partly free, and not free. (Free states include the islands of Cape Verde and Mauritius, not shown on the map.) While there is greater democracy in Africa today, democratic rights and civil liberties in many countries are fragile and cannot be taken for granted.

Reconciling with the Past

As more African states move toward freedom and democracy, some governments have attempted to make peace with their pasts through **truth and reconciliation commissions**. The commissions are meant to create a public record of violence, oppression, and other state violations of people's rights. They begin the process of healing the political and social divisions and emotional scars that linger after prolonged periods of violence and oppression.

truth and reconciliation commission
a forum that allows both the victims of violence and oppression and the perpetrators of those acts to bear witness to their experiences

FIGHTING FOR FREEDOM: ARCHBISHOP DESMOND TUTU

The first truth and reconciliation commission was held in South Africa in 1995. A firm believer in the power of forgiveness and reconciliation, Archbishop Desmond Tutu was asked to head the commission. The vigorous South African peace activist first gained international attention through his tireless campaign to end apartheid in his homeland. For his efforts, he won the Nobel Peace Prize in 1984.

During the hearings at South Africa's Truth and Reconciliation Commission (TRC), more than 20 000 people testified about the human rights violations they experienced under apartheid. Though Tutu was satisfied with the outcome of the hearings, he expressed regret that few White South Africans came forward to speak. Nevertheless, he believed that the TRC played an important role in South Africa's peaceful transition to democracy.

> **However painful the experience, the wounds must not be allowed to fester. They must be opened. They must be cleansed. And the balm must be poured on them so they can heal. This is not to be obsessed with the past. It is to take care that the past is properly dealt with for the sake of the future.**

Archbishop Desmond Tutu, *The Truth and Reconciliation Commission of South Africa Report*, October 1998

FIGURE 9.24 Archbishop Desmond Tutu (1931–)

The Desmond Tutu Peace Centre opens in South Africa in 2010. Its mission is to promote peace, democracy, and justice, following the life and lessons of Archbishop Desmond Tutu.

Models of Democracy

Across Africa, people are acting on their rights of citizenship to pressure their governments to govern on behalf of all citizens. **Non-governmental organizations** (NGOs) are fighting for democracy and social justice, for gender equality and children's rights, and for the rule of law through transparent government. Modern technology has made it possible for groups across the continent to communicate with one another electronically. In doing this, they bring strong and effective voices for freedom and democracy in Africa.

non-governmental organization
a private charitable organization that provides international aid or relief, promotes economic equality and community development, and protects the environment

LIBERIA: FROM CHAOS TO STABILITY

Liberia was founded by enslaved Africans who were freed in North America more than 150 years ago. They returned to Africa with the hope of living in freedom. But for years that freedom eluded the people of Liberia as its rulers took power through force rather than free elections.

By 1980, Liberia was in chaos. An **autocratic** government, social inequalities, internal conflict, and a stagnant economy triggered a political coup and ushered in dictatorship and civil war. Over the next two decades, almost 300 000 people were killed and another 500 000 were forced to flee their homes. Roads, schools, medical clinics, and utilities were left in ruins. The economy collapsed as the country drowned in a sea of debt.

autocratic
a form of government in which political power is held by a single, self-appointed ruler

In 2003, a UN peacekeeping force arrived in Liberia to monitor a ceasefire. Plans were put in place to hold free and democratic presidential elections in 2005. The election was won by Liberian-born, Harvard-educated economist Ellen Johnson-Sirleaf. In the 1980s, she was imprisoned for criticizing Liberia's military regime. She was forced into exile twice to escape legal confrontations with the governments of the day. Johnson-Sirleaf returned to Liberia in 1997 to run, unsuccessfully, for president.

FIGURE 9.25
Ellen Johnson-Sirleaf (1938–)

Fondly known by the steely nickname the "Iron Lady," Ellen Johnson-Sirleaf is the first woman to be elected as head of state in Africa. Her victory revived a nation's hope and restored Liberia's international reputation.

In the 2005 election, Johnson-Sirleaf campaigned on the promise of freedom, justice, and equality in a new Liberia. She vowed to tackle the country's $3.5 billion (US) national debt, to fight corruption, and to improve gender equality in Liberia.

> **The administration must endeavour to give Liberian women prominence in all affairs of our country. We will empower all Liberian women in all aspects of our national life. We will support and increase the weight of law . . . and deal drastically with crimes that dehumanize. We will enforce without fear of failure the laws against rape. . . . We will encourage all families to educate children especially the girls.**
>
> Liberian president Ellen Johnson-Sirleaf, *Democracy Now!* January 17, 2006

1	**Transparent, corruption-free government accountable to the people**
2	**Peace and security, by maintaining UN forces until new personnel can be assembled**
3	**Rebuilding infrastructure, including roads, schools, and medical facilities**
4	**Economic growth through a balanced budget and a revitalized agricultural industry**

FIGURE 9.26 Four key principles of democracy in Liberia

The Liberian government adopted four key principles in its efforts to rebuild the country. As a result of Johnson-Sirleaf's efforts, Liberia has obtained greater economic stability and prosperity.

GHANA: COMMITTED TO DEMOCRACY

In the 1970s and 1980s, Ghana experienced back-to-back **coups**. Then, under pressure from external development partners, Ghana's military leader, Jerry Rawlings, announced free elections. He ran for president himself and won two terms. After his second term expired in 2000, the country's new constitution required that he resign and allow the people to elect a new leader. Rawlings hand-picked his successor but his candidate was defeated by rival John Kufuor. Many observers expected Rawlings to try to cling to power. But he surprised them all by stepping aside for the newly elected leader.

coup
an attempt to chang
government by the
threat or use of forc

Kufuor served as president for two terms. In December 2008, he resigned after new elections were held. The election was an important landmark for democracy in Africa. Many countries, such as Mauritania, Nigeria, and Burundi, have had their democratic governments overthrown by coups after their elected leaders refused to give up power after being defeated at the polls. Many political scientists measure the stability of a country's democratic principles by the successful handover of power by two consecutive leaders. By this standard, Ghana is a model of democracy in Africa.

FIGURE 9.27 Waiting to vote in Accra, Ghana, December 7, 2008

On December 7, 2008, more than 12.4 million registered voters in Ghana were eligible to vote for one of eight candidates for president. Voter turnout was almost 70 percent. In contrast, voter turnout in the federal election in Canada in October 2008 was just 59 percent.

What conclusions can you draw from these statistics?

FIGURE 9.28 Protests during the Zimbabwe election, 2008

Elections in Zimbabwe in 2008 contrasted starkly with the election in Ghana. The governing party, led by Robert Mugabe, terrorized the opposition through unlawful detentions, beatings, torture, and murder. When votes were cast on March 28, Morgan Tsvangirai had won the most votes but not a majority. This forced another round of voting. But in the face of more threats and violence, Tsvangirai withdrew. Mugabe then declared himself the winner and in December 2008 declared "Zimbabwe is mine." Many Zimbabweans took to the streets demanding free and fair elections.

Human Rights

In 2008, Amnesty International identified several ongoing human rights violations in Africa, including:

- threats against people who criticize governments or political parties
- the imprisonment of political dissidents and people of conscience
- the maiming and murdering of civilians
- the use of the death penalty
- arbitrary detention and torture
- the recruitment of child soldiers
- discrimination and violence against women

Today, Africa is developing its own initiatives to promote and protect human rights. The African Commission on Human and Peoples' Rights oversees human rights issues across the continent. The African Charter of Human and Peoples' Rights reflects the cultural values of African nations by emphasizing the importance of community and family in addition to the rights of the individual. The African Court on Human and Peoples' Rights hears cases involving human rights violations. In addition, most democracies in Africa have established national human rights commissions. There are also hundreds of African NGOs working to protect human rights and promote social justice at national, local, and grassroots levels.

WOMEN'S RIGHTS

Perhaps one of the most pressing issues in Africa today is women's rights. Until recently, the rights of women were largely ignored. Yet women are the leading players in feeding the people of Africa. They work longer hours than men but earn substantially less money. In many cases, they are grossly underpaid—or not paid at all.

> **No [East African] woman is unemployed. Only a few are paid.**
>
> An Ethiopian woman, in "Discussion and Debate: Women and Employment in Ethiopia," *Reflection*, December 2001

Few African women work in salaried or clerical positions. A lack of education and reproductive choices, limited mobility, and discrimination in the workplace all restrict women's job opportunities outside of farming. In addition, women are affronted by such human rights violations as forced marriages, physical and sexual abuse, and property and inheritance discrimination.

Experts believe that empowering women and investing in women's rights will help to achieve many of the Millennium Development Goals. Equal rights will empower women and will set them on the path to full and productive lives. And when women's lives improve, so do the lives of their children and families. Healthy, educated, and empowered families will lead to more economically productive societies.

HADIJATOU MANI: A STORY OF COURAGE

The story of the gross violation of one woman's human rights made international headlines in 2008. When she was 12 years old, Hadijatou Mani was sold into slavery to a Nigerian man for $500 (US). She was forced to work as a domestic and farm worker. During this time she was repeatedly raped and forced to bear the man's children. In 2005, after 10 years in captivity, she was finally given her freedom.

In April 2008, Mani took her case to the Community Court of Justice in West Africa. She charged the government of Niger with failing to pro-

tect her from slavery. In October 2008, the court found the Niger government guilty and awarded Mani $20 000 (US) in compensation.

> **No one deserves to be enslaved. We are all equal and deserve to be treated the same. I hope that everybody in slavery today can find their freedom. No woman should suffer the way I did.**
>
> Hadijatou Mani, "Court Rules Niger Failed by Allowing Girl's Slavery," *The New York Times*, October 28, 2008

FIGURE 9.29
Hadijatou Mani (1984–)

Today, in Africa as well as other places around the world, thousands of women are enslaved, often in the sex trade. The court's ruling in Mani's case will force all 15 countries in West Africa to take action against slavery.

REVIEW AND REFLECT

1. What initiatives are the leaders of Africa taking to improve conditions in Africa?
2. How effective do you think truth and reconciliation commissions are in addressing past injustices? Give reasons for your response.
3. In a Venn diagram, compare and contrast the road to democracy in Liberia and Ghana.
4. To what extent do you believe that empowering women will help Africa achieve the Millennium Development Goals? Discuss your ideas with a partner.

Economic Development and Foreign Aid

Africa is a continent of great natural diversity and wealth. It is rich in many different natural resources. As Figure 9.30 reveals, it contains significant amounts of many of the world's mineral reserves.

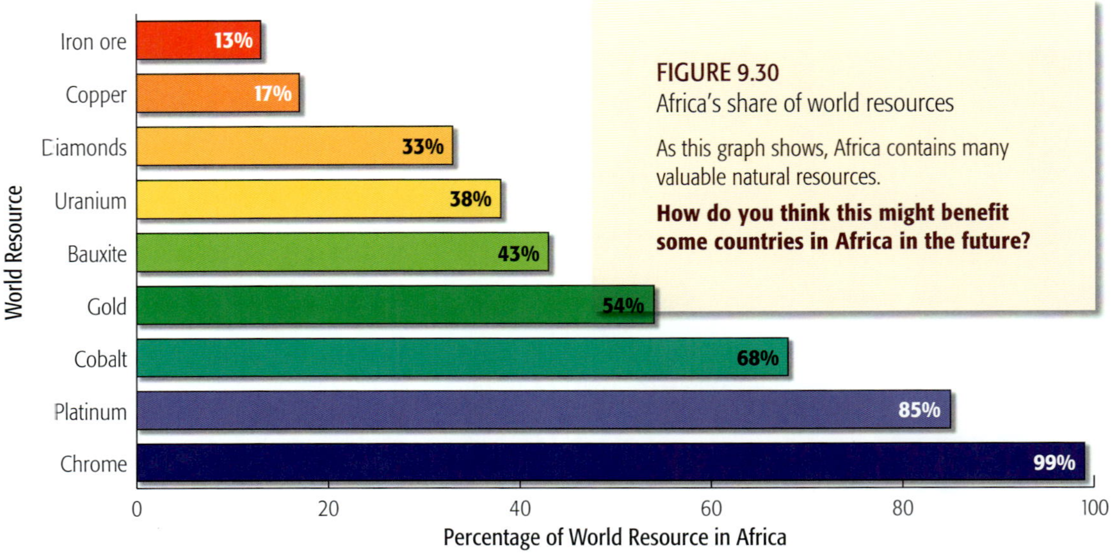

FIGURE 9.30
Africa's share of world resources

As this graph shows, Africa contains many valuable natural resources.

How do you think this might benefit some countries in Africa in the future?

Developing Oil and Gas Reserves

Africa is rich in oil and natural gas. It holds 9.5 percent of the world's known oil reserves and accounts for 12 percent of the world's oil production. Currently, five countries—Nigeria, Angola, Libya, Algeria, and Egypt—account for 85 percent of oil production. But several other countries produce modest amounts of oil and oil exploration is ongoing in many other countries. Africa also holds more than 8 percent of proven gas reserves and produces 6.5 percent of the world's natural gas.

Most oil and gas production is controlled by transnational corporations, with American companies dominating the field. The United States is looking to West Africa to help it meet its future energy needs. Some industry analysts predict that by 2015, West Africa will be supplying 25 percent of all oil imported by the United States.

The competition for valuable resources like oil and gas has raised some concerns that energy-hungry countries like the United States and China might trigger conflicts in politically unstable oil-producing countries. The competition for oil and gas reserves has already bred corruption,

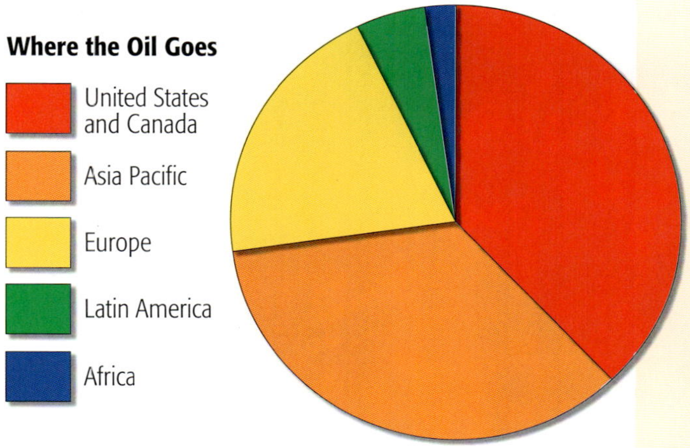

FIGURE 9.31 Destination of oil exports from West Africa, 2008

As the world's oil supplies begin to dwindle in traditional oil-producing regions like the Middle East, there will be growing competition for Africa's oil.

Which countries or regions do you think will be in the greatest competition for oil? Why?

poverty, and war in countries like Nigeria and Angola. These valuable resources generate millions of dollars that can be used to finance local conflicts. In Nigeria, for example, the Movement for the Emancipation of the Niger Delta attacks foreign-owned pipelines in an effort to force the government to share oil revenues with the poor people of the Niger Delta. The challenge for African oil-producing countries, then, is to use the profits from oil production to create sustainable and broad-based economic development.

Blood Diamonds

In recent years, international attention has been focused on resource exploitation through the illegal trade in diamonds. In some countries that are in conflict in Africa, diamonds are a form of currency. *Blood diamonds* or *conflict diamonds* are mined in war zones and sold illegally to finance internal conflicts and wars. In places like Sierra Leone and Angola in the 1990s, rebels kidnapped and tortured young people and forced them to work in the diamond fields. They committed atrocities, such as cutting off a person's hand as a warning not to steal any diamonds.

In response, governments of 71 countries negotiated a deal called the Kimberley Process to monitor and control diamond production and trade. Every diamond must have a government certificate guaranteeing that it is conflict-free. Though today countries like Sierra Leone are at peace, in places where conflicts are ongoing, such as the Democratic Republic of the Congo, there is the risk of a continued illegal trade in blood diamonds.

FIGURE 9.32 *Blood Diamonds* (2006)

The movie *Blood Diamonds* focused attention on the illegal trade in conflict diamonds. Set in Sierra Leone in 1999 during the civil war there, the film shows the horrors of the illegal diamond trade—violence, destruction, kidnapping, and drugging children.

The Price of Resource Exploitation

As with all resource exploitation, harvesting Africa's natural resources comes with a price to the environment. Today, many African countries require companies to assess and report on the impact their activities will have on the environment before they grant them licences to develop natural resources.

Relying on exporting natural resources also leaves Africa vulnerable to downturns in the global economy. It also diverts development money away from other economic sectors, such as manufacturing, which might help many countries in Africa diversify their economies.

Foreign Aid

African countries receive hundreds of billions of dollars in foreign aid. *Bilateral aid* is negotiated between individual donor countries and their African recipients. *Multilateral aid* is funding provided to international organizations such as the World Health Organization (WHO) and programs operated by the United Nations. *Charitable aid* is money donated by NGOs such as the International Red Cross and Oxfam. Canada distributes most of its foreign aid through the Canadian International Development Agency (CIDA).

Humanitarian aid provides short-term emergency assistance following natural or human-made disasters such as floods, droughts, and cyclones. Food, water, medical supplies, money, and personnel are dispatched to relieve the hardships in places affected by these emergencies.

Long-term aid for sustainable development is used to promote economic and social development. In Canada, CIDA sponsors medical personnel, engineers, farmers, teachers, technicians, and other advisers to work with local people to find permanent solutions to economic development. CIDA donates money to fund projects that benefit local communities and family-run businesses. It includes both **project aid** and **program aid**. However, Canada has been criticized by international NGOs for failing to live up to its promises to increase aid to Africa.

project aid
infrastructure projects such as schools, irrigation systems, and sewage treatment plants

program aid
health and educational services

FIGURE 9.33 A small-scale irrigation project in Malawi, 2007

Too often, foreign aid is misdirected, unfairly distributed, or misused on ill-conceived projects. Aid benefits people most when it is channelled into small-scale local projects like this one. Small businesses are better able to meet the needs of local people using local resources. They ensure that the profits remain in the community instead of in a corporate headquarters somewhere else in the world.

Most aid to Africa is *tied aid*—that is, aid that also benefits the donor country. Typically, between half and two-thirds of Canada's aid requires the African recipients to buy Canadian goods and services in return. In 2008, however, Canada promised to untie all aid by 2012–13.

Many people are critical of development aid. They claim aid is often used to further the foreign policy objectives of competing global powers. Powerful countries like the United States, China, and Russia use aid to promote their values in and influence over a region and to expand their own markets.

Microcredit: Changing the Face of Africa

Microcredit provides low-income, self-employed people with financial assistance to build small businesses and lift themselves out of poverty. Loans of between $50 and $500 are provided to people who are not eligible for traditional credit. The money is used to buy the tools and materials the borrowers need to launch their businesses and develop sustainable, long-term solutions to their economic problems.

Most microcredit programs require that borrowers take part in building their communities by providing mutual support. The programs educate the micro-entrepreneurs in basic health care, sanitation, family planning, and financial management. Microcredit funding is used to develop a variety of small businesses throughout Africa, including homes to care for the millions of children who have been orphaned by AIDS.

FIGURE 9.34 A microfinanced movie theatre run by women in Nairobi, Kenya

Women run the most successful businesses launched through the microcredit program. Microcredit has empowered many women and has enabled them to gain greater economic independence to provide for themselves and their families.

REVIEW AND REFLECT

1. What should be done to ensure that oil reserves in West Africa benefit the countries and people of that region?
2. Define the term *microcredit* in your own words and describe how this program addresses the issue of poverty. Share your ideas with a partner.

:XPRESSIONS

'RESERVING AND 'ROMOTING CULTURE 'HROUGH MICROFINANCE

many countries in Africa, artists and performers receive micro- ·edit financing for cultural projects. These projects include creating :s and crafts, forming theatre troupes, funding cultural festivals, oducing feature films, and establishing cultural conservation ntres. These facilities help to build sustainable cultural businesses. ey create self-employment, generate income, and support con- mer consumption.

Microcredit responds directly to the needs of local communities. ielps to ensure that people participate in promoting their cultural ritage. At the same time, it supports sustainable tourism, which nefits local economies and helps to alleviate poverty.

Yet microfinancing can do more than just promote African cul- re. It can help to preserve cultural artifacts and keep them in their omeland. As you discovered in Chapter 2, national cultural trea- res from throughout Africa grace the exhibit halls of many West- n museums and galleries. This loss of cultural heritage began ıring the days of European colonialism, but it continues today. The cent growth of tourism in the countries of Africa and the rising lue of African art in international markets are accelerating the loss the cultural heritage of many African communities. Many people ll pillaged artifacts and family heirlooms to art collectors, antique alers, and tourists to generate income for their families. Although any governments in Africa have banned the trade in cultural tifacts, it continues to thrive illegally in the black market.

In the Dogon village of Fombori, in Mali, the community has veloped its own local initiative to preserve its cultural heritage. e CultureBank is a microfinance institution, a community useum, and an education centre all rolled into one. It provides nall business loans to local villagers. In turn, they must put up ltural objects as collateral for their loans. This allows the com- unity to maintain ownership of its cultural heritage while provid- g financial assistance to local entrepreneurs. The CultureBank is e first institution of its kind worldwide. It provides a model for her nations seeking to preserve their cultural heritage.

ind Out More

orking with a partner, do some research to find out how your local ltural heritage is being preserved in your community.

FIGURE 9.35 Tourists buying arts and crafts in the village of Ireli, Mali

Artisans combine ancestral knowledge and skills with modern techniques and technologies to create arts and crafts that reflect their cultures. Tourists can buy these arts and crafts in local villages and city markets. Microcredit helps the artisans improve their productivity and the quality of their goods and expand their marketing resources.

FIGURE 9.36 Dogon cultural artifacts

The influx of tourists and their buying power persuade many poor people in towns and villages in African countries to sell cultural objects in exchange for hard currency. Many communities are being stripped of their cultural heritage as statues, masks, carvings, and other art forms are sold to foreigners.

The Impact of Globalization on Africa

globalization
the integration of world economies through trade, the flow of capital, the exchange of information and technology, and the movement of people

Globalization is a complex issue. Not only does it affect economies through international trade, it also influences social and political aspects of societies around the world. Through the process of globalization, the world's citizens are becoming increasingly interconnected and interdependent. Yet people disagree over whether globalization is a positive or negative force. Some believe it benefits countries because it spreads trade, wealth, and prosperity around the world. Others believe it has a negative impact because it increases the gap between rich and poor nations. While globalization provides immense opportunities, it also poses significant risks, especially for fragile economies.

Trade Inequities

Many people in Africa support globalization. They want transnational corporations to invest money and create jobs in their countries. But they also believe that the world's wealthy countries do not treat them fairly in trade negotiations. Since Western governments hold the real power in the World Trade Organization (WTO), African countries are forced to trade by their rules.

subsidy
a grant by a government to assist an enterprise that is considered to benefit the public

One of the biggest areas of debate is the issue of farm **subsidies**. Many developed countries subsidize their farmers. This allows them to export their products to Africa at lower prices. This is turn jeopardizes crop production in Africa. An example is the cotton industry in West and Central Africa. Between 10 and 15 million people earn their living producing cotton. It is fundamental to their economy and vital to their well being.

> Cotton allows us to send our children to school, care for our health and buy agricultural tools, which allow us to have enough to eat and to produce enough cereal stocks.
>
> François Traoré, president of the Association of African Cotton Producers, November 2005

Yet billions of dollars in government subsidies have allowed American and European cotton producers to flood world markets. This has led to the loss of hundreds of millions of dollars in West and Central African economies, and a devastating blow to those economies and their people's way of life.

> Some years ago, cotton for us was a source of wealth. But these days it has become our burden, a cause of poverty.
>
> Amadou Toumani Touré, president of Mali, November 2005

FIGURE 9.37 An anti-globalization protest in Nairobi, Kenya, 2006

Those who oppose globalization in Africa cite the fact that, while international trade has tripled since 1980, Africa's share of global exports has declined from 5 percent to less than 2 percent.

The Debate Over Globalization

The debate over globalization extends beyond trade inequities. One Nigerian journalist, Sunday Dare, believes that globalization has led to damaging partnerships between some corrupt African rulers and greedy transnational corporations. He accuses some African rulers of issuing licences to TNCs to exploit their countries' rich natural resources. In exchange, these corrupt rulers receive huge amounts of money, which they use to hold onto power by issuing bogus contracts or other payoffs to political friends and allies.

For their part, the TNCs prey on weak countries with corrupt governments, low labour costs, and no environmental standards in order to maximize their own profits while contributing little to local economies. Dare believes these partnerships encourage government corruption and create greater economic hardships.

Others believe that globalization has the potential to help economic development in Africa. In 2005, representatives from Africa, the United States, and China met to discuss global trade relations. They stated that globalization is the key to overcoming poverty. They recommended that governments:

- encourage investment by foreign companies that provide access to technology and international markets
- develop natural resource industries through partnerships between public and private enterprise
- attract businesses in the fields of transportation, communication, energy, and finance
- improve competitiveness in world trade by lowering trade and investment barriers and reducing government bureaucracy

The Role of China in African Trade

In the new millennium, China has emerged as one of the leading players in the African economy. Between 2000 and 2005, trade between China and the countries of Africa skyrocketed to $50 billion (US). China is now Africa's third-largest trading partner after the United States and the European Union.

China's interest in Africa is in obtaining natural resources to fuel its own growing economy. It has invested huge amounts of money in African economies. Yet there are problems associated with this investment. China often supports projects that are harmful to local environments. Many Chinese workers have migrated to Africa to work in Chinese-backed industries, thereby depriving Africans of jobs. China has flooded Africa with cheap manufactured goods that not only hurt local African-owned businesses but reduce opportunities to establish a broader industrial base in many African countries.

The Brain Drain

Globalization has also contributed to Africa losing educated people to other countries. This has an impact on both the economies and the social structures of many African countries.

Residents of Africa who leave their homelands to attend universities abroad often choose to remain there after they graduate. Because of high unemployment and poor wages, students who remain at home to study are recruited overseas once they enter their professions, especially in fields such as medicine, engineering, and academics. In some parts of sub-Saharan Africa, half of all university graduates immigrate to the West. In fact, Africa is losing as many as 20 000 professionals each year. This is forcing many African countries to spend billions of dollars annually to lure thousands of **expatriate** professionals back to work in Africa.

expatriate
a person who has taken up residence in a foreign country

FIGURE 9.38 Celebrating graduation

To escape war and political instability, many students choose to study abroad. Often they establish personal relationships, so they are reluctant to return home. Those who study in Africa are often lured away by the greater economic opportunities available in other parts of the world.

THE CONSEQUENCES OF THE BRAIN DRAIN

What are the consequences of Africa's brain drain? A shortage of doctors and nurses hurts the health-care system. The loss of engineers, technicians, and scientists restricts economic growth. The loss of professionals slows down the

development of a strong and prosperous middle class. This in turn reduces the tax base for African governments, which contributes to the cycle of poverty and political instability.

The Global Financial Crisis

In 2009, the global financial crisis that brought chaos to the world economy left unanswered many questions about globalization, world trade, and economic development. The crisis threatened to undermine Africa's development goals. The African Union and the African Development Bank (ADB) called on the World Bank to increase its financial support for developing economies in Africa. In response, the World Bank pledged to triple its loans to developing countries around the world, including those in Africa.

The immediate impact of the financial crisis was the depreciation of African currencies and plunging stock markets. Over the longer term, the global financial slowdown will reduce Africa's trade opportunities and its access to foreign investment capital. It will also likely reduce the amount of foreign aid African countries receive, as well as the amount of remittances sent home by family members living abroad. The economic uncertainty is expected to last for some time. Its long-term impact on globalization and development in Africa is impossible to predict.

The Future of Africa

While Africa faces many challenges in the 21st century, positive changes have already begun. The new African Union is working to end internal conflicts, strengthen human rights, promote economic cooperation and development, and give Africa a stronger voice in the global community. But perhaps the greatest hope for the future is the people of Africa. Across the continent, civil action groups are demanding that their leaders stamp out corruption, restore democracy, and be accountable for their actions. People are working at the grassroots level to increase food production, solve environmental problems, and train community health workers. These initiatives create real hope for the future. But they alone cannot meet all of Africa's challenges. The governments of Africa, the international corporations that do business in Africa, and the global community must work together to build a better future on the African continent.

REVIEW AND REFLECT

1. In a comparison organizer, highlight the pros and cons of globalization for Africa. Then express your own opinion in a written explanation.
2. Do you believe that a decrease in the brain drain in the countries of Africa would reduce poverty? Give reasons for your ideas.

The Historian's Craft

HISTORICAL MINDEDNESS

In earlier Historian's Craft features, you learned how historians—and history students—pursue their intellectual curiosity and develop research, interpretation, and presentation skills. In this final feature, you have the opportunity to build on another key aspect of the historian's craft—the mindset of the historian.

HISTORY IS ALIVE

Sometimes history is portrayed as a dead subject dealing with events long past and people long dead. Yet, for historians, history is alive because they are always finding new evidence or new perspectives on existing evidence. For example, historians have gained a new understanding about some of the causes of poverty in sub-Saharan Africa through the evidence they have discovered from the shrinking of Lake Chad over the past few decades.

History is also alive for historians because they recognize how it influences today's world. For example, you could not understand the challenges in meeting the Millennium Development Goals in Africa without knowing the history of the continent over the last century.

HISTORY HAS VALUE

Historians find both personal pleasure and career satisfaction in studying history. But if you look around, you will see that other people find pleasure in history, too, through history-based movies, television, theatre, books, and video games and by visiting museums, art galleries, and historic sites.

You might choose a career in history, as a teacher, professor, writer, archivist, or museum worker. But even if you have other career interests, the skills you develop in your history classes will serve you well. History prepares you for understanding people's life stories, other political positions, and different points of view. Such understanding is essential in life, whether you are pursuing higher education, travelling, working in the global economy, or communicating electronically with people around the world.

HISTORY IS PERSONAL

Historians find personal satisfaction in history. They often present personal perspectives on historical topics. As you worked through this book, you inevitably made history personal to you, too. You found topics that interested you on a personal level. You empathized with historical figures in a way that no one else did. You may have recognized a personal link between your family's history and broader events, such as the flight of refugees from internal conflicts and war.

In recent times, historians have become interested in historical consciousness. They study how individuals make sense of history in a personal way based on their own history, their family's history, and their social, economic, and cultural background. For example, if you had donated to the Green Belt Movement, you would have felt a more personal connection to the issue of deforestation and the planting of trees in Kenya that would be different from your classmates. Being aware of how you personally respond to historical events enriches your understanding of history. This is a key part of historical mindedness.

TRY IT!

With two classmates, choose one topic from this chapter that you all found especially interesting. Write down the reasons why you personally found it interesting and why the topic has special meaning for you. Then compare your notes with the notes your two classmates made. How did each of you respond to this topic? What are the similarities and differences in your responses?

STUDY HALL

KNOWLEDGE & UNDERSTANDING

1. Review the Millennium Development Goals from the beginning of this chapter. Then prepare a list of criteria you would use to judge the current effectiveness in achieving these goals in Africa.
2. Explain the importance of education and health care to economic productivity in Africa.
3. Discuss the following questions:
   a. What conditions can lead to civil war?
   b. Why are civil wars so difficult to resolve?
   c. What is the most effective way to end civil war?
   d. What impact do you think intervention by external forces has on civil war?
4. What role can Canada play in supporting microcredit programs in the countries of Africa?

THINKING

5. Does the West have a responsibility to do more to fight poverty in African states? Why or why not?
6. In some countries in Africa, children are forced to become soldiers. What do you think it would be like to be a child soldier? What impact do you think being forced to be soldiers has on the children? Discuss your ideas with a partner.
7. Brainstorm a list of the main challenges in promoting democracy and human rights in Africa.
8. Discuss the following question: "Is it possible to ensure that protecting human rights is a central goal in all Canadian peacekeeping missions in Africa?"

APPLICATION & COMMUNICATION

9. Imagine you are a reporter for *Friends of the Earth* magazine. You are on assignment to interview Dr. Wangari Maathai in Kenya about the Green Belt Movement. Develop ten questions you would ask her about her environmental goals that will give your readers a clear understanding of her initiatives.
10. Research two countries in Africa to compare and contrast what positive measures they are taking to respond to the HIV/AIDS crisis. Then present your findings to the class in a format of your choice.
11. After the genocide in Rwanda, world leaders vowed such atrocities would never be allowed to happen again. Yet, as you have learned in this chapter, genocide is still taking place in Africa. Do some further research into current conflicts in Africa. Then write a newspaper editorial expressing your views about what Canada and the world should do to respond to cases of genocide.
12. There are many African-led initiatives all across the continent working to improve the lives of the people of Africa. Do your own research to find out about one organization based in Africa. Then prepare a visual presentation highlighting the work this organization does. Be sure to include descriptions and captions to explain your visual information.

Glossary

A

abolitionist
a person who favours banning a practice or institution

alliance
a union for a common purpose

Almoravid
the Spanish name of a Muslim dynasty in North Africa and Spain

anthropologist
a person who studies human beings, especially their societies and customs

apartheid
an official policy of racial segregation involving political, social, legal, and economic discrimination against non-Whites

apprentice
a person who learns a trade by being employed in that business for a period of time

archaeologist
a person who studies human history and prehistory through the excavation of sites and the analysis of physical remains

Ark of the Covenant
a wooden box lined with gold containing the two tablets on which, according to the Christian faith, God wrote the Ten Commandments

asientos
contracts issued by non-Spanish merchants and financiers by King Charles I of Spain

assegais
a light spear with a short shaft and long blade for close combat, used by the Bantu peoples of southern Africa

assimilate
to absorb a group of people into one's culture

Assyrians
people from the ancient country of Assyria, now northern Iraq

atrocity
an appalling act or condition, especially of extreme cruelty

autocratic
a form of government in which political power is held by a single, self-appointed ruler

B

BCE
Before the Common Era

bias
a prejudice that makes it hard to judge fairly

bipedalism
the process of walking upright on two legs, a major milestone in human evolution

bovid
a family of hoofed, hollow-horned animals

bush meat
meat from the rainforest wildlife of Africa

C

carnivore
an animal that feeds on flesh

caste
a hereditary social class

castrate
to remove a man's reproductive organs, making him unable to have children

cataract
a cloudiness on the lens of an eye

CE
the Common Era

CEO
chief executive officer—the executive responsible for the operations of a business

chattel
a personal possession that is the legal property of the owner and can be bought, sold, or bequeathed at the owner's discretion

Christian evangelicals
a religious group that believes people should change their moral values and repent their sins and that promotes social reform and missionary work

collective agreement
a contract between labour and management for wages, benefits, and working conditions

colons
White colonists from France

concubine
a woman who lives with a man without being married, with few rights and low social status

conscription
required service in the armed forces

coup
an attempt to change a government by the threat or use of force

D

dialect
a form of speech peculiar to a particular region

diaspora
a group of people who are dispersed around the world

dictator
a leader who holds absolute power over a people

domestic slavery
a form of slavery that forces people to work in other people's households for little or no pay

Duvalier dictatorships
the oppressive regimes of François Duvalier and his son Jean-Claude in Haiti between 1957 and 1986

dynasty
a line of hereditary rulers

E

emancipation
the act of setting someone free

endangered
in danger of becoming extinct

Enlightenment
a philosophical movement in Europe in the 18th century in which reason and the rights of the individual were emphasized over traditional institutions, customs, and morals

entrepreneur
a person who organizes, operates, and assumes the risks of a business venture

environmental racism
intentionally locating hazardous waste dumps, landfills, incinerators, or other polluting industries near Black or First Nations communities

estate slavery
a form of agricultural slavery in which large numbers of enslaved workers perform labour in an impersonal relationship with the landowner, who has absolute power over them

ethnic cleansing
creating an ethnically homogeneous region by using force or intimidation to remove people of a particular ethnic or religious group from a territory

Eurocentric
focused on Europe and European peoples, especially in relation to historical and cultural influences

expatriate
a person who has taken up residence in a foreign country

expropriate
to take away property from its owner

F

factories
trading posts

Free French forces
French resistance soldiers who continued the war against Germany following the fall of France in 1940

French Revolution
the overthrow of the French monarchy between 1789 and 1799 that united various groups in French society against the established order

G

genealogical
concerning the line of descent traced continuously from an ancestor

genocide
the mass murder of human beings, particularly of a race, nation, or culture

globalization
the integration of world economies through trade, the flow of capital, the exchange of information and technology, and the movement of people

grassroots
efforts involving ordinary people working at a fundamental level

greenhouse gas
any of the gases in the atmosphere that absorb radiation and contribute to the warming of the Earth's atmosphere

H

harem
the part of a Muslim household reserved for the wives and concubines of the male head of the household

herbivore
an animal that feeds on plants

hominids
a species that includes the human family

house arrest
to be confined to one's home by court order

Hutu
the larger class of peasants or commoners in Rwanda

I-J

imperialism
the expansion of a country's political and economic influence through the seizure of new territory and/or the imposition of its values, beliefs, and culture on other peoples

indentured servant
a person who is contracted into the paid service of another for a specified period of time

indigenous
born in a region

Industrial Revolution
the transformation of society from an agricultural economy to an industrial economy characterized by manufacturing, which began in Britain in the mid-19th century

infrastructure
a state's physical assets such as roads, bridges, dams, power grids, and pipelines

institutional racism
a social pattern that imposes oppressive or negative conditions against a group based on race

internally displaced person
someone who flees his or her home to take shelter in a safer part of the country

Iron Age
the archaeological period that began around 1200 BCE when iron replaced bronze in the making of weapons and tools

K

King Solomon
(ca. 1000 BCE–922 BCE) in the Bible, one of the greatest kings of Israel, who ruled over a kingdom comprising most of the modern Middle East

Kiswahili
a Bantu language mixed with Arab elements, from the Arab word *sawahil*, meaning "coast"

knobkerry
a short wooden club with a heavy knob on one end

L

landed immigrant
a person who has relocated and changed his or her permanent residence to a country in which he or she is not a citizen

League of Nations
an international organization formed in 1920 to promote international peace and cooperation

lineage
line of descent; family or descendants

liquidation
the taking apart of a business or a political organization

Loyalists
people who remained loyal to Britain following the American Declaration of Independence in 1776 and who migrated from the United States to British North America

lynch mob
a gang that seizes people and puts them to death, especially by hanging, for alleged offences, immediately and without a legal trial

M

manumission
the act of setting a person free from slavery or bondage

martyr
a person who suffers or dies for the sake of a moral principle or political cause

mercantile
of or relating to merchants or trade

Middle Passage
the long journey of kidnapped African peoples across the Atlantic Ocean from Africa to the Caribbean and the Americas

mortar
a mixture of lime with cement, sand, and water used to bond bricks or stones

Mossi
an African people living in what is now Burkina Faso and Côte d'Ivoire

Muhammad
(ca. 570–632 CE) the Arab prophet and founder of Islam born in Mecca

mummified
embalmed and preserved

myth
a symbolic account of the origin of things

mythology
a collection of stories and traditions about people and institutions

N

Nation of Islam
a Black Islamic organization founded around 1930 that became prominent under the influence of Malcolm X; its members are known as Black Muslims

national self-determination
the right of a people of a defined territory to choose political independence

nationalism
a patriotic feeling toward one's country

nationalizing
transferring the ownership and control of a private business or property to the government

neo-colonialism
the continuation of foreign influence in the economic and political affairs of former colonies

non-governmental organization
a private charitable organization that provides international aid or relief, promotes economic equality and community development, and protects the environment

nuclear family
a family unit consisting of a mother, a father, and their children

O

oral tradition
the telling of stories and histories by word of mouth

P

paleoanthropology
the study of the origins of humankind

Pan-Caribbean
countries in the Caribbean that are connected politically, historically, or culturally

pandemic
an epidemic spread over a large geographic area that affects vast numbers of people and challenges a society and its economy

paternalistic
a policy or practice of treating or governing people by providing for their needs without giving them rights and responsibilities

perspective
a view of the world that has developed from a people's collective experience

political dissident
someone who protests or disagrees with established political policies

polygamy
being married to more than one spouse at the same time

post-traumatic stress
an anxiety disorder that develops after being exposed to a terrifying event or ordeal

Prazeros
people of Afro-Portuguese ancestry

prejudice
a preconceived opinion for or against a person or group

primary source
a first-hand account or an artifact created by people who witnessed or participated in a historical event

primate
the highest order of mammals

program aid
health and educational services

project aid
infrastructure projects such as schools, irrigation systems, and sewage treatment plants

propaganda
information spread to persuade people to adopt an attitude, accept something as fact, or to change their behaviour in a particular way

protectorate
a relationship of protection and partial control assumed by one power over another

proverb
a short saying that embodies a general truth

public housing
government-owned housing rented to low-wage earners

puritanical
a strict religious moral behaviour, especially one that opposes pleasure

Q

Quakers
a Christian religious society dating back to 17th-century England

Queen of Sheba
(ca. 1000 BCE–901 BCE) a mysterious and powerful woman who is immortalized in the world's great religious works, including the Bible and the Qur'an

R

racial profiling
any action that relies on stereotypes about race, colour, ethnicity, ancestry, religion, or place of origin to single out a person for closer scrutiny rather than on reasonable suspicion

radiocarbon dating
the determination of the approximate age of an ancient object, such as a fossil, by measuring the amount of carbon 14 it contains

refugee
a person who flees his or her home by escaping to another country

reptile
a cold-blooded, scaly animal

revivalism
religious fervour that leads to a spiritual awakening

S

sanctions
penalties levelled against a government to punish it for breaking an international law or holding opposing principles

Santeria
an African-based religion similar to voodoo that combines the worship of Yoruban gods with the worship of Roman Catholic saints

scorched earth
a military strategy in which anything that might be useful to the enemy is destroyed, including food supplies, shelter, transportation and communication facilities, and industries

secede
to formally withdraw from an alliance or union

segregation
the separation or isolation of a race, class, or culture through enforced residence in a restricted area or by other discriminatory social barriers

seigneur
a holder of land in New France

sorcerer
a living person who possesses special knowledge that allows him or her to use the spiritual powers of the ancestors

sovereignty
the absolute independence of a community or nation

stereotype
a preconceived and oversimplified impression of the characteristics of a person or situation

subsidy
a grant by a government to assist an enterprise that is considered to benefit the public

sultan
the ruler of a Muslim country

Swahilis
people of Afro-Arab ancestry

T

transnational
involving more than one country

transnational corporation
an international corporation that operates in two or more countries

transnational family
a family whose members live in more than one country

tribute
a donation given as a sign of respect or to ensure peace and protection

truth and reconciliation commission
a forum that allows both the victims of violence and oppression and the perpetrators of those acts to bear witness to their experiences

Tuareg
African traders living in North and West Africa

Tutsi
in traditional societies, the aristocratic or upper-class minority in Rwanda

U

UNESCO World Heritage Site
an area or structure designated by the United Nations for preservation because of its global historical and cultural significance

universal suffrage
the right to vote for all adults

urban renewal
the process of rejuvenating poor, rundown districts of a city through redevelopment

V-Z

voodoo
a religion practised primarily in the Caribbean, particularly in Haiti, that involves witchcraft and ancestor worship

Index

A

B

C

D

E

F

G

H

I

J

K

L

M

N

O

P

Q

T

U

V

W

Z

Credits

IMAGES

Cover

Gavin Hellier/JAI/Corbis.

Introduction

Page x: TIMOTHY A. CLARY/AFP/Getty Images. Page xi (top to bottom): SIMON MAINA/AFP/Getty Images; Ron Sachs-Pool/Getty Images.

Chapter 1

Page 3: Jeremy Woodhouse/Masterfile. Page 6: © Anthony Bannister; Gallo Images/CORBIS. Page 7: © Alain Nogues/Corbis. Page 8: © Danita Delimont/Alamy. Page 11 (clockwise from top left): Eric Baccega/A.G.E. Fotostock//First Light; Istock.com; Istock.com; Istock.com. Page 13: © Fridmar Damm/zefa/Corbis. Page 14: © Frans Lanting/Corbis. Page 15 (top to bottom): © Wolfgang Kaehler/CORBIS; © Frans Lemmens/zefa/Corbis. Page 16: © Tibor Bognar/Corbis. Page 17: Joseph Sohm-Visions of America/Getty Images. Page 20: Royalty-free/Corbis. Page 21: © Martin Barlow/Art Directors/Alamy. Page 22: Nimba (mixed media) by Guinean Musée des Arts d'Afrique et d'Océanie, Paris, France/Giraudon/The Bridgeman Art Library. Page 23 (left to right): Elephant mask, Grasslands, Cameroon, 1900–50 (cotton cloth, flannel, glass, raffia cloth, indigo dye and cane) by Bamileke Culture (20th century) Museum of Fine Arts, Houston, Texas, USA/The Bridgeman Art Library; Kifwebe Mask, Luba Culture, from Democratic Republic of Congo (wood) by African Private Collection/Photo © Heini Schneebeli/The Bridgeman Art Library. Top corners: (left) Jeremy Woodhouse/Masterfile; (right) Joseph Sohm-Visions of America/Getty Images.

Chapter 2

Page 27: F. Lukasseck/Masterfile. Page 31: Larry Fisher/Masterfile. Page 32 (top to bottom): Patrick Landmann/Getty Images; Marc Deville/Getty Images. Page 33: © Helene Rogers/Alamy. Page 35: Andrew McConnell/Getty Images. Page 37 (left to right): AFP/Getty Images; Ethan Miller/Getty Images. Page 38: Egyptian/Getty Images. Page 40: © John Warburton-Lee Photography/Alamy. Page 41: © imagebroker/Alamy. Page 42: © Carol Lee/Alamy. Page 43: SuperStock/MaXx Images. Page 45: Philippe Bourseiller/Getty Images. Page 46: © David C Poole/Robert Harding World Imagery/Corbis. Page 47: First Day of the Yam Festival, Ghana, from "Mission from Cape Coast to Ashantee" by T.E. Bowditch, 1819 (coloured print) British Museum, London, UK/The Bridgeman Art Library. Page 48: © Charles O. Cecil/Alamy. Page 49: © Gavin Hellier/JAI/Corbis. Page 51: The Granger Collection, New York. Page 52: Entrance of Heinrich Barth's (1821–65) Caravan into Timbuktu in 1853, from "Travels and Discoveries in North and Central Africa" by Barth, engraved by Eberhard Emminger (1808–85) published 1857 (colour engraving) by Johann Martin Bernatz (1802–1878) (after) Bibliothèque Nationale, Paris, France/Archives Charmet/The Bridgeman Art Library. Page 54: © Sebastien Cailleux/Corbis. Songhai Ruins. Page 55: The Granger Collection, New York. Page 57: Awaiting an Audience (oil on panel) by Rudolphe Ernst (1854–1932) Private Collection/Photo © Bonhams, London, UK/The Bridgeman Art Library. Page 59: © Images of Africa Photobank/Alamy. Page 60 (top to bottom): © Robert Harding

World Imagery/Corbis; © Gary Cook/Alamy. Page 62: © Ariadne Van Zandbergen/Alamy. Page 63: © Ariadne Van Zandbergen/Alamy. Page 64: Warrior figure, Nok, Nigeria (terracotta) De Meulder Collection, Belgium/Photo © Heini Schneebeli/The Bridgeman Art Library. Page 65 (left to right): © Picasso Estate/SODRAC 2009. Head of a Woman, 1907 (oil on canvas), Picasso, Pablo (1881–1973)/© The Barnes Foundation, Merion, Pennsylvania, USA/© DACS/The Bridgeman Art Library; Miniature mask, Dan, Liberia, Ivory Coast (wood) Private Collection/Photo © Heini Schneebeli/The Bridgeman Art Library. Top corners: (left) Jeremy Woodhouse/Masterfile; (right) F. Lukasseck/Masterfile.

Chapter 3

Page 69: Galen Frysinger. Page 71: The Granger Collection, New York. Page 74: The Slave Market at Ak-Hissar, Turkey, c. 1830–35 (colour litho), Leblanc, Theodore (1800–37) (after)/Bibliothèque des Arts Décoratifs, Paris, France/Archives Charmet/ The Bridgeman Art Library. Page 75: "Tippo-Tip," Zanzibar, c. 1890 (photo with gelatin printing-out paper), Dias, E.C. (fl. 1890)/Private Collection/ © Michael Graham-Stewart/The Bridgeman Art Library. Page 77: The Granger Collection, New York. Page 79: Unknown. Page 80: Slaves Carrying a Barrel and Black People from Different Nations, from "Voyage Pittoresque et Historique au Brésil," engraved by Thierry Freres, 1839 (colour litho) by Jean Baptiste Debret (1768–1848) (after) Bibliothèque Nationale, Paris, France/Archives Charmet/The Bridgeman Art Library. Page 81: Whipping a slave in punishment (coloured engraving) by American School Private Collection/ Peter Newark American Pictures/The Bridgeman Art Library. Page 85 (top to bottom): Rue des Archives/ The Granger Collection, New York; Slave in a Wood Yoke, c. 1840 (ink and washes on paper) by English School (19th century) Private Collection/© Michael Graham-Stewart/The Bridgeman Art Library. Page 86: Olaudah Equiano alias Gustavus Vassa, a slave, 1789 (mezzotint), British Library, London, UK/© British Library Board. All Rights Reserved/ The Bridgeman Art Library. Page 88 (top to bottom): The Granger Collection, New York; © Ariadne Van Zandbergen/Alamy. Page 89: A slave auction in the Deep South, c. 1850 (coloured engraving), American School, (19th century)/Private Collection/Peter Newark American Pictures/The Bridgeman Art Library; African slaves being taken on board ship bound for USA (coloured engraving), American School, (19th century)/Private Collection/Peter Newark American Pictures/The Bridgeman Art Library. Page 92: The Abolition of the Slave Trade, 1792 (coloured etching) by Isaac Cruikshank (1764–c. 1811) Private Collection/Michael Graham-Stewart/The Bridgeman Art Library. Page 93 (top to bottom): Slaves from Africa packed on the deck of a slaver ship bound for America (engraving), American School/Private Collection/Peter Newark American Pictures/The Bridgeman Art Library; Dumping slaves overboard due to reasons ranging from sickness to rebellion (engraving) by American School Private Collection/Peter Newark American Pictures/The Bridgeman Art Library. Page 94 (left to right): Death of Captain Ferrer, the Captain of the Amistad, July 1839, from "A History of the Amistad Captives," by John W. Barber, 1969 reprint of 1840 edition (engraving) (b&w photo), American School, (19th century)/Library of Congress, Washington D.C., USA/The Bridgeman Art Library; Joseph Cinque (c. 1813–79) the slave rebel (coloured engraving), American School, (19th century)/Private Collection/Peter Newark American Pictures/The Bridgeman Art Library. Page 96 (left to right): A Slave Sale notice published in a newspaper in Charleston, South Carolina, 1766 (print), American School, (18th century)/Private Collection/Peter Newark American Pictures/The Bridgeman Art Library; Slave Auction in Charleston, 1860–61 (engraving) (b/w photo), French School, (19th century)/Musée des Beaux-Arts, Chartres, France/ Giraudon/The Bridgeman Art Library. Page 97: The Granger Collection, New York. Page 99 (clockwise from top): © Danita Delimont/Alamy; Hola Images/ Getty Images; David Sanger/Getty Images. Page 100: Toronto Star/The Canadian Press (Tyler Anderson). Page 101: Unknown. Page 102: The Granger Collection, New York. Page 105: The Canadian Press (Tim Krochak). Page 106: Rex Features/The Canadian Press (Ian Dickson). Top corners: (left) Galen Frysinger; (right) The Granger Collection, New York.

Chapter 4

Page 110: © Nik Wheeler/CORBIS. Page 111: The Granger Collection, New York. Page 112: An open-air school in French speaking Africa, before 1914 (b/w photo) by French Photographer (20th century) Bibliothèque des Arts Decoratifs, Paris, France/ Archives Charmet/The Bridgeman Art Library. Page 113: King Mutesa of Buganda, from a photo (oil on canvas) by Dorothy Stanley, nee Tennant (1855–1926) Private Collection/The Bridgeman Art Library. Page 114 (top to bottom): Portrait of Rene Caillie (1799–1838), French explorer of north-west Africa, 1830 (oil on canvas) by Amelie Legrand de Saint-Aubin (b. 1798) Musée des Arts d'Afrique et d'Océanie, Paris, France/Lauros/Giraudon/The Bridgeman Art Library; © Nik Wheeler/CORBIS. Page 115 (top to bottom): The explorer David Livingstone (1813–73) and his meeting with Stanley (1840–1904) at Ujiji on 27th October 1871, trade card advertising "Poulain" chocolate (colour litho) by French School (19th century) Private Collection/ Archives Charmet/The Bridgeman Art Library; © Kennan Ward/CORBIS. Page 116 (top to bottom): Sir Henry Morton Stanley (1840–1904) African explorer, 1890 by Emily M. Merrick (b. 1842) © Royal Geographical Society, London, UK/The Bridgeman Art Library; © Frans Lanting/Corbis. Page 118: © Bettmann/CORBIS. Page 121: The Granger Collection, New York. Page 123 (top to bottom): Unknown; © Bettmann/CORBIS. Page 126: © Bettmann/CORBIS. Page 127: The Granger Collection, New York. Page 128: The Ashanti king; Prempeh, early twentieth century (b/w photo) by Private Collection/Archives Charmet/The Bridgeman Art Library. Page 129: Fred Mayer/ Hulton Archive/Getty Images. Page 130: © Stuwdamdorp/Alamy. Page 131: The Granger Collection, New York. Page 132: Portrait of the Negus of Ethiopia, Menelik II (1844–1913), illustration from "Je Sais Tout" magazine, c. 1900 (colour litho), Buffet, Paul (1864–1941)/Bibliothèque des Arts Decoratifs, Paris, France/Archives Charmet/ The Bridgeman Art Library. Page 133: Hulton Archive/Getty Images. Page 136: The Battle of Isandlwana: The Last Stand of the 24th Regiment of Foot (South Welsh Borderers) during the Zulu War, 22nd January 1879, c. 1885 (oil on canvas) by Charles Edwin Fripp (1854–1906) National Army Museum, London/The Bridgeman Art Library. Page 137: © Hulton-Deutsch Collection/CORBIS. Page 139: Per-Anders Pettersson/AfriLife/africanpictures.net. Page 140: Castelnau/George Eastman House/Getty Images. Top corners: (left) Galen Frysinger; (right) © Nik Wheeler/CORBIS.

Chapter 5

Page 145: © Trinity Mirror/Mirrorpix/Alamy. Page 147: Joy Martyr-André. Page 148: A Slave Auction at the South, from "Harper's Weekly," 13th July 1861 (engraving) (b&w photo) by Theodore Russell Davis (1840–94) (after) Library of Congress, Washington D.C., USA/The Bridgeman Art Library. Page 149: Eli Whitney's (1765–1825) Cotton Gin, operated by black slaves, 1793 (colour litho), American School, (18th century)/Private Collection/ Peter Newark American Pictures/The Bridgeman Art Library. Page 151 (top to bottom): Branding irons with owners' initials (iron), English School/ © Wilberforce House, Hull City Museums and Art Galleries, UK/The Bridgeman Art Library; Branding slaves on the coast of Africa, prior to embarkation, 1845 (litho) by American School (19th century) Private Collection/Peter Newark American Pictures/ The Bridgeman Art Library. Page 152: Painting by Annie Beaugrand-Champagne. Page 154: The death of Major Peirson at St. Helier, retaking Jersey from the French, 8 January 1781, from "Illustrations of English and Scottish History" Volume II (engraving) by John Singleton Copley (1738–1815) (after) Private Collection/Ken Welsh/The Bridgeman Art Library. Page 155: The Granger Collection, New York. Page 158: Fugitive slaves fleeing from the Maryland coast to an Underground Railroad depot in Delaware, 1850 (coloured engraving) by American School (19th century) Private Collection/Peter Newark American Pictures/The Bridgeman Art Library. Page 160: Hulton Archive/Getty Images. Page 161: The Granger Collection, New York. Page 162: Courtesy of the Black Cultural Centre. Page 163: Nat Turner (1800–31) with fellow insurgent slaves during the Slave Rebellion of 1831 (coloured engraving) by American School (19th century) Private Collection/Peter Newark American Pictures/ The Bridgeman Art Library. Page 164: Image

C-06124 courtesy of Royal BC Museum, BC Archives. Page 166: The Granger Collection, New York. Page 168: The Granger Collection, New York. Page 169: Archives of Ontario, I0027815. Page 170: The Canadian Press (Andrew Vaughn). Page 171: Courtesy of Black Cultural Centre, Nova Scotia. Page 172: Glenbow Archives na-4210-1. Page 173 (top to bottom): The Granger Collection, New York; The Granger Collection, New York. Page 174 (top to bottom): The Granger Collection, New York; Istock.com. Page 175 (left to right): The Granger Collection, New York; © Underwood & Underwood/CORBIS. Page 177: AP/The Canadian Press (Bebeto Matthews). Page 178 (top to bottom): © CORBIS; Corcoran Gallery of Art, Washington, D.C. Page 179: Glenbow Archives nc-6-11624a. Page 180: Pierre Obendrauf, The Gazette, Montreal. Page 181: Courtesy of The Black Cultural Centre, Nova Scotia. Page 182: © Michael Ventura/Alamy. Page 184: Julian Wasser//Time Life Pictures/Getty Images. Page 186: Unknown. Page 187: Republished with permission from The Halifax Herald Ltd. Page 188 (top to bottom): Robert Parent//Time Life Pictures/Getty Images; Bentley Archive/Popperfoto/Getty Images. Page 189: CSU Archives/Everett Collection/The Canadian Press. Top corners: (left) © Trinity Mirror/Mirrorpix/Alamy; (right) Joy Martyr-André.

Chapter 6

Page 193: Slaves Fell the Ripe Sugar, Antigua, 1823 (print) by William Clark (fl. 1823) British Library, London, UK/© British Library Board. All Rights Reserved/The Bridgeman Art Library. Page 195: Montpelier Estates, St James, from "A Picturesque Tour of the Island of Jamaica," engraved by Fielding, 1824 (colour litho) by James Hakewill (1778–1843) (after) Yale Center for British Art, Paul Mellon Collection, USA/The Bridgeman Art Library. Page 199: Unknown. Page 200: The Granger Collection, New York. Page 201: The Granger Collection, New York. Page 203: © Lee Karen Stow/Alamy. Page 206: Michael Ochs Archives/Getty Images. Page 209: © Esther Anderson/Corbis. Page 211: Unknown. Page 213: © Bettmann/CORBIS. Page 214: © Bettmann/CORBIS. Page 216: The Granger Collection, New York. Page 218: © ANDRES STAPFF/Reuters/Corbis. Page 219: The Granger Collection, New York. Page 220 (left to right): The Punishment of Slaves, illustration for "Voyage Pittoresque et Historique au Brésil," 1839 (colour litho), Debret, Jean Baptiste (1768–1848) (after)/Bibliothèque Nationale, Paris, France/Archives Charmet/The Bridgeman Art Library; The Granger Collection, New York. Page 221: © RICKEY ROGERS/Reuters/Corbis. Page 222: The Granger Collection, New York. Page 223 (top to bottom): Unknown; AP/The Canadian Press (Silvia Izquierdo). Page 224 (clockwise from top left): Mark Leibowitz/Masterfile; Mark Leibowitz/Masterfile; © Worldwide Picture Library/Alamy; SambaPhoto/Roberto Stelzer/Getty Images. Page 225: AP/The Canadian Press (Damian Dovarganes). Top corners: (left) © Trinity Mirror/Mirrorpix/Alamy; (right) Slaves Fell the Ripe Sugar, Antigua, 1823 (print) by William Clark (fl. 1823) British Library, London, UK/© British Library Board. All Rights Reserved/The Bridgeman Art Library.

Chapter 7

Page 229: Photofest. Page 230: © S. Hilton-Barber/AfriPics.com. Page 231: Drum Social Histories/Baileys African History Archive/africanpictures.net. Page 232: W.E.B. Du Bois Library/University of Massachusetts. Page 233: © Bettmann/CORBIS. Page 234: General Rommel (1894–1944) Commander in Chief of the African Corps, visiting the battlefield at Sollum, published in "Signal," September 1941 (photo) by Moosmuller (fl. 1941) Private Collection/Archives Charmet/The Bridgeman Art Library. Page 235: The Art Archive/Culver Pictures. Page 238: Senegalese woman, c. 1900 (b/w photo), French Photographer, (20th century)/Private Collection/Giraudon/The Bridgeman Art Library. Page 239 (all photos): Istock.com. Page 240: Free France in French Equatorial Africa, Brazzaville, General Charles de Gaulle (1890–1970) making a speech at the Eboue stadium, 26th October 1940 (b/w photo), French Photographer, (20th century)/Archives de Gaulle, Paris, France/Giraudon/The Bridgeman Art Library. Page 242: © Bettmann/CORBIS. Page 244: KAMBOU SIA/AFP/Getty Images. Page 245: © Bettmann/CORBIS. Page 246: © Manuel Litran/Corbis. Page 247: © Bettmann/CORBIS. Page 248: © Bettmann/CORBIS. Page 250: Hulton Archive/

Getty Images. Page 251: Archive Photos/Getty Images. Page 252: Eliot Elisofon//Time Life Pictures/Getty Images. Page 253: Drum Social Histories/Baileys African History Archive/africanpictures.net. Page 254: © Bettmann/CORBIS. Page 256: Keystone/Getty Images. Page 257: Unknown. Page 258: © Louise Gubb/CORBIS SABA. Top corners: (left) © Trinity Mirror/Mirrorpix/Alamy; (right) © Louise Gubb/CORBIS SABA.

Chapter 8

Page 263: AP/The Canadian Press (Martin Meissner). Page 265: Courtesy of the artist, David Vasquez. David Vasquez is a Canadian multimedia artist who was born in the Dominican Republic. Many of his works have African themes. Some of his other works can be viewed at his website at davidvart.com. Page 266: Tannis Toohey/Toronto Star. Page 268: The Canadian Press (Chuck Stoody). Page 269 (both images): Courtesy of The Black Cultural Centre. Page 270: Courtesy of Cornwallis Street Baptist Church. Page 271: Halifax Daily News/The Canadian Press (Ryan Taplin). Page 274: Republished with permission from The Halifax Herald Ltd. Page 275: Halifax Chronicle Herald/The Canadian Press (Peter Parsons). Page 276: Republished with permission from The Halifax Herald Ltd. Page 280: Photo by Aaron Leighton. Page 281: Sgt Serge Gouin, Rideau Hall © 2009 Office of the Secretary to the Governor General of Canada. Page 284: The Canadian Press (Robert Wagenhoffer). Page 286: Colin McConnell/Toronto Star. Page 288: Courtesy of The Ontario Black History Society. Page 289: Carlos Osorio/Toronto Star. Page 292: Michael de Adder/Artizans.com. Page 293: Toronto Star/The Canadian Press (Paul Irish). Page 294: The Canadian Press (Paul Chiasson). Page 295: Jason Blaney/Getty Images. Page 296: The Canadian Press (Aaron Harris). Page 297: The Canadian Press (Paul Lapid). Page 298: The Canadian Press (Sean Kilpatrick). Page 299: Ron Bull/Toronto Star. Top corners: (left) AP/The Canadian Press (Martin Meissner); (right) David Vasquez.

Chapter 9

Page 303: PIUS UTOMI EKPEI/AFP/Getty Images. Page 305 (top to bottom): Justin Sullivan/Getty Images For The Clinton Foundation; IBRAHIM AL-OMARI/AFP/Getty Images. Page 307: © Louise Gubb/CORBIS SABA. Page 308 (top to bottom): © Atlantide Phototravel/Corbis; © Howard Davies/CORBIS; Per-Anders Pettersson/Getty Images. Page 310: Liz Marshall/Stephen Lewis Foundation. Page 311: ALEXANDER JOE/AFP/Getty Images. Page 313: RICCARDO GANGALE/AFP/Getty Images. Page 314: GIANLUIGI GUERCIA/AFP/Getty Images. Page 316: © Christopher Morris/Corbis. Page 318: © Lynsey Addario/Corbis. Page 319: MUSTAFA OZER/AFP/Getty Images. Page 320: RODGER BOSCH/AFP/Getty Images. Page 324: Amy Graves/Getty Images. Page 325: AP/The Canadian Press (Pewee Flomoku, File). Page 327 (top to bottom): PIUS UTOMI EKPEI/AFP/Getty Images; ALEXANDER JOE/AFP/Getty Images. Page 329: Rex Features/The Canadian Press. Page 332: © Warner Bros/courtesy Everett Co/The Canadian Press. Page 333: © FAO/23346/A. Proto. Page 334: Brent Stirton/Getty Images. Page 335 (top to bottom): Jose Azel/Aurora/Getty Images; Travel Ink/Getty Images. Page 337: SIMON MAINA/AFP/Getty Images. Page 338: Eric Miller/Independent Contributors/africanpictures.net. Top corners: (left) AP/The Canadian Press (Martin Meissner); (right) PIUS UTOMI EKPEI/AFP/Getty Images.

TEXT

Page 139: Poem by Dr Mongane Wally Serote. Reprinted by permission.
Page 185: Reprinted by arrangement with The Heirs to the Estate of Martin Luther King Jr., c/o Writers House as agent for the proprietor New York, NY. Copyright 1963 Dr. Martin Luther King Jr.; copyright renewed 1991 Coretta Scott King.
Page 208: Reproduced by permission of the Estate of Louise Bennett Coverley.